GUIDE TO THE
YUCATAN
PENINSULA

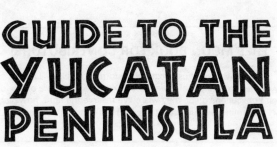

FREE MOON BOOK FOR CONTRIBUTORS!

For all those who send us substantial information, we will send a free copy of the next edition of *Guide to the Yucatan Peninsula* or any other Moon Publications guide they wish. We reserve the right, however, to determine what is "substantial". Thank you for your help.

GUIDE TO THE
YUCATAN
PENINSULA

CHICKI MALLAN

PHOTOS BY
OZ MALLAN

moon
PUBLICATIONS

Please send all comments,
corrections, additions,
amendments and critiques to:

**CHICKI MALLAN
MOON PUBLICATIONS
P.O. Box 1696
Chico, CA 95927, USA**

GUIDE TO THE
YUCATAN PENINSULA

Published by
Moon Publications
P.O. Box 1696
Chico, California 95927, USA
tel. (916) 345-5473/5413

Printed by
Colorcraft Ltd., Hong Kong

© Chicki Mallan 1986

Library of Congress Cataloging in Publication Data

Mallan, Chicki, 1933-
Guide to the Yucatan Peninsula.

Bibliography: p. 305
Includes index.
1. Yucatan Peninsula—Description and travel—
Guide-books. I. Title.
F1376.M27   1986   917.2'604834   86-23500
ISBN 0-918373-11-5

Printed in Hong Kong

"Each stone is part of an allegory or fable, hidden from us, inscrutable under the light of the feeble torch we may burn before it, but which, if ever revealed, will show that the history of the world yet remains to be written."

—John Lloyd Stephens, 1841
Incidents of Travel in Yucatan

ACKNOWLEDGEMENTS

It takes so many more people than just the author to come up with a book. And though words can't really express my feelings, I'd like to say *muchas gracias* from the bottom of my heart to everyone involved with bringing this book together. First, where would an author be without a publisher willing to listen to still another idea — *viva!* Bill Dalton. If I were passing out gold statues, the "most impressive" award would go to Editor Deke Castleman. Behind every writer is a great editor and Moon has the finest! Deke was always there with encouragement and advice, patience and impatience, harangues and kudos — and always with an incomparable eye for perfection (and a lot of laughs on the way). And to another valuable colleague, Dave Hurst, production manager/art director extraordinaire. What a pleasure to work with a craftsman who never loses his cool nor his artistic eye working with disorganized authors. Beauty and organization just keep tumbling from his fertile mind. He is responsible for the fine layout and design of the entire book. And to Kathy Escovedo Sanders for her excellent painting on the cover of the book as well as the bannner art for the chapter headings — even when a brand new baby came along, vying with the Yucatan for attention. To Diana Lasich for her fine illustrations and Louise Foote for her precise map work (and her wonderful sketch of *wild canaries;* Mark Morris for his technical contributions and Louise Shannon on the typesetter, along with computer wizard Randy Smith, always ready with the right answer when the computer (or the author) glitched down. One cannot forget the "front office" and Donna Galassi who makes sure the rest of the world discovers the Moon Travel Books, and does it in style! Thanks to the rest of the Moon crew for providing without a doubt the most relaxed loving atmosphere of any publishing house: Howard, Rick, Asha, and Jackie. **others:** Dr. Jess White, manatee specialist at the Miami Seaquarium. Joanne Andrews of Merida, expert on Yucatan orchids. Fellow author Dave Stanley for digging deep enough to find out which 5 reefs are *really* the longest in the world (and sharing the info!). To Senor Javier Rivas and the Ministry of Tourism for their many kindnesses in Mexico, Mexicana Airlines, Aeromexico, Charlotte McCarthy, Hill and Knowlton, Inc. Advertising Agency. Also, to California State University at Chico for two helpful interns: Kathy Brooks, semester-long girl-friday and intern Julie Van Wyk, top-notch library researcher. Both made the nuts and bolts part of the job go much smoother. To good friend Phyl Manning who always found time to listen to the latest about *the book.* I save the best *sports* for last. To my great kids, Patti and Bryant Lange, who knew immediately when they came home from school if dinner would be good or *just quick* by listening for the sound of the printer. And how can words express *thanks* to photographer/husband Oz, who cheerfully went places and took outstanding pictures in unlikely spots: climbing every tall pyramid, waiting patiently in bug-infested jungles for animals that sometimes never did show themselves, wading through miles of estuaries loaded with equipment in search of the fleeing flamingo and even enduring a search and near-arrest by soldiers after straying too close to a Guatemalan refugee camp — all in good humor and with unfailing love and encouragement. These are the people that make a book.

CONTENTS

LIST OF MAPS

CHARTS

IS THIS BOOK OUT OF DATE?

Most people who enjoy Mexico are aware that many changes are taking place, mostly with the fluctuating *peso*. Even while producing this book, we were aware that prices would be out of date before the book was published. However, most travelers like an idea of what to expect in the pocketbook when planning a trip. Prices will be higher than we have indicated, especially when designated in *pesos;* when specified in U.S. dollars expect a slight increase, but not overwhelming. Use these prices only as a general guide.

We want to keep our book as up to date as possible and would appreciate your help. If you find a hot new resort or attraction, or if we have neglected to include an important bit of information, please let us know. Our mapmakers take extraordinary care to be accurate, but if you find an error or if you find anything contrary to what we have told you, jot it down in the margin of the book. When you return home, send us the book and we'll send you a new copy.

We're especially interested in hearing from female travelers, backpackers, RVers, outdoor enthusiasts, expatriates, and local residents. We're interested in any comments from the Mexican tourist industry including hotel owners and individuals who specialize in accommodating visitors to their country.

If you feel you have outstanding photos or artwork and care to send duplicate slides or drawings for an upcoming edition, you will be given full credit and a free book. Materials will only be returned with a self-addressed stamped envelope. Moon Publications will own all rights. Address your letters to:

Chicki Mallan
Moon Publications
Box 1696
Chico, CA 95927

ABBREVIATIONS

a/c — air conditioned	L — left	R — right
C — Centigrade	m — meter	RT — round trip
C. — century	min. — minute	s — single occupancy
d — double occupancy	N — north	S — south
E — east	OW — one way	t — triple occupancy
ha — hectare	pd — per day	tel. — telephone number
I. — island	pn — per night	W — west
km — kilometer	pp — per person	

INTRODUCTION

THE LAND AND SEA

The Yucatan Peninsula occupies an area of approximately 113,000 square kilometers, with a shoreline of over 1,600 kilometers. Geographically, the Peninsula includes the Mexican states of Yucatan on the N coast, Campeche on the W along the Gulf of Mexico, Quintana Roo on the E along the Caribbean coast, the whole country of Belize, and a corner of Guatemala. Geologically, the Yucatan is a flat shelf of limestone and coral composition; the abundant limestone provided the early Maya with sturdy material close at hand to create the mammoth structures that have survived hundreds of years. Limestone was readily cut with hand-hewn stone-cutting implements. This geology, however, also creates a problem for the primary necessity of life — water. In the northern region of the flat Yucatan are no rivers or lakes. Only in the extreme S is one river, the Rio Hondo, which cuts a natural boundary between Belize and Mexico, at the city of Chetumal.

Cenotes (Natural Wells)

Limestone and coral create eerie shorelines, caves, and (fortunately) water holes. Like a stone sponge, rain is absorbed into the ground and delivered to natural stone-lined sinks and underground rivers. When flying over the Peninsula you can see circular ground patterns caused by the hidden movement of underground rivers and lakes. The water level rises and falls with the cycle of rain and drought. The constant ebb and flow erodes underground around the moving water, creating steep-walled caverns; the surface crust eventually caves in exposing and allowing access to the water. Around these sources of water Maya villages grew. Some of the wells are shallow, 7 m below the jungle floor; some are treacherously deep, with the surface of the water as much as 70-90 m deep. In times of drought, the Maya carved stairs into slick limestone walls or hung long ladders into abysmal hollows leading to underground lakes

THE YUCATAN

U.S.A.

GULF
OF
MEXICO

MEXICO

THE YUCATAN
PENINSULA

BELIZE

AREA DESCRIBED
IN TEXT
0   500 km

PACIFIC OCEAN

GUATEMALA

to obtain precious water. John Stephens' book, *Incidents of Travel in The Yucatan,* covers the 1841 expedition of Fredrick Catherwood and Stephens. Catherwood's realistic art reproduces accurately how the Indians survived in the northern part of the Peninsula from year to year with little or no rainfall by burrowing deep into the earth to retrieve water. The two American explorers observed long lines of naked Indian men carrying the precious liquid from deep holes back to the surface in calabash containers.

The Peninsula Coast

The W and N coast is composed of many lagoons, sandbars, and mangrove swamps. The E coast is edged with coral reefs; several islands lie offshore—Cozumel, Isla Mujeres, and Contoy. The fifth largest reef in the world, the Belizean Reef, extends from the tip of Isla Mujeres 280 km S to the Bay of Honduras. Many varieties of coral—including rare black coral found at great depths—grow in the hills and valleys of the often deep reef that protects the E coast of the Peninsula. In many places along the reef it is illegal to dive for the coral, and where it is permitted it's a dangerous (but money-making) occupation. Since tourists are willing to buy it, the local divers continue to retrieve it from the crags and crevices of underwater canyons. The coral ridges of Yucatan's reef attract curious divers from all over the world.

AGRICULTURE

The land in the northernmost part of the Yucatan was described by Diego de Landa, an early Spanish priest, "as a country with the least earth ever seen, since all of it is one living rock." Surprisingly, the thin layer of soil supports agriculture. This monotonous landscape is a stony plain dotted with a multitude of sword-shaped plants called henequen. The Spanish settlers on the Peninsula made vast fortunes growing and selling henequen (used for rope making) at the turn of the century. However, it was the Maya that showed the Spanish its value; it was used in many ways, but especially for building their houses. Without nails or tools, the house was "tied together" with henequen fiber twisted by hand into sturdy twine. Wherever *palapa*-style structures are built today by the Indians, the same nail-free method is used.

Food Crops

With careful nurturing of the soil, the early Indians managed to support a large population of people on the land. Though the rainfall in the far N is spotty and unreliable, the land is surprisingly fertile and each year produces corn and other vegetables on small farms. Toward the NW of the Peninsula, where tradewinds bring more rain, the land is greener. As you travel south the desert gradually becomes green until you find yourself in a jungle plain at Quintana Roo fringed by the turquoise Caribbean. Along the coast of Quintana Roo remnants of large coconut plantations, now broken up into small tracts and humble *ranchitos,* are being developed by farmers with modest government assistance. It's commonplace to see copra lining the roadside, drying in the sun. Different parts of the Peninsula produce different crops. In most areas juicy oranges grow which you can find for sale everywhere; in the marketplace and along the road the green peel is often removed, the sweet fruit ready to eat. In the southern state of Tabasco, the cacao bean is cultivated. Introduced by the Maya, the bean was actually used as a form of money. The first chocolate drink was developed by the

Maya and presented to the Spanish. Today chocolate is manufactured and shipped all over the world from Mexico. Bananas of many kinds from finger-size to 15-inch red plantains are grown in thick groves close to the Gulf of Mexico coast. Tabasco bananas are recognized worldwide as among the finest.

REEFS ALONG THE YUCATAN PENINSULA

The sea is a magical world unto itself. Man is just beginning to learn of the wonders that take place within its depths. Some dreamers predict that a time is coming when oceans of the world will provide man with all the nutrients he needs, and that people will live comfortably side by side with the fish in the sea. For now, men and women are content just to look at what's there.

Coral
From tiny polyps grow spectacular coral reefs. Coral is a unique limestone formation that

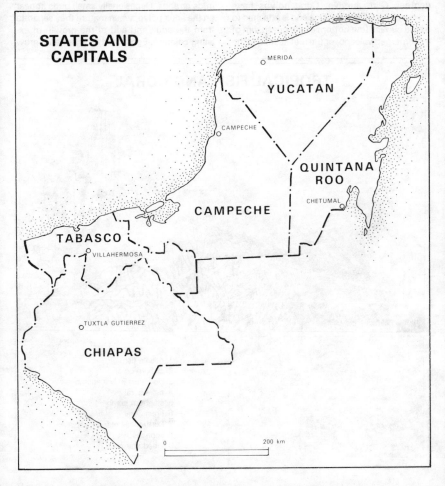

STATES AND CAPITALS

MERIDA

YUCATAN

CAMPECHE

QUINTANA ROO

CHETUMAL

CAMPECHE

TABASCO

VILLAHERMOSA

TUXTLA GUTIERREZ

CHIAPAS

0   200 km

grows in innumerable shapes: delicate lace, trees with reaching branches, pleated mushrooms, stove pipes, petaled flowers, fans, domes, heads of cabbage, and stalks of broccoli. Corals are formed by millions of tiny carnivorous polyps that feed on minute organisms and live in large colonies of flamboyantly colored individual species. These small sea creatures can be less than a cm long or as big as 15 cm in diameter. Related to the jellyfish and sea anemone, polyps need sunlight and clear saltwater not colder than 20 degrees C to survive. Coral polyps have cylinder-shaped bodies. One end is attached to a hard surface (the bottom of the ocean, rim of a submerged volcano, or the reef itself) and the other, mouth end is circled with tiny tentacles that capture its minute prey with a deadly sting.

Colonies are formed when polyps attach themselves to each other. Stony coral, for example, makes the connection with a flat sheet of tissue between the middle of both bodies. They develop their limestone skeletons by extracting calcium out of the seawater and depositing calcium carbonate around the lower half of the body. They reproduce from buds or eggs. Occasionally small buds appear on the adult polyp; when mature they separate from the adult and add to the growth of existing colonies. Eggs, on the other hand, grow

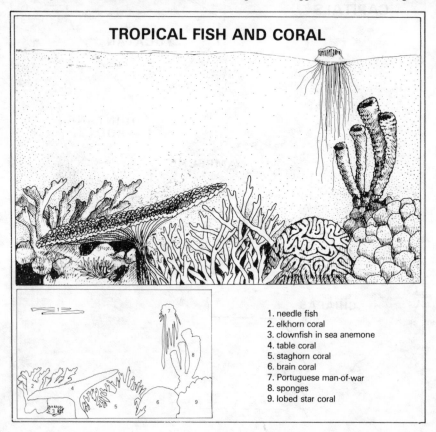

TROPICAL FISH AND CORAL

1. needle fish
2. elkhorn coral
3. clownfish in sea anemone
4. table coral
5. staghorn coral
6. brain coral
7. Portuguese man-of-war
8. sponges
9. lobed star coral

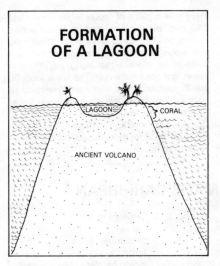

FORMATION OF A LAGOON

LAGOON — CORAL

ANCIENT VOLCANO

The Yucatan Peninsula has a barrier reef extending from the tip of Isla Mujeres to Sapodilla Cay in the Gulf of Honduras. This reef is known by various names (Belizean Reef is the most common), and it's 280 km long, fifth longest in the world. The beauty of the reef attracts divers and snorkelers from distant parts of the world to investigate the unspoiled marinelife.

LONGEST REEFS IN THE WORLD

Great Barrier Reef, Australia	2000 km
New Caledonia, S. Barrier Reef	600 km
New Caledonia, N. Barrier Reef	540 km
S. Louisiade Archipelago Reef, PNG	350 km
Belize Reef	280 km
Great Sea Reef — Ethel Reef, Fiji	279 km

into tiny forms that swim away and settle on the ocean floor. When developed the egg begins a new colony.

A Reef Grows

As these small creatures continue to reproduce and die, their sturdy skeletons accumulate. Over eons broken bits of coral, animal waste, and granules of soil all contribute to the strong foundation for a reef, which slowly rises toward the surface. A reef must grow from a base no more than 25 m below the water's surface and in a healthy environment can grow 4-5 cm a year. One small piece of coral represents millions of polyps and many years of construction.

Reefs are divided into 3 types: atoll, fringing, and barrier. An atoll can be formed around the crater of a submerged volcano. The polyps begin building their colonies on the round edge of the crater, forming a circular coral island with a lagoon in the center. Thousands of atolls occupy tropical waters of the world. A fringing reef is coral living on a shallow shelf that extends outward from shore into the sea. A barrier reef runs parallel to the coast. Water separates it from the land, and can be a series of reefs with channels of water in between. This is the case with some of the largest barrier reefs in the Pacific and Indian Oceans.

The Meaning Of Color

Most people interested in a reef already know they're in for a brilliant display of colored fish. In the fish world, color isn't only for exterior decoration. Fish change hues for a number of reasons, including anger, protection, and sexual attraction. This is still a little-known science. For example, because of its many colors, marine biologists are uncertain how many species of groupers there are — different species or different mood? A male damsel fish clearly imparts his aggression — and his desire for love — by turning vivid blue. Some fish have as many as 12 recognizable different color patterns they can change within seconds. These color changes, along with other body signals, combine to make communication simple between species. Scientists have discovered that a layer of color-bearing cells lies just beneath a fish's transparent scales. These cells contain orange, yellow, or red pigments; some contain black, and others combine to make yellow or green. A crystalline tissue adds white, silver, or iridescence. Color changes when the pigmented cells are revealed, combined, or masked, creating the final result. Fish communicate in many surprising ways including electrical impulses and flashing bioluminescence (cold light). If fish communication intrigues you, read Robert Burgess' book titled *Secret Languages Of The Sea* (Dodd, Mead and Company).

Conservation

The Mexican government has strict laws governing the reef, to which most divers are more than willing to comply in order to preserve this natural phenomenon and its inhabitants. It takes hundreds of years to form large colonies, so please don't break off pieces of coral for souvenirs. After a very short time out of water the polyps lose their color and you have only a piece of chalky white coral—just like the pieces you can pick up while beachcombing. Strict fines await those who remove anything from the reef. Spear fishing is allowed in some areas along the Yucatan coast, but not on the reef. The spear must be totally unmechanical and used free-hand or with a rubber band only (no spear guns). If you plan on fishing, write to Oficina de Pesca, 1010 2nd Ave., Suite 1605, San Diego CA 92101, tel. (619) 233-6956 for more details; fishing license is required.

SPECIES OF FISH IN THE CARIBBEAN

blue chromis	french grunt	sergeant major
toadfish	spotted drum	big eye
porkfish	angel fish	bluestriped grunt
trunkfish	barred cardinal	butterfly
queen angelfish	trumpetfish	indigo hamlet
grouper	sand tilefish	barracuda
stoplight parrotfish	triggerfish	hogfish

SHELLS YOU MIGHT FIND ON THE BEACH

horse conch	queen conch	West Indian fighting conch
cowrie	olive	West Indian top
prickly cockle	cut-ribbed ark	turkey wing

SPONGES TO LOOK FOR

tube	encrusting	basket
vase	rope	barrel

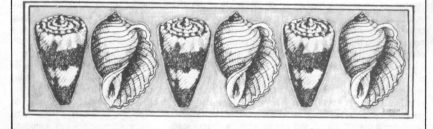

FAUNA

Many exotic animals are found in the thick jungles, upper rainforests, and flatlands of the Yucatan Peninsula; many don't occur elsewhere in Mexico. With patience it's possible to observe animals not normally seen in the wild. If you're serious about this venture, bring a small folding stool (unless you prefer to sit in a tree), a pair of binoculars, possibly a camera, and plenty of bug repellent! The distribution of animal and plant life is a direct result of the climatic zones which are affected by different altitudes and proximity to the sea.

REPTILES

Reptiles thrive in Yucatan's warm sunny atmosphere—man is their worst enemy. Though against the laws of most countries today, in the past some species were greatly reduced in number because the reptile was hunted for its unusual skin. Snake and crocodilian skin when tanned makes sturdy, attractive, waterproof leather, previously used in luggage, shoes, and ladies handbags. A few black-marketeers still take their toll on the species.

Iguana
This species—American lizards *Iguanidae*—includes various large plant eaters typically dark in color. Seen everywhere on the Peninsula, they come in many sizes with slight variations in color. The young iguana is bright emerald green and tamed. This common lizard grows to one m long, has a blunt head and long flat tail. Bands of black and gray circle the body, and a serrated column traces down the middle of its back almost to the tail.

Very large and shy, the lizard's forelimbs hold the front half of its body up off the ground while the two back limbs are kept relaxed and splayed alongside its hind quarters. However, when frightened, the hind legs do everything they're supposed to and the iguana crashes quickly (though clumsily) into the brush searching for its burrow and safety. They are as frightened of you as vice versa, and move quickly to hide once they discover an outsider. Though not aggressive, if cornered they will bite and use their tail in self-defense. They most enjoy basking in the bright sunshine along the Caribbean. Though they are herbivores, the young also eat insects and larvae. Certain varieties in some areas are almost hunted out—for instance, the spiny-tailed iguana in the central valley of Chiapas has been nearly eliminated. A moderate number are still found in the rocky foothill slopes and thornscrub woodlands.

iguana

From centuries past are recorded references to the medicinal value of this lizard, which partly explains the active trade of live iguanas in the marketplace of some parts of the Peninsula. Iguana stew (especially from the spiny-tailed iguana) is believed to cure or relieve various human ailments such as impotence. Another reason for their popularity at the market is their delicate white flesh that tastes much like chicken but is much more expensive.

Other Lizards

You'll see great variety of lizards, from a skinny 2-inch miniature gecko to a chameleon-like black anole that changes colors to match the environment either when danger is imminent or as subterfuge to fool the insects that it preys on. At mating time, the male anole's bright red throat-fan is puffed out to make sure that all female lizards will see it. Some are brightly striped in various shades of green and yellow; others are earth colors that blend with the gray and beige limestone which dots the landscape. Skinny as wisps of thread running on hind legs or chunky and waddling with armor-like skin, the range is endless — and fascinating!

Coral Snake

Commonly seen from southern Yucatan to Panama, these coral snakes grow much larger (1-1½ m) than the ones in the southern U.S. The body is slender, with no pronounced distinction between head and neck. In N. and S. America are several genera of true coral snakes, which are close relatives of cobras. Many false coral snakes (with similar coloring) are around, though harmless. Nocturnal, they spend the day in mossy clumps, under rocks or logs.

Note: The two N. American coral snakes have prominent rings round the body in the same sequence of black, yellow or white, and red. They don't look for trouble and seldom strike, but they will bite if stepped on; their short fangs, however, can be stopped by shoes or clothing. Even though the Mexicans call this the "20-minute snake" (meaning if you are bitten and don't get antivenin within 20 minutes, you die), it's actually more like a 24-hour period. According to Mexico's Instituto Nacional de

Hygiene, an average of 135 deaths per year (mostly children) are reported for the country, the number declining as more villages receive antivenin.

Chances of the average tourist being bitten by a coral (or any other) snake are rare. However, if you plan on extensive jungle exploration, check with your doctor before you leave home. Antivenin is available in Mexico, and it's wise to be prepared for an allergic reaction to the antivenin with antihistimine and adrenalin. The most important thing to remember if bitten: *don't panic and don't run.* Physical exertion and panic cause the venom to travel through your body much faster. Lie down and stay calm; have someone carry you to a doctor.

Tropical Rattlesnake

Called *cascabel* in Mexico and Mesoamerica. This species is the deadliest and most treacherous of all rattlers. It differs slightly from other species by having vividly contrasting neck bands. Contrary to public myth, this serpent doesn't always rattle a warning of its impending strike. It grows 2-2½ m long and is found mainly in higher, drier areas of the tropics.

Cayman

The cayman is part of the crocodilian order; crocodiles' and alligators' habits and appearance are very similar. The main difference is the underskin. The cayman's skin is reinforced with bony plates on the belly making them useless for the leather market (lucky them!); alligators and crocodiles, with smooth belly skin and sides, in some parts of the globe have been hunted almost to extinction. There are laws that now protect the crocodilia, though certain world governments allow farming the animal for leather production.

Of the five species of cayman, several frequent the brackish inlet waters near the estuaries on the N edge of the Peninsula, along the Rio Lagartos (loosely translated to mean "River of Lizards"). They are broad snouted, and often look as though they sport a pair of spectacles. A large cayman can be 2½ m long, very dark gray/green, with eyelids that look swollen and wrinkled. Some species have eyelids that look like a pair of blunt horns. They are quicker than alligators and have longer, sharper teeth. Their disposition is vicious and treacherous; don't be fooled by the old myth that on land they're cumbersome and slow moving. When cornered they move swiftly and are known for not liking people. The best advice one can heed is to give the cayman a wide berth when spotted.

Sea Turtle

At one time many species of giant turtles hugged the coastal regions of the Yucatan, laying their eggs in the warm Caribbean sands. They produced thousands of eggs that hatched; though many didn't survive birds, crabs, and sharks, thousands of young managed to return each year to their birthplace. The Sea Turtle Rescue organization claims that in 1947, during one day, over 40,000 (Kemp's ridley) sea turtles nested on the one Mexican beach instinct returns them to each year. In 1984 less than 500 Kemp's ridleys nested during the entire season.

In spite of concentrated efforts by the Mexican government, the number of turtles is still decreasing. They were a valuable source of food for the Maya Indians for centuries. But only in recent years has the wholesale theft of turtle eggs coupled with the senseless slaughter of the lovely hawksbill (for its beautiful shell, known as tortoiseshell) begun to deplete the species. Refrigeration and freezer holds enable large fishing boats to capture thousands of turtles at one time, and smuggle meat by the ton into various countries to be canned as soup or frozen for the unwary consumer: processors often claim the turtle meat in their product is from the legal freshwater variety.

Another cause of the problems is the belief that turtle eggs cure impotence. Despite huge fines for anyone possessing turtle eggs, every summer nesting grounds along the Yucatan Peninsula are raided. There *is* a hunting season for these threatened creatures (though never during nesting season), and therefore the meat is legal on menus throughout the Peninsula. Though some restaurants serve turtle meat, not true for the eggs! They are forbidden fruit anytime of the year.

hitching a ride on a giant turtle

Ecological organizations are trying hard to solve the problem of the dwindling turtle population. Turtle eggs are kept in captivity; when the hatchlings break through the shells, they are brought to the beach and allowed to rush toward the sea to hopefully imprint the natural sense of belonging here, so that they will then return to their place of "birth." Afterwards, the hatchlings are scooped up and placed in tanks, and allowed to grow larger before being released into the open sea to increase their chances of survival. All of these efforts are in the experimental stage; the results will not be known for years. For more information write to the Sea Turtle Rescue Fund, 624 9th St. N.W., Washington, D.C. 20001.

ENDENTATA

Nine-Banded Armadillo

This strange creature looks like a miniature prehistoric monster. The size of a small house dog, its most unusual feature is the tough coat of armor plate which encases it. Even the tail has its own armor! Flexibility comes from nine bands (or external "joints") that circle the midsection. Living on a diet of insects, its extremely keen sense of smell can locate grubs 15 cm underground. The front paws are sharp,

enabling it to dig easily into the earth and build underground burrows. After digging the hole, the animal carries up to a bushel of grass down to make its nest. Here it sleeps during the day, and bears and rears its young. Unlike some armadillos that roll up into a tight ball when threatened, this species will race for the burrow instead, stiffly arch its back and wedge in so that it cannot be pulled out. The tip of the Yucatan is a favored habitat due to its little rain and warm temperatures; too much rain floods the burrow and can drown young armadillos.

Giant Anteater

This extraordinary cousin of the armadillo measures 2 m long from the tip of its tubular snout to the end of the bushy tail. Its body is shades of brown-gray; the hindquarters become darker in tone while a contrasting wedge-shaped pattern of black outlined with white decorates the throat and shoulder. This creature walks on the knuckles of its paws, keeping the foreclaws razor sharp. If threatened, anteaters can be deadly; more important, they are capable of ripping open the

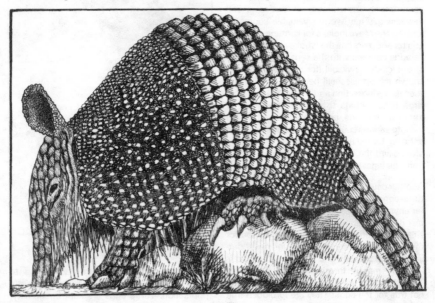

armadillo

The giant anteater's forelimbs have undergone anatomical changes making them effective shovels.

leathery mud walls of termite or white ant nests, the contents of which are a main diet source. After opening the nest, the anteater begins flicking its darting viscous tongue. Ants don't have a chance; they stick to the long tongue that quickly transfers them into a toothless, elongated mouth.

Tapirs

South American tapirs are found from the southern part of Mexico to the S of Brazil. A stout-bodied animal, it has short legs and tail, small eyes, and rounded ears. The nose and upper lip extend into a short but very mobile proboscis. Totally herbivorous, tapirs usually live near streams or rivers in the forest. They bathe daily and also use the water as an escape when hunted either by man or by its prime predator, the jaguar. Shy, unaggressive animals, they are nocturnal with a definite home range, wearing a path between the jungle and their feeding area. If attacked, they lower their head and blindly crash off through the forest; they've been known to collide with trees and knock themselves out in their chaotic attempt to flee!

Peccary

Next to deer, peccary is the most widely hunted game on the Yucatan. Other names for it are musk hog and javelina. Some compare peccaries to the wild pigs found in Europe; in fact, they're part of an entirely different family. Two species found on the Peninsula are the collared peccary and the white-lipped peccary.

The feisty collared peccary stands 50 cm at the shoulder and can be one m long, weighing as much as 30 kg. It's black and white with a narrow semi-circular collar of white hair on the shoulders. In Spanish *javelina* means "spear," descriptive of 2 spear-like tusks that protrude from its mouth. This more familiar peccary is found in desert, woodland, and rainforests, and travels in groups of 5-15. Also with tusks, the white-lipped peccary is reddish-brown to black and has an area of white around the mouth. This larger animal can grow to 105 cm long. This peccary is found deep in tropical rainforests and lives in herds of 100-plus.

"CATS"

Seven species of cats are found in N. America, four tropically distributed. The jaguar is the one most coveted by sportsmen. This robust cat is heavy chested with sturdy-muscled forelegs. Its tail is relatively short and it has small rounded ears. Color ranges from tan on the top to white on the underside. The male can weigh 65-115 kg, females 45-85 kg. Largest of the cats on the Peninsula, it's about the same size as a leopard. Other cats found in Yucatan are ocelot and puma. In tropical forests the large cats are the only predators capable of controlling hoofed game such as deer, peccary, and tapir. If hunting is poor and times are tough, the jaguar *(el tigre)* will go into the rivers and scoop fish with its large paws. The river is a favorite spot for the jaguar to hunt the large tapir when it comes to drink.

MANATEE

Probably the most unusual mammal. Though today seldom seen, this enormous animal, often referred to as the sea cow, at one time roamed the shallow inlets, bays, and estuaries of the Gulf of Mexico and Caribbean in large numbers. The manatee is said to be the basis of myths and old seamen's references to mermaids. In S. America this particular mammal is revered by certain Indian tribes. The manatee image is frequently seen in the art of the ancient Maya, who hunted it for its flesh. In modern times, the population has been reduced by the encroachment of large numbers of people in the manatees' habitats along the riverways and shorelines. Ever-growing numbers of boats with motors inflict often deadly gashes on the nosey creature.

The manatee is an elephantine mammal of immense proportions with gentle manners and the curiosity of a kitten. It weighs 30-35 kg at birth and is gray with a pinkish cast; it can then grow to 3-4 m long and weigh over a ton. Shaped like an Idaho potato, it has a spatulate

a close-up of the truncated snout and prehensile lips of the manatee, which surprisingly is a distant relative of the elephant

tail, 2 forelimbs with toenails, pebbled coarse skin, tiny sunken eyes, numerous fine-bristled hairs scattered sparsely over its body, and a permanent Mona Lisa smile. The head of the mammal seems small for its gargantuan body, and its pre-proboscidean lineage includes dugongs (in Australia), hyrax, and elephants. The manatee's truncated snout and prehensile lips help to push food into its mouth. The only aquatic mammal that exists on vegetation, the manatee grazes on bottom-growing grasses and other aquatic plant life. It ingests as much as 225 kg per day, cleaning rivers of oxygen-choking growth. It is unique amongst mammals in that it constantly grows new teeth — worn teeth fall out and are replaced. Posing no threat to any other living thing, it's been hunted for its oil, skin, and flesh, which is said to be tasty. The mammal thrives in shallow warm water; on the Yucatan Peninsula the manatee has been reported in shallow bays between Playa del Carmen and Punta Allen, but very infrequently anymore. In neighboring Guatemala, the government is sponsoring a manatee reserve in Lago de Izabal. In the U.S. the mammal is found mostly in the inshore and estuarine areas of Florida. It is protected under the Federal U.S. Marine Mammal Protection Act of 1972, the Endangered Species Act of 1973, and the Florida Manatee Sanctuary Act of 1978. It is estimated their population numbers about 2,000.

BIRDS OF THE YUCATAN PENINSULA

Since a major part of the Peninsula is still undeveloped and covered with trees and brush, it isn't surprising to find exotic, rarely seen birds all across the landscape. The Mexican government is beginning to realize the great value in this (almost) undiscovered treasure trove of nature (attracting both scientists and laymen) and is making initial efforts to protect their nesting grounds. The birds of the Yucatan have until recent years been free of pest sprays, smog, and human beings encroaching on their land. If you're a serious bird-watcher, you know all about the Yucatan Peninsula. Undoubtedly, however, change is

a flock of Celestun's flamingoes in flight over the estuaries near the Gulf Coast

coming as more people intrude into the range-land of the birds, exploring these still undeveloped tracts on the Peninsula. Hopefully, stringent regulations will take hold before many of these lovely birds are chased away or destroyed.

Quintana Roo is one of the better ornithological sites. Coba, with its marsh-rimmed lakes, nearby cornfields, and relatively tall, humid forest, is worth a couple of days to the ornithologist. One of the more impressive birds to look for is the keel-billed toucan, often seen perched high on a bare limb in the early hours of the morning. Others include *chachalacas* (held in reverence by the Maya cult), screeching parrots, and occasionally, the occellated turkey.

Flamingos

In the far N of the Peninsula at Rio Lagartos, thousands of long-necked, long-legged flamingos are seen during the nesting season. They begin arriving around the end of May when the rains begin. This homecoming is a breathtaking sight: a profusion of pink/salmon colors clustered together on the white sand or sailing across a blue sky, long curved necks straight in flight, the flapping movement exposing the contrasting black and pink on the underside of the wings. The estimated population of flamingos on the Peninsula is 5,000-7,000. Many of these American flamingos winter in Celestun, a small fishing village on the NW coast a few km

N of the Campeche-Yucatan state border. Celestun lies between the Gulf of Mexico and a long tidal estuary known as La Cienega. If you're visiting Merida and want to see flamingos, it's a closer drive to Celestun (about one hour) than to Rio Lagartos (about 3 hours). Don't forget your camera and color film!

Estuary Havens

The estuary near Celestun plays host to hundreds of other species of birds (see "Celestun,"

just one in Quintana Roo's treasure trove of birds

p. 107). A boat ride into the estuary will give you the opportunity to see a variety of ducks; this is a wintering spot for many flocks on N. American species. Among others you'll see the blue-winged teal, northern shoveler, and lesser scaup, along with a variety of wading birds feeding in the shallow waters, including many types of heron, snowy egret, and (in the summer) white ibis. Seven species of birds are endemic to the Yucatan Peninsula: occellated turkey, Yucatan poorwill, Yucatan flycatcher, orange oriole, black catbird, yellow-lored parrot and the quetzal.

Quetzal

Though the ancient Maya made abundant use of the dazzling quetzal feathers for ceremonial costume and headdress, they hunted other fowl in much larger quantities for food; nonetheless, the quetzal is the only known bird from the pre-Columbian era that is almost extinct. (The Guatemalan government has established a quetzal sanctuary not too far from its capital, Coban. The beautifully designed reserve is open to hikers with several km of good trails leading up into the cloud forest. Definitely worth a few days detour to search out this gorgeous bird. The tourist office, IN-GUAT, in Coban hands out an informative leaflet with a map and description of the quetzal sanctuary.)

Rare sightings are reported from thick rainforests in Chiapas. This bird grew long curly vibrant blue-green feathers used exclusively for clothing and head-dressing nobility. The ancient craft of weaving cloth with feathers was nearly lost, and only recently has been reintroduced in isolated places.

INSECTS

Any tropical locale has literally thousands of insects. Some are annoying (mosquitos and gnats),

some are dangerous (black widows, bird spiders, and scorpions), and others can cause pain when they bite (red ants), but many are beautiful (butterflies and moths), and *all* are fascinating studies in evolved socialization and specialization.

Butterflies And Moths

The Yucatan has an abundance of beautiful moths and butterflies. Of the 90,000 types of butterflies in the world, a large percentage are seen in the Yucatan.

DIFFERENCES BETWEEN MOTHS AND BUTTERFLIES

1. Butterflies fly during the day; moths fly at dusk or night.

2. Butterflies rest with their wings folded straight up over their bodies; most moths rest with their wings spread flat.

3. All butterflies have bare knobs at the end of both antennae (feelers); moths' antennae are either plumy or hairlike and end in a point.

4. Butterflies have slender bodies; moths are plump. Both insects are of the order *lepidoptera*. So *lepidopterists* bring your nets! For you are in butterfly heaven in the jungle areas of the Yucatan Peninsula.

You'll see, among others, the magnificent blue morpho, orange-barred sulphur, the copperhead, cloudless sulphur, malachite, admiral, calico, ruddy dagger-wing, tropical buckeye, and emperor. Trying to photograph a butterfly (live) is a testy business. Just when you have it in your cross hairs, the comely critter flutters off to another spot!

FLORA

Flora of the Yucatan Peninsula varies widely from N to S, even E to west. The N part of the Peninsula gets little rain compared to the S; this landscape is arid, with vegetation described as cacti-thorn scrub forest, or sub-deciduous. The Peninsula is a flat plain with no rivers and few lakes until you get into the S end, where rainforest conditions are the norm. The Yucatan is subject to tropical storms and occasional hurricanes. Although these tremendous winds seldom reach the interior, they are a factor in periodically damaging vegetation in their path. They also pick up and disperse seeds from the Caribbean basin (where the storms originate), spreading plants and flowers across political boundaries.

The Forests

Tropical evergreen forests are found along the Peninsula's Gulf of Mexico coast. Among the plantlife are mangroves, bamboo, swamp cypresses, plus ferns, vines, and flowers creeping from tree to tree creating a dense growth. On top-most limbs, orchids and air ferns reach for the sun. In the southern part of the Peninsula (Chiapas and Tabasco) is classic tropical rainforest. Here are the tall mahogany, *campeche, sapote,* and *kapok,* also covered with wild jungle vines.

Palms

A wide variety of palm trees and their relatives grow on the Peninsula — tall, short, fruited, even oil producers. Though similar, various palms have distinct characteristics. Royal palm is tall with a smooth trunk. Queen palm is often used for landscaping, and bears a sweet fruit. Thatch palm is called *chit* by the Indians; the frond of this tree is used extensively on the Peninsula for roof thatch. Coconut palm serves the Yucatecan well. One of the 10 most useful trees in the world, it produces oil, food, drink, and shelter. The tree matures in 6-7 years and then for 5-7 years bears the coconut, a nutritious food that is also used for copra, valued as a money crop for the locals. Hene-

quen is a cousin to the palm tree; from the fiber comes twine, rope, matting, and other products. New uses are constantly being sought since this plant is common and abundant.

From Fruit To Flowers

The following is a small sampling of the many trees that grow on the Peninsula. Yucatan grows delicious sweet and sour oranges, limes, and grapefruit. Avocado is abundant, and the papaya tree is practically a weed. The mammey tree grows tall (15-20 m) and full, providing not only welcome shade but also an avocado-shaped fruit, brown on the outside with a vivid salmon-pink flesh that makes a sweet snack (a flavor similar to a yam). Another unusual fruit tree is the *guaya,* also called the sea grape. This rangy evergreen thrives on sea air and is commonly seen along the coast and throughout the Yucatan Peninsula. Its small green leathery pods grow in clumps like grapes and contain a sweet, yellowish, jelly-like flesh — tasty! The calabash tree, a friend to the Indian for many years, provides a gourd used for containers.

The tall ceiba is a very special tree to those close to the Maya religious cult. Considered the tree of life, even today it remains undisturbed whether it has sprouted in the middle of a fertile *milpa* (corn field) or anywhere else. At first glance when visiting in the summer, it

Isla Mujeres wildflowers

would seem that all of Yucatan favors the beautiful *flamboyanes* (royal poinciana). As its name implies, when in bloom it is the most flamboyant tree around, with wide-spreading branches covered in clusters of brilliant orange/red flowers. These trees line sidewalks and plazas, and when clustered together present a dazzling show.

a ruffled orchid of Yucatan

Orchids

While traveling through remote areas of the Peninsula, one of the more exotic blooms, the orchid, is often found on the highest limbs of tall trees. Of the 71 species reported on the Yucatan, 20% are terrestrial and 80% are epiphytic, which grow attached to a host plant (in this case trees) and derive moisture and nutrients from the air and rain. Both species grow in many sizes and shapes, from a tiny button, spanning the length of an extended branch, to those with ruffled edges, to deep tiger-striped miniatures. The lovely flowers come in a wide variety of colors, some subtle, some brilliant.

Nature's Hothouse

In spring, flowering trees are a beautiful sight—and sound, attracting hundreds of singing birds throughout the mating season. While wandering through jungle landscapes, you'll see thriving in the wild a complete gamut of plants that we so carefully nurture and coax to survive in a pot on a windowsill at home. Here in its natural environment, the croton exhibits wild colors; the pothos grows 30-cm leaves; and the philodendron splits every leaf in gargantuan glory.

White and red ginger are among the more exotic herbs that grow on the Peninsula. Plumeria (in Hawaii called frangipani) has a wonderful fragrance and is seen in many colors. Hibiscus and bouganvillea bloom in an array of bright hues. A walk through the forest will introduce you to many delicate strangers in the world of tropical flowers. But you'll find old friends too, such as the common morning glory creeping and climbing for miles over bushes and trees. You'll notice thick viny coils that thicken daily. Keeping jungle growth away from the roads and utility poles and wires is a constant job because humid warm air and ample rainfall encourage a lush green wonderland.

HISTORY

THE ANCIENTS

Earliest Man

During the Pleistocene Ice Age (50,000 B.C.) when the level of the sea fell, men and animals crossed the Bering land bridge from Asia to the American continent. For nearly 50,000 years, man made an epic trek southward until approximately 1,000 B.C., when it is believed that the first Indians reached Tierra del Fuego, located at the tip of S. America.

As early as 10,000 B.C., Ice Age Man hunted woolly mammoth and other large animals roaming the cool moist landscape of central Mexico. Between 7,000 and 2,000 B.C., society evolved gradually from hunting and gathering to truly agricultural. Such crops as corn, squash, and beans were independently domesticated in widely separated areas of Mexico after about 6,000 B.C. The Preclassic Period, during which the remains of clay figurines presumed to be fertility symbols announced the rise of religion in Mesoamerica, began around 2,000 B.C.

Around 1000 B.C. the Olmec Indian culture spread and the first large-scale ceremonial centers grew along Gulf Coast lands. Much of Mesoamerica was touched and influenced by the spread of this often sinister religion of strange jaguar-like gods, by the New World's first calendar, and a beginning system of writing.

Classic Period

The arrival of the Classic Period, about A.D. 300, began what would be hailed as the peak of cultural development among the Maya Indians as well as cultures in other parts of Mexico. Until A.D. 900, phenomenal progress was made in the development of artistic, architectural, and astronomical skills. The most impressive buildings were constructed during this period, and the codices (folded bark books) were written and filled with hieroglyphic symbols putting forth complicated mathematical calculations of time: days, months and years. Only the priests and privileged held this knowledge, continuing to learn and develop, until for some still unexplained reason (see p. 25 for speculation) there was a sudden halt to this Classic growth.

Postclassic

After A.D. 900, the Toltec influence took hold. This marked the end of the most artistic era; a new militaristic society built a blend of ceremonialism, civic and social organization, and conquest. The Toltecs were achieving their highest expression as Cortez' fleet appeared on the horizon of the Yucatan Peninsula.

COLONIAL HISTORY

Conquered

Following Columbus' arrival in the New World, other adventurers traveling the same seas quickly found the Yucatan Peninsula. In 1519, 34-year-old Hernan Cortez in an insubordinate act sailed from Cuba, without the authority of the Spanish governor, taking 11 ships, 120 sailors, and 550 soldiers. His attack began on the Yucatan coast, encompassed most of Mexico, and continued through years of bloodshed and death for many of his men. (It didn't *really* end on the Peninsula until the Chan Santa Cruz Indians finally signed a peace treaty with the Mexican federal government in 1935, over 400 years later.) The destruction and elimination of most Indian cultures that had existed throughhout Mexico for thousands of years had been accomplished. By the time of Cortez' death in 1547 (while exiled in Spain), the Spanish military and Franciscan friars were well entrenched in the Yucatan.

Diego de Landa

The Franciscan priests were shocked at what they believed to be influences of the devil, such as body mutilation and human sacrifice, in the

Hernan Cortez

name of the Maya religion. The Franciscans felt it their duty to God to eliminate these ceremonies and all traces of the Maya cult, and gather them into the fold of Christianity. Friar Diego de Landa, who later became a bishop, was instrumental in destroying thousands of their idols. He oversaw the burning of 27 codices, filled with characters and symbols that he could not understand but believed to contain nothing but superstitions and evil lies of the devil. Since then, only 3 others have been found and studied, but are still largely undeciphered. While Landa was directly responsible for destroying the history of these ancient people, he did in fact redeem himself before his death by writing the most complete and detailed account of the life of the Maya in his book *Relacion de las Cosas de Yucatan.* Landa's book described daily living in great detail, including growing and preparing food, the structure of society, the priesthood, and sciences. Although he was aware of their sophisticated "count of ages," he didn't understand it. Fortunately, he left a one-line

PRE-COLUMBIAN?

The word *pre-Columbian* establishes the time before Columbus discovered the New World. His arrival on the scene was the catalyst that would bring to an end the cultures of the period that were then thriving. Some of the ancient cultures had died out many years before the Spanish arrival; but some continued beyond 1492, as in the case of the Aztec culture which continued until about 1521. The Maya endured (though in much smaller numbers) until well toward the end of the 16th century.

formula which, used as a mathematical and chronological key, opened up the science of Maya calculations and their great knowledge of astronomy.

Landa was called back to Spain in 1563 after complaints from colonial civil and religious leaders accusing him of "despotic mismanagement." He spent a year in prison, and while his guilt or innocence was being decided, he wrote his book in defense of the charges. During his absence, his replacement, Bishop Toral, acted with great compassion toward the Indians. Landa was ultimately cleared and allowed to return to the New World in 1573 where he took up the duties of bishop and quickly resumed his previous methods of proselytizing. He lived in Yucatan until his death in 1579.

Franciscan Power

Bishop Toral was cut from a different cloth. A humanitarian, he was appalled by the unjust treatment of Indians. Though Toral, after Landa's imprisonment, tried to impose sweeping changes sending his suggestions to Europe, he was unable to make inroads into the power held by the Franciscans in the Yucatan. Defeated, he ultimately retired to Mexico; it wasn't until a short time before his death (1571) that his reforms were implemented with the "Royal Cedula" which prohibited friars from shaving heads, flogging the Maya, and having prison cells in monasteries, and called for the immediate release of all Indians held prisoner.

Catholicism

Over the years, the majority of Indians were indeed baptized and made part of the Catholic faith. In fairness, most priests did their best to educate the people, teach them to read and write, and protect them from the growing number of Spanish settlers who used them as slaves. The Indians, then and now, practice Catholicism in their own manner, which is combined with the beliefs of their ancient cult handed down through centuries. These mystic yet Christian ceremonies occur in baptism, marriage, courtship, illness, farming, house-building, and fiestas.

Further Subjugation

While the rest of Mexico dealt with the problems of economic colonialism, the Yucatan Peninsula had an additional set: the harassment by vicious pirates who made life on the Gulf coast tenuous. Around 1600, when production of silver began to flag, Spain's economic power faltered. In the following years, *haciendas* (self-supporting estates or small feudal systems) began to thrive. Before these *haciendas, ejidos* (pre-Columbian villages of Indians jointly owning the land and living in a communal society) defined the living situation. But between 1700 and 1810, as Mexico endured several government upheavals in Europe, Spanish settlers on the Peninsula began exploiting the native Maya in earnest. The passive Indians were ground down, their

old Franciscan church in Muna

lands taken away, and their numbers greatly reduced by white man's epidemics and mistreatment.

Caste War

The Spaniards grabbed the Maya land, relentlessly planted it with tobacco and sugarcane year after year until the soil was worn out. Coupled with the other abuses it was inevitable that the Indians would ultimately explode in a furious attack. This bloody uprising, in the 1840s, is called the Caste War. Though the Maya were farmers, not soldiers, this savage war saw the Indians taking revenge on every white man, woman, and child by means of rape and violent murder. The few European survivors made their way to the last Spanish strongholds of Merida and Campeche. The governments of these two cities appealed for help to Spain, France, and the United States. No one answered the call, and it was apparent that the remaining two cities would soon be wiped out. But the fates would not have it that way. Just as the governor of Merida was about to begin evacuating the city, the Maya picked up their primitive weapons and walked away.

Sacred Corn

Attuned to the signals of the land, the Maya knew that the appearance of the flying ant was the first sign of rain. Corn was their sustenance, a gift from the gods, without which they would not survive. When the rains come, the corn must be in the soil, otherwise the gods would be insulted. When, on the brink of destroying the enemy, the winged ant made an unusually early appearance, the Indians turned their backs on certain victory and returned to their villages to plant corn.

This was just the breather the Spanish settlers needed. Help came from Cuba, Mexico City, and 1,000 U.S. mercenary troops. Vengeance was merciless. Most Maya, no matter his beliefs, were killed. Some were taken prisoner and sold to Cuba as slaves; others left their villages and hid in the jungles, in some cases for decades. Between 1846-1850 the population of the Yucatan Peninsula was reduced from 500,000 to 300,000. Guerilla war ensued, the escaped Maya making sneak attacks. Parts of the Peninsula along the Caribbean coast

were considered a dangerous no-man's land for almost another hundred years. (In 1936, President Lazaro Cardenas declared Quintana Roo a Territory under the jurisdiction of the Mexican government; in 1974, with the promise of the birth of tourism, the Territory was admitted to the Federation of States of Mexico.)

Growing Maya Power

In this coastal area of Quintana Roo, the Chan Santa Cruz Indians revived the cult of the "talking cross." The cross was a pre-Columbian symbol representing gods of the 4 cardinal directions. As a result of the words from the talking cross, shattered Indians came together in large numbers and began to organize. The community guarded the cross's location where advice strengthened the Maya. This was a religious/political marriage, with a priest, a master spy, and a ventriloquist in charge, all wise leaders who knew their people's desperate need for divine leadership.

The community, located close to the Belize border (at that time known as British Honduras), did a thriving business with the British, selling timber and buying arms. With these arms, in 1857 the Indians took advantage of the internal strife that weakened relations between Spanish Campeche and Merida, ending with Campeche seceding from the state of Yucatan in 1857. The Indians seized the Fort at Bacalar, putting them in control of the entire Caribbean coast, from Cabo Catouche to the border of British Honduras, and in 3 years destroyed numerous towns, slaughtering or capturing thousands of whites.

The Indians of the community of Chan Santa Cruz became known as Cruzobs. For years they murdered their captives, but starting in 1858 they took lessons from the colonials and began to keep the whites for slave labor in the fields and forest; women were put to work doing household chores and some were concubines. For the next 40 years, the Chan Santa Cruz Indians kept the E coast of the Yucatan for themselves; a shaky truce with the Mexican government endured. The Indians were financially independent, self governing, and with no roads in, totally isolated from technological advancements beginning to take place in other parts of the Peninsula. They were not at war so long as everyone left them alone and stayed away.

The Last Stand

It was only when Porfirio Diaz took power in 1876 that the Federal government began to think about the Yucatan Peninsula. It rankled Diaz that a handful of Indians had been able to keep the Mexican army at bay. Under the command of army General Ignacio Bravo a new assault on the Indians was made. The army captured a village, laid railroad tracks, and built a walled fort. Supplies got through the jungle to the fort by way of the railroad, but General Bravo also suffered at the hands of the clever Indians. The army and its general were besieged for a year until reinforcements arrived from the capital and the upstarts were finally put down. Even then the Indians demanded (and received) a negotiated settlement. When agreement was reached the Chan Santa Cruz Indians signed a peace treaty with the Feds. Now came a time of new beginnings, new growth, a new century.

MODERN TIMES

Meanwhile, in the northern part of the Peninsula, prosperity settled upon Merida, capital of the state of Yucatan. In 1875, the henequen boom began. Twine and rope, made from the sword-shaped leaves of this variety of the agave plant, was in demand all over the world. Merida became the jewel of the Peninsula. Spanish *haciendas* with their Indian slaves cultivated the easily grown plant, and for miles, the outlying areas were planted with the henequen that required little rainfall and thrived in the Peninsula's thin rocky soil. Beautiful mansions were built by the entrepeneurs who led the gracious life, sending their children to Europe to be educated, taking their wives by ship to New Orleans, looking for new luxuries and entertainment. Port towns were developed on the Gulf coast, and a 2-km-long wharf, built to accommodate the large ships that came for *sisal* (hemp from the henequen plant), was named Progreso. The only thing that didn't change was the lifestyle of the

Maya woman wearing handsewn huipil

peone. The Indian peasants' life was still oppressive and they had no human rights; they labored long hard hours to keep henequen production up. The Indians lived in constant debt to the company store, where their meager *peso* wage was spent, setting up a cycle of bondage that exists to this day in Merida. During this time in Merida, the lovely *huipil* (Indian dress) was mandated to be worn by all *mestizos* (those of mixed blood) on the Peninsula.

Hacienda Wealth

The outside world was becoming aware of the Peninsula, its newly found economic activity, and its rich *patrones.* In 1908, an American journalist, John Kenneth Turner, stirred things up when he documented how difficult (for the Indians) and prosperous (for the owners) life was on a henequen plantation. From this time forward, change was inevitable. Wealthy *hacienda* owners were compelled to pay (in 1915) an enormous tax to then President Venustiano Carranza. This tax was extracted under duress and the watchful eye of General Alvarado and 7,000 armed soldiers who needed the money to put down revolutionists Emiliano Zapata and Pancho Villa in the northern sections of Mexico. Millions of *pesos* changed hands. The next thorn in the side of the *hacienda* owners was the upstart Felipe Carrillo Puerto, the first Socialist governor of Merida. Under his tutelage the Indians set up a labor union, educational center and political club — "leagues of resistance." These leagues gave the *peones* the first hope ever held out to them. Through the leagues, workers wielded a power wealthy Yucatecans were forced to acknowledge. Carrillo pushed on, making agrarian reforms at every turn. He decreed that abandoned *haciendas* were up for appropriation. He was very successful, so much so that his opponents began to worry seriously about the power he was amassing. His followers were growing; conservatives knew he must be stopped and saw only one way out. In 1923 Felipe Carrillo Puerto was assassinated — but not his cause.

The Revolution

A continual fight for freedom from the power

This bust of Benito Juarez — one of Mexico's most respected presidents — can be seen in central plaza on Isla Cozumel.

held by wealthy landowners followed Carrillo's murder. In the south, Emiliano Zapata was demanding land reform; shortly thereafter, the Revolution put an end to the uneven control of wealth in the country. The new Constitution (1917) saw the large *haciendas* divided, giving the country back to the people and making sweeping political changes. The education of all children was decreed, and schools were built to implement it. Power of the church was curtailed and land redistributed. Sadly, the *ejido* was a casualty in this war of ideals and these communal groups were broken up. Turmoil continued and it wasn't until recent years that the Indians have benefited from this land division, when President Lazaro Cardenas (1934-40) gave half the usable land in Quintana Roo to the poor.

Mexican Unity

Between 1934-40, the Mexican government nationalized most of the foreign companies that were taking more out of the country than they were putting in. Mexico passed through a series of economic setbacks but gained a unity and a nationai self-confidence that enthusiastically heralded the economic strides to come. Like a crawling child wanting to walk, the country took many falls. But progress continued, the people of the country saw more jobs, fairer wages, and more products on the market — until the 1970s.

Inflation began to grow, and by 1976 it was totally out of hand. Mexico was pricing itself out of the market, both for tourists and capital investors. Ultimately, a change in the money policy let the *peso* float and find its own value against the dollar. This legislation brought back tourists and investors. The condition of the *peso* is a boon for visitors, but a burden for the people. The belief is that enough foreigners coming and spending their money will create more jobs so that in time the economic condition will remedy itself. Based on this belief, smart Mexican businessmen began developing the natural beauty of the Yucatan Peninsula, and indeed visitors are coming from all over the world.

ECONOMY

Mexico is trying valiantly to pull itself out of the realm of a developing country and continues to make rapid strides in economic growth. The average yearly wage per person has grown to the equivalent of US$1800, but inflation defeats the gains that have been made. The country has many natural resources to work with; however, if it can begin to control the inflation problem perhaps then it will be able to make use of the resources and provide enough jobs to keep up with the rapid population growth.

World's Largest City
Mexico is suffering from a population explosion. Mexico City, with 16 million people, is the largest city in the world. Each year 600,000 people enter the city's job market; only 400,000 jobs are available. Roughly 65% of the national population resides in cities, partly due to continuing migration from rural areas. In addition, a certain number of young Mexican adults, many accompanied by their families, try to make their way across the U.S. border, where there's more hope of getting jobs; about 6 million Mexicans presently live in the U.S. Because of this leave-the-land movement, the country's agriculture suffers. Mexico imports corn, cereals, and sugar, among others, and exports coffee, cotton, sisal, honey, bananas, and beef cattle.

Industries
Mexico's chief industries are oil, mining, and tourism. After the oil industry was nationalized in 1938, a time of transition slowed down production. Pemex, the state oil corporation, does not belong to the Organization of Petroleum Exporting Countries (OPEC) but keeps its prices in line with it. Most of the oil produced in Mexico is shipped to the U.S. (its number one customer), Canada, Israel, France, and Japan. Rich in natural gas, the country sends the U.S. 10% of its total output. Two-thirds of Mexico's export revenue comes from fossil fuels.

Mexico is still the world's largest producer of silver and fluorspar. It also processes large quantities of barite, antimony, bismuth, cop-

The local fishermen's cooperative operates from Cozumel's old downtown pier.

per, sulphur. Other minerals mined are gold, tin, manganese, zinc, coal, and iron. Although mining has always been important to the economy of Mexico, growth of the industry is slow, about a 2% increase per year. Around 60% of the country's industrial plants are concentrated around Mexico City, though the government is developing petrochemical processing industries along the U.S. border.

The Yucatan

Without question the leading money-maker on the Peninsula is the oil business. Along the Gulf coast from Campeche south into the state of Tabasco the oil industry is booming. Yucatan cities are beginning to show the signs of good financial health. Yucatecan fisheries are abundant along the Gulf coast. At one time fishing was not much more than a "ma and pa" business here, but today fleets of large purse seiners with their adjacent processing plants can be seen just south of the city of Campeche and on Isla del Carmen. With renewed interest in preserving the fishing grounds for the future, the fishing industry could continue to thrive for many years.

In the Yucatan Peninsula, "finishing" plants are enthusiastically being developed. Products from the U.S. such as dresses and leather goods are begun in the States, then sent to Mexico to be completed by the cheaper labor force.

Tourism is developing into the number two contributor to the economy. Going with a good thing, the government has set up a National Trust to begin a program of developing beautiful areas of the country to attract visitors. Cancun is one successful result. Where once was an overgrown sandbar is now one of Mexico's most modern and popular resorts. Other naturally attractive sites are earmarked for future development. Extra attention is also being given to archaeological zones ignored for hundreds of years: building restrooms, ticket offices, and fences to keep out vandals.

Travel in Mexico gets better every day. For the Mexican people, the deflated *peso* is a sock in the eye. For the traveler in Mexico, the dollar is worth more than ever. Now is definitely the time to take a vacation in the Yucatan Peninsula.

THE PEOPLE

For hundreds of years, scholars of the world have asked, what happened to the Maya people? Their magnificent structures, built with such advanced skill, still stand. Many carvings, unique statuary, and even a few colored frescoes remain. All of this art depicts a world of intelligent human beings living in a well-organized, complex society. It's apparent their trade and agricultural methods supported a large population. Scholars agree the Maya was the most advanced of all ancient Mesoamerica cultures. Yet, all signs point to an abrupt work stoppage. After around A.D. 900, no buildings were constructed, and no *stelae*, carefully detailing names and dates to inform future generations of their roots, were erected. So what happened? Where did the people go?

Traveling through the Peninsula, it becomes apparent that *the people* didn't go anywhere! In every village you are greeted with the same faces and profiles that are frozen in carved panels displayed on elegant structures throughout Mayaland.

A Society Collapses

Priests and noblemen, the guardians of re-ligion, sciences, and the arts, conducted their ritual ceremonies and studies in the large stone pyramids and platforms today found in ruins throughout the jungle. More specific questions could be: what happened to the priests and noblemen? Why were the centers abandoned? What happened to the knowledge of the intelligentsia who studied the skies, wrote the books, and designed the pryamids? Theories abound! Some speculate about a revolution of the people or decentralization with the arrival of outside influences. Others suggest the Indians tired of subservience, and were no longer willing to farm the land to provide food, clothing, and support for the priests and nobles. Whatever happened, it's clear that the special knowledge concerning astronomy, hieroglyphics, and architecture was apparently not passed on to the descendents of the Maya. Sociologists who've lived with Indians in isolated villages are convinced that this privileged information is no longer known by today's Maya. Why did the masses disperse, leaving once-sacred stone cities unused and ignored? It's possible that lengthy periods of drought, famine, and epidemic caused the peo-

A balloon is fun in any language.

ple to leave their once glorious sacred centers. No longer important to their day-to-day existence, these structures were ignored for a thousand years to face the whimsy of nature and its corroding elements. These questions may never be answered with authority.

However, there's hope in today's technology. The astronauts, for example, have seen many wonders from outer space, spotting within the thick uninhabited jungle of the Yucatan many untouched structures, large treasures of knowledge just waiting to be rediscovered. As new discoveries are made, the history of the Maya develops new depth and breadth.

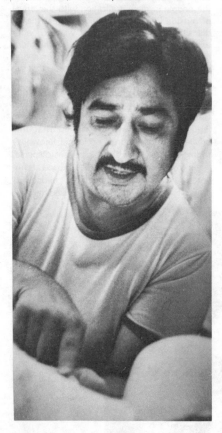

contraption used to flatten the heads of the newborn

Modern Times

Today's knowledge of the Maya is gathered from varied sources: archaeologists, ethnologists, art historians, and linguists continue to unravel the ongoing mystery with constant new discoveries of temples and artifacts that each have a story to tell. Native writings such as the *Chalam Balam* follow the history and traditions of the period just before the Spanish came, and a few books written soon after the Spanish conquest provide vivid firsthand accounts of Maya life in its last days of cultural purity, especially Landa's complete description of Maya life, *Relaciones de las Cosas*.

PHYSICAL CHARACTERISTICS

Maya men and women average 1.62 and 1.50 m tall respectively. Muscular bodied, they have straight black hair, round heads, broad faces with pronounced cheekbones, aquiline noses, almond-shaped dark eyes, and eyelids with the epicanthic or Mongolian fold (a prolongation of a fold of the upper eyelid over the inner angle or both angles of the eye). Some of the highland groups, such as the Tzeltals and Tzotzils, have

mestizo hat maker

elongated heads—perhaps as a result of their centuries-long geographic and genetic isolation.

Stylized Beauty

Bishop Diego de Landa writes in his *Relaciones* that when the Spanish arrived, the Maya still practiced the ancient method of flattening a newborn's head with a press made of boards. By pressing the infant's forehead, the fronto-nasal portion of the face was pushed forward, as can be seen in carvings and other human depictions from the pre-Columbian period. This was considered a very important sign of beauty. Further, they dangled a bead in front of a baby's eyes to encourage cross-eyedness, another Maya beauty mark. Dental mutilation was practiced by filing the teeth to give them different shapes or by making slight perforations and inlaying pyrite, jade, or turquoise. Tattooing and scarification were accomplished by lightly cutting a design into the skin and purposely infecting it, creating a scar of beauty. Adult noblemen often wore a phony nosepiece to give the illusion of an even longer nose

sweeping back into the long flat forehead.

The Maya Bloodline

In the past, few outsiders ever stayed long in the Yucatan. Wherever the Spanish had a stronghold, the purity of Spanish blood precluded contact with the Indian slaves. Mixed marriages were not permitted. Even as recently as the turn of this century, cities boasted of a pure line of Spanish blood: specifically Izamal and Merida. Similarly, isolation of the Indian people kept the Maya pure. The resemblance to the people of a thousand years ago is understandable, but still amazing!

Today, 75-80% of the entire population of Mexico is estimated to be *mestizo* (mixed blood, mostly Indian and Spanish), with 10-15% pure Indian. (For comparison, as recently as 1870, pure-blooded Indians made up over 50% of the population.) While no statistics are available, it's believed most of the 15% of the population who are pure Indian live on the Peninsula.

Maya bullfighters

ANCIENT CULTURE
OF THE YUCATAN PENINSULA

RELIGION AND SOCIETY

The Earth

The Maya saw the world as a flat layered square. At the 4 corners (each representing a cardinal direction) stood 4 bearded gods called Becabs that held up the skies. In the underworld, 4 gods called Pahuatuns steadied the earth. Both the skies and underworld were divided in layers, with a determined number of steps up and down. The gods and each direction were associated with colors: black for west, white for north, yellow for south, and most important, red for east. In the center of the earth stood the Tree of Life, *la ceiba*. Its powerful roots reached the underworld, and its lofty foliage swept the heavens, connecting the two. The *ceiba* was associated with the color blue-green *(yax)* along with all important things — water, jade, and new corn.

The Indians were terrorized by the underworld and what it represented: odious rivers of rotting flesh and blood, and evil gods such as Jaguar God of the Night, whose spotty hide was symbolized by the starry sky. Only the priests could communicate with and control the gods. For this reason, the populace was content to pay tribute to and care for all the needs of the priests.

Ceremonies

Ceremony appears to have been a vital part of the daily lives of the Maya. Important rituals took place on specific dates of their accurate calendar; everyone took part. These often bizarre activities were performed in the plazas, on the platforms, and around the broad grounds of the temple-cities. Some rituals were secret and only priests took part within the inner sanctums of the temple. Sweat baths commonly found at the centers were also incorporated into the religion.

Other ceremonies included fasts, abstinences, purification, dancing, prayers, and simple sacrifices of food, animals, or possessions (jewelry, beads and ceramics) amid clouds of smoky incense. The later Maya took part in self-inflicted mutilation of the body. Frequently found depictions (in carvings) show the Indian

symbolic
Chaac nose

A CEREMONY FOR CHAAC

Anyone fortunate enough to be invited to a Maya ritual should by all means attend and be grateful for the honor. Many rites are used for many occasions, and all are a fascinating marriage of Catholic and Maya mysticism. At a *Chachaac* rite, a Maya priest and the people beseech the rain god Chaac for help. The first surprise is the altar (in this case in a clearing in a jungle) made of poles and branches that would be at home in a Catholic church. With distinct corners and a tall candle on each, the altar has been dedicated to the 4 cardinal points—sacred in the Maya cult. In the center is a crucifix with a Christus dressed not in a loincloth, but in a white skirt embroidered with bright red flowers like a *huipil.*

The priest is brought offerings of cigarettes, soda pop, sometimes food, even a raw chicken. A small group of onlookers finds stones and sits down for the ceremony (usually men only) in front of the priest.

Some of the cigarettes are placed on one end of the altar next to small gourd bowls. On the ground nearby lays a plastic-covered trough made from a hollowed log. At the beginning of the ceremony (dusk), the priest lifts a plastic sheet, and pulls something from a pocket in his workshirt, and drops it into the log. He then pours water into a bucket, adding ground corn and mixing it with a small bundle of leaves and kneels on an old burlap sack with his young helper beside him. The two of them pray quietly in Maya dialect to Chaac for quite awhile. At some unseen signal, one of the men in the group throws incense on a shovel of hot coals, and the priest begins praying in Spanish. Everyone stands up and chants Hail Marys and Our Fathers. The priest dips his sheaf of leaves in a gourd and scatters consecrated water in all directions—now the ceremony begins in earnest.

Young boys sitting under the altar make frog sounds (a sign of coming rain) while gourds of the sacred corn drink *zaca* are passed to each person. Christian prayers continue, and more *zaca* is passed around, several hours passing with rests in between. Bubbling liquid sounds come from the log trough. It's a mixture of honey, water, and bark from a *balche* tree. The priest takes intermittent naps between rounds of prayers. The men occasionally stop and drink beer, or smoke a cigarette from the altar. The young acolyte gently nudges the napping priest and the praying starts again. Each round of prayers lasts about 45 minutes, and the nine rounds continue throughout the night. No one leaves, and the fervency of the prayers never diminshes.

At dawn, after a lengthier than usual round of prayers, the priest spreads out polished sacred divination stones on the burlap sack and studies them for some time. Everyone watches him intently and after a long silence, he shakes his head. The verdict is in; there would be no rain for the village this planting season.

The sun comes up and the men prepare a feast. Chaac must not be insulted despite the bad news. Thick corn dough cakes, layered with ground squash seeds and marked with a cross are placed in a large pit lined with hot stones. The cakes are covered with palm leaves and then buried with dirt. While the bread bakes and the gift-chicken stews in broth, blood, and spices, gourds of *balche,* Coca Cola, or a mixture of both are passed around to all—for as long as they can handle it. The mixture is not fermented enough to be as hallucinogenic as it is proclaimed, but enough to make the outsider quite ill. The rest of the morning is spent feasting and drinking. Chaac had spoken, so be it.

The priest accurately forecast the weather that night; no rain fell the rest of that spring or summer. The villagers didn't raise corn in their *milpas* that year.

pulling a string of thorns through a hole in his tongue or penis and the blood that ensued. The most brutal were sacrifices including death by a variety of causes. Sacrificial victims were thrown into a sacred well; if they didn't drown within a certain length of time (often overnight), they were rescued and then expected to relate their conversation with the spirits that lived in the bottom of the well. Other methods of sacrifice were spearing, beheading, or removing the heart of the victim with a knife and offering it—still beating!—to the spirits.

Sacrifices were made to gain the approval of the gods. Although old myths and stories claimed young female virgins were most often sacrificed in the sacred *cenotes*, after dredging and diving in the muddy water in various ruins on the Yucatan Peninsula, it turns out most of the victims were young children, both male and female.

Time

The priests of the Classic Period represented time as a parade of gods that were really numbers moving through Maya eternity in careful mathematical order. They were shown carrying heavy loads with tumplines around their heads. The combination of the gods and their burdens reflected the exact number of days gone by since the beginning of the Maya calendar count. Each god has particular characteristics, such as Number Nine, an attractive young man with the spots of a serpent on his chin, sitting leaning forward, jade necklace dangling on one knee. His right hand reaches up to adjust his tumpline. His load is the screech owl of the *baktun* (the 144,000-day period). Together, the two represent 9 times 144,000, or 1,296,000 days; the number of days elapsed since the beginning of the Maya day count and the day the glyph was carved, maybe 1,275 years ago. Archaeologists call this a Long Count date. Simpler methods also were used, including combinations of dots and bars (ones and fives, respectively, with special signs for zero). Most Mayanists agree that the date of the beginning of the Long Count was August 10, 3114 B.C.

Status

If this sounds complicated to you, it's no dif-

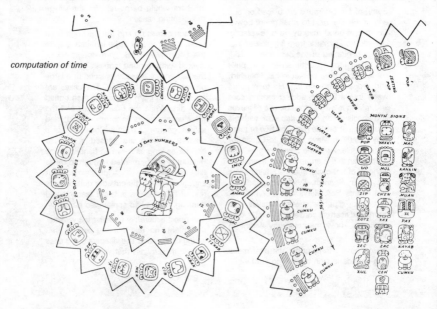

computation of time

ferent than the complex, stratified society that made up the Maya civilization. The society of many classes was headed by the Elite who controlled matters of warfare, religion, government, and commerce. Also in this group were the architects who designed the magnificent temples and pyramids. Skilled masons belonged to a class that included servants of royalty. Priests directed the people in participation in a realm governed by a pantheon of gods who demanded constant homage and penance.

Farmers were instrumental in maintaining the social order. They battled the hostile environment, constantly fighting the jungle and frequent droughts. Their creativity enabled them to win out most of the time; slashing fields from rainforest, constructing raised plots in swampy depressions, and building canals to bring the water where it was needed. In some areas they even terraced the land to conserve soil and make ultimate use of water. The result, with the use of tools of stone, wood, and hand labor, was sufficient to feed a population that ultimately grew to large numbers. Often overseen by the priests, all of these matters maintained a close relationship to the Maya religion.

THE ARTS

Pottery

The Maya were outstanding potters. Some of the earliest Maya pottery art is dated to 36 B.C. and found at Izapan. Evidence of advancement is apparent with the variety of new forms, techniques, and artistic motifs that developed during the Classic Period. Growth has been traced from simple monochrome ceramics of early periods to bichrome and then later to rich polychrome; polychrome drawings on pottery work has been found with recognizeable color still visible. Three-legged plates with a basal edge and small, conical supports, as well as covered and uncovered vessels, were prevalent. A screw-on lidded jar was found in 1984 in Rio Azul, a Maya site in an isolated corner of Guatemala; an amazing find!

The figurines, especially those found in graves on the island of Jaina, were faithful reproductions of the people and their times.

Maya pottery

Many decorated pottery vessels used for everyday purposes tell us something about these people that enjoyed a touch of class along with the mundane. Decorative motifs ranged from simple geometric designs to highly stylized natural figures to simple true-to-life reproductions. We have learned much from their realistic representations of their bodies (even those that were pathologically deformed), and garments and adornments that were typical of their time. Through this precise method we get a glimpse into the lives of people of all social classes: common men and women, noblemen and priests, musicians, craftsmen, merchants, warriors, ballplayers, even animals. Many of these clay figurines were made to be used as flutes, whistles, ocarinas, rattles, or incense holders. Noteworthy are the quantity of female figurines that appear to represent the fertility goddess Ixchell.

Sculpture

The Maya used their great talent for sculpture almost exclusively for the decoration of ritualistic temples and sanctuaries. They employed a variety of techniques, depending on the areas and what natural resources were available. They excelled in free-standing stone carving, such as the *stelae* and altars. In areas where stone wasn't as available, such as Palenque, stucco art is outstanding. The Indians added rubber to the plaster-and-water mixture creating an extremely durable surface that would polish to a fine luster. In Palenque you'll see marvelous examples of stucco bas-reliefs adorning pyramids, pillars, stairways, walls, friezes, masks and heads. Sculpting was done not only in stone, but also in precious materials such as gold and silver. Some of their finest work was done in jade, a substance they held in great reverence.

Painting

Paints were of mineral and vegetable origin in hues of red, yellow, brown, blue, green, black, and white. Mural painting reached a high degree of expression with the Maya. The murals, found in several ancient sites, depict everyday life, ceremonies, and battle scenes in brilliant colors. Bright color was also applied to the carved stone structures, pyramids and *stelae.* Today all color has disappeared from the outside of these buildings along with most of the finishing plaster that was used as a smooth coating over large building stones. When Cortez' men first viewed the coast of Tulum, it must have been quite a thing to behold: brilliantly colored buildings in the midst of lush green jungle, overlooking a clear turquoise sea!

SCIENCE

Inscriptions of the Maya relate to calculations of time, mathematics, and the gods. Astronomy was also a highly developed science integrated within the cult. The Maya shared their concept of zero and calendar system with other Mesoamerican groups. But they went on to perfect and develop the sophisticated calendar system that turns out to be more exact to a ten-thousandth of a day than the Gregorian Calendar in use today.

Hieroglyphics

Hieroglyphics used in scientific calculations and descriptions are seen everywhere on the Yucatan Peninsula: in carved panels in the temples, decorating steps on pyramids, and in *stelae* commonly installed in front of the great structures, carrying pertinent data of building and people of that era. The most important examples of the system are the three codices that were not destroyed by the *conquistadores.* In the codices, symbols were written carefully on pounded fig bark with the use of brushes and various dyes developed from plants and trees. Similar to Maya fine art, it was the upper class and priests who learned, developed, and became highly skilled with hieroglyphics. When they suddenly and inexplicably stopped functioning around A.D. 900, long before the Spanish arrived on the Peninsula, all science and artwork ceased.

ring at Chichen Itza ball court

MAYA "BASKETBALL"

Ballparks were prevalent in the ceremonial centers located throughout the Yucatan Peninsula. Though today's Maya is peaceful, at one time bloody games were part of the ancient cult as seen from the remaining art work (as in a panel in Chichen Itza's Temple of the Bearded Man). The carvings graphically show that either the losing or (as a few far-out scientists have suggested) winning team was awarded a bloody death. The players were heavily padded with leather, and the object of the game was to hit a hard rubber ball into a cement ring attached to a wall 8 m off the ground. Legend says the game went on for hours and the winners (or losers) were awarded clothes and jewelry from the spectators.

HOUSING

Thanks to remaining stone carvings, we know how the ancient Maya lived. We know that their houses were almost identical to the *palapa* huts that many people still live in today. Huts were built with tall thin sapling trees placed close together forming the walls, then topped with a *palapa* roof. This type of house provided cool circulation through the walls, and the thick *palapa* roof allowed the rain to run off easily, keeping the inside snug and dry. In the early years there were no real doors and few furnishings. Then (as now), families slept in hammocks, the coolest way to sleep. For the rare times that it turned cold, tiny fires were built on the floor below the hammocks to keep the family warm. Most of the cooking was done either outdoors or in another hut. Often a small group of people (extended families) built their huts together on one plot and lived almost a communal lifestyle. If one member of the group brought home a deer, everyone shared in this trophy. Though changing, this is still commonplace throughout the rural areas of the Peninsula.

Yucatan hammocks have a reputation for being the best in the world. Many local people sleep in them and love it. Hamacas are cool, easy to store, make wonderful cribs that babies cannot fall out of (at least not easily), and come in a variety of sizes.

It's important to know the size you want when shopping. The Yucatecans make a matrimonial which is supposed to be big enough for 2 persons to sleep comfortably; for even more comfort, ask for the familiar, weavers say the whole family fits! A good hammock stretches out to approximately 5 m long (one-third of which is the woven section), and the width 3-5 m pulled out (gently, don't stretch!). Check the end strings, called brazos; there should be at least 100 to 150 triple loops for a matrimonial.

A variety of materials is used: synthetics, henequen, cotton, and linen. It's a toss-up whether the best is pure cotton or linen. The finer the thread the more comfortable; the tighter the weave the more resilient. Experts say it takes 8 km of thread for a matrimonial.

SPANISH CULTURE

Cortez' arrival was greeted by a peasant culture. The large ceremonial centers had long been abandoned. According to Bishop de Landa, the people still practiced the ancient cult, but the huge stone monoliths were already being overtaken by the jungle. It was inevitable that the Spanish culture would ultimately supplant the Indians'. Their books were destroyed and they were overpowered by the Spanish belief that Maya ways were evil. Ultimately, the old beliefs were mixed in a strange rendition of Christianity. Surprisingly, the Catholic priests accept this marriage of religion, and it can be seen today in many of the functions and holiday celebrations. In small rural pockets that have had little contact with the modern world, certain customs and ceremonies still take place, but in secret. The Maya learned their lessons the hard way, and some believe that they still maintain an underground pipeline of

*turn-of-the century Spanish
mansion in Merida*

the ancient culture. However, as more tourists and travelers come into the area, this culture and the old ways are becoming diluted with progress.

TODAY'S CULTURAL CHARACTERISTICS

Language
The farther away you go from a city, the less Spanish is spoken—only Maya or a dialect of Maya is heard. The government estimates that of the 10 million Mexican Indians in the country, about 25% speak only an Indian dialect. Of the original 125 native languages, 70 are still spoken. Of this number, 20 are different Maya languages, including Tzeltal, Tzotzil, Chol, and Yucatan Maya. Though mandatory education in Mexico was initiated in 1917, like most laws, this one didn't reach the Yucatan Peninsula till quite recently. Despite efforts to integrate the Indian into Mexican society, many remain content with the status quo. Schools throughout the Peninsula use Spanish-language books, even though many of these children speak only some form of Maya. In some of the smaller schools in rural areas (such as in Akumal), bilingual teachers (Spanish and local dialects) are recruited to help children make the transition.

Higher Education
For years, students wanting an education on the Peninsula had to travel to Merida to the university. The numbers going on to university grows with each generation, and universities are slowly being built. Two colleges are now available in Merida (Yucatan state), and one each in Campeche and Tabasco. The state of Quintana Roo still does not have a university for its youngsters.

Today's Housing
The major difference in today's rural housing is the growth of the *ranchito*. Only one hut sits on a family farm where corn is raised, and sometimes a few pigs and turkeys, maybe even a few head of cattle. The Indians have become slightly more comfortable with a table and chairs, a lamp, and maybe a metal bathing tub as the only furniture in the room. In the S,

*Maestro Federico holds the attention of his young students at
Akumal's 2-room school house where children 4-16 attend class.*

huts are often built of planks and tin roofs. In
the N more are constructed with stucco walls.
The only modern touch to the hut design is the
frequently seen electric meter and wires poking through even the sapling walls. Many huts
may have electric light and often radios, but
few have refrigeration.

Family

Small children in Mexico are treated with great
love and caring. Until recently families always
had many children. A man validated his
masculinity with a large family; the more
children, the more respect. The labor around
the family plot was happily doled out to each as
they came along. Today's young couples encounter the same problem that plague parents
everywhere: the expense of raising children is
growing. Just to provide the basics—food,
clothing, housing—is creating havoc for the
poorer families. Though education is free,
many rural parents need their children to help
with work on the *ranchito*. That and the cost of
books still prevent many Yucatecan children
from getting an education. Gradually this is
changing, and the government is trying to im-
press the people with the importance of
schooling by providing one in all areas.

FIESTAS AND CELEBRATIONS

Mexico knows how to give a party! Everyone who visits the Yucatan should take advantage of any holidays falling during the visit. Workers are given a day off on legal holidays, and the biggest fiestas take place on the following dates each year.

As well as the public festivals listed, a birthday, baptism, saint day, wedding, a leaving, a returning, a good crop, or many more reasons than we'd ever think of are good excuses to celebrate with a fiesta. One of the simplest but most charming celebrations of a holiday is on Mother's Day in Playa del Carmen. Children both young and old serenade mothers (usually this means a live band), theirs and other people's, with beautiful songs under their windows in the evening of the special day. If invited to a fiesta, join in and have fun. Even the most humble family manages to scrape together money for a great party on these occasions.

Village Festivities

More money means fancier fireworks. Half the fun is watching preparations which generally take all day, with everyone involved. Both big and little kids get goosebumps of excitement watching the *specialiste* wrapping and tying bamboo poles together with mysterious packets of paper-wrapped explosives. At some point this often tall *castillo* (structure holding the fireworks) will be tilted up and admired by all. Well after dark, at the height of the celebration, the colorful explosives are set off with a spray of light and sound, to appreciative cheers of delight.

Village fiestas are a wonderful time of dancing, music, noise, colorful costumes, good food and usually lots of drinking. A public fiesta is generally held in the central plaza, surrounded by temporary stalls where you can get Mexican fast food: tamales, both sweet and meat, *bun-*

Have you ever danced with a bottle on your head? These dancers do it in style.

Sunday evening in the plaza is always a party.

uelos (sweet rolls), tacos, *refrescos* (soft drinks), *churros* (fried dough dusted with sugar—taste like donuts), *carne asada* (barbecued meat), and plenty of beer chilling in any convenient ice-filled container.

Beware "The Egg"
You'll find innocent-looking little old ladies selling the "dreaded eggshell" filled with confetti, ready to be smashed on an unsuspecting head. So be prepared if you're the only gringo around! Your head or any convenient part of the body will be pummeled with the colorful bombs by anyone tall enough. This is followed by a quick getaway and lots of giggles from onlookers. The more you respond with good nature and even a forced smile, you will continue to be the target—and what the heck, whether the headache is from too much beer or too many eggs doesn't matter. Besides, it might be time for you to plunk out a few *pesos* for your own bombs! This is part of joining in—and having fun!

A Marriage Of Cultures
Many festivals in Mexico are in honor of religious feast days. You'll see a unique combination of religious fervor and ancient cult mixed with plain old good times. In the church plaza, dances that have been passed down from family to family since before Cortez introduced Christianity to the New World continue for hours. Dancers dress in symbolic costumes of bright colors, feathers and bells, reminding crowds of onlookers about their

Maya past. Inside the church is a constant stream of candle-carrying devout, some traveling long distances to *perigrinate* (a devout journey), sometimes even traveling several km entirely on the knees to the church repaying a promise made to a deity months before in thanks for a personal favor: a healing, job found, or who knows what.

Some villages offer a *corrida* (bull fight) as part of the festivities. Even a small town will have a simple bull ring. In the Yucatan these rings are frequently built of bamboo. In Maya fashion, no nails are used—only twine (made from henequen) to hold together a two-tiered bull ring! The country *corrida* has a special charm. If celebrating a religious holiday, a procession carrying the image of the honored deity might lead off the proceedings. The bull has it good here; there are no blood-letting ceremonies and the animal is allowed to live and carry on his reproductive activites in the pasture. Only a tight rope around its middle provokes sufficient anger for the fight. Local young men perform in the arena with as much heart and grace as professionals in Mexico City. And the crowd shows its admiration with shouts, cheers, and of course, *musica!*—even if the band is composed only of a drum, a trumpet, and a guitar. Good fun for everyone, even those who don't understand the art of the *corrida*.

Religious Feastdays
Christmas and Easter are wonderful holidays.

continued on page 42

FIESTAS AND CELEBRATIONS

Jan. 1: **New Years Day.** Legal Holiday.

Jan. 6: **Dia De Los Reyes Magos.** Day of the Three Kings. On this day Christmas gifts are exchanged.

Feb. 2: **Candelaria.** Candlemas. Many villages celebrate with candlelight processions.

Feb. 5: **Flag Day.** Legal holiday.

Feb./Mar.: Date determined by Easter **Carnival.** The week before Ash Wed., beginning of Lent, moveable. Some of the best festivals of the year are held this week. In Merida, Isla Mujeres, Cozumel, Campeche: parades with colorful floats, costume balls and sporting events. Chetumal: a parade with floats, music, and folk dances from all over Mesoamerica.

Mar. 21: **Birthday Of Benito Juarez** (1806). Legal Holiday.

Mar. 21: **Chichen Itza.** Vernal Equinox, a phenomenon of light and shadow displaying the pattern of a serpent slithering down the steps of the Pyramid of Kulkucan.

May 1: **Labor Day.** Legal holiday.

May 3: **Day Of The Holy Cross.** Dance of the Pig's Head performed during fiestas at Celestun, Felipe Carrillo Puerto, and Hopelchen.

May 5: **Battle Of Puebla,** also known as **Cinco De Mayo.** In remembrance of the 1862 defeat of the French. Legal Holiday.

May 12-18: **Chankah Veracruz** (near Felipe Carrillo Puerto), honoring the Virgin of the Immaculate Conception. Maya music, bullfights, and religious procession.

May 15: **San Isidro Labrador.** Festivals held at Panaba (near Valladolid) and Calkini (SW of Merida).

May 20-30: **Becal.** Jipi Fiesta in honor of the plant *jipijapa,* used in making Panama hats, the big money-maker for most of the population.

June 29: **Day Of San Pedro.** All towns with the name of San Pedro. Fiestas held in Sanahcat and Cacalchen (near Merida), Tekom, and Panaba (near Valladolid).

Early July: **Ticul** (near Uxmal). Week-long fiesta celebrating the establishment of Ticul. Music, athletic events, dancing and fireworks.

Sept. 15: **Independence Day.** Legal holiday.

Sept. 27-Oct. 14: **El Senor De Las Ampollas** in Merida. Religious holiday. Big fiesta with fireworks, religious services, music and dancing.

Oct. 4: **Feast Day Of San Francisco De Asisi.** Usually a week-long fiesta precedes this day in Uman, Hocaba, Conkal and Telchac Pueblo (each near Merida).

Oct. 12: **Columbus Day.** Legal holiday.

Oct. 18-28: **Izamal.** Fiesta honoring El Cristo de Sitilpech. A procession carries an image of Christ from Sitilpech to the church in Izamal. Religious services, fireworks, music, dancing. Biggest celebration on the 25th.

Oct. 31: **Eve Of All Souls Day.** Celebrated all through the Yucatan. Flowers and candles placed on graves, the beginning of an 8-day observance.

Nov. 1-2: **All Souls Day And Day Of The Dead.** Graveside and church ceremonies. A party-like atmosphere in all the cemeteries. Food and drink vendors do a lively business, as well as candy makers with their sugar skulls and skeletons. A symbolic family meal is eaten at the gravesite.

Nov. 8: **Conclusion Of El Dia De Muerte.** Day of the Dead.

Nov. 20: **Dia De La Revolucion.** Revolution Day of 1910. Legal Holiday.

Dec. 8: **Feast Of The Immaculate Conception.** Fiestas at Izamal, Celestun (including a boat procession), and Chompoton (boat procession carrying a statue of Mary, waterskiing show, other aquatic events, dancing, fair).

Dec. 12: **Our Lady Of Guadalupe.**

Dec. 25: **Christmas.** Legal Holiday.

BULLFIGHTING

The bullfight is not for everyone. Many foreigners feel it's inhumane treatment of a helpless animal. There is bloodletting at most of these spectacles. If you can't tolerate this sort of thing, you'd probably be happier not attending a bullfight.

Bullfighting is big business in Mexico, Spain, Portugal, and S. America. The *corrida de toros* (running of the bulls) is made up of a troupe of well-paid men all playing an important part in the drama. Each Sunday and holiday 50,000 people fill the country's largest arena (in Mexico City) for each performance. The afternoon starts off (promptly at 1600) with music and a colorful parade of solemn pomp with *matadores* and *picadores* on horseback, *banderilleros,* plus drag mules and many ring attendants. The *matadores* ceremoniously circle the crowded arena to the roar of the crowd. The afternoon has begun!

The *matador* is the star of the event. This ceremony is a test of a man and his courage. He's in the arena for one purpose—to kill the bull—but bravely, with classic moves and within a given length of time. Ideally, the *matador* stands tall and straight. With graceful passes of the cape he works the bull *around* his still body, bringing the huge beast (and its lethal horns) closer each time. If he knows his business and has a sense of the

dramatic, the *matador* manages to work the crowd into a frenzy and at just the right moment, turns his back on the bull and requests permission from the judge to kill the bull. If he has been brave and daring, maintained his posture and command of the bull with elegant style and timing, the crowd roars its approval and the judge nods his permission. If he has not fulfilled all of these requirements, the onlookers then roar their *disapproval* with him or even a bull that is not courageous. With permission to proceed to the *hour of truth,* he dedicates the bull either to a special person in the crowd by throwing his *montera* (hat) to the honored person or with a broad gesture with his hat to the crowd dedicates the kill to the entire arena. And now he must show his real talent.

A trumpet sounds the beginning of a 16-minute period, the last *tercio*. The bull must be killed within that time limit. The large cape is traded for the *muleta,* a smaller "killing" cape. At just the right moment and with great cunning, he slips the *estoque* (sword) into the bull's neck. If he's an artist, he will sever the aorta and the huge animal immediately slumps to the ground and dies instantly. If the *matador* displays extraordinary grace, skill, and bravery, the crowd awards him the ears and the tail, and their uncontrollable adulation. If he misses he could be killed by the bull or his own sword. If it takes several thrusts of the sword, the crowd feels they have been cheated (and certainly it's hard on the bull). If the 16-minute period passes and the bull is still alive, the *matador* is humiliated and ordered from the ring. The bull is lured into the corral, slaughtered and sold.

Bullfighting has long been one of the most popular events in Mexico. Aficionados of this Spanish artform thrill to the excitement of the crowd, the stirring music, the grace and courage of a noble *matador,* and the bravery of a good bull. A student of Mexican culture will want to witness the *corrida de toros* to learn more about this powerful art. And *art* is the key word. A bullfight is not really a fight; it is an artistic scene of pageantry and ceremony that's been celebrated all over Europe since the Middle Ages.

Records of the first primitive bullfight come to us from the island of Crete, 2,000 years before Christ. At the same time in Spain savage wild bulls roamed the Iberian peninsula. When faced with killing one of these vicious animals, young men would "dance" as close as possible to the brute to show their bravery before finally killing the animal with an axe.

The Romans began importing Spanish wild bulls for Colosseum spectacles and even Julius Caesar is said to have gotten in the ring with a wild bull. The Arabs in Spain stimulated *tauromachia* (bullfighting).

In 1090, El Cid (Rodrigo Diaz de Vivar), the hero of Valencia and subject of romantic legend, is believed to have fought in the first *organized* bull festival. With great skill he lanced and killed a wild bull from the back of his horse. In that era, only noblemen were allowed to use a lance, and the *corrida* soon became the sport of kings. Bullfighting quickly became popular, and it was *the* daring event for the rich. A feast day celebration wasn't complete without a *corrida de toros* and the number of noblemen killed while participating in this event began to grow.

To stop the *corrida,* Pope Pius V issued an edict threatening to excommunicate anyone killed while bullfighting. This didn't dull the enthusiasm of the Spanish; the edict was withdrawn and the fights continued. Queen Isabella and King Philip ordered bullfighting by nobles halted. The fights ceased just about the time a new brave twist changed the spectacle. Who knows whether it was out of respect for their monarch that they quit, or because they were being over-shadowed by the common man who showed amazing courage facing the bull without a horse.

Forbidden to use the lance, commoners began fighting bulls on foot, using a cape to hide the sword and confuse the bull. This was the beginning of the *corrida* as we know it today.

The modern *corrida* has changed little in the past 200 years. The beautiful clothes, originally designed by the Spanish artist Goya, are still used. Richly embroidered silk capes draped over the railing of the arena add a gala touch. Even at the smallest Yucatecan village *corrida,* the traditional costume design persists. Though made of simple cotton (rather than rich satin and gold-trimmed silk) and delicately embroidered with typical designs of the Yucatan, the *matador* is impressively dressed.

Gone are the wild bulls; the animals are now bred on large Mexican ranches just for the bullring. Only the finest—those showing superior strength, cunning and bravery—are sent to the ring, trained for years for one shining day.

The season begins in December and lasts for three months. The rest of the year it's the *novilleros* (neophyte bullfighters) that are seen in plazas across the country. They must prove themselves in the arena before they are acknowledged (and highly paid) *matadores*. Bullfighting is as dangerous now as when the pope tried to ban it in the 16th century. Almost half of the most renowned *matadores* in the past 250 years have died in the ring.

Bullfights take place regularly on Sunday afternoons and for special events. The best seats are on the shady side of the arena, *la sombra,* and are more costly. Bring a hat, binoculars, sunscreen, and small change for the soda/beer vendor. Don't carry a weapon (even a penknife) and be prepared for a possible quick frisk as you enter the arena (they seldom frisk women). Ask at your hotel or local travel agency for ticket information.

Many fiestas are held in honor of a religious occasion with processions like this one at Chan-Kom to lead off the festivities.

continued from page 37

The *posada* (procession) of Christmas begins 9 days before the holiday, when families and friends take part in processions which portray Mary and Joseph and their search for lodging before the birth of Christ. The streets are alive with people, bright lights, colorful nativity scenes. Families provide swinging *pinatas* (pottery pots covered with *papier mache* in the shape of a popular animal or perky character filled with candy and small surprises). Children and adults alike enjoy watching the blindfolded small fry swing away with a heavy board or baseball bat while an adult moves and sways the *pinata* with a rope, making the fun last, giving everyone a chance. Eventually, someone gets lucky, smashes the *pinata* with a hard blow (it takes strength to break it) and kids skitter around the floor retrieving the loot. *Pinatas* are common, not only for Christmas and Easter but also for birthdays and other special occasions in the Mexican home.

The Fiesta And Visitors
A few practical things to remember about fiesta times: Cities will probably be crowded. If you know in advance that you'll be in town, make hotel and car reservations as soon as possible. Easter at any of the beach hotels on the Peninsula will be crowded, and you may need to reserve as far as 6 months in advance. Respect the privacy of people. If you want to take pictures, ask permission first. Some of the best fiestas are in more isolated parts of the Yucatan and its close neighbors. In San Cristobal de las Casas, for instance, the Indians have definite feelings and religious beliefs about having their pictures taken and are known to show their feelings violently. In Chiapas it is especially repugnant to the people for you to click your camera in church; ask permission of the priest in charge.

ACCOMMODATIONS

Today's Yucatan offers a wide variety of accommodations. If your lifestyle is suited to outdoor living, beach camping is wonderful along the Caribbean coast. If you prefer the convenience of a hotel, there's a myriad to choose from in all price ranges, and if you like the idea of light housekeeping including your own food preparation, condos are available in some locales.

CAMPING

RVs

Ten years ago there were almost no campgrounds with hookups. But now with an increasing number of Mexican families beginning to show an interest in RVs, more campgrounds are popping up in the Yucatan Peninsula. Though you still cannot find a book that lists only Yucatan campgrounds, the Secretaria de Turismo in Mexico D.F. publishes a guidebook in Spanish that lists most of the campgrounds in all of Mexico (see "Booklist"). RV campgrounds are listed in specific travel chapters of this book.

You must obtain a vehicle permit when entering the country in an RV (see p. 76). Camping with a vehicle, you're at liberty to become a "luxury camper," bringing all the equipment you'll need (and more!). A van or small camper truck will fit on almost any road you'll run into. With an RV you can "street camp" in the city. The parking lot of a large hotel (check with the manager) or a side street near a library or museum is generally safe and offers some entertainment possibilities.

Vehicle Supplies

A few reminders and some common-sense planning make a difference when traveling and camping with a vehicle. Near both the Caribbean and Gulf coasts are many swampy areas so check for marshy ground before pulling off the road. When beach camping park above the high-tide line. Remember that gas stations are not as frequently found in the Yucatan as in most parts of Mexico. If you plan on traveling for any length of time, especially in out-of-the-way places, carry extra gas, and fill up whenever the opportunity arises. Along with your food supply always carry enough water for both the car and the passengers. Be practical and come prepared with a few necessities:

VEHICLE SUPPLIES

Couple extra fan belts
Long towing rope or chain
Bottle of Windex
Set of spark plugs
Points and condenser
Emery boards
Feeler gauge (to set the points)
Oil and gas filter
Gas can
Oil
Fuses
Extra tire, patch kit
Air supply
Good sized machete to hack your way
  through vines and plants
Shovel
Flares
Flashlight
A few basic tools
Paper towels.

Sleeping Outdoors

Sleeping under a jeweled sky in a warm clime can be either a wonderful or excruciating experience. Two factors that will make or break it are the temperature in conjunction with your personal body thermostat and the mosquito population in the immediate vicinity. Some campers sleep in a tent to get away from biting critters, which helps, but is no guarantee; also, heat hangs heavy inside a closed tent. Sleeping bags cushion the ground but tend to be much too warm. If you have a bag that zips across the bottom, it's cooling to let your feet hang out (well marinated in bug repellent or wearing a pair of socks, a dark color the mosquitos might not notice). An air mattress softens the ground (bring along a patch kit). Mexican campers often just roll up in a lightweight blanket covering all skin, head, and toes to defy possible bug attacks.

The most comfortable (according to Yuc-

atecans and backpackers) is to sling a hammock between two palm trees protecting yourself with a swath of mosquito netting and bug repellent. Some put a lightweight blanket between them and the hammock strings. Many homey resorts provide *palapa* hammock-huts for a very small fee that usually includes water (to wash); these places are great if you want to meet other backpackers. Hammock-huts are most frequently found along the Caribbean and Gulf coasts.

When camping near the sea, before you choose your sleeping spot check out:

- The highwater mark.

- The proximity of swampy marshland. The location of coconuts in the trees. Rake the ground of all bits of sharp coral, spiny plants, or anything else that could give your air mattress a "let down" during the night.

- Be sure to clean up all foodstuffs around your sleeping area. Hanging food supplies from a tree is one answer, but not the tree you're sleeping in—unless you yearn for the closeness of curious nocturnal creatures.

- Keep a raincover handy for unexpected showers during the night. Large sheets of plastic are always handy to have around.

HOTELS

Though the Yucatan Peninsula is behind the rest of Mexico in developing facilities to attract and accommodate tourists, it's catching up rapidly. In the larger cities modern hotels are springing up faster than any guidebook can keep track of them.

Reservations

Traveling during high season (15 Nov. to 15 April) requires a little planning if you wish to stay at the popular hotels. Make reservations in advance. Most hotels can be contacted through a travel agency or auto club. If not, write to them direct and enclose a deposit check for one night (if you don't know how much, guess). Ask (and allow plenty of time) for a return confirmation. If traveling any other time of the year, hotel rooms are usually easy to find.

The Mexican government-owned chain, El Presidente, is either adapting old mansions, convents, and other unique structures for use as hotels, or building new ones. These hotels offer modern conveniences such as private bathrooms, a/c, good beds, nightclub, and dining facilities. Most have swimming pools, entertainment, and accept credit cards. Via a toll-free number (1-800-472-2427), the El Presidente chain will make reservations with a credit card and you'll receive a confirmation by mail. Refunds are possible with advance notification within a given time limit. The El Presidente chain ranges in price from moderate (most of the Peninsula) to expensive (in Cancun).

Uxmal's Hotel Mayaland has a lovely old colonial design with broad open corridors, using wrought iron, colorful tile, and heavy wood furniture.

Luxury

Familiar American hotel chains such as the Holiday Inn, Hyatt, and Sheraton are usually top of the line in luxury as well as expense. Luxury hotels are found in Campeche, Merida, Cozumel, and Villahermosa, but most are in Cancun. Cancun has a master plan for development and claims that it will not become another Miami or Waikiki—so far so good. Cancun in fact has the most expensive hotels on the Peninsula, yet you can still find small unassuming accommodations in the downtown area for a lot less money.

Colonial

In large cities (such as Merida, Campeche, Valladolid), the downtown areas offer many small hotels that ooze with nostalgia. Some were originally mansions dating from turn-of-the-century "henequen days." They aren't modern, the paint is peeling here and there, and maybe the tiles are beginning to chip, but spacious rooms, gracious design, and fanciful trim are very colonial in flavor, providing an insight into the Yucatan past. Relaxing courtyards with water bubbling from archaic fountains surrounded by tropical plants offer a shady respite from the noon-day sun. These hotels are old elegance (with emphasis on the "old") but are usually quite reasonably priced and can be a pleasurable experience.

Budget Inns

Travelers looking to spend nights cheaply inside can find overnight accommodations in most towns and cities. The large cities like Merida, Campeche, and Villahermosa all have many clean, enjoyable budget hotels. It might take a little (or a lot of) nosing around (starting out early in the day makes it easy) but this type of hostelry is available and offers a good way to the see the city and meet the friendly people of the city as well.

In small towns, ask at the local cantina, cafe, or city hall for a hotel or boarding house-type accommodation. These hotels are usually clean, and more than likely you'll share a toilet and (maybe) a shower. Sometimes you'll share the room itself, a large area with enough hammock hooks scattered around the walls to handle

Some beach huts offer little more than sapling walls, thatch roof, and hammock hooks; this one goes further with hanging beds and mosquito netting.

several travelers. The informed budget traveler carries his hammock (buy it in Yucatan if you don't already have one—they're the best made) when wandering around the Peninsula. When staying in the cheaper hotels in out-of-the way places, don't expect free bottled drinking water, toilet paper, soap, or dining rooms; and credit cards are *not* accepted. However, the price will be right and the family that runs it will offer a cultural experience that you won't forget.

Youth hostels, though few and far between, are good bargains on the Peninsula, especially

in Cancun. Youth Hostels on or near the Yucatan Peninsula:

CREA Cancun
Km 3, 200 Boulevard Kukulcan
Zona Hotelera
Cancun, Quintana Roo, Mexico.

CREA Campeche
Av. Agustin Melgar S/N, col. Buenavista
Campeche, Campeche, Mexico.

CREA Chetumal
Alvaro Obregon y General Anaya S/N.
Chetumal, Quintana Roo, Mexico.

CREA Tuxtla Gutierrez
Calz. Angel Albino Corzo No. 1800
Tuxtlan Gutierrez, Chiapas, Mexico.

For more information write to:
CREA, Agencia Nacional de Juvenil
  Glorieta Metro Insurgentes
Local CC-11 col. Juarez
C.P. 06600 Mexico, D.F.
Tel. 525-25-48/525-29-74

Condominiums

Condomania hasn't hit much of Yucatan—yet! Cancun is the exception, with hundreds of condos lining the beach; Isla Mujeres and Cozumel have a few. If vacationing with family or a group, condo living can be a real money-saver while still enjoying the fine services of a luxury hotel. Fully equipped kitchens make cooking a snap. In many cases the price includes daily maid service. Some condos welcome you with a refrigerator stocked with food basics (like the Condumel on Isla Cozumel) which you are not required to use. You pay only for the foods and beverages that you use each day. Details are given in the appropriate travel sections.

FOOD

Many of the crops now produced by American farmers were introduced by the Maya, including corn, sweet potatos, tomatos, peppers, squash, pumpkin, and avocados. Many other products favored by Americans are native to the Yucatan Peninsula: pineapple, papaya, cotton, tobacco, rubber, vanilla, and turkey.

EARLY AGRICULTURE

Enriching The Soil
Scientists believe priests studied celestial movements. A prime function performed in the elaborate temples (built to strict astronomical guidelines) may have been to chart the changing seasons and to decide when to begin the planting cycle. Farmers used the slash-and-burn method of caring for their soil (and still do today). When the time was propitious (before the rains began in the spring), Indians cut the trees on their land, leaving stumps about half a meter above ground. Downed trees were spread evenly across the landscape in order to burn uniformly; residue ash was left to nourish the soil. At the proper time, holes were made with a pointed stick and precious maize kernels were dropped into the earth, one by one. At each corner (the cardinal points) of the cornfield, offerings of *pozole* (maize stew) were left to encourage the gods to give forth great rains. With abundant moisture, crops were bountiful and rich enough to provide food even into the following year.

The Maya knew the value of allowing the land to lay fallow after two seasons of growth, and each family's *milpa* (cornfield) was moved from place to place around the villages which were scattered through the jungle. Often, squash and tomatos were planted in the shade of a towering corn stalk to make double use of the land. Today, you see windmills across the countryside (many stamped CHICAGO, INC.); and with the coming of electricity to the outlying areas, pumps are being used to bring water from underground rivers and lakes to irrigate crops. Outside of irrigation methods, the Maya follow the same ancient pattern of farming as that of their ancestors.

Maize

Corn was the heart of Maya nutrition, eaten at each meal of the day. From it the Indians made tortillas, stew, and beverages both alcoholic and non-alcoholic. Because growing corn was such a vital part of Maya life, it is represented in drawings and carvings along with other social and religious symbols. Corn tortillas are still a main staple of the Mexican people. Native women in small towns can be seen early in the morning carrying bowls of corn kernels on their heads to the tortilla shop for grinding into tortilla dough. This was done by hand for centuries (and still is, in isolated places). With the advent of electricity to the Peninsula it's so much quicker to pay a *peso* or two and

making tortillas by hand

zap—tortilla dough! Others pay a few more *pesos* (price is controlled by the government) and buy their tortillas by the kilo hot off the griddle. It's amazing that the Maya came up with the combination of corn and beans without a dietician telling them it was a perfect protein for their diet. The Maya did not raise cattle, sheep, or pigs before Spanish times.

GASTRONOMICAL ADVENTURE

Taste as many different dishes as possible! You'll be introduced to spices that add a new dimension to your diet. Naturally, you won't be wild about everything—it takes awhile to become accustomed to squid served in its own black ink, for instance! A hamburger might not taste like one from your favorite fast foodery in California. It should not come as a shock to find your favorite down-home Tex-Mex enchiladas and tacos are nothing like those you order in Mexican restaurants. Be prepared to come into contact with new and different tastes—you're in *Mexico*, after all!

Seafood

You won't travel far before realizing that one of Yucatan's specialties is fresh fish. All along the Caribbean and Gulf coasts are opportunities to indulge in piscine delicacies: lobster, shrimp, red snapper, sea bass, halibut, barracuda, and lots more. Even the tiniest cafe will prepare sweet fresh fish "a la Veracruz" using ripe tomatos, green peppers, and onions. Or if you prefer, ask for the fish *con ajo,* sauteed in garlic and butter—scrumptious! Most menus offer an opportunity to order *al gusto* (cooked to your pleasure).

Try the unusual! Conch *(KAH-nk)* has been a staple in the diet of the Maya along the Caribbean coast for centuries (see pp. 258-9). It's often used in *ceviche.* Some consider this raw fish; actually, it's marinated in a vinegar or lime dressing with onions, peppers, and a host of spices—no longer raw and very tasty! Often conch is pounded, dipped in egg and cracker crumbs, and sauteed quickly (like abalone steak in California), with a squirt of fresh lime. Caution: if it's cooked too long it becomes tough and rubbery.

CORN AND THE CHACS

Families today still maintain a small *milpa,* or corn field. It is handled in much the same manner as in their ancestors' days, even down to a Chac ritual. Performed at the end of each April, the ceremony arouses Chacs from their seasonal sleep. The Chacs, age-old deities, are treated with great respect: to anger the Chacs could mean a drought. Without the yearly rains the corn crop will surely fail.

Corn was an important part of Maya life; legendary beliefs of man's beginnings were intertwined with the magic of corn. This is seen in many of the remaining carvings and drawings (such as a fresco at the ruins of Tulum showing man's feet as corn). The crop was so significant to the Maya that everything else would stop when the signs implied it was time to plant the fields. In ancient times the priests calculated when it was time to fire the fields before the rains. This was done by relating the ritual calender to the solar year, as at Chichen Itza during the vernal equinox. Today the farmer observes nature's phenomena such as the swarming of flying ants and the rhythm and frequency of croaking frogs—a Yucatecan version of a Farmer's Almanac.

Corn, one of the main staples of the Mexican diet, is still planted in the centuries-old method of the Maya. First the trees and grasses are cut, then set aflame. The field is left until all the trees are reduced to ash, and then a stick is used to poke a hole into the earth into which seeds are dropped one by one.

This mural, "The Creation of Maya Man" by Raul Anguiano, was inspired by the myth of creation as read in "Popul Vuh." It can be seen in Maya Hall at the Anthropological Museum in Mexico City.

If you happen to be on a boat trip where the crew prepares a meal of fresh fish on the beach, more than likely you'll be served *tik n' chik*. The whole fish (catch of the day) is placed in a wire rack and seasoned with onions, peppers, and *achiote,* a fragrant red spice grown on the Peninsula since the time of the Maya. Bishop Diego de Landa identified *achiote* in his *Relaciones* written in the 1700s.

Wild Game

The Yucatecans are hunters, and if you explore

TORTILLAS

One of the fascinating operations in the public market is watching the tortilla machine. Always the busiest shop, housewives line up to buy 2, 4, or 6 kg of tortillas every day. Still the staple of the Mexican diet, many women still make them by hand at home, but a large percentage buy them for a reasonable price, saving hours of work on the *metate* and the griddle. It's easy to spend 20 minutes in fascinated concentration observing the 20-kg plastic sacks of shucked corn kernels stacked in a corner of the stall, the machinery that grinds it, the pale yellow dough, the unsophisticated conveyor belt that carries it across the live-flame cooking surface, the patrons who patiently line up for the fresh results, and the baker who might even hand you several tortillas hot off the fire along with a friendly smile that says thanks for being interested.

the countryside very much, you'll commonly see men and boys on bicycles, motorscooters or horses with rifles slung over their shoulders and full game bags tied behind them. Game found in the jungle varies, but *venado* (venison) is the most common menu item. Hunters take their extra catch to the marketplace for a quick cash sale. A *comida corrida* (set lunch) often includes *venado* as part of the meal. *Pato* (wild duck) is served during certain times of the year and is prepared in several ways that must be tried.

Restaurants

Most small cafes that cater to Mexican families are open all day and late into the night. The Mexican custom is to eat the heavier meal of the day between 1300-1600. In most of these family cafes a generous *comida corrida* is served at this time. If you're hungry and want an economical (filling) meal, that's what to ask for; though you don't know exactly what's coming, you get a table full of many delights. Always expect a large stack of tortillas, and 5 or 6 small bowls filled with the familiar and the unfamiliar: it could be black beans, a cold plate of tomatos and the delicious Yucatan avocado, *venado* (deer), *pollo pibyl* (chicken in banana leaves), fish, and whatever. Cafes in the larger hotels that cater to tourists don't serve this set meal. Late in the evening a light supper is served from 2100-2300. Hotels with foreign tourists offer dinner earlier to cater to British and American tastes. Some restaurants add a service charge onto the bill. If so, the check will say *incluido propina*. It's still gracious to leave a few coins for the waiter. If the tip isn't added to the bill, leaving 10-15% is customary.

Strolling musicians are common in Mexican cafes. If you enjoy the music, P100-200 is a considerate gift.

In certain cities, it's common at cafes that cater to Mexicans to serve free snacks in the afternoon with a beer or cocktail. The Cafe Prosperidad (Calle 56 No. 456-A) in downtown Merida is very generous with their *antojitos* (snacks). The place is always packed with locals for the *comida corrida* complete with live entertainment and waitresses wearing a long version of the *huipil*. Here you'll get the real

Small fondas *offer fast foods in most public markets.*

essence of the city, and you may be the only gringo present. Remember, we didn't say the cafe is spotless!

Yucatan has its own version of junk food. You'll find hole-in-the-wall *torta* (sandwich) stands, and the same goes for tacos, tamales, *liquidos* (fruit drinks), as well as corner vendors selling mangos on a stick, slices of pineapple, peeled oranges, candies of all descriptions, cotton candy, and barbecued meat. The public markets have foods of every description, usually very cheap. In other words, there's a huge variety to choose from, so have fun.

A ploy that many seasoned adventurers use when they're tired of eating cold food from their backpacks is: in a village where there isn't

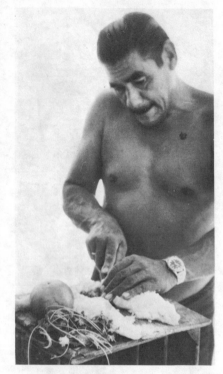

making fresh ceviche

a cafe of any kind, go to the local cantina (or grocery store, church, or city hall) and ask if

there's a housewife in town who (for a fee) would be willing to include you at her dinner table. Almost always you'll find someone, usually at a fair price (determine price when you make your deal). With any luck you'll find a woman renowned for not only her *tortillas por manos* but also for the tastiest *poc chuc* this side of Tikal. You gain a lot more than food in this arrangement; the culture swap is priceless.

Food Safety

When preparing your own food in the back-country, a few possible sources of bacteria are fresh fruit and vegetables, especially those with a thin skin that don't get peeled, like lettuce or tomatos. When washing these foods in local water (and they should definitely be washed thoroughly before consuming), add either bleach or iodine to the wash water. Soaking all together in a container or plastic bag for about 20 minutes is easy; Ziploc bags are essential to carry. If at the beach and short of water, substitute sea water (for everything but drinking). Remember not to rinse the bleached food with contaminated water, just pat dry and if you have a distasteful lingering flavor, a squirt of lime juice tastes great and is very healthy. Some foods nature has packaged hygienically; a banana has its own protective seal so is considered safe (lucky! — since they're so abundant on the Peninsula). Foods that are cooked and eaten immediately are considered safe.

...so this is where a chocolate bar comes from!

1. beautiful Mexican woman; 2. spinning henequen twine;
3. puppy love; 4. Chapultepec Castle guard

ACTIVITIES

DIVING

Not everyone who travels to the Yucatan Peninsula is a diver or even a snorkeler—at first! One peek through the looking glass—a diving mask—changes that situation. The Caribbean is notoriously one of the most seductive bodies of water in the world. Turquoise blue and crystal clear with perfect tepid temperature, the protected Yucatan coast (thanks to off-shore reefs) is ideal for a languid float during hot humid days.

You'll find that the sea is where you'll want to spend a good part of your trip. So even if you never considered underwater sports in the past, you'll be willing—no, eager!—to learn. It's easy for the neophyte to learn how to snorkel. Once you master breathing through a tube, then it's just relax and float. Elements of time disappear as you are introduced through a 4-inch glass window to a world of fish in rainbow colors of garish yellow, electric blue, crimson and a hundred shades of purple. The longer you look, the more you'll discover: underwater caverns, tall pillars of coral, giant tubular sponges, shy fish hiding on the sandy bottom, and delicate wisps of fine grass.

Diving Wonderland

For the diver, there's even more adventure. Reefs, caves, and rugged coastline harbor the unknown. Ships wrecked hundreds of years ago hide secrets as yet undiscovered. Swimming among the curious and brazen fish puts you literally into another world, a world to be investigated. This is raw excitement!

Expect to see magnificent marinelife along with an astounding variety of fish, crustaceans, and corals. Even close to shore, these amazing little animals create exotic displays of shape and form, dense or delicate depending on species, depth, light, and current. Most need light to survive; and in deeper, low-light areas, some species of coral take the form of a large plate, thereby performing the duties of a solar collector. Sponge is another curious underwater creature. It comes in all sizes, shapes, and colors, from common brown to vivid red.

Be Selective

Diving lessons are offered at almost all the dive shops on the Peninsula. Before you make a commitment, ask about the instructor and check his accident record, then talk to the harbormaster in the community or, if a small village, the local cantina. Most of these divers (many are American) are conscientious, but a few are not, and the locals know whom to trust. Also, check with your divemaster about emergency procedures before your boat heads out to sea.

Bringing your own equipment to Mexico might

snorkeling in Xelha Lagoon

save you a little money, depending on the length of your trip and means of transportation. But if you plan on just a couple of weeks and are joining a group onboard a dive boat by the day, it's generally little more for tank rental and sometimes not worth the hassle of carrying your own.

Choose your boat carefully. Look it over first. Some aren't much more than fishing boats, with little to make the diver comfortable. Don't neglect to ask questions. Most of the dive masters who take divers on their boats speak English. Does it have a platform to get in and out of the water? How many tanks of air may be used per trip? How many dives? Exactly where are you going? How fast does the boat go and how long will it take to get there? Remember some of the best dive spots might be farther out at sea. A more modern boat (though costing a little more) might get you extra diving time.

Detailed information is available for divers and snorkelers who wish to know about the dive sites they plan to visit. Once on the Yucatan Peninsula, pamphlets and books are available in dive shops. Look for Ric Hajovsky's comprehensive pamphlet on the reefs, the depths, and especially the currents. Wherever diving is good, you'll almost always find a dive shop. There are a few high adventure dives where diving with an experienced guide is recommended (see "Diving" in "Cozumel," p. 228).

Finally, a safety recompression chamber is located on the island of Cozumel: tel. 2-01-40.

DIVING HAZARDS

Underwater

A word here about some of the less inviting aspects of marine society. Anemones and sea urchins are everywhere. Some can be dangerous if touched or stepped on. The long-spined black sea urchin can inflict great pain and its poison can cause an uncomfortable infection. Don't think that you're safe in a wet suit and booties *or even if wearing gloves!* The spines easily slip through the rubber skin. In certain areas, such as around the island of Cozumel, the urchin is encountered at all depths

and is very abundant close to shore where you'll probably be wading in and out of shallow water; keep your eyes open. If diving at night, use your flashlight. If you should run into one of the spines, remove it quickly and carefully, disinfect the wound, and apply antibiotic cream. If you have difficulty removing the spine, or if it breaks, see a doctor — pronto!

First Aid

Cuts from coral will often cause an infection, even if only just a scratch. Antibiotic cream or powder will usually take care of it. If you should get a deep cut, or if minute bits of coral are left in the wound, a serious and long-lived infection can ensue. See a doctor.

If you should get a scrape on red coral you'll feel a burning sensation for a few minutes — to 5 days. On some, it causes an allergic reaction and will raise large red welts. Cortisone cream will reduce inflammation and discomfort. While it wouldn't be fair to condemn all red things, you'll notice in the next few paragraphs that the following creatures to avoid are all red!

Fire worms (also known as bristle worms) should be avoided. If touched, they will deposit tiny cactus-like bristles in your skin. They can cause the same reaction as fire coral. Scraping the skin with the edge of a sharp knife (as you would to remove a bee stinger) might remove the bristles. Don't get cut! Any leftover bristles will ultimately work their way out, but you can be very uncomfortable in the meantime. Cortisone cream helps to relieve this inflammation, too.

Several species of sponges have fine sharp spicules (hard, minute, pointed calcareous or siliceous bodies that support the tissue of these invertebrates) that should not be touched with the bare hand. The attractive red fire sponge can cause great pain; a mild solution of vinegar or ammonia (or urine, if there's nothing else) will help. The burning lasts a couple of days, and cortisone cream soothes. Don't be fooled by dull-colored sponge. Many have the same sharp spicules, and touching them with a bare hand is risky at best.

Protect Your Hands And Feet

Some divers feel the need to touch the fish they swim with. A few beginners want an

parasailing on Cancun beaches

underwater picture taken of them feeding the fish — bad news! When you offer the fish a tasty morsel from your hand (even gloved), you could start an underwater riot. Fish are always hungry and always ready for a free meal. Some of those denizens of the deep may not be so big, but in the frenzy to be first in line, their very efficient teeth have been known to miss the target. Another way to save your hands from unexpected danger is by keeping them out of cracks and crevices. Moray eels live in just those kinds of places in a reef. A moray will usually leave you alone if you do likewise, but its many needle-sharp teeth (eels have a lot!) can cause a painful wound that's apt to infect.

A few sea-going critters resent being stepped on and they can retaliate with a dangerous wound. The scorpion fish, hardly recognizable with its natural camouflage, lies hidden most of the time on a reef shelf or the bottom of the sea. If you should step on or touch it you can expect a painful, dangerous sting. If this happens, see a doctor immediately.

Another sinister fellow is the ray. Several varieties in the Caribbean include the yellow and southern sting rays. If you leave them alone they're generally peaceful but if they get stepped on they zap you with a tail that carries a poisonous sting, which can cause anaphylactic shock. Symptoms include respiratory difficulties, fainting, and severe itching. Go quickly to the doctor and tell him what caused the

sting. One diver suggests a shuffling, dragging-of-the-feet sort of gate when walking along the bottom of the ocean. If bumped, the ray will quickly escape, but if stepped on it feels trapped and uses the tail for protection.

Jellyfish can also inflict a miserable sting. One does not want to come in contact with the long streamers of the Portugese man-of-war, and some of the smaller ones are just as deadly.

Don't let these what-ifs discourage you from an underwater adventure, though. Thousands of people dive in the Caribbean every day of the year and a small percentage of accidents occur.

EMERGENCY NUMBERS

channel 16 (canal numero diez y seis)

Divers Alert Network (DAN) Dial this number for info about Cozumel's recompression chamber or for assistance in locating a chamber in the U.S.A.	(919) 684-8111
Air-Evac International located in San Diego Cal.	(619) 278-3822
Life Flight (air ambulance service) Houston, TX.	(713) 797-4357 (800) 854-2567

OTHER WATER SPORTS

With so many fine beaches, bays, and coves, all water sports are available. Because so many beaches are protected by the reef that runs parallel to the Yucatan's E coast, calm swimming beaches are easy to find and many hotels have pools. Waterskiing is good on Nichupte Bay in Cancun; parasailing is popular there also. Lessons for windsurfing are given, with rental boards available at most of the resort areas: Cozumel, Cancun, Akumal, and Playa del Carmen.

FISHING AND HUNTING

Fishing

A fishing license is required for all persons 16 years or older, good for 3 days, one month, or a year, available for a small fee at most fresh- and saltwater fishing areas from a local delegate of the Fishing Secretariat. Ask in the small cafes at the more isolated beaches. Check with the closest Mexican consulate where you can get a permit for your sports-fishing craft; you can also get up-to-date information there on fishing seasons and regulations which vary from area to area. Fishing gear may be brought into Mexico without customs tax; however, the customs office at the border crossing from Brownsville, Texas, into Mexico is notorious for expecting their palms greased before allowing the RVer or boater to cross the border. If you find yourself in this position start with $1 bills (be prepared; have lots of them with you) — several people may need to be soothed before you can cross. If you choose not to pay the bribe, they can keep you hanging for hours, even days, before they allow you to cross the border. Sadly, it's a no-win situation. For more fishing information write to: General de Pesca, Av. Alvaro Obregon 269, Mexico 7, D.F.

Hunting

A seasonal small-game license (including birds) must be purchased from the state where the hunting is intended. Any Mexican Consulate or tourist office will provide information on obtaining a firearms permit as well as current hunting season dates and regulations, which vary yearly. Big-game hunting requires a special one-time permit (expensive) from the Mexican Department of Wildlife. Start making your preparations well in advance of your hunting date. For more hunting information write: Direccion General de Caza, Serdan 27, Mexico D.F. After obtaining Mexican information, write to the Dept. of Wildlife in Washington D.C., or go to the nearest customs office and ask for the booklet on "Pets and Wildlife." This lays out the U.S. government rules and regulations on importing game.

The safest and least confusing way to go hunting is to either travel from the States with an American guide (check with your travel agent or hunting club) that makes the trek each year, or to make arrangements in advance with a hunting lodge in Mexico, such as the one listed in Campeche (see p. 161). Another source of hunting lodges information is the back ad sections of *Field And Stream* and *Hunter* magazines. By mail they walk you through the whole planning procedure, but allow *plenty* of time!

OTHER SPORTS

Tennis courts are scattered about the Peninsula; the large hotels at Cancun, Akumal, Cozumel, and Villahermosa have courts. Bring your own rackets. Golf courses are few, but you can plan on playing in Merida and Cancun.

OTHER ACTIVITIES

Birdwatching is wonderful throughout the Yucatan. From N to S the variety of birds is broad and changes with the geography and the weather. Bring binoculars and wear boots and lightweight trousers if you plan on watching in jungle areas. Studying **tropical flora** is also a popular activity. For this you most certainly will be in the backcountry — don't forget bug repellent and be prepared for an occasional rain shower, even in the dry season. For most orchids and bromeliads look up in the trees. However, Yucatan does have its ground orchid to look for. Remember, don't take anything away with you except pictures.

Photography

There's a world of beauty to photograph between the sea, the people, and the natural landscape of the Peninsula. If you plan on videotaping, check with your local Mexican Tourist Office for information on what you can bring into the country. Most archaeological zones prohibit tripods. For the photographer who wants to film *everything*, small planes are available for charter in the larger cities and resorts. In Cancun, for instance, you can take pictures from a plane that gives an air tour of about 15 minutes over the resort and surrounding coast. Per person price is US$12. For further photography info see p. 73.

GETTING THERE AND AROUND

For centuries, getting to the Yucatan Peninsula required a major sea voyage to one of the few ports on the Gulf of Mexico, followed by harrowing and uncertain trips on land limited to mule trains and narrow paths through the tangled jungle. Today the Peninsula is accessible from anywhere in the solar system! Arrive via modern airports, a network of new (good) highways, a reasonably frequent train schedule, and an excellent bus service that reaches an incredible number of small villages in remote areas as well as the large cities.

BY CAR

An international driver's license is not required to drive or rent a car in Mexico. However, if you feel safer with it, get one from an auto club. At AAA in California you need two passport pictures and a $5 fee along with a current driver's license from your home state. It's another good form of identification if you should have an accident or other driving problem.

When you cross the border from the U.S. into Mexico, your car insurance is no longer valid. You can buy insurance from AAA or an auto club before you leave home. Numerous insurance agencies at most border cities sell Mexican insurance: Sanborn's is one of the largest. Ask Sanborn's for their excellent free road maps of the areas you plan to visit. For more information write: Sanborn's Mexican Insurance Service, P.O. Box 1210, McAllen, TX 78501, tel. (512) 682-3401.

In the last 15 years highway construction has been priority work on the Peninsula. A growing number of fine roads throughout have been well engineered. However, before taking your car into the country, consider the condition of the car and the manufacturer. Will parts be available in the event of a breakdown? Volkswagon, Renault, Ford, General Motors, and Chrysler have Mexican branches and parts should be available. If you drive an expensive foreign sports car or a large luxury model, you might be better off to make other arrangements. Repairs might be unavailable and you could be stranded in an unlikely place for days waiting for a part. It's always wise to

Small planes make frequent trips between cities on the Peninsula.

make sure you and the mechanic understand the cost of repairs before he begins — just like at home! **Note:** Selling your car in Mexico is highly illegal.

Highways to Yucatan

In California, main highways cross the Mexican border from San Diego to Tijuana and from Calexico to Mexicali. From Arizona go through Tuscon to Nogales. From Texas, El Paso leads to Juarez, Eagle Pass to Piedras Negras, Laredo to Nuevo Laredo, and Brownsville to Matamoros. From each of these gateways, good highways bring you to the capital of the country, Mexico City.

From the capital the easiest and most direct route to Merida and other Peninsula cities is on Mex. 190d, a toll road to Puebla. At Puebla there's an interchange with Mex. 150D, another tollway that parallels the older free road (Mex. 150). On 150D you cross the plateau climbing to 2,385 m at the summit of the Cumbres de Maltrata, after which a 22½-km road curves and drops you down quickly. Though this road is often foggy, it beats the alternative on 150 which hairpins through the Cumbres de Acultzingo, a narrow, heart-thumping drop of 610 m in only 11 km. Mexico 150D eliminates going through Mt. Orizaba; the old road (150) takes it in. In Cordoba the roads meet (the end of 150D); continue on 150 to the humid coastal plain. At Paso del Toro turn SE onto 180 which leads to Veracruz. Following 180 takes you through Coatzacoalcos to Villahermosa. From here you can continue on 186 which loops SE, close to Palenque, and then N through

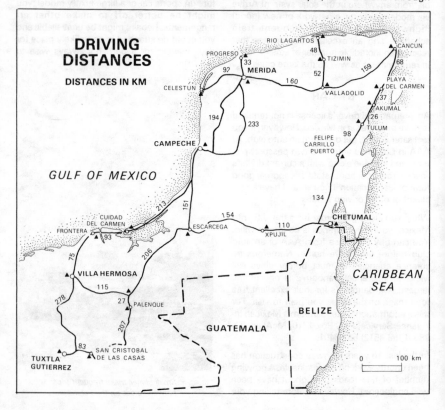

DRIVING DISTANCES

DISTANCES IN KM

AIRLINES SERVING THE YUCATAN PENINSULA

Airline	To	From
American	Cancun, Cozumel	Dallas, Ft. Worth
Aeromexico	Cozumel, Mexico, Merida, Chetumal Monterrey, Cancun	Houston, Los Angeles
Continental	Cancun, Cozumel	Los Angeles, Houston, Denver, San Francisco
Eastern	Cancun	New Orleans
LACSA	Cancun	Guatemala, Costa Rica New Orleans
Mexicana	Cancun, Cozumel	Miami, Dallas Philadelphia
United	Cancun	Chicago

Escarcega where the road meets 261. Stay on 186, travel due E across the Peninsula to Chetumal on the Caribbean coast. At Chetumal 307 follows the coast NE to Cancun. From Cancun take 180 SW to Merida.

Another option from Villahermosa is to take 180 following the Gulf coast. This route includes several ferry boats (that have frequently interrupted schedules due to rough seas), takes you through Isla del Carmen, Champoton, Campeche, and then on to Merida. With *no* delays figure the trip from Villahermosa and Champoton to take about 8½ hours.

Just past Villahermosa, 186 provides the fastest route to Champoton. Take 186 to Escarcega, turn onto 261 and follow it for 85 km to Champoton. Though longer, this is a much faster uncomplicated route and avoids several ferry boats.

Driving Tips
In Yucatan, it's recommended you don't drive outside the cities at night unless it's a necessity. The highways have no streetlights — it's hard to see a black cow on a black road in the black night. Also, pedestrians have no other place to walk; shoulders are non-existent on Yucatan roads. Public phones are few and far between, and gas stations close when the sun goes down. If you should have a problem while

driving during daylight hours on a *main road,* it's suggested that you stay with your car. The Green Angels, a government-sponsored tow truck service, cruise the roads several times a day on the lookout for drivers in trouble. They carry gas and small parts, and are prepared to fix flats. Each car is equipped with a CB radio and the driver is trained to give first aid, or will call a doctor that is always on duty. If you foolishly decided to travel an isolated road after dark, and break down, your best bet is to lock yourself in and stick it out for the night; go for help in the morning. The Mexican people are friendly, especially when they see someone in trouble; sometimes you have more help than you want.

BY PLANE

Today, planes fly to one of several international airports on the Peninsula. The newest and most modern is at Cancun, Yucatan's most sophisticated resort. Jets arrive daily with connections from most countries in the world. It's also possible to fly internationally to the small island of Cozumel, to Merida (capital of the state of Yucatan), to Villahermosa (in Tabasco), and to Campeche, (capital of the state of Campeche). Most small cities throughout the Peninsula have landing strips for use by private planes and small commuter airlines.

AIR ROUTES TO CANCUN

NEW YORK
LOS ANGELES
DALLAS
HOUSTON
MIAMI
LA HAVANA
TO PARIS
TO MADRID
GUADALAJARA
MEXICO CITY
CHETUMAL
CANCÚN

BY TRAIN

For many years Mexico has had a fairly efficient railway service. Traveling by train is relaxing and the scenery is outstanding. You can make an entire trip from the States to Merida by rail. From several stateside cities along the border, buses or trains drop off passengers at Mexican train connections. For example, you can catch a Greyhound bus at the Los Angeles main terminal which crosses the border into Mexicali. Here you board a 1st-class train to Mexico City (48 hours) and for US$91, 2 people can travel in a private compartment with 2 beds and a bathroom; dining car, a/c, daily departures, reservations necessary. In the Los Angeles area call Orozco Travel, (213) 626-2291. In Mexico City at the train station you transfer to the daily train to Merida.

It's possible to travel by rail from the Yucatan to most cities in Mexico. The prices are cheap, and for approximately double the price of a 1st-class ticket you can get a sleeping car (a *good* bargain). For 1st-class you need reservations; even if there's not a dining car (ask), you can bring a lunch, or depend on the (frequent) stops at stations along the way where vendors sell everything, including Mexican fast food, tamales etc. For information on other departure points along the border, plus schedules, prices, etc., it's wise to go direct to the railway companies; schedules and prices change frequently. Some travel agents have train information, but not all. Government tourist offices can give you schedules and prices for a specific trip or for further information write:

Mexican National Railways
489 Fifth Ave., Suite 2601
New York, NY 10017
tel. (212) 682-1494

BY BUS

Bus service to the Peninsula is very efficient. The price will fit the most meager budget, scheduling is frequent, and even the smallest village is accessible from most cities in northern Mexico. From the U.S. it's smart to make reservations with Greyhound or Trailways to your final destination on the Peninsula. The bus driver will take you to the border and then

These kids are combining culture with cooling in the giant fountain at Mexico's Anthropological Museum.

THE ANTHROPOLOGICAL MUSEUM OF MEXICO

Passing through Mexico City? Many flights to the Yucatan Peninsula from the U.S. stop in Mexico City for a change of planes. Though it would take days to really tour the capital city properly, a highly informative adjunct to your trip to Mayaland would be three days in Chapultepec Park. The park covers 4 sq km, with a children's playground, a lake with boating activity, water birds including lovely white and black swans, a botanical garden, zoo, Chapultepec Castle (made famous by Maximilian and Carlotta, short-term king and queen from France), and two important museums: Anthropological and Modern Art. The park is the scene of concerts, theater, children's programs, picnics, and much more. People of the city come to enjoy cultural offerings plus grass, trees, and a feeling of being in the country.

The Anthropological Museum complex was built in 1963-4, beautifully designed by Pedro Ramirez Vasquez. The museum presents a surprisingly harmonious example of contemporary architecture. Incorporated in the roof is an enormous stone umbrella supported on a column 12 m high with a curtain of water dropping into a basin below.

As you enter the museum the shop on the L has a great selection of catalogs, brochures and informative books (in several languages) on many subjects, including the Indian cultures of ancient Mexico, and an excellent museum guide. Some of the finer reproductions of Maya art are available here at reasonable prices. Unfortunately, the store doesn't ship to the States, so you must either lug your purchases around with you on the rest of your trip or take the time to wrap and ship them yourself.

If time is limited, there are well-informed English-speaking guides. For a moderate fee you can join a small group tour that will give you concentrated information either on the entire museum or the salons you're interested in. Each culture is represented in its own well-organized salon. Tickets (small fee) to the museum are sold in the vestibule at the main entrance of the two-story building.

In the Salon of the Maya you'll see some of the finest treasures found on the Yucatan Peninsula. The terra-cotta figures from the island of Jaina are remarkable portrayals of people of various lifestyles. Reproductions of the colored frescoes found in Bonampak are outstanding, as are the delicate carvings from Chichen Itza.

A theft during the Christmas season of 1985 saw the tragic loss of some spectacular remnants of Maya history. The fabled jade mask of Pacal from the Temple of the Inscriptions at Palenque was among the valued pieces stolen.

If you plan on staying awhile, budget travlers can find a good selection of hotels all over the large city plus 3 youth hostels:

SETEJ, Cozumel 57 (tel. 286-91-53), 4 blocks S of Metro Sevilla station (Line 1), which is on Av. Chapultepec. Between Zona Rosa and Chapultepec Park.

CREA Hostel (IYHF), one block S of Villa Olimpica, on Insurgentes Sur, tel. 286-91-53.

International Mexicano Norteamericano de Relaciones Culturales, Hamburgo 115, between Genova and Amberes, in Zona Rosa (no phone).

If money is not a problem, the El Presidente Hotel in Chapultepec Park is within walking distance of all the park attractions. Mexico City has a plethora of hotels to fit every pocketbook and if you're looking for a luxurious splurge, this is where you'll find sophisticated, beautiful inns that compete with any in the world.

help you make the transfer (including your luggage) to a Mexican bus line. This service saves you a lot of time and confusion when in a strange bus station. When making return reservations, make them straight through across the border, even if only to the first town on the U.S. side; again you will have an easier time crossing the border and making the connection.

Class Choice

You have a choice of super-deluxe, deluxe, 1st, 2nd, and 3rd class. Third-class passengers can bring their animals (and often do); buses are older models usually, with no toilets or a/c. Third-class bus tickets can be as cheap as a ticket to a baseball game in the U.S. First-class and above buses have assigned seats, are more comfortable, and still very moderately priced. Make reservations in advance. Your ticket will say *asiento* (seat) with a number. Some 1st-class buses sell food and drinks on board. If you're traveling a long distance, buy 1st-class; the difference in comfort is worth the small added expense. Second- and 3rd-class buses stop for anyone who flags them, and at every small village along the way. First-class operates almost exclusively between terminals. This cuts a lot of time off a long journey.

Luggage

If it fits in the overhead rack almost anything can be carried on board. Usual allowance is 25 kg, but unless you're ridiculously overloaded, no one ever objects to what you bring aboard. If a driver should refuse your load, usually you can come to an amicable (monetary) agreement. Larger luggage is carried in the cargo hold under the bus where breakables have a short lifespan. Purses and cameras are best kept between your feet on the floor, rather than in the overhead rack, just in case. Luggage should always be labeled with your name inside and out.

Seat Comfort

Seats in the middle of the bus are a good choice. When choosing a seat, if you can, pick the shady side of the bus during the day: going S sit on the left (E) side and going N sit on the right. At night sit on the right, eliminating the glare of oncoming headlights. Steer clear of seats near the bathroom, usually the last few rows. They can be smelly and the aisle traffic and constant door activity can keep you awake. Bring a book and ignore the bus driver and his abilities; in other words, just relax.

OTHER TRANSPORTATION

By Ship

Cruise ships stop over at several ports on the Caribbean coast of the Yucatan. Many lines will take you one way and drop you off either at Cancun, Cozumel, or Playa del Carmen. Check with Princess Lines and Carnival Cruises; your travel agent can give you the name of others that stop along the Yucatan coast. New cruise ships are continually adding the Mexican Caribbean to their list of ports of call. Cruise passengers are offered the opportunity to take shore excursions from the Yucatan coast ports to Chichen Itza, Tulum, Coba, and Xelha. Shopping and beach time is also included. For less adventurous travelers, this may be your only chance to visit Maya archaeological zones.

Group Travel

If you prefer to go with a group, travel agents have many choices of escorted tours. You pay a little extra, but all arrangements and reservations are made for you to tour by plane, train, ship, or RV caravan. Also, special-interest groups with a guest expert are another attraction. For instance, archaeology buffs can usually find a group through a university that includes a knowledgeable professor to guide them through chosen Maya ruins. Evenings are spent together reviewing the day's investigation and discussing the next day's itinerary. Ar-

---

LUGGAGE TIP

Both in large and small terminals, look for a sign that says GUARDA EQUIPAJE if you wish to leave your luggage for a few hours or even overnight. Your ticket may be all you need, though others charge a small fee. Ask if there's a time limit.

chaeology laymen will find many opportunities, including trips offered through Earthwatch, Box 403, Watertown, MA 02172, an institute of volunteers where participants can physically work on a dig under the supervision of professionals (among other options); destinations change regularly. The Intercare Organization, FACHCA Director, Box 8561, Moscow, Idaho 83843, for nursing home administrators and related fields, travels to cities around the globe visiting nursing homes, comparing and learning about facilities similar to their own with lectures and seminars. *Transitions Abroad,* 18 Hulst Rd., Box 344, Amherst, MA 01004, is a magazine that offers information about study and teaching opportunities around the world. Travel agencies, student

---

LOS TOPES

When you see a sign that says "TOPE," slow down! You'll soon learn it means a traffic bump is imminent. They are often very high, sometimes with spikes sticking up, and if you hit them fast they can cause severe damage to your car, as well as your head! *Topes* signs precede almost every town and school on the Yucatan Peninsula.

---

publications, and professional organizations can give you more information. It's a good way to mix business with pleasure, and in certain instances the trip is tax deductible.

CAR RENTAL TIPS

Renting a car in Mexico is usually a simple matter, but can be much more costly than in the U.S. —and always subject to Murphy's Law. If you know exactly when you want the car and where, it's helpful to make reservations in the States in advance. Renting a car once in Mexico you pay the going rate, which can add up to about $60 per day for a small car; most offices give little or no weekly discount. This is not to say that you can't take part in the favorite Mexican pastime, bargaining. You might get lucky. *If* it's just before closing time, and *if* someone cancelled a reservation, and *if* it's off season on the Peninsula, it's possible to get a car for a good rate. However, that's a lot of *ifs* to count on when you want and need a car as soon as you arrive. Also, it's often difficult to get a car without reservations and you may have to wait around for one to be returned.

Affordable Mexico
Representatives of Hertz, Avis, and Budget can be found in many parts of Mexico. These are separate franchises. Though not run by the mother companies, U.S. corporate offices will honor a contract price made in the States previous to your arrival in Mexico. If you should run into a problem, and you still want the car, pay the higher price and write a brief protest on the contract right then. Hertz runs a special

deal a good part of the year called "Affordable Mexico." In 1986 the rate for a VW bug or Renault was US$178 per week, including Mexican tax and car insurance, and unlimited km. You can only get this rate by making the deal in the U.S. in advance. If you belong to an automobile club, many offices will give you another 10-20% discount (have your membership card) when returning the car and making the final calculation. This is the cheapest fee for car rentals in Mexico, and unless you plan to use a car for only one or two days, the price is definitely right. Hertz, Avis, and Budget list toll-free 800 phone numbers in the yellow pages of all U.S. cities. You need a major credit card to make phone reservations.

Getting The Car
Another advantage to making reservations in advance is the verification receipt you receive. Hang onto it; it's like money in the bank. When you arrive at the airport and show your verification receipt (be sure you get it back), a car is almost always waiting for you. Once in awhile you'll even get an upgrade for the same fee if your reserved car is not available. On the other side of the coin, be sure that you go over the car *intimately* before you take it far. Drive it around the block and check it out.

CAR RENTAL TIPS

☐ Spare tire and working jack.

☐ All doors lock.

☐ Make sure the seats move forward, have no sprung backs, etc. All windows should lock, unlock, roll up and down properly. Trunk should lock and unlock.

☐ Proper legal papers for the car, with address and phone numbers of associate car rental agencies in cities you plan to visit in case of an unexpected car problem.

☐ Horn, emergency brake, and foot brakes should work properly.

☐ Clutch, gear shift, all gears, and don't forget reverse.

☐ Directions to the nearest gas station; the gas tank may be empty. If it's full it's wise to return it full, since you'll be charged top dollar per liter of gas.

☐ Ask to have any damage, even a small dent, missing door knob, etc. noted on your contract, if it hasn't already.

☐ Note the hour you picked up the car and try to return it before that time: a few minutes over will get you another *full* day's rental fee.

Payoff Time

When you pick up your rental car, the company makes an imprint of your credit card on a blank bill, one copy of which is attached to the papers you give the agent when you return the car. Keep in mind that if you're driving for a long period, 3-4 weeks, the car agency has a limit of how much you can charge on one card at one time (ask the maximum when you pick up the car). If you go over the limit be prepared to pay the balance in cash or with another credit card. If you pick up a car in one city and return it to another there's a hefty drop-off fee (per km). Most agents will figure up in advance exactly how much it will be so there aren't any surprises when you return the car.

In 99 cases out of 100, all will go smoothly. However, if you run into a problem or are overcharged, don't panic. You might be at an office that never heard of Affordable Mexico, even though it is specified on your verification. Go ahead and pay (with plastic money), save all your paper work, and when you return to the States, make copies of everything, call the company, and chances are very good that you'll get a refund.

Insurance

Mexican insurance from the rental car agency runs about US$6 per day and covers only 80% of damages (a fact which many travelers are unaware of). However, it's dangerous to skip insurance; in most cases in Mexico, when there's an accident the police take action first and ask questions later. With an insurance policy, most of the problems are eased over. The rental agency also offers medical insurance for US$4 per day. Your private medical insurance should cover this (check) and if not, many traveler's-cheque packages come with some sort of medical insurance for a small extra fee.

WHAT TO TAKE

Whatever time of year you travel to the Yucatan you can expect warm weather, which means you can pack less in your suitcase. If you plan on a one-destination trip to a self-contained resort hotel and want a change of clothes each day, most airlines check 2 suit-cases, and you can bring another carry-on bag that fits either under your seat or in the overhead rack. But if you plan on moving around a lot, keep it light.

Experienced women travelers pack a small foldable purse into their compartmented carry-on which then gives them only 2 things to carry while en route. And be sure to include a few overnight necessities in your carry-on in the event your luggage doesn't arrive when you do. Valuables are safest in your carry-on and under the seat in front of you between your feet whether you're on a plane, train, or bus.

Security

It's smart to keep passports, traveler's cheques, money, and important papers on your person at all times. The do-it-yourselfer can sew inside pockets into clothes; buy extra long pants that can be turned up, sewn ¾ of the way around, with a piece of Velcro used for easy opening and closing. Separate "shoulder-holster"-type pockets, moneybelts, and pockets that hang around the neck and fit in-side clothing—all made of cotton—are avail-able commercially. If you're going to be backpacking and sloshing in jungle streams etc. put everything in Ziploc plastic bags before placing them in pockets. It's always a good idea to write down document numbers (such as passports); keep them separated in your luggage and leave a copy with a friend back home. This expedites replacement in case of loss.

Clothing

A swim suit is a must, and if you're not staying at one of the larger hotels, bring a beach towel. In today's Yucatan, *almost* any clothing is ac-ceptable. If traveling the winter months of Nov., Dec., and Jan. it's a good idea to bring

along a light wrap because it can cool off in the evening. The rest of the year you'll probably carry the wrap in your suitcase. For women, a wrap-around skirt is a useful item that can quickly cover up shorts when traveling through the villages and some cities (many small villagers really gawk at women wearing shorts and whatever you do, don't enter a church wearing them). The wrap-around skirt also makes a good shawl when it cools off. Cotton underwear is the coolest in the tropics, but nylon is less bulky and dries overnight, cutting down on the number needed. Be sure that you bring broken-in, comfortable walking shoes. Blisters can wreck a vacation almost as much as a sunburn.

Campers

For the purist who vows to cook every meal, here's a list for a handy carried kitchen:

Single-burner stove, 2 fuel cylinders (fuel not allowed on commercial airlines).
One large sharp machete-type knife; one small, sturdy, sharp knife.
Pair of pliers—good hot pot grabber.
Plastic pot scrubber.
Can opener (with bottle hook).
Hot pad, 2 if there's room.
2 pots that nest, one Silverstone skillet.
 Wire holder to barbecue fish or meat over open fire.
Small sharpening stone.
Soap and laundry detergent.
Plate, cup, fork,and spoon, plastic or metal.
2 large metal cooking spoons.
One long-handled wooden spoon.
One egg spatula.
3 fast-drying dish towels (not terrycloth).
Plastic Ziploc bags, large trash bags.
Paper towels or napkins.
2 or 3 plastic containers with tight-fitting lids, nested.
Coffee drinkers that don't like instant will want a coffee pot.
Several short candles and matches.
Flashlight (batteries are usually easy to find).

Backpackers

If you plan on hitchhiking or using public transportation, don't use a large external frame pack; it won't fit in most small cars or public lockers. Smaller packs with zippered compartments that will accommodate mini-padlocks are most practical. A strong bike cable and lock secures the pack to a YH bed or a bus or train rack. None of the above will deter the real criminal, but might make it just difficult enough to discourage everyone else.

Experienced backpackers travel light with a pack, an additional canvas bag, small waterproof, mosquito-proof tent, hammock and mosquito netting. What camping supplies to bring depends on your style of traveling.

Necessities

Anyone planning an extended trip in Mexico should bring an extra pair of glasses or carry the lens prescription; the same goes for medication, though many pharmacies sell prescription drugs over the counter (make sure it's written in general terms).

Reading Materials

Avid readers in any language besides Spanish should bring a supply of books; English-language reading materials are available in limited quantities, mostly in big hotel gift shops and only a few book stores.

HEALTH CARE

TURISTA

Some travelers to Mexico worry about getting sick the moment they cross the border. But with a few simple precautions, it's not a foregone conclusion that you'll come down with something in the Yucatan. The most common illness to strike visitors is *turista,* Montezuma's Revenge, the trots, or in plain Latin—diarrhea. No fun, it can cause uncomfortable cramping, fever, dehydration, and the need to stay close to a toilet for the duration. It's caused, among other things, by various strains of bacteria managing to find your innards, so it's important to be very careful of what goes into your mouth.

Possible Causes

Statistics show that the majority of tourists get sick on the third day of their visit. Interested doctors note that this traveler's illness is common in every country. They say that in addition to bacteria a change in diet is equally to blame, and suggest that the visitor slip slowly into the eating habits of Mexico. In other words, don't blast your tummy with the *habanera* or *jalapeno* pepper right off the bat. Work into the fried food, drinks, local specialties, and new spices gradually; take your time changing over to foods that you may never eat while at home,

including the large quantities of wonderful tropical fruits that you'll want to eat every morning in the tropics. Blame is also shared by mixing alcohol with longer than usual periods of time in the tropical sun.

It's The Water

While these theories are valid for the rest of Mexico, in Yucatan water is probably the worst culprit. Many parts of the Peninsula have modern sewage systems, but the small villages and more isolated areas still have little or none. So all waste is redeposited in the earth and can contaminate the natural water supply. While in these places you should take special precautions.

In the backcountry, carry your own water, boil it, or purify it with chemicals, whether the source is out of the tap or a crystal-clear *cenote.* That goes for brushing your teeth as well. If you have nothing else, a bottle of beer will make a safe (though maybe not sane) mouth rinse. If using ice, ask where it was made and if it's pure. Think about the water you're swimming in; some small local pools might be better avoided.

The easiest way to purify the water is using purification tablets; Hidroclonozone and Halazone are two, but many brands are available at drugstores in all countries, and in Mexico ask at the *farmacia.* Another common method is to carry a small plastic bottle of liquid bleach (8-10 drops per quart of water) or iodine (called *yodo,* 5-7 drops per quart). Whichever you use, let the water stand for 20 minutes to improve the flavor. If you're not prepared with any of the above, boiling the water for 20-30 minutes will purify it. Even though it takes a heck of a lot of fuel when you're carrying it on your back, don't get lazy in this department. You can get very sick drinking contaminated water and you can't tell by looking at it—unless you travel with a microscope!

When camping on the beach where fresh water is scarce, use seawater to wash dishes and even yourself. Liquid Ivory or Joy detergents both suds well in saltwater. It only takes a small squirt of the detergent to do a good job. (A rub of soap on the bottom of pots and pans before use over an open fire makes for easy cleaning of the soot after cooking.)

In the larger cities purified water is generally provided in bottles in each room, or if the hotel is large enough it maintains its own purification plant on the premises. In Cozumel, for example, the Sol Caribe Hotel has a modern purification plant behind glass walls for all to see, and they're proud to show it off and explain how it works. If the tap water is pure, a sign over the spigot will specify this—except in Cancun, which with a modern infrastructure, brags they're the only Mexican city in which every tap gives purified water. If you're not sure about the water, ask the desk clerk; he'll let you know the status—they prefer healthy guests that will return.

Other Sources of Bacteria

Handling money can be a source of germs. Wash your hands frequently, don't put your fingers in your mouth, and carry individual packets of disinfectant cleaners, like Wash Up, that come in tiny foil packets, and are refreshing in the tropic heat. Hepatitis is another bug that can be contracted easily if in the neighborhood.

When in backcountry cafes, remember that fruit and vegetables, especially those with a thin skin that is eaten (like tomatoes), are a possible source of bacteria. If you like to eat food purchased from street vendors (and some

shouldn't be missed), use common sense. If you see the food being cooked (killing all the grubby little bacteria) before your eyes, have at it. If it's hanging there already cooked and nibbled on by small flying creatures, pass it by. It may have been there all day, and what was once a nice sterile morsel could easily have gone bad in the heat, or been contaminated by flies. When buying food at the marketplace to cook yourself, use the hints given in "Foods," p. 52.

Treatment

Remember, it's not just the visiting gringo who gets sick because of bacteria. Many Mexicans die each year from the same germs, and the Mexican government is working hard to remedy these problems. Tremendous improvements have taken place, and it ultimately will be accomplished all over Mexico, but it's a slow process. In the meantime, many careful visitors come and go each year with nary a touch of *turista*. If after all your precautions you still come down with traveler's illness, many medications are available for relief. Most can be bought over the counter in Mexico, but in the States you'll need a prescription from your doctor. Lomotil is common, and it certainly turns off the faucet after a few hours of dosing; however, it has the side effect of becoming a plug. It does not cure the problem, only the symptoms. If you quit taking it too soon your symptoms reappear and you're back to square one. In its favor, Lomotil probably works faster than any of the other drugs, and if you're about to embark on a 12-hour train ride across the Peninsula you might consider Lomotil a lifesaver. A few other over-the-counter remedies are Keopectate in the U.S., Immodium and Donamycin in Mexico. If you're concerned, check with your doctor before leaving home.

For those who prefer natural remedies, lime juice and garlic are both considered good bacteria killers—good preventatives. They need to be taken in large quantities. Douse everything with the easily available lime juice (it's delicious on salads, fresh fruit, and in drinks). You'll have to figure your own ways of using garlic (some believers carry garlic capsules, available in most health food stores in the U.S.). *Pero Te* (dog tea) is used by the Mexicans, as well as the juice of a fresh coconut (don't eat the oily flesh, it makes your problem worse!). Plain boiled white rice soothes the tummy. While letting the ailment run its course stay away from spicy and oily foods and fresh fruits. Don't be surprised if you have chills, nausea, vomiting, stomach cramps, and run a fever. This could go on for about three days. But if the problem persists, see a doctor.

SUNBURN

Sunburn can spoil a vacation quicker than anything else. Approach the sun cautiously. Expose yourself for short periods the first few days; wear a hat and sunglasses. Use a good sunscreen, and apply it to all exposed areas of the body (don't forget your feet, hands, nose, back of the knees, and top of the forehead— especially if you have a receding hairline). Remember that after every time you go into the water for a swim, sunscreen lotion must be reapplied. Even after a few days of desensitizing the skin, when spending a day snorkeling, wear a T-shirt in the water to protect the exposed back, and thoroughly douse the back of the neck with sunscreen lotion. PABA (para amino benzoic acid) solutions offer good protection and condition the skin. It's found in many brand names and strengths and is much cheaper in the U.S. than in the Yucatan. The higher the number, the more protection.

If you still get a painful sunburn, do not return to the sun. Cover up with clothes if it's impossible to find protective deep shade (like in the depths of a dark, thick forest). Even in the shade (such as under a beach umbrella), the reflection of the sun off the sand or water will burn your skin. Reburning the skin can result in painful blisters that easily become infected. Soothing suntan lotions, coconut oil, vinegar, cool tea, and preparations like Solarcaine will help relieve the pain. Mostly a cure takes just a couple of days out of the sun. Drink plenty of liquids (especially water) and take tepid showers.

HEALING

Most small cities on the Yucatan have a resident doctor. He may or may not speak English, but will usually make a house call. When staying in a hotel, get a doctor quickly by asking the hotel manager; in the larger resorts, an English-speaking doctor is on call 24 hours a day. If you need to ask someone to get you a doctor, say *"necessito doctor, por favor!"* Emergency clinics are found in all but the smallest village, and a taxi driver can be your quickest way to get there when you're a stranger in town. In small rural villages, if you have a serious problem and no doctor is around, you can usually find a *curandero*. These healers deal with the old natural methods (and maybe just a few chants thrown in for good measure). This person could be a help in a desperate situation away from modern technology.

Self Help

The smart traveler carries a first-aid kit of some kind with him. If backpacking, at least carry the following:

> Alcohol
> Adhesive Tape
> Aspirin
> Baking Soda
> Bandaids
> Cornstarch
> Gauze
> Hydrogen Peroxide
> Iodine
> Insect Repellent
> Lomotil or ?
> Needle
> Pain Pills
> Antibiotic Ointment
> Pain Killer
> Sunscreen
> Tweezers
> Water Purification Tablets

Many of these products are available in Mexico, but certain items, like aspirin and bandaids, are sold individually in small shops and are much cheaper bought in your hometown. Even if not out in the wilderness you should carry at least a few bandaids, aspirin, and an antibiotic ointment or powder or both. Travelers should be aware that in the tropics, with its heavy humidity, a simple scrape can become infected more easily than in a dry climate. So keep it as clean and as dry as possible.

Another great addition to your first-aid kit is David Werner's book, *Where There Is No Doc-* tor. Also published in Spanish, it can be ordered from Hesperian Foundation, Box 1692, Palo Alto, CA 94302. David Werner drew on his experience living in Mexico's backcountry to create this practical informative book.

Shots
Check on your tetanus shot before you leave home; especially if you're backpacking in isolated regions.

SIMPLE FIRST AID GUIDE

Acute Allergic Reaction
This, the most serious complication of insect bites, can be fatal. Common symptoms are hives, rash, pallor, nausea, tightness in chest or throat, trouble in speaking or breathing. Be alert for symptoms. If they appear, get prompt medical help. Start CPR if needed and continue until medical help is available.

Animal Bites
Bites, especially on face and neck, need immediate medical attention. If possible, catch and hold animal for observation taking care not to be bitten. Wash wound with soap and water (hold under running water for 2-3 min. unless bleeding is heavy). *Do Not* use iodine or other antiseptic. Bandage. This also applies to bites by human beings. In case of human bites the danger of infection is high.

Bee Stings
Apply cold compresses quickly. If possible, remove stinger by gentle scraping with clean fingernail and continue cold applications till pain is gone. Be alert for symptoms of acute allergic reaction or infection requiring medical aid.

Bleeding
For severe bleeding apply direct pressure to the wound with bandage or the heel of the hand. Do not remove cloths when blood-soaked, just add others on top and continue pressure till bleeding stops. Elevate bleeding part above heart level. If bleeding continues, apply pressure bandage to arterial points. *Do Not* put on tourniquet unless advised by a physician. *Do Not* use iodine or other disinfectant. Get medical aid.

Blister On Heel
It is better not to open a blister if you can rest the foot. If you can't, wash foot with soap and water; make a small hole at the base of the blister with a needle sterilized in 70% alcohol or by holding the needle in the flame of a match; drain fluid and cover with strip bandage or moleskin. If a blister breaks on its own, wash with soap and water, bandage, and be alert for signs of infection (redness, festering) that call for medical attention.

Burns
Minor burns (redness, swelling, pain): apply cold water or immerse burned part in cold water immediately. Use burn medication if necessary. **Deeper Burns** (blisters develop): Immerse in cold water (not ice water) or apply cold compresses for 1-2 hours. Blot dry and protect with sterile bandage. *Do Not* use antiseptic, ointment or home remedies. Consult a doctor. **Deep Burns** (skin layers destroyed, skin may be charred): cover with sterile cloth; be alert for breathing difficulties and treat for shock if necessary. *Do Not* remove clothing stuck to burn. *Do Not* apply ice. *Do Not* use burn remedies. Get medical help quickly.

continued

Cuts

For small cuts wash with clean water and soap. Hold wound under running water. Bandage. Use hydrogen peroxide or other antiseptic. For large wounds see "Bleeding." If a finger or toe has been cut off, treat severed end to control bleeding. Put severed part in clean cloth for the doctor (it may be possible to reattach it by surgery). Treat for shock if necessary. Get medical help at once.

Diving Accident

There may be injury to the cervical spine (such as a broken neck). Call for medical help. (See "Drowning.")

Drowning

Clear airway and start CPR even before trying to get water out of lungs. Continue CPR till medical help arrives. In case of vomiting, turn victim's head to one side to prevent inhaling vomitus.

Food Poisoning

Symptoms appear a varying number of hours after eating and are generally like those of the flu—headache, diarrhea, vomiting, abdominal cramps, fever, a general sick feeling. See a doctor. A rare form, botulism, has a high fatality rate. Symptoms are double vision, inability to swallow, difficulty in speaking, respiratory paralysis. Get to emergency facility at once.

Fractures

Until medical help arrives, *Do Not* move the victim unless absolutely necessary. Suspected victims of back, neck, or hip injuries should not be moved. Suspected breaks of arms or legs should be splinted to avoid further damage before victim is moved, if moving is necessary.

Heat Exhaustion

Symptoms are cool moist skin, profuse sweating, headache, fatigue, drowsiness with essentially normal body temperature. Remove victim to cool surroundings, raise feet and legs, loosen clothing and apply cool cloths. Give sips of salt water—1 teaspoon of salt to a glass of water—for rehydration. If victim vomits, stop fluids, take the victim to emergency facility as soon as possible.

Heat Stroke

Rush victim to hospital. Heat stroke can be fatal. Victim may be unconscious or severely confused. Skin feels hot, is red and dry, with no perspiration. Body temperature is high. Pulse is rapid. Remove victim to cool area, sponge with cool water or rubbing alcohol; use fans or a/c and wrap in wet sheets, but do not over-chill. Massage arms and legs to increase circulation. *Do Not* give large amount of liquids. *Do Not* give liquids if victim is unconscious.

Insect Bites

Be alert for acute allergic reaction that requires quick medical aid. Otherwise, apply cold compresses, soothing lotions.

Ivy, Oak, or Sumac

After contact, wash affected area with alkali-base laundry soap, lathering well. Have a poison-ivy remedy available in case itching and blisters develop.

Jellyfish Stings

Symptom is acute pain and may include feeling of paralysis. Immerse in ice water from 5-10 min. or apply aromatic spirits of ammonia to remove venom from skin. Be alert for symptoms of acute allergic reaction and/or shock. If this happens, get victim to hospital as soon as possible.

Malaria

If traveling where malaria is prevalent, check with your physician before leaving about the advisability of taking chloroquine or Fansidar. These medications can cause side affects so it's important that good medical advice is followed. Centers for Disease Control can give you further information.

Mosquito Bites

Apply cold compresses and a mild lotion to relieve itching. If bites are scratched and infection starts (fever, swelling, redness), see a doctor.

Motion Sickness

Get a prescription from your doctor if boat traveling is anticipated and this illness is a problem. Many over-the-counter remedies are sold in the U.S.: Bonine is one. If you prefer not to take chemicals or get drowsy something new, called the Sea Band, is a cloth band that you place around the pressure point of the wrists. For more information write:

Sea Band,
1645 Palm Beach Lake Blvd.
Suite 220
W. Palm Beach, FL 33401
(305) 684-4508

Medication that's administered in adhesive patches behind the ear is also available by prescription from your doctor.

Muscle Cramps

Usually a result of unaccustomed exertion. "Working" the muscle or kneading with hand relieves cramp. If in water head for shore (you can swim even with a muscle cramp), or knead muscle with hand. Call for help if needed.

Mushroom Poisoning

Even a small ingestion may be serious. Induce vomiting immediately if there is any question of mushroom poisoning. Symptoms — vomiting, diarrhea, difficult breathing — may begin in 1-2 hours or up to 24 hours. Convulsions and delirium may develop. Go to a doctor or emergency facility at once.

Nosebleed

Press bleeding nostril closed or pinch nostrils together or pack with sterile cotton or gauze. Apply cold cloth or ice to nose and face. Victim should sit up, leaning forward, or lie down with head and shoulders raised. If bleeding does not stop in 10 min. get medical help.

Obstructed Airway

Find out if victim can talk by asking "Can you talk?" If he can talk, encourage victim to try to cough obstruction out. If he can't speak, a trained person must apply the Heimlich method. If you are alone and choking, try to forcefully cough object out. Or press your fist into your upper abdomen with a quick upward thrust, or lean forward and quickly press your upper abdomen over any firm object with rounded edge (back of chair, edge of sink, porch railing). Keep trying till the object comes out.

Plant Poisoning

Many plants are poisonous if eaten or chewed. Induce vomiting immediately. Take victim to emergency facility for treatment. If the leaves of the diffenbachia (common in the Yucatan jungle) are chewed, one of the first symptoms is swelling of the throat.

Puncture Wounds

Usually caused by stepping on a tack or a nail. They often do not bleed, so try to squeeze out some blood. Wash thoroughly with soap and water and apply a sterile bandage. Check with doctor about tetanus. If pain, heat, throbbing, or redness develop, get medical attention at once.

Rabies

Bites from bats, raccoons, rats, or other wild animals are the most common threat of rabies today. Try capturing the animal, so it can be observed; do not kill the animal unless necessary and try not to injure the head so the brain can be examined. Avoid getting bitten. If the animal can't be found, see a doctor who may decide to use antirabies immunization. In any case, flush bite with water and apply a dry dressing; keep victim quiet and see a doctor as soon as possible.

Scorpion Sting

Stings of the more poisonous kinds can be fatal, especially in young children. Follow directions for snakebites and get medical attention as soon as possible. Most doctors in the Yucatan carry scorpion antivenin.

continued

Scrapes

Sponge with soap and water; dry. Apply antibiotic ointment or powder and cover with a non-stick dressing (or tape on a piece of cellophane). When healing starts, stop ointment and use antiseptic powder to help scab form. Ask doctor about tetanus.

Shock

Can be a side effect in any kind of injury. Get immediate medical help. Symptoms may be pallor, clammy feeling to the skin, shallow breathing, fast pulse, weakness, or thirst. Loosen clothing, cover victim with blanket but do not apply other heat, and place him lying on his back with feet raised. If necessary, start CPR. *Do Not* give water or other fluids.

Snakebite

If snake is not poisonous, toothmarks usually appear in an even row (an exception, the poisonous gila monster, shows even tooth marks). Wash the bite with soap and water and apply sterile bandage. See a doctor. If snake is poisonous, puncture marks (1-6) can usually be seen. Kill the snake for identification if possible, taking care not to be bitten. Keep the victim quiet, immobilize the bitten arm or leg, keeping it on a lower level than the heart. If possible, phone ahead to be sure antivenin is available and get medical treatment as soon as possible. *Do Not* give alcohol in any form. If treatment must be delayed and snakebite kit is available, use as directed.

Spider Bites

The black widow bite may produce only a light reaction at the place of the bite, but severe pain, a general sick feeling, sweating, abdominal cramps, and breathing and speaking difficulty may develop. The more dangerous brown recluse spider's venom produces severe reaction at the bite, general-ly in 2-8 hours, plus chills, fever, joint pain, nausea and vomiting. Apply a cold compress to the bite in either case. Get medical aid quickly.

Sprain

Treat as a fracture till injured part has been X-rayed. Raise the sprained ankle or other joint and apply cold compresses or immerse in cold water. If swelling is pronounced, try not to use the injured part until it has been X-rayed. Get prompt medical help.

Sunburn

For skin that is moderately red and slightly swollen, apply wet dressings of gauze dipped in a solution of 1 tablespoon baking soda and 1 tablespoon cornstarch to 2 quarts of cool water. Or take a cool bath with a cup of baking soda to a tub of water. Sunburn remedies are helpful in relieving pain. See a doctor if burn is severe.

Sunstroke

This is a severe emergency. See "Heat Stroke." Skin is hot and dry; body temperature is high. The victim may be delirious or unconscious. Get medical help immediately.

Ticks

Cover ticks with mineral oil or kerosene to exclude air from ticks and they will usually drop off or can be lifted off with tweezers in 30 minutes. To avoid infection, take care to remove whole tick. Wash area with soap and water. Check with doctor or health department to see if deadly ticks are in the area.

Wasp Sting

Apply cold compresses to the sting and watch for acute allergic reaction. If such symptoms develop, get victim to medical facility immediately.

CAMERAS AND PICTURE TAKING

Bring a camera to the Yucatan! Nature and Maya combine to provide unforgettable panoramas, well worth taking home with you on film to savor again at your leisure. Many people find simple cameras such as Instamatics or disc-types easy to carry and uncomplicated. Others prefer 35mm which offers higher-quality pictures, are easier than ever to use, and available in any price range. They can come equipped with built-in light meter, automatic exposure, self-focus, and self-advancing—with little more to do than aim and click.

Film
Reasons to bring film with you are: it's cheaper and more readily available in the States. Reasons *not* to bring lots of film are: if you're backpacking, space may be a problem, and heat can affect film quality, both before and after exposure. Even in a car, heat is something to consider. To protect the finished product, carry film in an insulated case, something as simple as a styrofoam cooler (the size that handles a 6-pack). Or you can be more sophisticated by buying (for greater cost) a soft-sided insulated bag sold in some camera shops or ordered out of a professional photography magazine. Ideally, it's best to plan ahead and pick up a limited quantity of film when you come across the right shop.

X-Ray Protection
If you bring your film from home remember to take precautions when traveling by plane. Each time film is passed through the security X-ray machine, a little damage is done. It's cumulative, and perhaps one time won't make much difference, but most photographers won't take the chance. Request hand inspection. With today's tight security at airports, some guards insist on passing your film and camera through the X-ray machine. It's wise to pack it in protective lead bags even when in your checked luggage. Lead-lined bags are available at camera shops in two sizes. The larger size holds up to 22 rolls of 35mm film. The smaller size holds 8 rolls. If you use fast film, ASA 400 or higher, buy the double lead-lined bag designed to protect more sensitive film. It's also efficient to carry an extra lead-lined bag to carry your film-loaded camera if you want to drop it into a piece of carry-on luggage (and for non-photographers, it protects medications from X-ray damage).

If you decide to request hand examination (rarely if ever refused at a Mexican airport), make it simple for the security guard. Have the film out of boxes, placed together in one clear plastic bag that you can hand him for quick examination both coming and going. He'll also want to look at the camera; load it after crossing the border. If you hand-carry your equipment in a camera case, expect to have to unpack it for examination.

Film Processing

For processing film the traveler has several options. Most people take their film home and have it processed at a familiar lab. However, if the trip is lengthy and you are shooting lots of film, it's impractical to carry it all around for a couple of months. One-hour photo labs are found in the larger cities and resort areas on the Peninsula, but they only handle color prints; color slides must be processed at a different lab, which usually takes a week or two. If you'll be passing through the same city on another leg of your trip, the lab is a good cool place to store your slides while you travel. Just tell the

labman when you think you'll be picking them up. Another option is to buy prepaid Kodak mailers before you leave home and simply drop the film in post offices (preferably in larger cities) as you travel. Be sure to put your own country's postage on the inside envelope that will be sent to your home address. Some photographers don't trust the mail and won't let their film out of sight until they reach their own favorite lab, but with the Kodak label all over the yellow envelopes, problems with the mail are rare.

Camera Protection

Take a few precautions with your camera while traveling. At the beach remember that a combination of wind and sand can really gum up the works and scratch the lens. On 35mm cameras keep a clear skylight filter instead of a lens cap so it can hang around the neck or over the shoulder always at the ready for that spectacular shot that comes when least expected. And if something is going to get scratched, better a $7 filter rather than a $300 lens. It also helps to carry as little equipment as possible. If

Photographer Oz Mallan displays a convenient belt with all equipment (except cameras) hanging from it in army-surplus pouches. This is at Chichen Itza in front of Chac Mool, abandoned hundreds of years ago before the carvers completed it.

you want more than candids and you carry a 35mm camera, basic equipment can be simple. A canvas bag is lighter and less conspicuous than a heavy photo bag. At the nearest surplus store you can find small military bags, and webbed belts with eyelet holes to hang canteen pouches and two clip holders. These are perfect size to hold one or two extra lenses (safely tucked into a canteen pouch), and another filled with film. They're comfortable hanging on the hips, and free the hands while climbing pyramids or on long hikes.

Safety Tips

Keep your camera dry; carrying a couple of big Ziploc bags is instant protection. If you plan to be in small boats that put you close to the water, keep the cameras temporarily in the zipped bags when not in use. Don't *store* cameras in plastic bags for any length of time, because the moisture that builds up in the bag is the same as being in the rain. It's always wise to keep the cameras out of sight in a car or when camping out. Put your name and address on the camera. Chances are if it gets left behind or stolen it won't matter whether your name is there or not, and don't expect to see it again; however, miracles do happen.(You *can* put a rider on most homeowner's insurance policies for a nominal sum that will cover the cost if a camera is lost or stolen.) It's a nuisance to carry cameras every second when traveling for a long period. During an evening out, you can leave your cameras and equipment (out of sight) in the hotel room—unless it makes you

---

EFFICIENT GADGETS

2 Nikon 35mm cameras—one for black and white and one for color.

2 short zoom lenses, 43mm x 86 mm (which are almost always on the cameras).

1 long zoom lens, 70 x 210.

1 24mm wide-angle lens.

1 small strobe light.

A small clamp-on tripod.

A pair of polaroid filters. (A necessity in the brilliant Caribbean sun, sand, and sea. They cut a bit of the glare on the white beaches, and give a better separation of sky and clouds in the bright light.) It's a good idea to keep your cameras in *ready mode* (daylight setting when outdoors) at all times.

---

crazy all evening worrying about it!

Cameras can be a help and a hindrance when trying to get to know the people. Traveling in the backcountry you'll run into folks frightened of having their pictures taken. Keep your camera put away for just the right moment. The main thing to remember is: ask permission first, and then if someone doesn't want his/her picture taken, accept the refusal with a gracious smile and move on.

OTHER PRACTICALITIES

ENTRY AND DEPARTURE

U.S. and Canadian citizens can obtain a free Tourist Card with proof of citizenship (birth certificate, passport, voter's registration, or notorized affidavit) good for 180 days. It can be obtained at any Mexican consulate or tourist office, at all border entry points, or from airport ticket offices for those traveling by plane. Hang on to your Tourist Card for the entire trip. If visiting Mexico for 72 hours or less, a Tourist Card is not needed. Ask at the Mexican Consulate about extensions for longer periods. If you're a naturalized citizen, carry your naturalization papers or passport. Certificates of vaccination are not required to enter Mexico from U.S. or Canadian citizens; other nationals should check with a local Mexican consulate. Those under 18 without a parent or legal guardian must present a notorized letter from the parents or guardian granting permission to travel alone in Mexico. If a single parent is traveling with a minor, he or she should carry a notorized letter from the other parent granting permission. This is important going in both directions.

Bring A Passport

Hang onto your Tourist Card! You won't need it after you go through customs until it's time to leave the country. Then you must give it back. If you have a passport, bring it along even though it's not required (tuck your Tourist Card inside); it's the simplest ID when cashing traveler's cheques, registering at hotels, and going through immigration. If you're visiting an area that has a current health problem and you have a health card with current information, keep that with the passport also. Keep all documents in a waterproof plastic case and in a safe place. Write to the U.S. Secretary of State for the most recent information about isolated areas that might be on the list for immunization. If such is the case, you will need proof of vaccination to get back into the U.S. and perhaps other countries as well.

Driving Procedures

If traveling by car or RV, the Tourist Card serves as a vehicle permit when completed and validated at the border point of entry. Vehicle title or registration and driver's license are required. If you should happen to reach a remote border crossing at night, you may find it unmanned. *Do not* cross the border with your car until you have obtained the proper papers; if you do it will cause problems when you exit the country. Mexican vehicle insurance is available at most border towns 24 hours a day.

If traveling with a pet, a veterinarian's certificate verifying good health and a rabies inoculation within 6 months is required to bring dogs and cats into the country. This certificate will be validated by any Mexican Consulate for a small fee.

Purchases

When departing by land, air, or sea, you must declare at the point of re-entry into your own country all items acquired in Mexico. To facilitate this procedure, it is wise to register any foreign-made possessions with customs officials before entering Mexico, and to retain the receipts for purchases made while there. Limitations on the value of goods allowed to be imported duty-free vary from country to country and should be checked before traveling. U.S. citizens are allowed to carry through customs $300 of purchases per person duty free. However, about 2700 items are exempt from this limit, most of which are handcrafted or manufactured in Mexico. Consular offices or embassies in Mexico City can supply additional information on exempt items. Plants and certain foods are not allowed into the U.S. Authentic archaeological finds, colonial art, and other original artifacts cannot be exported from Mexico. And of course trying to bring pot or any other narcotic out of Mexico and into the U.S. is foolhardy. Jail is one place in Mexico a visitor should miss.

Bargaining

This is how a visitor really gets to know the people. Although the influx of many outsiders who don't appreciate the delicate art of bargaining has deteriorated this traditional verbal exchange, bargaining is still a way of life between Mexicans; it can still build a bridge between the gringo and the Yucatecan. Some Americans accustomed to shopping with plastic money either find bargaining distasteful or go overboard and insult the merchant by offering far too little. It would not be insulting to begin the bargaining at 50% below the asking price; expect to earn about a 20% discount (and new respect) after a lively repartee often filled with joviality between buyer and seller.

Shipping

Mailing and shipping from Mexico is easy within certain limitations. Packages of less than $25 in value can be sent to the U.S. The package must be marked "Unsolicited Gift —

You can buy a living jeweled beetle at the Merida market, but it won't clear U.S. Customs.

Under $25" and addressed to someone other than the traveler. Only one package per day may be sent to the same addressee. Major stores will handle shipping arrangements on larger items and duty must be paid; this is in addition to the $300 carried in person across the border.

COMMUNICATIONS

Telephone

Large cities in Mexico have direct dialing to the U.S., with international operators available to assist whenever necessary. Many cities in the Yucatan still have a less efficient system, and often a long-distance call can take several hours to place. For the cities that do have direct dialing, see chart on page 78.

Telegraph and Postal

Even the smallest village has a telegraph office. Wires can often be sent direct from the larger hotels. Night letters are available at a lower rate. All service must be prepaid. Almost every town on the Peninsula has a post office. If you can't find it by looking, ask — it may be located in someone's front parlor. Air mail postage is recommended for the best delivery. Post offices will hold mail for travelers one week if it is marked *a/c Lista de Correos* ("care of General Delivery"). Hotels will extend the same service for mail marked "tourist mail, hold for arrival."

Radio And Television

AM and FM radio stations, in Spanish, are scattered throughout the Peninsula. Television is becoming more common as well. In the major cities hotel rooms have TV entertainment. The large resort areas like Cancun have one or two cable stations from the U.S., on which you can expect to see all the major baseball and football events.

MONEY

Currency Exchange

The *peso,* the basic medium of exchange in Mexico, has floated on the free market since 1976. The money is issued in paper bills (50, 100, 500, 1,000, 5,000, and 10,000 denomina-

TELEPHONE AND EMERGENCY INFORMATION

Information (national)	01
Long-distance operator	02
Time	03
Information (local)	04
Police radio patrol	06
Bilingual emergency information	07
International operator (English)	09
Long-distance direct service	
station to station (nat'l)	91 plus area code and no.
person to person (nat'l)	92 plus area code and no.
Long-distance direct service	
station to station (int'l)	95 plus area code and no.
person to person (int'l)	96 plus area code and no.
Worldwide	
station to station	98
person to person	99

tions) and coins (1, 5, 10, 20, 50, and 100 *peso* pieces). Curiously, coins of smaller value are measured in *centavos* (10, 20, and 50), but no one is really sure what to use them for since nothing sells for *centavos.*

Usually your best rate of exchange is the bank, but small shops frequently give a better rate. Hotels notoriously give the poorest exchange. Check to see what fee, if any, is charged. In today's economy, it's common to have moneychangers approach you (in the bank) while you're waiting in line to exchange dollars and offer you better than the posted rate. There's no harm in this—except, can you tell the difference between counterfeit *pesos* and the real thing? You can learn the current exchange rate daily in all banks and most hotels. Try not to run out of money over the weekend because the new rate often is not posted until noon on Mon. and you will get the previous Fri. rate of exchange even if the weekend newspaper may be announcing an overwhelming difference—in your favor.

Insurance
When buying traveler's cheques in the States, look into Bank of America's *SafeTravel Network,* a package deal that provides medical coverage for 45 days and baggage insurance (over and above the airlines) all for US$10. This enables you to pass by the US$4 daily charged for medical insurance when renting a car. A bargain if you plan on at least a week's car rental.

Credit Cards
Major credit cards are accepted at all of the larger hotels, travel agencies, and many shops throughout the Peninsula. But don't take it for granted, ask. In rare instances you'll be asked to pay a fee on top of your charged amount. Gas stations *do not* accept credit cards.

Business Hours
Banks open from 0900-1330, Mon. to Friday. Business offices open from 0800 or 0900-1300 or 1400, then reopen at about 1530-1600, until 1800. Government offices are usually open from 0830-¡500. Stores in cities on the Peninsula are generally open from 1000-1900 or 2000, closing from 1300-1600. Government offices, banks and stores are closed on national holidays.

Tipping
Ten to 20% of the bill, if not already included, is standard. Tips for assistance with bags should be equivalent to US$.50 per bag. Chambermaids should receive about P100 per day. It is not necessary to tip taxi drivers unless they have performed a special service. Tour

METRIC CONVERSION TABLES

Mexico officially uses the metric system of weights and measures. The following tables will help you make quick conversion.

Liquid measure: To roughly convert liters to quarts and gallons—one liter is approximately one quart; four liters about one gallon. To be more exact, multiply liters by 2.642 and divide by 10 to obtain gallons.

Liters	U.S. Gals.
5	1.3
8	2.1
10	2.6
20	5.3
30	8.0
50	13.2

weight: to roughly convert kilos (kilograms, 1000 grams) to pounds—one kilo is about 2 lbs. More exactly, multiply kilos by 2.2046 to obtain lbs.

Kilograms	Pounds
0.5	1.1
1.0	2.2
5	11.0
10	22.0
25	55.1
50	110.2

distance: In order to convert kilometers (1000 meters) to miles—multiply by 0.6.

Kilometers	Miles
1	.625
8	5.0
25	15.6
60	37.5
100	62.5
110	68.75

Air pressure in automobile tires is expressed in *kilopascals*. Multiply pound-force per square inch (psi) by 6.89 to find *kilopascals* (kPa).

Temperature conversions:
To convert Fahrenheit to Celsius, subtract 32 from the Fahrenheit temperature, multiply by 5 and divide by 9.

To Convert Celsius to Fahrenheit, multiply by 9, divide by 5 and add 32.

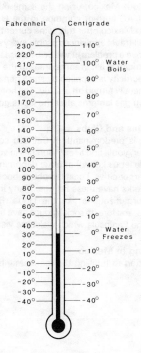

It helps to carry a small pocket calculator with you to make these conversions quickly.

guides should receive P200 for a half-day trip and P400 per day for longer trips. Gas station attendants are tipped P10 or P20 for pumping gas, cleaning the windshield, checking the oil and water, and providing other standard services. Often tips are the main part of the provider's income.

MISCELLANEOUS

Time
Campeche, Yucatan, and Quintana Roo are in U.S. Eastern Standard Time Zone. Chiapas and Tabasco are in the Central Time Zone.

Electricity
Electric current has been standardized throughout Mexico, using the same 60-cycle 110-volt AC current common in the U.S. All hotels in Mexico offer this same current, making small travel appliances usable everywhere. If you have a problem, it will be because there's no electricity at all. In some areas of the Peninsula, electricity is supplied by small generators and generally turned off at 2200. The hotels will offer you gas lanterns after the lights go out.

Churches and Clubs
Mexico is predominantly a Catholic country. However, you'll find a few churches (if you find a temple let us know!) of other denominations in the larger cities. Local telephone books and hotel clerks have these listings. Many international organizations like the Lions, Rotary, Shriners, and foreign social groups have branches on the Peninsula which welcome visitors.

Studying In Mexico
In addition to fulfilling the requirements for a Tourist Card, students must present documents to a Mexican consulate demonstrating that they have been accepted at an educational institution and that they are financially solvent. A number of courses and workshops are offered throughout Mexico lasting 2-8 weeks in addition to full-time study programs. The United Nations Institute of International Education can supply information on study projects in Mexico. Many adults as well as younger folks are taking part in language programs where the student lives with a family (that speaks only Spanish to them) for a period of 2-4 weeks and attends language classes daily. This total immersion into the language, even for a short time, is quite successful and popular as a cultural experience. See Appendix for more information.

Also write to the National Registration Center for Study Abroad (NRCSA), 823 North Second St., Milwaukee, WI 53203 or phone 1 (800)- 558-9988. Request their "Directory of Educational Programs," which describes programs in a number of cities in Mexico.

U.S. Embassies And Consulates
If an American citizen finds himself in a problem of any kind, contact with the nearest Consul will provide advice or help. Travel advisories with up-to-the-minute information about traveling in remote areas of Mexico are available. See Appendix for more information on U.S. embassies and tourist offices.

THE STATE OF YUCATAN

Yucatan is a triangle-shaped state bordered by the Gulf of Mexico to the N, the state of Quintana Roo on the E, and the state of Campeche on the west. It occupies 38,508 sq km and boasts a population of over 950,000 people. The climate is hot and humid during the summer months. Most of the rain falls between May and Oct. with only a slight variation of daytime temperatures of a few degrees between seasons. The average daytime temperature during the summer months is 37 degrees C (96 degrees F) and sticky. Fortunately a breeze blows through most of the year and the drier winter months seem much cooler. The state has no lakes or rivers, and is dependent upon natural wells called *cenote* from the Maya word *dzonot*.

History
Spaniards arrived in the early 1500s, confiscated the land of the Maya, forced them into slave labor, and established *haciendas* and cities. Ultimately the Indians rebelled and the state of Yucatan bore the brunt of the bloody Caste War of the mid 1800s between Maya Indians and Spanish colonialists. Over the years, through revolutions and the mellowing of time, Yucatan has seen many changes between people and government. The state has developed into a small business metropolis and is now the gateway to the Peninsula for both commerce and tourists.

Economy
Today the main industries of Yucatan are the cultivation and processing of henequen into hemp, fishing, commerce, and tourism. The seat of the government is (and has been for centuries) in the capital — Merida, which is also the largest city in the state. Yucatan, along with all of Mexico, is making sweeping changes to lure tourists from all over the world to visit its outstanding archaeological ruins.

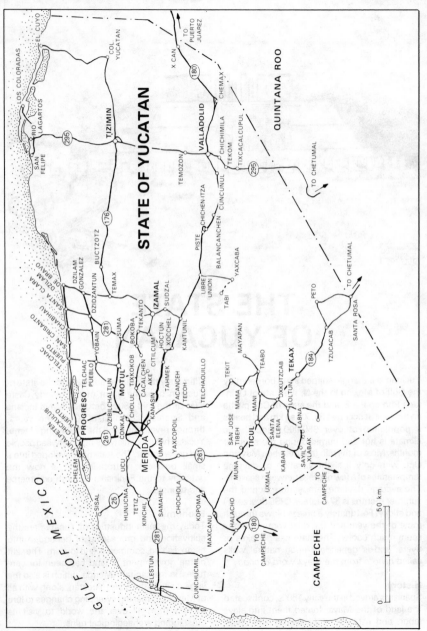

MERIDA AND VICINITY

Merida is the largest city on the Yucatan Peninsula, with a population of over 500,000. The colonial capital of the state of Yucatan displays the appeal and grace of old Europe—as it should since much of it was patterned after the design of Paris. The atmosphere is an exotic mix of a bloody past and cosmopolitan present. Heady Latin rhythms and the latest disco steps share billing with Maya and Spanish folkloric songs and dances. Free nightly concerts and other cultural gatherings throughout the week are well attended by local citizens as well as a few outsiders. Take several days to investigate the many museums, old churches, beautiful government buildings, monuments, and shady, tree-lined plazas everywhere. The longer you stay, the better you'll like this city of contradictions.

"The White City," as Merida has been called for centuries, is very clean. Sewage problems have been eliminated and potable water plants are scattered all around town. Most of the hotels have purification plants on site. Ask hotel personnel to be sure—or if there's a bottle of water in your room, you can be certain the water out of the tap is only for washing.

History
Merida was originally called T'ho or Ichcansiho (depending on which chronicler you read) by the Mayan inhabitants. The first Spaniards found a large Maya commercial center with ornate stone structures that reminded them of the Roman ruins in Spain's city of Merida—hence the name. Mexico's Merida was founded Jan. 6, 1542 by Francisco de Montejo, to celebrate his victory over the Indians after 15 years of conflict. The Maya Indians, now slaves of the Spanish invaders, were forced to dismantle their temples and palaces, and use the materials to build homes, offices, cathedrals, and parks they were not permitted to enjoy. Merida became the capital and trade center of the Peninsula, the seat of civil as well as religious authority. The Spaniards lived in fine houses around the central plaza in downtown Merida, while Indian servants lived on the outer edges of town. It wasn't until the late 1840s that they finally rebelled in the Caste War, one of the bloodiest wars in the history of Mexico (see "History," p. 20). To look at Merida today, one would never know of the enmity of the past. The people are happy and what appears to be an even mix of Indian, Ladino, and mestizo populate the city.

Economy
Merida's economy today is based on commerce and agriculture. Formerly this N part of the Peninsula was the hub of the henequen industry. Although henequen is no longer the vital money-maker that it once was, it still employs a very large percentage of people in and around Merida. Fishing has been a way of life for centuries along the Gulf coast; but only in recent years has the activity become mechanized and organized to a point where exporting fish (mostly to the U.S.) is now big business. Tourism is taking its place at the top of the money-making list. The state tourism departments are wielding more clout and the government is spending more to provide the traveler with good accommodations, improved highways, emergency road service, and bigger and better attractions; especially noted are the improvements at the sites of Maya ruins.

MAYA ARCHAEOLOGICAL ZONES IN YUCATAN

CHICHEN ITZA	UXMAL
IZAMAL	DZIBILCHALTUN
KABAH	SAYIL
LABNA	XLAPAK
MAYAPAN	

SIGHTS

CENTRAL PLAZA AREA

The large green central plaza is an oasis in the middle of this busy town, surrounded by aristocratic colonial buildings. Friends (and strangers) gather here all day and late into the night. In the old custom, sweethearts can sit on *confidenciales* (S-curved cement benches) allowing intimate *tete-a-tetes* — oh so close! — but without touching. White-sombreroed men gather early in the morning; visiting *mestizas* in their colorful *huipils* sit in the shade and share lunch with their children excited by the sights of the big city. Sidewalk cafes edge the park, and in the cool of evening locals and tourists enjoy music offered several times a week.

The narrow streets were originally designed for

the heart of Merida is the central plaza

calesas (horse-drawn buggies), sometimes called *pulpitos* by locals because they resemble a church pulpit. You can still ride the *calesa* through the old residential neighborhoods. From 0800-2200 on Sunday a major downtown section surrounding the central plaza is closed off to vehicular traffic. This is the ideal day to tour the city in a *calesa* and see beautiful old mansions built at the turn of the century or earlier. Like taxis, the horse-drawn buggies are not metered, so arrange your fee and route before starting out: average price is around P1000 per hour.

"Domingo en Merida"

A free guided walking tour of the historic structures in the center of town starts at 1000 on Sundays. This program, sponsored by the Dept. of Tourism, is called "Domingo en Merida"; check with your hotel for time schedule and meeting place. This is a good opportunity to see the inside of Montejo House (one of the oldest homes on the Peninsula) complete with narrative, along with surrounding government buildings. The buildings in Merida are dignified structures — some with magnificent facades created by European craftsmen — each with an intriguing story that contributes to the elegant heritage of this lovely city.

The Cathedral

The most prominent building on the plaza is the Cathedral. Built from 1561 to 1598 with stones taken from Maya structures on site, it is the largest church on the Peninsula and one of the oldest cathedral buildings on the continent. The prevalent architecture in Spain at the time is reflected in the Moorish style of the two towers. Surprisingly, the interior is stark in comparison to some of the ornately decorated churches in other parts of Mexico — during the Caste War and the Revolution of 1910, the church was stripped of its valuable trimmings. Note the impressive painting of the meeting between the nobles of the Maya Xiu clan and the Spanish invaders in 1541. This solemnly

1. brilliant blooms of the Yucatan; 2. *mamey* fruit from Cozumel; 3. wild orchid;
4. water lilies of Coba marsh; 5. scarlet ginger from Yucatan State;
6. *flamboyane* tree, Cozumel plaza

1. mom and baby manatee; 2. landing pelican; 3. a pair of macaws;
4. reef life near Cozumel; 5. iguana

portrays the Xiu tribe joining the Spaniards as allies—a trust that was violated, and the beginning of the end of the Maya regime.

Left of the main altar is a small chapel which houses an honored image of Christ called *El Cristo de las Ampollas* ("Christ of the Blisters") carved from a tree in Ichmul that is said to have been engulfed in flames but remained undamaged. Reportedly the wooden statue then went through another fire in a church, this time developing blisters as living skin would. The statue is honored with a fiesta each fall.

Palace of the Archbishop
Just south of the Cathedral facing the plaza, this once-elaborate building was the home of the archbishop. Since the Revolution when the church's power was restricted, the large structure has housed the local military post. Today, along with the military, an assortment of small shops offers everything (from art to clothing) a tourist or visitor could possibly need.

Casa Montejo
Facing the S edge of the central plaza is the **Banamex Bank** building. This was formerly the home of Francisco de Montejo, constructed in 1549 by his son Francisco de Montejo de Adelantado (The Younger), using talented Maya craftsmen and recovered stone. The unique carvings of Spaniards erectly standing at attention with their feet planted firmly on the heads of the Maya remain in place today—a blatant reminder of their dominance at the time, also rendered by Maya slaves. Today the bank takes up the entire structure, including a large second floor. You can see the enormous patio during business hours (0900-1300), or on Sun. mornings during the walking tour with the Domingo en Merida program.

Los Palacios
Opposite the NE corner of central plaza is the **Palacio de Gobierno**. Striking abstract murals painted by Fernando Castro Pacheco in 1978 decorate the interior walls and upper galleries. The brilliant colors variously represent the birth of the Maya, gods of wisdom, sale of slaves, and other social commentaries. This is the seat of government offices for the state of Yucatan; open daily to the public at no

downtown Merida

charge. **Palacio Municipal** (City Hall), located on the W side of the central plaza, is a gracious building dating back to 1543. Architecturally charming with its tall clock tower, it was renovated in the mid-1800s.

Archaeological Museum
On Paseo Montejo one of the most outstanding renovated structures is the **Palacio Canton**. This lovely rococo-facade building was built 1909-11 for General Francisco Canton Rosado, a former governor of Yucatan. It was designed by the same architect who built the Teatro Peon Contreras on Calle 60. The building served as the official state residence from 1948-1960. Today it is under the auspices of the National Institute of Anthropology and History, housing a small but impressive collection of fine art and historical artifacts of the

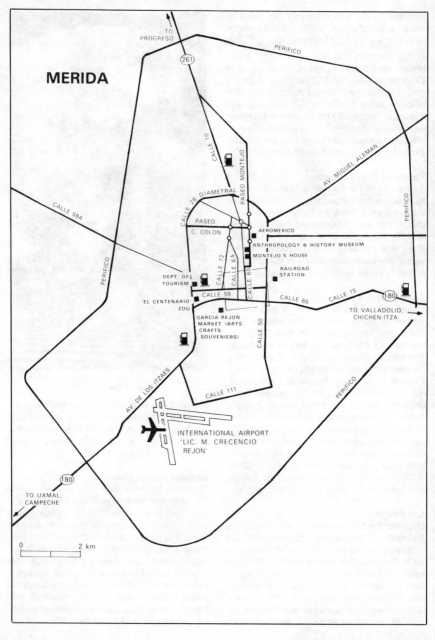

Maya past. A fine library contains a valuable collection of historical volumes that are available to the public at the museum.

DIVE SIGHTS

Cenote Dives

A surprise to most snorkelers is a unique diving opportunity in and around this inland city, Merida. Merida is only 9 m above sea level, and centuries ago the entire Peninsula was under the sea. An organization called the **Club de Espeleobuceo** makes diving expeditions to a half dozen locations around Merida. Some of these are *cenotes,* located on the grounds of old henequen haciendas, an added reason to make the trip. **Cenote-Noc-Ac** gives the diver a rare view of fossilized sharks teeth and snails. Espeleobuceo can be reached for further information and reservations in Merida; tel. 3-45-17/1-43-22, ask for Fernando Rosado.

PRACTICALITIES

ACCOMMODATIONS

Merida has hotels to fit everyone's expectations—and pocketbook. Large and modern, aged and plain, expensive or cheap, there's something for everyone! You can expect outstanding service, formal dining rooms, casual coffee shops, *tipico* and continental food, swimming pools, discos, indoor and outside bars, purified water, laundry service, TV, room service, tour service, and almost all accept credit cards.

Budget

Although there's no youth hostel, numerous small hotels close to the plaza offer economical shelter. **Hotel D'Farahon** is at the municipal market, up a flight of stairs 3 blocks SE of the plaza. Often filled early, the spartan rooms have ceiling fans and bathrooms; P720 s, P900 d, P1200 t, add P600 for a/c; Calle 65 #468; tel. 1-9l-92. For the money, **Hotel Macuy** can't be beat; NE of the plaza, it's in a quiet neighborhood, with a relaxing patio where a guest can lounge in the sun and read a book from a good choice of English-language paper-

Campers will find 2 trailer parks in the Merida vicinity: Paradise Park, 7 km SW of the city and Rainbow Park 8 km north.

backs provided by the management; P1500 s, P1550 d, 10 rooms; Calle 57 #48I; tel. I-I0-37. Facing the municipal bus station, **Hotel Rodriguez** is plain—except for its beautiful tile floors and bathrooms. The rooms in the back of the building are the quietest. Handy location, pleasant staff—ask for purified water at the desk. P1150 s, P1400 d, P1650 t, more for a/c; Calle 69 #478; tel. 1-43-00.

Moderate

For something a little nicer, many small hotels have been converted from lovely old colonial homes. These lodgings offer clean, comfortable rooms with a touch of old Mexico. Try the **Hotel Peninsular**; 2½ blocks SE of the central plaza, you'll spot the entrance with its bright green awning. Roomy and clean, it offers 2 double beds in each room, tiled bathrooms, courtyards, small pool in an attractive atrium with a good restaurant; P1250 s, P1600 double, extra for a/c; Calle 58 #519; tel. 3-69-02. At the **Gran Hotel**, a little bit of the good old days lingers on in the high ceilinged loggias, Corinthian arches, shiny tile floors, and dark woods of this Italianated turn-of-the-century building. Anyone who appreciates old elegance should at least take a look. Rates are P1700 s, P2300 d, P2700 t; extra for a/c. It's located in a small plaza behind the Cathedral; Calle 60 #496; tel. 1-76-20. Note: when checking into this hotel be sure to state at the outset that you don't want a/c (if you don't). Often the room they offer you is their *last room* and if it happens to be a/c they tack on an extra fee. It's best to get the price clarified up front. With a lot of 4-star features, 3-star **Hotel Caribe** is a good buy. The location is ideal, one block from the plaza and close to everything. It sports a/c and a swimming pool, clean restaurant downstairs serving good food with reasonable prices. Rates are P2400 s (fan), P2800 s (a/c); P2800 d, (fan), P3200 (a/c), P300 extra bed. Located on Calle 59 #500; tel. 4-90-34.

Expensive

Merida has a good choice of deluxe hotels. The prices range from P7000 to P10,000 for two. Starting at the low end of the price range, **Hotel Maria del Carmen** is 4 blocks W of the plaza. Pleasant carpeted rooms, swimming

pool, coffee shop, restaurant, a/c, and garage; P7000 s, P7500 d; located on Calle 63 #550; tel. 3-91-33. The **Casa del Balam** has been high on the ratings for years. Large, clean rooms are furnished with heavy dark wood in colonial-style furniture. All have twin beds except for the honeymoon suite which has a giant *matrimonial* (double bed) in an airy room with windows that open for a rooftop view of the entire city. On the lower floors you may not wish to open windows because of the traffic noises outside. The shady courtyard is planted with lush tropical plants; comfortable chairs placed under wide arches along the tile-corridors are perfect for relaxing or reading to the accompaniment of a splashing fountain. P7500 s, P8500 d, P11,000 suite; located on Calle 60 #488. **El President Panamericana** includes an entrance and large central courtyard that once belonged to a gracious mansion built at the turn of the century. Elegant wooden doors, spacious high-ceilinged rooms (now used as offices or banquet rooms), fine plaster carv-

courtyard of the Panamericana Hotel

ings topping Corinthian columns—brought from Europe to enhance the opulent structure years ago—are carefully maintained to add an old-world touch. The bedrooms were added onto the rear of the patio. The hotel offers elevators, rooms furnished in early-1900s' simplicity, private baths, a/c, swimming pool, patio bar/coffee shop, dining room, live entertainment, and credit cards accepted; P6500 s, P7400 d, P8300 t. Located on Calle 59 #455; tel. 3-91-11 or from the U.S., toll free 800-472-2427.

A few blocks walk fom the central plaza, the **Los Aluxes** is a multi-storied hotel providing courtesy valet parking for its guests. The hotel has a friendly staff, the kind that remembers your name as you come and go. Live music and excellent food served in the lobby dining room. An intimate bar/lounge provides mellow late night music. Good swimming in pleasant surroundings, plus a poolside bar, formal dining room, coffee shop, room service, tropical garden complete with fountain, one-day laundry service, travel agency, car rental, and credit cards accepted. Rooms carpeted and equipped with TV, and the suites, with individual terraces with tropical plants, are the best buy in Merida; especially nos. 317, 417, or 517. Rates: P8500 s or d, P9000 t or suite. Located at Calle 60 #444; tel. 4-21-99.

Luxury

The **Holiday Inn**, located a few km N of the downtown area, is the most expensive hotel in town. This is a well-designed, multi-storied, modern hotel with *all* the conveniences. It is often crowded with out-of-town conventions and banquets; P15,000 s or d, P2000 extra pp. Located at Colon and Calle 60; tel. 5-68-77.

FOOD AND ENTERTAINMENT

Cafes of every description are found in Merida. Yucatecan as well as Mexican food is included on most menus, and the "hot stuff" is served on the side so you needn't worry about the infamous habanera chiles making a sneak attack. Be sure to try Yucatecan salsa made from the usual chiles, cilantro, tomatoes, spices, and one addition—a dash of citrus fruit and rind

MERIDA ACCOMMODATIONS

The following list of Merida's hotels begins with the least expensive in ascending order:

D'Farahon	Calle 65 no.468	1-91-92
Posada Central	Calle 55 no.446	1-61-13
Rodriguez	Calle 69 no.478	1-43-00
Del Mayab	Calle 50 no.536	1-09-09
Mexico	Calle 60 no.525	1-92-55
Del Arco	Calle 63 no.452	1-31-92
Peninsular	Calle 58 no.519	3-69-02
Latino	Calle 66 no.505	1-48-31
Mody	Calle 86 no.243	5-21-01
Flamingo	Calle 57 no.485	1-77-40
Dolores Alba	Calle 63 no.464	1-37-45
Gran Hotel	Calle 60 no.496	1-76-20
Reforma	Calle 59 no.508	1-79-20
Montejo	Calle 57 no.507	1-45-90
Alfonso Garcia	Av. Aviacion 587	1-64-96
Del Parque	Calle 60 no.497	1-78-40
San Luis	Calle 61 no.534	1-75-80
Nacional	Calle 61 no.474	1-92-45
Posada Toledo	Calle 58 no.487	3-22-56
Principe Maya	Av. Aviacion km 5	4-04-11
Suites Imperial	Calle 17 no.191	7-17-22
Londres	Calle 64 no.456	1-35-15
Cayre	Calle 70 no.533	1-16-52
Caribe	Calle 59 no.500	4-90-31
Colonial	Calle 62 no.476	3-64-44
Colon	Calle 62 no.483	3-43-55
Bojorquez	Calle 58 no.483	1-16-20
Del Gobernador	Calle 59 no.535	1-35-14
Paseo de Montejo	Paseo Montejo 482	3-90-33
Autel	Calle 59 no.546	4-21-00
Panamericana	Calle 59 no.455	3-91-11
Maria del Carmen	Calle 63 no.550	3-91-33
Montejo Palace	Paseo de Montejo 483	4-76-44
Hacienda Inn	Av. Aviacion no.709	1-16-80
Conquistador	Paseo de Montejo	6-21-55
Casa del Balam	Calle 60 no.488	1-06-00
El Castellano	Calle 57 no.513	
Los Aluxes	Calle 60 no.444	4-21-99
Merida Mission	Calle 60 no.491	3-95-00
Holiday Inn	Colon and Calle 60	5-68-77

(mostly sour orange). If your palate is ready for a change from Yucatecan gourmet, Merida offers excellent Arabic, Chinese, and European food. For those traveling on a budget, it's a sim-

DOWNTOWN MERIDA

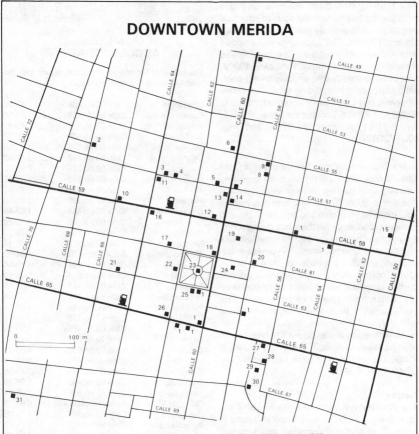

1. Bank
2. Hotel Paris
3. Viajes Estrada Travel Agents
4. Hotel Castellano
5. Pop Cafe
6. Santa Lucia Park
7. Hotel Casa del Balam
8. Hotel Bojorquez
9. Molica Tours
10. Hotel del Gobernador
11. Alberto's Continental Patio
12. Pancho Villa's Follies Restaurant & Disco
13. University of Yucatan
14. Jose Peon Contreras Theater (Information Center)
15. Los Almendros Restaurant
16. Central Telephone Office
17. Francimex
18. Government Palace
19. Hotel Caribe
20. Mexicana Airlines
21. Juan Gamboa Guzman Picture Gallery
22. City Hall
23. Central Plaza (Plaza de la Independencia)
24. Cathedral
25. Montejo Palace
26. Hotel Oviedo
27. Post Office
28. Telegraph Office
29. Municipal Market
30. Arts and Crafts Bazaar
31. Bus Station

Fondas, *Mexico's fast fooderies, are usually the most economical cafes around. The one pictured here is in Merida's municipal market on the 2nd floor.*

ple matter to find filling economical meals in Merida. As always the park vendors sell good tamales for about P100. Or if you prefer, *tortas* (sandwiches on a roll) made from meat, chicken, or cheese combinations are the same price.

Restaurants

In some *cantinas* in Merida when you order a cold beer in the middle of the afternoon, you'll be served tasty snacks (a more than ample lunch!). **La Prosperidad** is a popular spot. Meridanos crowd into the large cafe daily, for drinks, snacks, and good live music. Try it either for cold beer or for a large *tipico comida corrida* including a variety of dishes: *pollo pibyl, panuchos, venada escabeche, tortillas, rellenos,* cold chicken, and avocado—a big meal for P500. A spotless health food store serving great sandwiches and some vegetarian dishes is called **Proust** on Calle 60, #446; tel. 4-37-32—two doors from the Los Aluxes Hotel. A few other nice places well worth trying: **Albertos Continental** for excellent Lebanese cooking, plus continental and Yucatecan dishes. Romantic atmosphere, moderate prices. The building alone (dating from 1727) is a must see; Calle 64 and 57. **La Casona** has good Italian pasta in a former mansion. Dining in a patio (bug repellent!) overlooking a lush garden or an indoor formal dining room. Great capuccino, moderate prices; Calle 60 #434, tel. 3-83-48. **Kon Tiki** serves outstanding Chinese

food for a change of taste. Av. Colon and Calle 14. For the purist whose mouth waters for handmade tortillas, **Restaurant Los Almendros** is one of the few places where you can watch them made, and enjoy *poc chuc,* a zesty marinated meat dish.

Pancho's is a fun place with good Mexican food served by cloned Pancho Villa-type waiters right down to the hat and crossed ammunition belts; as the evening progresses, the disco music begins. For another spirited disco try the **Holiday Inn**. However, if you're feeling more in the mood for classic Mexican, spend an evening at **Tulipanes** or **La Ciudad Maya;** both serve good *tipico* food and put on exotic shows with authentic-looking costumes of the ancient Maya. If you're craving good pizza go to **Gatopardo's**, or on the same par, try **La Mansion**. Hamburger-heaven is an hour spent at **Tommy's;** or as the younger set claims, **Leo's** isn't just a hangout: the tacos are the best.

Drinks And Goodies

Yucatan offers several drinks not commonly found anywhere else: *horchata* (ground rice, raw sugar, cinnamon, water—and today—ice) and *posole* (made from ground corn). These two drinks are classic Maya specialties dating back hundreds of years; *posole* was described by Bishop Diego de Landa in the 16th C. as used for offerings to the gods when planting corn. These easy-to-find nourishing drinks quench your thirst, satisfy your sweet tooth, and are easy on the pocketbook, while providing a taste of everyday Maya life. In all honesty, one must *develop* a taste for them. On the other hand, the more modern Maya produce *licuados* (liquified fruit drink) that everyone loves at first sip. *Licuado* stands—filled by rows of bright colored fruit—are found all over the city. You can also buy fresh fruit cocktail from these vendors. Another Mexican treat called *champula* (an ice milk sherbet) is mixed in many tropical flavors.

Markets

Many women from the rural villages of Yucatan state still wear the white *huipil* (ee-PEEL). A lovely garment (first used by mestizo women at the insistence of hacienda patrons), it is edged with bright-colored embroidery

coming to the big city on market day

around the squared neck and hem, with a lace-finished petticoat peeking out below the dress. Most Merida women are fashion-conscious and vitally into the clothes of the 1980s, but *huipils* are worn almost exclusively by the women at market for the day.

At the **Mercado Municipal** many small *fondas* (food stalls) are on the second floor with a vast selection of fruits, vegetables, tortillas, sweets; these and other prepared foods are also scattered throughout the market. Don't overlook the *super mercado* surprisingly like any you'll find in the U.S. This is the easiest place to find scotch tape, boxed crackers and cookies, paper goods, canned or boxed sterilized milk, or dried pasteurized milk, dehydrated soup mixes, soap, and a number of other items that are often hard to locate in the public market unless you're a whiz in Spanish. Just as in the States, the supermarket is a cheap place to purchase liquor and beer. Mexican brandies (El Presidente and Don Pedro), or other liquors manufactured in Mexico (Kahlua and Xtabentum), often go on sale. Remember that imported liquors carry a high import tax making American gin or Canadian whiskey high priced in Mexico. (The same goes for American peanut butter or coffee.) If you haven't already, try the dark beer made in Yucatan, Leon Negra; or if you prefer light try Montejo and Carta Clara. For a special gift to take home, buy locally made Xtabentum. This liqueur, made from fermented honey and anise, has a spicy licorice flavor.

Music

Informal entertainment is provided for Merida's residents and visitors at parks throughout the city. Families and friends gather under the stars in the warm tropical night for a variety of music each evening year-round begining at 2100—free.

Teatro Peon Contreras

This theater, built in 1908 during Merida's rich period, was patterned on European design. A lovely old building, it continues to offer a variety of concerts and other entertainment, worth visiting just to see the classic interior. Located on Calle 60 and 57, admission varies depending on the event. For a list of attractions at the

MERIDA MUSIC

Monday: Behind the Municipal Palace, in the Garden of the Composers—regional music of Yucatan folkloric dancers, and the *Jaranera Orchestro.*

Tuesday: Same location—short international films about the arts in Yucatan and other countries. Plaza de Santiago—popular music of different eras.

Wednesday: Plaza de Santa Ana—semiclassical music and Yucatecan compositions, or visiting musical groups. Park of Santa Lucia—City String Ensemble offers semiclassical renditions.

Thursday: Plaza de los Heroes—traditional Yucatecan serenades. Santa Lucia Park—Folkloric dancers, guitars, troubadors, soloists, and guest artists.

Friday: Ermitage of Santa Isabel—romance night, serenades, jugglers, poets, legends and stories of ancient Merida.

For more information about these evening concerts, check at your hotel or any one of the city's tourist offices. This is casual entertainment, so don't hesitate to speak to your benchmate—very often you'll make friends with a great Meridano who will take delight in showing off his city, or at least give you the opportunity to ask questions or practice Spanish.

theater, tel. 4-92-90/4-93-89. Located in one corner of the theater building is the **State Tourist Office.** They speak English and give out lots of good information. If you have a problem and need assistance, call SECTUR, the federal tourism office, tel. 4-94-31/4-95-42.

For Children
Sunday is family day in Mexico, and Merida is no exception. The tree-shaded parks are popular for picnics, playing ball, buying giant colorful balloons, etc. Children's movies are offered from 1000 throughout the day at **Pinoc-**chio's **Movie House** located just across El Centenario Park. On Sun. festivals are held at **El Centenario Park** and **La Ceiba's Park,** at 1100; **Mulsay's Park** at 1800. Here children (and parents) are entertained by magicians, clowns, puppets, theater groups, and all take part in organized games which include the smallest child, and offer prizes for winning participants.

SHOPPING

Merida is definitely *the* place to shop on the Peninsula. Prices at the *mercado municipal* are hard to beat and you'll find a selection of quality crafts from all parts of Yucatan. Even if you're not interested in a shopping spree, take a trip through the busy market for a wonderful social and cultural experience.

Mercado Municipal
Along with the euphoric pleasures of color—bundles of brilliant flowers and rainbows of neatly stacked fruit and vegetable—watching the steady stream of people makes a visit to the market a bustling diverse entertainment. Here are foods of all description: cooked tamales, raw meat, live chickens and pungent odors from mounds of unusual-looking herbs, spices, and fruit. The candy man offers delicate sugar flowers, shoes, and skulls (if it's near the Day of the Dead holiday) for just a few *pesos.* Be sure to stop by the *tortilleria.* Upstairs, a series of tiny fast-food windows serves the cheapest meals in Merida: tacos, *tamales, tortas* and *licuado.*

Chattering merchants invite you to inspect (and bargain for) their colored woven hammocks, gleaming chunks of clear yellow *copal* (incense) in use since the early Maya, and *huaraches.* Narrow little gold-stalls have thousands of dollars worth of gold earrings along with charms and bangles of every description stored in their small glass cases. You'll see the common and the uncommon, ordinary and extraordinary. Some things you may not want to see, such as *mecech,* jeweled lapel beetles—the crawly kind outlawed in the U.S., or iguanas being skinned and fileted. The ordinary seems always in demand: woven belts, straw baskets of every shape, pottery bowls for every use, Panama hats in the final stages of manufacture, *guayerba* (wide-lapel cotton shirt) and *huipils* with thickly embroidered flowered borders in every color. Located at Calle 56 and 67.

Contraband Market

Don't miss the contraband market, just next door and part of the municipal market. Usually, a couple of burly men will approach you at the entrance and ask what you want (they want your dollars and can get it wholesale, whatever *it* is!). Tell them you're just looking. This market's even more crowded than next door (if possible), and louder: tape recorders blast out the latest rock and vie in decibels with lively Latin rhythms.

Antique Shops

A multitude of antique shops are sprinkled throughout Merida. The ones that are really junk shops are the most intriguing! If you like to get lost in dusty shelves of rare old books (if you can read Spanish, you're in luck), chipped 19th C. religious art, empty rococo frames,

mercado municipal

Lebanese shopkeeper weighing a gold piece

rows of dust-covered crystal chandeliers — then you must visit **Emilio's** shop off the central plaza. Often, you'll find Emilio himself and his two brothers, descendants of a large contingent of Lebanese who migrated at the turn of the century, spending a congenial time each day sipping peppermint tea around a cluttered wooden desk. Emilio will exchange dollars at a good rate or will hock your granddad's watch if you run out of money. But take care, he's the master bargainer of Merida. He can shut off the timid beginner in just under 3 seconds, and an expert will be nonetheless outstripped. At best the customer will be excused the tax — and at 15% that discount can be important.

Arts And Crafts

Each Sun. from 1000-1500, a **Bazaar of Arts**

and **Crafts** is held in the Centenario Park and Zoo. See artists and their paintings, sculpture, crafts and — to add a little zing — chess instructors go knight to rook with students. On the same day from 1000-1400 an **Antique and Crafts Bazaar** is held at Santa Lucia's Park. Sellers bring worn books, antique bric-a-brac, old stamps, furniture, typical clothing, and lovely art work — good browsing!

Maya Feather And Shell Art
The Maya created lovely art in a variety of forms. Using shells and feathers was considered a lost art for years; but more and more this form is surfacing in bazaars and tourist shops. The ancients used brilliant colored feathers to weave elegant garments from the richly hued birds of the Yucatan Peninsula, especially the blue-greens of the now seldomseen quetzal bird. Some fine examples of this art can be seen at the Anthropological Museum in Mexico City.

Books, Magazines, And Newspapers
As usual, the large hotel gift shops carry the best supply of English-language books, both fiction and pictorial books about the area. You can get American magazines and often *The News,* a Mexico City-published Englishlanguage newspaper. This paper can also be found at the small newsstand in the arcade on the N edge of the central plaza. **Discolibros**

Hollywood, located on the S side of Cepeda Peraza facing Calle 60, has a good selection of English paperbacks, plus the *New York Times Weekly Review* and *The News.* Another bookstore, **Dante's,** is on Calle 59 between 66 and 68.

Photo Supplies
A complete line of photo equipment, film and one-hour color processing can be found at **Omega,** Calle 60 off 59. Kodak and Fuji are most common here, a little more expensive than the States; but if you must buy film on the Peninsula, Merida's probably the least expensive place, and offers good processing services. Some travelers have found it convenient to buy Kodak mailers and drop them off at post offices (or large hotel mail pickups) along the way, with processed results sent directly home. (For more photo information, see "Cameras," p. 73.)

SERVICES

Remember that most businesses in Merida close between 1300-1600, and are open evenings until 1900.

Tourist Information
Several tourist information centers are found in Merida. One is at the Teatro Peon Contreras on

Freshest fruit and vegetables are from the mercado municipal.

Calle 60; another at the Palacio Gobierno (facing the N side of the main plaza). The address of the Office of Federal Tourism is Av. Itzaes 590, Calle 59, Merida, Yuc., Mexico (located across from Centenario Park), tel. (9 19 22) 1-59-89. Each of these offices gives information, maps, and other important literature. At the Contreras office, you can make reservations to Sound and Light Shows at Chichen Itza and Uxmal as well as buy tickets to other events.

Medical Or Emergency

For a medical emergency most hotels can provide the name of an English-speaking doctor (see "Health," p. 68). You can also contact the **Hospital O'Horan;** tel. 3-87-11. For severe emergencies, medical or otherwise, call the **U.S. Consulate,** 5-50-11/7-70-11. **The Dept. of Tourism** hot line number for all of Mexico is (5) 250-0123 24 hours daily. **The Green Angels,** the government-sponsored road service, cruise the main roads daily; they recommend staying with your car in the event of a breakdown if it's daylight (they don't cruise after 2100) and you're on a paved artery (they do not cruise dirt roads).

Police Dept.	3-34-56
Fire Dept.	1-41-22
Immigration	3-87-01

Banks

Banks are everywhere you look in Merida; hours are 0900-1200 Mon. through Friday. Get there early during the busy seasons, there's usually a line. On **Calle 65** alone are 5 banks. Changing traveler's cheques at a bank is usually more advantageous than at a hotel. Often shops will give an even better exchange than the bank (with a purchase); usually a sign is posted—if not ask. If you go to **Banamex** facing the S side of the central plaza, take a look around; until recently it was the home of the historic Montejo family.

Post Office

The post office and telegraph office are located on Calle 65, near the *mercado;* business hours are 0900-1900 Mon. to Fri., 0900-1300 on Saturday.

Long-Distance Telephone and Telegraph

For *larga distancia* telephone calls go to **Condesa,** Calle 62 and 59 or, to the bus terminal on Calle 69 #554. It's much cheaper than at your hotel where a service charge can be as high as 100%. If you must phone from the hotel, ask the service charge structure—it may be cheaper if you call collect, but you will still have an added charge. Telegrams can be sent from Calle 56 between 65 and 67; tel. 1-59-55, or from the bus terminal on Calle 69 #554.

Churches

Catholic churches are predominant in Merida. On the E side of the central plaza (Calle 60 at 61) the **Cathedral,** built in the late 16th C., is the largest church on the Peninsula; tel. 1-66-71. Other churches in Merida include **Santa Ana,** Calle 60 at 45, tel. 1-23-16; and **Santa Lucia,** Calle 60 at 55, tel. 3-10-66. A Presbyterian church, **El Divino Salvador,** with an English-speaking pastor, is located at Calle 66 #518; tel. 1-68-49.

Consulates

The **U.S. Consulate** is located at Paseo de Montejo at Av. Colon #453, tel. 7-70-11. The **Canadian Consulate** is on Calle 58 #450, tel. 1-67-94. The **British Consulate** is at Fraccionamiento Campestre IF 249 at 36, tel. 7-04-60.

Office of Federal Tourism in Merida
Itzaes 590, corner of Calle 59
Merida, Yuc., Mexico
Tel. (9 19 22) 1-59-89

TRANSPORT

GETTING THERE

Since the Spanish first settled the city of Merida, it has been the hub of travel and the easiest city on the Peninsula to get to by a variety of transport.

AIRLINES SERVING MERIDA

Flights from Merida International Airport cover most parts of Mexico and several points in the U.S. Airlines with offices in Merida are:

Aeromexico	Paseo Montejo no. 460
	7-90-00
Mexicana	Calle 58
	1-27-80
Eastern Airlines	Paseo de Montejo no. 496
	3-38-11
Continental Airline	Airport
	3-69-29
Lufthansa	Calle 56-A no. 494
	7-74-97
United Airlines	Airport
	3-90-45

With destinations to: Mexico City, Cancun, Oaxaca, Monterrey, Chetumal, Cozumel, Tijuana, Guadalajara, Puerto Vallarta, Houston, New York, Miami, Los Angeles. Please check with the airlines or a travel agent for prices and schedules. Merida customs, tel. 1-18-74; general airport info, tel. 1-42-21.

By Plane

Planes fly into the large airport from most cities in Mexico. The airport service road is located on Av. de Itzaes (Hwy. 180) 7 km SW of town. Cafe, post office, long-distance phone, money changer, car rental counters, and several gift shops are inside. The terminal is (usually) a/c. A taxi charges about P1000 *to* the airport but *from* the airport a collective cab will deliver you to downtown hotels for P250; buy your ticket at a counter in front of the air terminal. Hang onto your ticket until all packages, baggage, purses and carry-ons are accounted for at your destination. The cabbies in Yucatan have a great reputation for honesty, but there's no point in pushing your luck. For bus transportation from the airport into the downtown area, look for bus #79. It runs between the air terminal and a downtown bus stop on the corners of Calles 67 and 60; the fare is P20.

By Train

Look for the sign that says "Ferrocarriles Unidos del Sureste." Merida's train station is located on Calle 55 between Calles 46 and 48, 8 blocks NE of the central plaza. To walk downtown, turn W (right) from the main entrance along Calle 55 for 5 blocks to Calle 60; turn S (left) and 3 blocks will bring you to the plaza. An information booth is open from 0700-2200 daily; bus tickets are also for sale. Trains departing from Merida have no dining cars; either bring a lunch or plan on buying from the food vendors at each stop. For the

best information on train schedules, go direct
to the train station.

TRAIN SERVICE FROM MERIDA

Palenque	(12 hours)	Leaves daily at 2000
Mexico DF	(37 hours)	Leaves daily at 2000
Campeche	(5 hours)	Leaves daily at 0500, 2000, 2300.
Valladolid	(5 hours)	Leaves daily at 1510
Tizimin	(5 hours)	Leaves daily at 0530

By Bus

The main bus station is on Calle 69 between 68
and 70, tel. 1-91-50 (other stations noted
below). The station houses both 1st- and 2nd-
class companies. As you enter the station 1st-
class is on the left and 2nd-class on right, both
with baggage checking services. Ask at the information counter for latest schedules. Bus
transport on the Peninsula is excellent with
routes going to all parts of Mexico. The following list will get you going to many places — for
further information check at the bus terminal.

By Car

Driving into Merida, good highways approach
the city from all directions. Be prepared for
one-way streets, and avoid arriving on Sun. — a
large area in the center of town is closed off to
vehicles. If you don't know the city, it can be a
real headache to drive to your hotel, most of
which are located downtown. If you should
land in town on Sun., flag down a cabbie and
pay him to lead you to your hotel. He'll know
how to get around the detours — worth the few
pesos.

Car Rentals

Cars are available from several agencies in the
airport terminal building, downtown Merida,
and in most of the larger hotels. Advance reservations are advised during the busy winter
months.

GETTING AROUND

Merida is laid out in a neat grid pattern of one-
way numbered streets. The even numbered

BUS SCHEDULES

From **Autotransportes del Sureste**, 2nd-class.

Tuxtla Guitierrez	1330
Villahermosa	1100, 1330, 2230
Palenque	2330
Tenosique	2130
Campeche	0700, 1000, 1100, 1330, 1400, 2100, 2130, 2230, 2330

From *Autotransportes del Noreste,* 1st-class:

Tizimin (short route)	1000, 1930
Tizimin and Rio Lagartos	
	0700, 1400, 1730

From *Autotransportes de Pasajeros,* Calle 62 between 65 and 67; tel. 1-23-44.

Progreso	Leaves every 15 minutes from 0500 to 2100.
Dzibilchaltun	0500, 0715, 1215, 1615

From *Lineas Unidas del Sur de Yucatan,* Calle
50 between 65 and 67

Oxkutzcab	Check at station.

ADO (1st-class — *Autotransportes de Oriente*)

Sisal (1 ¼-hr. trip)	0500, 0630, 0800, 0900, 1100, 1200, 1300, 1400, 1430, 1600, 1630, 1700
Celestun (1 ½-hr. trip)	
	0500, 0600, 0700, 0800, 1000, 1120, 1200, 1340, 1400, 1600, 1830, 2000
Izamal	Leaves every 45 minutes.
Playa del Carmen	0030, 0600, 1100, 2330
Puerto Morelos	0600, 1100, 2330
Cancun and Puerto Juarez	
	0700, 0800, 0900, 1000, 1200, 1300, 1400, 1500, 1600, 1800, 2000, 2200, 2400
Tizimin	0630, 1700
Valladolid	0630, 1630, 1730
Chichen Itza	0630, (RT 0830-1500) 1630, 1730

For more detailed bus info to archaeological zones
check at the terminal. Buses travel to the following
sites: Chichen Itza, Ruinas Ake, Izamal, Uxmal,
Kabah, Coba, Tulum, and Dzibilchaltun. Ask a-
bout return trips; they're often not well scheduled.

CAR RENTALS

Hertz	1-38-28/or 1-93-33
Avis	1-07-99/or 1-45-99
Budget	1-82-23
Pan Am Rente	3-25-99
Max	1-08-08
Quick Rent	3-42-19
National	3-60-02

streets run E to W, the odd N to south. The central plaza is the center of town and you can easily walk to most downtown attractions, shops, and marketplace. Buses provide frequent service in and around the city and outlying areas. Bus stops are located at almost every corner along the main streets—P20 to any destination in the city. During the day, it's never more than 10 min. between buses; they run less frequently at night. For a complete bus schedule check with the tourism office at the Teatro Peon Contreras.

At one time, *calesas* were the only means of getting around the city; today they're a pleasant alternative. From near the plaza, *calesas* are a relaxing slow way to see aristocratic old houses with carved facades, marble entries, stone gargoyles, etched glass, wrought-iron fences, some with their elegance slipping, others well maintained over several generations in this European-flavored residential district.

Taxi Service

The gasoline taxi is fastest. You can always find one in a hurry—they're easily flagged all day and late into the evening, and any hotel will call one for you. After midnight you might have to telephone the company; a cafe or disco will call one for you, or tel. 1-23-00/1-12-21. All other hours call one of these numbers: 1-21-33/ 1-25-00/1-22-00. Taxis are not metered, so establish your fare in advance. The average fare around town is P700.

PROGRESO

Located on the Gulf of Mexico, Progreso is Merida's closest access to the sea, where Meridanos flock to escape the intense heat and sticky humidity of summer in "The White City." On a good wide highway, it's an easy 33-km drive between the capital of the state and its once-bustling seaport. During the halcyon days of the henequen industry, ships were a regular part of the scene along the calm Progreso waterfront and its aging 2-km-long wharf. Expansive mansions built by henequen entrepeneurs still line the water's edge just E of town; however, they are vacation homes now used mostly for rentals—adapting to the town's burgeoning new economy: tourism.

SIGHTS

Progreso is small (pop. 20,000), and with Yucalpeten taking over as the more important fishing port, the town leads a subdued existence most of the year. In July and Aug., however, most of Merida empties out and arrives at this beach. All the restaurants are open, the small shops take on a busy look, the beaches are filled with happy families enjoying the sun and the surf, and Progreso is transformed for the summer.

Wharf

Progreso's claim that its 2-km-long wharf is the longest stone wharf in the world was probably true—at the turn of the century when it was first built. For 100 years Progreso's wharf was the scene of heavy international shipping—the days when the henequen industry was in its prime. Today, only a small percentage of henequen products is shipped. In addition, the wharf has lost some of its impact since the protected new (1968) Yucalpeten harbor, 6 km W of Progreso, stole most of its thunder. Occasional ships still tie up at the Progreso wharf, which is open to the public, either on foot or in a vehicle as long as you don't try to park. Pier fishermen will find lots of company with abundant local advice and fish stories—in Spanish. They say early in the morning or late in the afternoon you have only to throw out your hook to catch a string in no time!

Beaches

Travelers just returning from the Caribbean side of the Peninsula will find the Gulf coast is different. The water doesn't have the crystalline clarity and flamboyant shades of blue that make the Quintana Roo coast famous. But the beach at Progreso is nothing to apologize for; it's open and broad with clean sand. Except for the stormy season (June through Oct.), the warm water is calm. It's possible to walk ½ km from shore into the sea and still have dry ears. A paved road and inviting palm-lined promenade wind along the breezy waterfront. The beach is dotted with *palapa* sunshelters and a few cafes. For the energetic it's an invigorating walk E along the shoreline from the wharf 7 km to Chixulub. Don't expect fascinating flotsam and jetsam, but you'll see shells aplenty—plus gangs of people in the middle of summer. During the winter, except on weekends, the beach is practically deserted.

PRACTICALITIES

Accommodations

Progreso has a limited choice of accommodations. However, the economy-minded traveler can usually find a room to fit his budget if he's not too fussy and it's not July or August. On Calle 79 are several budget hostelries. Also, take a look at **Hotel Rio Blanco**: it's not the newest or cleanest and hasn't been too well loved over the years—but if you're desperate the prices are moderate: P1600 s, P1900 d, on Calle 27 #148; tel. 5-0066. **Hotel Miramar** is a bit nicer and charges P1800 s, P2000 d. **Casa de Huespedes Bonanza** is cheap, but the nicest of these simple hotels is **Hotel Malecon. Hotel Costa Maya** is another hotel in the same category; in addition it provides accommodations for recreational vehicles in its parking lot located a short walk from a clean, pleasant beach. Some backpackers claim to use the beach for overnight sleeping, but if you ask the town authorities for permission, they make it clear that camping is not allowed and that they'll check you into their "free" hotel involuntarily if caught. Beaches E and W of town are more likely places to camp than in the center of the promenade that the town is trying to dress up to attract more tourists.

Food

Progreso's cafes are typical of Mexican seaside resorts: if you like sweet, fresh-caught fish you're in luck—but it's hard to find much else. For a change of menu, as you approach town on the main road, look for an open wooden

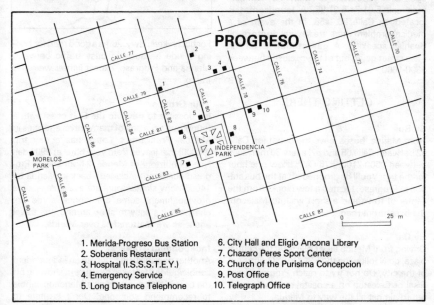

1. Merida-Progreso Bus Station
2. Soberanis Restaurant
3. Hospital (I.S.S.S.T.E.Y.)
4. Emergency Service
5. Long Distance Telephone
6. City Hall and Eligio Ancona Library
7. Chazaro Peres Sport Center
8. Church of the Purisima Concepcion
9. Post Office
10. Telegraph Office

building with a sign that advertises *POLLO CARBON* (barbecued chicken), P700 per whole chicken. Walk along Calle 79 for several budget cafes. Try **Soberani's** (of chain fame) located at Calle 30 #138; **El Cordobes**, an unpretentious restaurant on the plaza, serves a few hearty and economical dishes.

In the off season, if you're looking for breakfast on the waterfront when most cafes are closed until later in the day, don't hesitate to walk into one of them. The cook/owner/family are usually there early. With a friendly request they'll fix you something—usually *huevos motulenos* (Yucatecan egg dish). More than likely you'll have a porch/dining room all to yourself while you watch birds diving for their breakfast in a deserted sea. During the summer, cafes come to life along the promenade in pleasant outdoor surroundings overlooking the beach and waterfront. They often feature live loud music. A cinema shows mostly Mexican films.

Services
On the main street are the **post office** and the **telephone/telegraph office**. Two **banks** are open 0900-1230 Mon. to Friday. For **taxi service** call 5-01-71/5-01-85. A **laundromat** is located on Calle 36, #58. In the event of a medical problem there are several **doctors**, all Spanish speaking. A **gas station** is on the main street going out of town; closed between 1300-1600.

GETTING THERE

By Bus
From Merida, buses leave the depot (on Calle 62 between Calle 65 and 67) every 30 min. daily between 0500-2100, P75 OW; allow one hour for the trip. You'll be dropped off at the bus station in Progreso, located a few blocks from the center of town and a short walk to Malecon, the beachfront road.

By Car
Driving from Merida take Calle 60 at the central plaza, go N following the PROGRESO signs out of the city. Do not try to reach Progreso from Sisal or Celestun on a coastal road; you must return almost all the way to Merida.

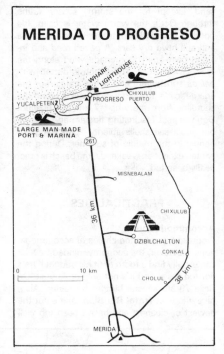

MERIDA TO PROGRESO

For hitchhikers, Hwy. 260 is a good road for finding a ride because of busy traffic between Merida and Progreso; expect lighter weekend traffic.

Tour Groups
It's possible to travel to the Gulf coast with a tour group from any of many travel agencies in Merida. **Francimex Tours** has a day trip (P4000) that leaves from your hotel at 0900 daily: a 2-hour tour of Merida, 2-hour stay in Progreso (lunch not included), back in Merida by 1400. Many similar tours are available—some provide lunch, some are longer, some are cheaper—it's easy to shop around, the travel agencies are scattered all over Merida.

Independent Tours
Another possibility is to locate an independent cabbie/guide that takes pleasure in showing off the best in his country. Ask a Meridano cabbie to recommend someone. Don't hesitate to

haggle over the rate which, depending on time of year and number of tourists, is negotiable. For a full day ending back in Merida, the fee will probably be the same for one to 4 passengers—ask. This can be a good deal if you're traveling with others; if traveling alone

pass the word around your hotel. Tell the driver where you wish to go and what you want to see, how long you expect to be gone, your budget limitations for cafes and drinks, and then rely on his judgement.

EAST OF PROGRESO

CHIXULUB

The coastal road from Progreso (E of the wharf) wanders behind a long string of summer houses for 7 km to Chixulub. Many are available as rentals. Summer is high season, with prices in the same stratosphere. In the winter months the rental fees are quite reasonable, about P55,000-P60,000 monthly. Check with the proprietor of the Restaurant El Cordobes in Progreso for detailed rental information.

Chixulub is a small fishing village with a dilapidated, half-missing wooden pier that no longer accommodates vehicles. However, the nimble-footed local pier fishermen hop across its missing planks and always come in with a good catch. This is a picturesque beach: broad, white, with a collection of worn fishing boats often beached on their side. If you decide to stay a day or two for some quiet time, there's one small inn, **Hotel Cocoteras**. Strolling around the small fishing village, you'll run into a *panaderia* (bakery) where you can buy a tasty

small loaf of French bread for P100 or *pan dulce* for just P40 each, a small Conasuper market, and seasonal fruit and vegetable stands by the side of the road.

Boat Builder
You'll also discover a talented boat builder who constructs pirate-style boats in his yard on a side street just up from the beach. When completed, the all-natural wood boats are sailed to Cancun or Cozumel where they're used to carry about 70 passengers on Robinson Crusoe trips along the Caribbean coast. Though the builder (Juan Jose) has one or two power tools, most of the work is done by hand. The results are terrific! If the boat didn't look so new you'd not be surprised to see swashbuckling Jean Lafitte at the helm. If you're lucky, you might see a launching. With a lot of help from friends, relatives, neighbors, or onlookers like yourself, the boat is inched down the street and then across the beach bit by bit on timbers laid on the ground. A network of lines and pulleys keeps everything taut and upright. When the boat finally splashes into the water there's a big celebration.

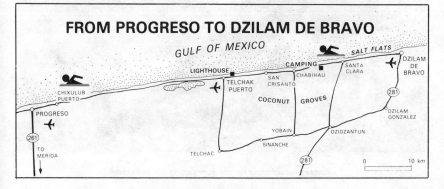

FROM PROGRESO TO DZILAM DE BRAVO

FROM CHIXULUB TO DZILAM DE BRAVO

Continuing along the coast E from Chixulub, the road parallels the sea for 75 km to Dzilam de Bravo. Along the way are several small villages, all tuned in to life on the sea. Forty km past Progreso is **Telchac Puerto,** the largest of these villages. On the road going into town a large coconut grove shelters an outdoor cafe called **Los Cocos** — prices reasonable and surroundings tropical. Investigate the lighthouse, the small flotilla of fishing boats, and on the E side of town, a *balneario* (day-use swim resort) with dressing rooms, *palapa* sunshelters, and a restaurant serving fried fish, beer and soda pop.

Between Telchac Puerto and Dzilam de Bravo the road passes 3 small villages. On this section of the coast road you'll see copra drying in the sun and a salt works. Just beyond the small village of **Chabihau** is a narrow strip of sandy beach good for camping. About 10 km farther is **Santa Clara,** located on the inland side of a small lagoon and crossed by many causeways. Investigate them to find several good beaches.

Dzilam De Bravo

The coastal road from Progreso ends at Dzilam de Bravo. In order to go farther around the Peninsula to San Felipe or Rio Lagartos, you must first return S on any one of the paved roads from the small towns, then catch another northbound road. All the paved roads return to Merida. About 13 km before Dzilam de Bravo, there's a small village cemetery where a wooden grave marker has the name Jean Lafitte. Historians question the validity of his burial here, since after his departure in 1826 there's no record of his return. However, Pierre Lafitte, his brother, is known to be buried in the cemetery. The Yucatecan fishermen held Lafitte in great esteem because of his good treatment of local sailors. Today you can see Jean's marker, authentic or not, where it was moved to, at the museum in Xelha National Park on the Caribbean coast of Quintana Roo. If you decide to spend the night in Dzilam de Bravo, stay at the simple **Hotel Dzilam,** P2000 d.

A rickety wharf stops no one from getting out to the end.

WEST OF PROGRESO

Yucalpeten

On the Progreso Hwy. S of the city, turn R (W) at the junction. This road, which parallels the coast, goes to Yucalpeten, an active shipping and fishing port, and a popular vacation spot for Mexican families and students on *temporada* (summer break). The government runs a large hotel on the beach called **ISSTEY,** a 2-story, modern cement building with 2 adult swimming pools and a shallow one for kids. It's moderately priced, very clean, and each room has a bathroom with a shower. The rooms vary in size from doubles to family units with cooking facilities. The larger units provide hammock hooks to sleep more people than the number of beds. In July and Aug. it's crowded and noisy with fun-seekers of all ages. In the middle of the week during winter months the place is seldom filled and makes a good stopover along the coast; P2500 double. On the beach alongside the hotel is a *balneario,* which has a large pavilion with a cafe, dressing rooms, showers, *palapa* sun shelters, and easy access to the ocean (small fee). A few km beyond Yucalpeten, the road continues through **Chelem** and **Chuburna**. Both small towns cater to summer tourists with *balnearios* and open-air cafes serving fresh fish. During

the yearly migration season, when hundreds of birds pass by, most of these cafes serve a local delicacy, *pato* (duck), cooked in several different spicy sauces.

DZIBILCHALTUN

To the archaeologist, Dzibilchaltun (dseeb-eelchall-TOON) represents a valuable 19 sq km of land. This is the oldest continuously used Maya ceremonial and administrative center on the Peninsula: from 2000 B.C. until the conquest. The map of the site shows close to 8,400 fallen structures. To the layman it does not offer the visual displays of the more fully reconstructed sites. For the amateur archaeologist, however, Dzibilchaltun is fascinating.

Sights

Dzibilchaltun was unknown to the world at large until 1941 when archaeologists George W. Brainerd and E. Wyllys Andrews IV began their explorations. By 1965 several important buildings had been uncovered and repaired. Probably the most remarkable structure is the **Temple of the Seven Dolls,** where 7 primitive clay dolls were found buried under the floor of the temple. These crude figurines

Today's rural dwellings are of the same design as their Maya ancestors.

included various deformities, such as a hunch-back and a distended stomach. Possibly they were part of a ritual for protection against ill-nesses and deformities.

Anyone who has read E. Wyllys Andrews and Luis Marden articles in the Jan. 1959 issue of *National Geographic* will enjoy visiting the *cenote* called **Xlacah** (shla-KAH) where the dive that was described took place. This natural pool is 44 m deep and clear — (not all *cenotes* have such clarity) and though work continues on and off, you can swim when workers are absent. Thousands of artifacts from ancient ceremonial rites were reclaimed from this sacred well, and a limited number are on display at the small museum on the grounds.

Getting There

Direct buses depart from the 2nd-class bus sta-tion in Merida on Calle 62 no. 524 (tel. 1-2344) 4 times a day: 0500, 0715, 1215, 1615. The 30-min. (P60) ride is a good way to get to the site. The return trip isn't so dependable — it's best to go on one of the early buses if you want to return to Merida in the afternoon. Don't plan on catching a return bus after the 1615 bus's ar-rival at the ruins. Another alternative is to travel from Merida on the Progreso bus which leaves from the same 2nd-class station every 15 minutes from 0500-2100, and will drop you off at the crossroads on Hwy. 273 to the Dzi-bilchaltun archaeological zone (when you board the bus be sure to tell the driver where you wish to get off). This alternative leaves you

with a 4-km walk to the ruins. A return bus can be caught at the same spot. If driving, go from Merida on Hwy. 273, and look for the Club de Golf La Ceiba, then continue 1½ km beyond and turn L (E) on the side road for 4 km to the entrance of Dzibilchaltun.

SISAL

Sisal is another port town that's lost most of its zing since henequen production fell off, slip-ping from a bustling, prosperous seaport to a small sleepy Gulf village. Walk through the old customs house for a taste of colonial days. A short pier off the main road makes a good spot to photograph the beached fishing boats. The beach E or W of town is clean, though the water can be silty in the afternoon when the breeze picks up. There are several lighthouses along this coast, and often with just a smile and your best Spanish (even if your best is not too good), you'll be permitted to climb the old stair-way and take a look around. The lighthouse in Sisal, however, is a private home, and you must ask permission to visit their tower, a solid red-and-white structure located on the main road a block from shore. The view is worth the climb! A P200 tip to the child who leads you up the stairway would be appreciated. If you have the urge to fish, you can easily make a deal with a resident fisherman to take you along for a reasonable fee. Sisal is a good place to catch red snapper and sea bass.

Accommodations And Food

There's little choice of accommodations at Sisal. The **Club Felicidades** located E of the pier (a 5-min. walk on the beach), offers 13 rooms with bathrooms that wouldn't receive a gold star for cleanliness. A double bed in each room takes care of one or two people for the same price, P1000. **Club de Patos** is a bit nicer, and a little higher priced. You can also contact the manager of the **Conasuper** 4 blocks from the waterfront; he rents 2 rooms without beds (bring your hammock) in a building near the water. Each room has an oddly arranged bathroom, P500 pp. Find fresh seafood in a tired-looking cafe at the **Club Felicidades**; depending on the time of year, you may have to wait while the proprietor sends a fleet-footed messenger to the closest fisherman to buy fish.

Getting There

Buses for Sisal are available from the Merida bus station at Calles 67 and 50 every 30 min., 0500-1900, a 2-hour ride, P150. Return to Merida from the Sisal bus station in town, 2 blocks from shore. Buses to Merida leave frequently from 0515-2020. If you're driving some maps show a coastal road from Chuburna to Sisal; it does not exist! Mexican maps often show roads that are in the *planning* stage. To drive to Sisal from Merida, leave the city on Calle 60 going W, follow the signs that say SISAL-HUNUCMA. At Hunucma take Hwy. 25 to Sisal.

CELESTUN

A narrow finger of land separates the estuaries of Rio Esperanza from the Gulf of Mexico. On the tip of the one-km strip is a small fishing village, Celestun, which attracts Mexican visitors to its fine swimming beach on the N edge of town. Tourists wishing a luxury seaside resort should look elsewhere, but anyone who takes pleasure in studying birds will want to stop and stay a few days. During winter months, when birds are migrating from the cold climates of the N, many stop over at Celestun for a pause on their way to S. America. Others make their home here until nature directs them back north. One of the most startling in hue of the many winged inhabitants is the flamingo, with an "S"-shaped neck and long spindly legs with webbed feet that enable it to walk through shallow water. Its color ranges from pale coral to flame red with black wing tips; and when a group of flamingos is seen standing on a beach, the vibrant colors melting together is a wonderful stroke to the senses. It's not unusual to see the blue egret or an anhinga perched on a dry stump of a tree drying out its wings.

Sights

The best time for birdwatching is in the morning before the day warms up. Protect yourself from the sun — wear a hat and use sunscreen if you plan on spending a few hours in an open boat on the estuary. Fishing boats along the Rio Esperanza can be hired to go into estuaries to see the birds. Open launches available for hire dock under the bridge that spans the river one km before you reach town. These vessels are a little rickety, and some make so much noise they scare off the birds. Talk with your boatman and make sure he's willing to stop frequently for pictures. The gracious Ositas family (on shore under the bridge) regularly takes people to see the flamingos. The captain will turn off the motor and quietly pole the boat as close as possible without scaring off the flock. Expect to pay approx. P6000 per boat load.

Other than birds, Celestun offers little entertainment. The plain central plaza is a gathering place for townspeople, but everything moves in slow gear. Across the plaza is a simple stucco church, and on the opposite side the market opens early until 1300. The beach on the N edge of town is white and clean, but the choppy water gets silty in the afternoon with the rising wind. In the morning, it's a beautiful walk along the beach which meanders for miles. Many small cafes spill out onto the sand; parents sit at white tin tables that say SUPERIOR, enjoy fried fish and beer, and watch their children play in the surf close by. Except for July and Aug., you and the fishermen have the beach to yourselves. For the artist and photographer, the harbor, with its hundreds of boats, fishermen, curious traps and mended nets stretched out to dry, provides endless and colorful subjects. **Note:** Photographers, protect your lenses from blowing sand on this coast.

Accommodations

Several hotels in Celestun are all in the budget category; the nicest are on the seafront. **Hotel San Julio,** constantly blown by the wind, maintains clean simple accommodations with private bathrooms. Through the patio there's easy access to the beach. Located on Calle 12 #92 (tel. 1-85-89 in Merida for reservations); P1400 s, P2000 d. Another smaller hotel right on the beach is **Hotel Gutierrez.** Though spartan, it has 10 comfortable rooms, each with 2 double beds and private bathroom. The 3-storied stucco hotel is cooled with ceiling fans and breezes from the sea, especially the front rooms. The tile-floored rooms are extremely clean, with purified water and cold soda for sale in the lobby; P1300 s and P2000 d, Calle 12 #22. Also on the same street (which faces the beach) is **Posada Martin,** simple and reasonable, on Calle 12 #76. The local police do not object to people sleeping on the beach, but a combination of wind and sand cause gritty discomfort. Those driving vans and campers are free to park on the beach, but pick a spot close to the road where the sand isn't so soft that you get stuck.

Food

A few small seafood cafes edge the beach. **Playarita** and **Restaurant Celestun** are the cleanest and both serve good food. Try a generous fresh shrimp cocktail (P500) that ranks with any restaurant any place in the world. This is fish country and the closer you

get to Campeche, the bigger the shrimp! Meet the incoming fishermen if you want to buy fresh-caught fish. The market is active with a good supply of fresh fruit and vegetables, but closes at 1300. The *panaderia* makes good bread, P50 per loaf, and the *tortilleria* opens early in the morning.

Services

The **bank** cashes traveler's cheques Mon. to Fri. from 0900-1330, located on Calle 12 #103. The **long-distance telephone** office (really a private home without a sign) is located on the corner of Calles 9 and 12 across from the plaza, open 1600-1800. The **post office** is just as difficult to find; but if you must mail a letter or buy stamps, it's just beyond the Restaurant El Camaron toward the sea in a home at Calle 7, open Mon. to Sat. 0800-1200. You'll find a **gas station** in town.

Getting There

From Merida, buses go out from the Autotransportes del Sur station, Calle 50 #531 at Calle 67, leaving hourly from 0500-1400 and every 2 hours from 1400-2000. Return trips begin early and follow the same schedule, 0430-2030. The trip (OW) takes about 1½ hours, and the fare is P250 OW. From Merida by car follow the signs out of town marked SISAL-HUNUCMA. At Hunucma go to Kinchil and pick up Hwy. 281 to Celestun. There isn't a coastal road from Sisal to Celestun.

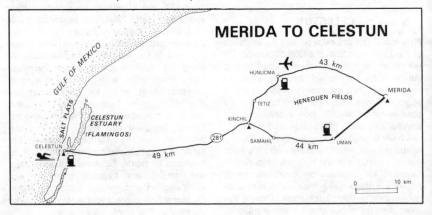

MERIDA TO CELESTUN

EAST AND NORTH COAST OF YUCATAN

IZAMAL

Izamal is a fine old colonial town (pop. 20,000) with Maya origins. Arriving Spaniards were determined to alter the importance of Izamal as a pilgrimage destination. They lost no time tearing down most of the religious Maya ceremonial centers; to add insult to injury, they used the same stones to construct their own city buildings and churches. The original Maya city that the Spaniards destroyed was called It-zamna (variously translated as "City of Hills" or "Dew from Heaven"). The present-day colonial town is mostly ignored by tourists because its location is off the tourist track and it lacks such amenities as modern hotels. However, the town is well worth a detour.

Sights
The most imposing structure in the small town is the yellow **Convent of Saint Anthony de Padua,** a church-convent complex built on what looks like a broad hill. Actually the hill is

the base of a Maya temple, Popul-Chac, that was destroyed in the 1600s. The immense base measures 180 m long and stands 12 m high. Designed by by Fray Juan de Merida, construction began in 1533. Wander through the church grounds, and in one of the stark stone cells you'll see a huge caldron, metal tools, and a hanging rack still used to make candles for church use. The buildings surround a grassy courtyard (8,000 sq m, the largest in Mexico) with 75 arches—once a glorious yellow, now faded and splotched with age. The town plaza is surrounded by buildings all the same color, condition, and arched design: massive porticoed stone pillars and sheltered walkways. During the colonial period, the city must have been a shiny jewel in New Spain's showcase. Because most of the structures in Izamal are the same color, it's often referred to as *Ciudad Amarilla* ("City of Yellow").

Archaeological Zone

Itzamna was already an ancient city when the Spaniards arrived. Although the archaeologists date it from the Early Classic Period (A.D. 300-600), pottery, carbon-dated to 1000 B.C., has been found. When standing on one of the stone stairways on the grounds near the church, you have a good view of the pyramid called **Kinich Kakmo,** dedicated to the sun god. When you try to track it down from street level the structure mysteriously eludes you, even though the site is only 2½ blocks NE of the main plaza! One of the tallest pyramids in the Western Hemisphere, it has been only partially restored. If you decide to climb to the top, be aware that the upper stairway is not completely reconstructed. Once on the peak you'll have a striking view of the surrounding brush-covered landscape. Looking E, you can see for 50 km to Chichen Itza. As is the case with hundreds of pyramids on the Peninsula, one day it will be excavated and if ancient rumors are true, scientists will find the burial chamber of an honored ruler.

Practicalities

Most travelers to Izamal just pass through, stopping long enough to take a look around, which even with a climb to the top of the local pyramid Kinich Kakmo should take no more than a couple of hours. However, if you decide to spend the night, there are 3 (at least) accommodations to look for, all simple and close to the main plaza. Ask for: **Hotel Kabul, Hotel Toto,** or **Hotel Canto,** whose rates average US$4-6. You'll see several cafes, one under the arches of a yellow building near the plaza across from the bank. A few small stores sell minimal basics. The bank doesn't cash traveler's cheques.

Transport

Driving on 180 from Merida, turn left (N) at Hoctun and after traveling 24 km you'll reach Izamal. Highway 180 is a well-used road and hitching is comparatively simple. Along the road from Hoctun any 2nd-class bus will stop for you with a wave of your arm .

At any hour of the day, you'll find a queue of *calesas* which serve as taxis parked in front of a broad stairway leading to the church and courtyard. These tiny buggies do an active business carrying locals (often whole families) around town. The *calesas* are not impractical bits of nostalgia for the tourists to look at and admire (though you will), they're the only transportation some families have.

horse-drawn taxis waiting for local fares in Izamal

CHICHEN ITZA

A large restored site, Chichen Itza is a 1 ½-hour drive from Merida, a favored destination of those fascinated with Maya culture. Chichen Itza is a mingling of two distant cultures: ancient Maya and later arriving Toltecs. The oldest buildings are good examples of Late Classic Maya construction from the 5th C. to the 1100s when the Toltecs invaded and then ruled Chichen Itza for 200 years. The Toltecs built new structures and added on to many already in place—all bear a remarkable similarity to those in the ancient Toltec capital of Tollan (today called Tula) 1200 km away in the state of Hidalgo. Those 2 centuries of mingling cultures added a new dimension to 800 years of Maya history. The carvings found on buildings of different eras vary between the rain god Chac (early Maya) to the cult of the feathered serpent (late Mexicanized Maya). Though Chichen Itza was most likely abandoned toward the end of the 13th C., Maya were still making pilgrimages to the sacred site when Montejo the Younger, the Spaniard who played a role in ultimately subjugating the Maya, settled his troops among the ruins of Chichen Itza in 1533. However, although they placed a cannon on top of the pyramid of Kukulcan, they were unable at that time to conquer the elusive Indians, and left Chichen Itza after a year for the coast. The pilgrimages continued.

Today, a different breed of pilgrim comes to Chichen Itza from all over the world to walk in the footsteps of great rulers, courageous ball players, mysterious priests, and simple peasants. Chichen is considered the best restored archaeological site on the Peninsula. Restoration, begun in 1923, continued steadily for 20 years. Work is still done intermittently, and there are enough unexcavated mounds to support continued exploration for many years into the future.

Travel Tips

You can easily walk the 10-sq-km grounds; 2 days is a relaxing way to do it. Wear walking shoes for this entire expedition: climbing around in sandals can be uncomfortable and

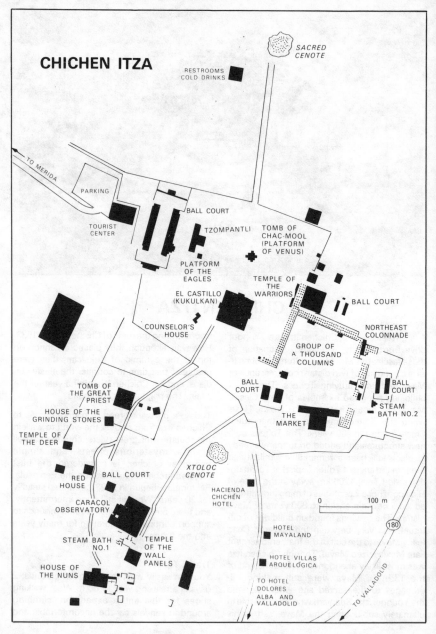

unsafe. For some a short walk around the grounds will satisfy their curiosity, and they can say they've "been there." For a ruins-nut, however, the best advice is to spend the night either at a close hotel where you can be up and on the grounds as soon as the ticket taker is there (usually 0800), or at Piste with a good shot at getting to the site as early as possible. Two good reasons for arriving early are the weather (it's much cooler in the early hours) and the absence of the crowds that arrive later in tour buses. With 2 days you can study these archaeological masterpieces in leisure, have a chance to climb at your own pace, and be there at the odd hours when the inner chambers open (only for short periods each day). This also allows time to return to your hotel for a leisurely lunch (maybe a swim), a short siesta, and an afternoon return visit (free with your ticket). The ruins are open daily from 0800-1700, although some of the structures have special hours (posted on the buildings or ask at the entrance). Admission is P40 pp, and small parking fee to use the parking lot.

SIGHTS

This large park-like area is easy to stroll. Eighteen structures have been excavated, many of those restored. The uses for these buildings are not truly understood. Archaeologists can only study and guess from the few *real* facts that have been found. Near the Sacred Cenote a snack bar sells cold drinks, light snacks, postcards, and a few curios. A clean restroom is available at the back of the *palapa* building.

Temple Of The Warriors
On a 3-tiered platform, the **Temple of the Warriors** stands next to the impressive **Group of a Thousand Columns**—reminiscent of Egypt's Karnak. Many of the square, stone columns have carvings still in excellent condition. In 1926 during restoration, a subtemple found underneath was named **Chacmool Temple**. The former color on the columns of the inner structure is still slightly visible. Close to the Thousand Columns on the E side of the plaza is a simple sweat house cleverly constructed with an oven and a channel under the floor to carry off the water thrown against the hot stones to create steam. Indian sweat houses are a combination religious and health-giving experience still used today on American Indian reservations.

The Platforms
Strolling the grounds you'll find the **Platform of Venus** and another called **Platform of Tigers and Eagles**. The flat square structures with a low stairway on each of 4 sides were used for ritual music and dancing and, according to Diego de Landa (infamous 16th C. Franciscan bishop), farce and comedy were presented for the pleasure of the public.

Temple of the Bearded Man
At the N end of the ballpark sits the handsome
continued on page 116

carved serpents on top of the Temple of the Warriors

ONGOING ARCHAEOLOGICAL RECONSTRUCTION OF CHICHEN ITZA

While walking through Chichen Itza, it's common to see areas with a concentration of loose stones close together. Even a layman can sense that at one time this was more than likely a structure that finally fell victim to the elements. Crews working under the auspices of the Anthropological Museum in Mexico City work at different archaeological zones during the winter months (dry season). In November 1985, workers spent a few months at Chichen Itza. An area N of the sweat house (8 m by 12 m) was covered with stones marked with identifying numbers and laid out in neat rows by a crew of 3 local men. A photographer from San Miguel Allende had his Hasselblad camera set up on a tripod in the grass with several studio lights (working off portable power) aimed at a small platform. The crew carried the stones, all about 39-45 cm in diameter, to the platform. Here they were photographed one by one and then returned to their numbered spot on the ground.

Each stone is numbered and photographed.

The photos are taken to the museum in Mexico City and with the help of modern laser equipment and computers the structures are scientifically reconstructed. Detailed drawings done by Fredrick Catherwood in 1841 and published in John Stevens *Incidents Of Travel In Yucatan* have been a tremendous visual aid to the scientists. Catherwood's engravings are the earliest accurate reproductions of the Maya ruins and since that time the elements have further deteriorated many of the buildings pictured in his drawings—some are completely down.

It often takes years before real progress is recognized at the archaeological zones. Money is the biggest limitation and field work takes place only about 3-5 months a year. When a structure is ultimately finished it's a work of art and a close duplication of the original.

Photos and high tech equipment enable archaeologists to rebuild structures as originally built.

a completed effort

continued from page 113

Temple of the Bearded Man. Two graceful columns frame the entrance into a smallish temple with the remains of decorations depicting birds, trees, flowers, and the earth monster. It's doubtful whether anyone will ever know if the unusual acoustics here were used specifically for some unknown display of histrionics, or if it's accidental that standing in the temple one can speak in a low voice and be heard a good distance down the playing field, well beyond what is normal (much like in the dome of St. Peter's Cathedral in Rome). Was this the "dugout" from which the coach whispered signals to his players down field?

Great Ball Court

Of several ball courts at Chichen Itza, the most impressive is the **Great Ball Court**, the largest found yet in Mesoamerica. On this field, life and death games were played with a hard rubber ball in the tradition of the Roman Coliseum. The playing field is 85 m by 35 m, with two 8-m-high walls running parallel to each other on each side of the playing field. The players were obliged to hit the ball into carved stone circles embedded into the vertical walls 8 m above the ground using only their elbow, wrist, or hip. The heavy padding they wore indicates the game was dangerous; it was also difficult and often lasted for hours. The winners were awarded jewelry and clothing from the audience. The losers lost more than jewelry and valuables, according to the carved panels on the site—they lost their *heads* to the winning captain!

Temple Of The Jaguar

On the SE corner of the ballpark. The upper temple was constructed between A.D. 800-1050. To get there you must climb a steep stairway at the S end of the platform. Two large serpent columns with their rattlers high in the air frame the opening into the temple. The inside of the room is decorated with a variety of carvings and (almost visible) remnants of what must have been colorful murals.

Sacred *Cenote*

Today's adventurer can sit in the shade of a *palapa* terrace and enjoy a cold drink next to

With Temple of the Bearded Man in the background, the largest ball park on the Peninsula is this one at Chichen. The game hinged around players getting the ball into the ring, 8 m above.

the sacred *cenote* (say-no-TAY). This natural well is 300 m N of the Tomb of Chacmool. The roadway to the sacred well, an ancient *sacbe,* was constructed during the Classic Period. The well is large, 6 m in diameter with walls 20 m above the surface of the water (34 m deep) where human bones were found. On the edge of the *cenote* is a ruined sweat bath probably used for purification rituals before sacrificial ceremonies.

In 1885, Edward Thompson was appointed United States Consul in nearby Merida. A young writer greatly interested in the archaeological zones surrounding Merida, he eventually settled in Chichen Itza and acquired the entire area, including an old hacienda (for only US$75). For many years he studied Diego de Landa's account of human sacrifice still going on at the time of the Spanish conquest. Stories of young virgins and valuable belongings thrown into the well at times of drought over hundreds of years convinced him there was treasure buried in the muddy *cenote* bottom. From 1903-07, with the help of Harvard's Peabody Museum, he supervised the first organized dive into the well. Less than 50 skeletons were found, mostly those of children, male and female, smashing the virgin myth. Precious objects of jade, gold, copper, plus stone items with tremendous archaeological value were also dredged from the muddy water.

Thompson set off an international scandal when he shipped most of these important finds to the Peabody Museum by way of diplomatic pouch. He was asked to leave Yucatan and for years (1926-1944) a lawsuit continued over the booty. Ironically, the Mexican court ruled in favor of Peabody Museum, claiming that the Mexican laws concerning archaeological material were inadequate. After the laws were toughened up, the Peabody Museum, in a gesture of friendliness, returned many (but not all) of the artifacts from Chichen Itza's well of sacrifice.

The next large-scale exploration of the well was conducted in the 1960s, sponsored by the National Geographic Society with help from CEDAM (a Mexican organization of explorers and divers noted for their salvaging operation in the Caribbean of the Spanish ship *Mantanceros*). As Thompson suspected before his untimely departure, there was much more treasure in the *cenote* to be salvaged. Hundreds of pieces (including gold, silver, obsidian, copper bells, carved bone and other artifacts, plus a few more skeletons) were brought to the surface. In order to see in this well, thousands of gallons of chemicals (a unique experiment by the Purex Co.) were successfully used to clarify the water.

Observatory

One of the most graceful structures at Chichen Itza is the **Caracol**, a 2-tiered observatory shaped like a snail, where advanced theories of the sun and moon were calculated by Maya astronomers. Part of the spiral stairway into the tower/observatory is closed to tourists in an effort to preserve the decaying building. The circular room is laid out with narrow window slits placed facing S, W, the summer soltice, and the equinoxes. The priests used these celestial sightings to keep (accurate) track of time in their elaborate calendrical system.

Caracol

Kukulcan

The most breathtaking place to view all of Chichen Itza is from the top of **Kukulcan**, also called El Castillo. At 24 m it's the tallest and most dramatic structure on the site. This imposing pyramid, built by the Maya on top of another smaller pyramid, was probably constructed at the end of a 52-year cycle in thanksgiving for allowing the world to survive the elements—maybe even Halley's Comet! Halley's swept by this part of the earth A.D.

Kukulcan, also known as El Castillo

837 (and most recently in 1986): the construction of the second temple was approximately A.D. 850.

Kukulcan was built according to strict astronomical guidelines. Giant serpent heads repose at the base of each of 4 sides of 91 steps with one more to the top for a total of 365 — one step for each day of the year. On 22nd March and September (days of equinox) between 1200 and 1700, the sun casts an eerie shadow of a serpent slithering down the steep steps of the pyramid, giving life to the giant heads at the base. A visit including March 21 and 22 is a good time to observe the astronomical talents of the Maya.

Be sure to make the climb into the inner structure of Kukulcan where you'll see a red-painted jade-studded sculpture of a jaguar, just as it was left by the Maya builders over a thousand years ago. Check the visiting hours since the inner chamber is not always open.

Others

The largest building on the grounds is the **Nunnery**, named by the Spaniards. From the looks of it and its many rooms, it was a palace of some sort built during the Classical Period. Meaning "Wall of Skulls," **Tzompantli** is a platform decorated on all sides with carvings of skulls, anatomically correct but with eyes staring out of large sockets. This rather ghoulish structure also depicts an eagle eating a human heart. It is presumed that ritualistic music and dancing on this platform culminated in a climax of sacrificial death for the victim, his head then left on display, perhaps with others already in place in a gory lineup. It's estimated the platform was built between A.D. 1050-1200 after the intrusion of the Toltecs.

A much-damaged pyramid, **Tomb of the High Priest** is intriguing because of its burial chamber found within. Sometimes referred to as Osario (Spanish for "ossuary," a depository for bones of the dead), the pyramid at one time had 4 stairways on each side (like El Castillo) and a temple at the crest. From the top platform a vertical passageway lined with rock leads to the base of this decayed mound. There, from a small opening, some stone steps lead into a cave about 3 m deep. Seven tombs were discovered containing skeletons and the usual funeral trappings of important people, including copper and jade artifacts.

PRACTICALITIES

Accommodations

Only a few hotels are within walking distance of the ruins, all in the moderate price range. **Hotel Mayaland** is an old colonial with private bath, dining room, swimming pool, and lovely gardens. Rates: US$54 d, including breakfast, reservations suggested. From the U.S., tel. 1-800-223-4084. **Hotel Hacienda Chichen Itza** contains original bungalows of the early archaeologists. The narrow-gauge railroad tracks used in the 1920s for transportation and hauling still go through outlying areas of the hotel; not used today. This hotel has lots of history, plus private bathrooms, a pool, dining room, and part of the rustic original hacienda. This hotel isn't used in the summer unless the traffic through Chichen is heavy. Rates US$53 d, includes breakfast, reservations suggested; from U.S. tel. 1-800-223-4084. **Villa Arquelogica,** owned by Club Med, is the newest hotel at Chichen Itza. Almost deluxe small rooms, private bath, swimming pool, bar, covered patio, dining room, and a unique library filled with books concerning the Maya and the pertinent area. Rates US$48 d, breakfast included, reservations suggested; from U.S. tel. 1-800-528-3100.

Two km or more from the ruins are: **Hotel Dolores Alba**, 2.2 km E of the ruins, rustic, clean, with swimming pool, private bath, and dining room. Here, also, small trailers, campers and vans are welcome to park in the hotel parking lot. There are some electrical hookups and the hotel swimming pool is available to guests. About P800 per vehicle per night. Mailing address: Calle 63 #464, Merida 97000, Mexico. Rates: US$15. **Hotel Mision Chichen**, 2 km W of the ruins on Hwy. 180, rustic, pool, a/c, dining room, credit cards accepted. Rates US$40 d, including lunch. Reservations suggested; tel. from U.S. 1-800-223-4084. Nearby,

you'll find the **Piramide Inn Trailer Park.** With cement pads, electrical and water hookups, the park is peaceful, grassy, tree shaded, and guests may use the swimming pool across the street. Rates about P500 pp per night.

Food And Entertainment

The only restaurants within walking distance of the site are at the hotels. Check the hours since they're usually open for lunch only between 1230-1500. Bring your swim suit — lunch guests are welcome to use the pool, a refreshing break in a day of climbing and exploring the ruins. Every evening a **Sound and Light Show** is presented in 2 languages at the ruins. The English version is usually the second one of the evening and the fee is around P500. Other than that there's no organized entertainment in Chichen Itza. However, the guests of the nearby hotels are generally well-traveled people, many with exciting tales to tell. Sitting under the stars on a warm night with a cold *cerveza* swapping adventure yarns is a delightful way to spend many an evening.

Chichen Itza's House of the Nuns

column carving at the Temple of the Warriors, also known as the Temple of 1,000 Columns; in reality there are only 400

TRANSPORT

Chichen Itza lies adjacent to Hwy. 180, 121 km E of Merida, 213 km W of Cancun, and 43 km W of Valladolid. If traveling by car you have many options (see map). The roads to Chichen Itza are in good condition, as long as you slow down for the *topes* (traffic bumps) found before and after every village and school. Hitchhiking at the right time of day will put you in view of many autos on Hwy. 180, but be settled before dark or you may spend the night on the roadside; there's little traffic on this road after sunset.

By Bus

From Merida, buses leave the 2nd-class bus station regularly and stop at Piste, 2½ km W of the Chichen Itza ruins (allow 2 hours), or ask the bus driver if he'll drop you even closer at the fork in the road where the old highway gets closest to the ruins. First-class (ADO) buses take you to the parking lot of the ruins, but ask when you get on the bus in Merida. ADO buses arrive about every hour from 0900-1700; less frequently earlier and later. Many budget travelers stay in Piste, from where taxi fare is approximately P800 (and negotiable!) or a 30-min. walk to the ruins. Buses leave from Cancun and Puerto Juarez (3-hour trip) to Piste; ask about the return schedule, and from Valladolid (½-hour trip) frequently.

By Plane

Small planes offer commuter service to Piste from Cozumel, Chetumal, Merida, and Cancun. Check with Aerocaribe, in Cancun tel. 4-12-31, in Cozumel 2-08-77 for information and reservations.

Escorted Tours

Escorted tours on modern a/c buses leave daily from Merida, Cozumel, and Cancun — day trips or overnighters. Check with your hotel, or any travel agency. Many travel agents offer a variety of tours and prices; check around before you make a decision. The following 2 tours with the Francimex Agency from Merida to Chichen Itza will give you an idea of price and time schedule. On the first, the bus leaves Merida 0900 taking you to the ruins with an English-speaking guide. After a couple of hours at the archaeological zone, at about 1300 you're taken to Piste for lunch at Xaybe, a simple cafe serving typical Yucatecan food. From there you return to Merida between 1600-1800; cost pp is about US$15.50. The second tour, which serves 2 purposes, originates in Merida at 0900, stops at the ruins for sightseeing, and again in Valladolid for lunch, then continues on to Cancun, arriving approx. 1800. Your luggage is safe in the same bus for the entire trip. So, although you don't spend a great deal of time at the ruins, you have the opportunity to make a brief visit enroute while transferring from Merida to Cancun. Fare is US$55 pp including lunch.

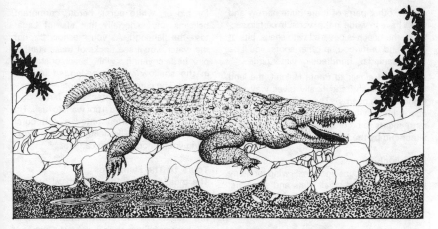

RIO LAGARTOS

A little more than 100 km from Valladolid on the most northerly point of the Yucatan Peninsula, the small fishing village of Rio Lagartos is known for its colonies of flamingos that return each year to nest. In April, May, and June, literally thousands of pink and cerise *Phoenicopterus ruber* flamingos are in the shallow estuaries every place you look building their nests. The locals are very protective of their flamingos; during the reproductive season, visitors are not allowed to disturb the birds whle they guard their strange-looking mud nests which are exposed above the surface of the water. The sounds of outsiders cause them to rise in flight, often knocking fragile eggs from the nests. The rest of the year, it's an easy matter to rent a boat and guide; from Nov. to March there aren't as many birds, but the young are just beginning to color. At hatching, flamingos are mostly white, and at 3 months the black feathers along their wings begin to grow.

The town of Rio Lagartos is an amazing small community. Like the birds, people build their homes in swampy water that seems to submerge a good bit of the land. If you're lucky, you might be able to watch as cement for a foundation is poured right into the water.

Besides the growing number of birdwatchers, which is still infinitesimal compared to the visitors of most other cities on the Peninsula, the main industry is fishing; many folks also work 16 km E at the Las Coloradas salt factory (in operation since Maya days). Most of the employees of the factory today are still Maya.

SIGHTS

Beach Hiking

Rio Lagartos ("Lizard River") at one time was home to numerous crocodilians but before anyone realized what was happening, the animal was hunted out. Today, unless you set up camp in a mangrove-lined swamp, the only crocs you're likely to see are 2 kept in a fenced mud wallow on the beach near the hotel.

The small spit of land called Rio Lagartos Peninsula that separates the lagoon from the sea is 9½ km long from the head of the lagoon to Punta Holohit. This is a good walk for beach hikers. Chances are you'll not see another soul; the utter isolation encourages the wildlife you *will* encounter. Wear some type of protective covering for your feet since some parts of this peninsula are covered with brush including cactus; other parts of it are quite narrow and you'll have to wade in the water. In certain sections, the beach is covered with shells, bits of coral, and driftwood; in other spots, you'll be accompanied by hundreds of water birds.

As you get closer to Punta Holohit, the land becomes marshy and finally gives way to a lagoon (3 are nearby). The end of the marsh is about 1½ km from Punta Holohit. Make arrangements to be dropped off or picked up at either end by the Nefertiti Hotel van.

Birdwatching
The shallow lagoons and canals wind for many km in and around small islets and sandbars. This is the ideal place for birdwatching. Look

Flamingos lay one egg in a cone-shaped mud nest.

for plover, white egret, heron, cormorant, pelicans and especially that star of Lagartos—the flamingo. As you meander through the water, you'll see flocks of these startling pink birds covering a white beach or standing in the shallow water one-legged in large groups. The combination of colors—blue sky, white sand, green water, pink birds—is a breathtaking effect you'll not want to rush. The sandy beach is often tinted a soft coral, covered with the silky feathers of flamingos. Bring your binoculars and camera.

Tours To The Flamingos
The most versatile and economical trips are preplanned through the Hotel Nefertiti; several package deals are posted on the wall behind the desk. The different options include 2½-hour or full-day trips. You have a choice of boat or car transport. A combination (full-day) trip includes a van tour of the Las Coloradas salt factory, a swim in the Gulf, lunch, a boat trip to see the flamingos, and a visit to El Cuyo, the small fishing village at the head of the Rio Lagartos lagoon. Hotel Nefertiti tours to the flamingos: short trip with a group, P2000 pp; full-day trip with a group, P3500 boat and van; hotel van of 10 persons, P800 pp.

For the average visitor, one of these trips will satisfy the desire to see the flamingos and is most economical. If, however, you want more time to observe them or take pictures, make arrangements with a guide for a private trip. One guide who can be highly recommended is Luis Carmel—ask for him at the hotel. If you're traveling by car he'll take you first in *your* car to his small boat anchored off a rickety wooden dock about 25 km from the Nefertiti. From here you travel in his very noisy but ample-sized open launch. Bring protection from the sun (it's an open boat), water, and lunch if you can talk Luis into spending the day. Luis, an agreeable guy, doesn't seem to mind as you sit quietly on the shore of one of the small islands that dot the estuaries and wait for the birds to forget the noise of your earlier approach. He's also well versed in the habits of flamingos, willing to tell you how they build a nest, how, if a storm hits at nesting time, the usually calm water sweeps away their one egg, and how some shady characters (not locals) steal eggs and young

Crooked dock and open launch can be the means to a fine day of birdwatching at Rio Lagartos.

birds to sell on the black market, an illegal activity since this is a national park.

Although Luis is friendly, he is also very shrewd, so get all the particulars straight before you begin your trip: how long it will last, how much for each person, and where you will be going. During the heavy tourist season (Dec., March, April, July, and Aug.), expect the price to be higher. Don't forget your Spanish dictionary, for Luis, along with most of the local guides, speaks little English. Serious photographers: bring your long lens (a tripod helps, too) since most of your pictures will be taken with the birds in flight, seldom closer than 300 meters.

Swimming

For swimming, go to the N side of the Rio Lagartos Peninsula, a narrow strip of land that separates Gulf water from shallow estuaries. The only way there is by boat, and the easiest and most economical is a small shuttle run by the Nefertiti Hotel, P200 pp RT (with a minimum of 5 people—find other travelers at the hotel or on the beach). The driver will drop you off at the beach and return for you at an agreed time. This beach is very isolated, and although there's usually a breeze, it's hot with no shade. Bring protection from the sun's intense glare, plus food and water—there are no facilities of any kind and very likely you will be the only visitors. Beware of the sudden drop-off when you go into the surf; within a meter of shore the water is waist deep. The sea here has a slight current and is not clear, so snorkeling isn't worth the effort of carrying equipment. As for fishing, don't bother in the estuaries: they're so shallow that you'll foul up your line. On the seaward side, it's possible to find a sand bar where you'll probably have luck. If your Spanish is good, you might be able to arrange (for a fee) a trip with a fisherman in his boat. Bring your own equipment.

PRACTICALITIES

Accommodations

Hotel Nefertiti is the only hotel in Rio Lagartos. It's located on the waterfront; you can't miss it, the only multi-storied building in town. The rooms are spartan, not noted for cleanliness, have bathrooms and (usually) hot water; rates are P1800 s or d, P2500 t, P500 pp extra. An alternative is to inquire at the cafe on the plaza; there may be a place that you can hang your hammock for a reasonable fee.

lobby of the Nefertiti Hotel, the only one in Rio Lagartos

Camping

Along the shore about one km E of Nefertiti Hotel, you'll come across a lovely *cenote*. Circling the *cenote* is a parking lot with little else in the area, but it's a beautiful, clean, and pleasant stopover for picnicking and swimming. It makes a quiet, deserted campground at night, but expect lots of company during the day when families and kids come to swim and have a good time, especially on a weekend. Another alternative for camping is the **Rio Lagartos Peninsula** (see above). About 5 km from Punta Holohit is a large flat area where the peninsula is so wide that you needn't worry about surf hitting your campsite. Don't forget your toothbrush, for there's no corner drugstore close by—nor even a corner.

Food And Entertainment

Again you have a limited choice in Rio Lagartos. The **Hotel Nefertiti Restaurant** is about

as good as it gets. The seafood is always fresh; and though the decor is garish, the prices are moderate and you'll come away satisfied. For something cheaper, try the **Restaurant Negritos**, located on the plaza; it serves mostly seafood. The small market has a limited selection but will keep body and soul together nicely. If you have transportation, a pleasant surprise is the food at the **Restaurant El Payaso** in San Felipe, 12 km W of Rio Lagartos (see below). At night, music from the Hotel Nefertiti disco, called **Los Flamingos**, filters across the water to engulf the hotel (including almost every room). If you happen to have quarters overlooking the disco, you might as well use the free ticket they presented you with when you checked in because you'll "enjoy" the music one way or another.

Services

Few services exist in this small town. Bring plenty of film for your camera, and don't bother even to look for a long-distance phone. The basketball court you may have noticed in the center of town is really the central plaza. On one side, you'll find the Catholic church, on the other, city hall. The local authorities are helpful and willing to answer questions—when their office is open.

GETTING THERE

By Bus

From Valladolid, it's a 2-hour bus trip to Rio Lagartos—which does not include the layover in Tizimin, where you have time to look the town over as you wait for your transfer. There are no direct buses to Rio Lagartos. The bus drops you off in front of the Restaurant Negritos, which also sells bus tickets.

By Car

At Valladolid, Hwy. 180 (heading N) junctions with 295 through Tizimin, ending in Rio Lagartos 103 km later. Beware of the *topes* (traffic bumps)! You'll find these all over Mexican highways to slow the traffic down as it approaches a village or a school. However, the *topes* (sometimes called *punta* or "bridge") in this northern section of the Peninsula are higher and more deadly than most. If you hit these at any speed over 20 km an hour, the underside of your car will be destroyed— quickly! The highway in this N country has little traffic and it's easy to find yourself speeding right along the 2-lane road—and a *tope* sign gives short warning. Gasoline is available along this route; you'll find **Pemex** stations at Valladolid, Tizimin, and Rio Lagartos. On the Yucatan, one should never let fuel get too low: although stations may be closely spaced, they suffer occasional non-delivery—leaving them empty for as much as a day or two. Top off your tank frequently. Driving along this part of the Peninsula, you'll find the landscape arid and dry, mostly inhabited by range cattle. As is recommended in all of Yucatan, don't drive at night. It's very dark; animals often lie in the middle of the road; or worse, pedestrians walk invisibly in the road, not seen until hit.

Cycles
The roads on most of the Peninsula are flat. Highway 295 between Valladolid and Rio Lagartos is especially inviting to bikers. Though it is 103 km, the road has comparatively little traffic. Don't count on any commerce once past Tizimin until you reach Rio Lagartos, and as described, that's minimal.

Tours
If in Merida and you would like to see Rio Lagartos and the birds, contact the **Yucatan Trails Travel Agency**, which offers a 2-day birdwatching excursion. This includes an overnight stop at the Hotel Nefertiti.

LAS COLORADAS

This small settlement is named for the color (mineral-laden reds and purples) of marshy swamps that surround the village. These ponds have been producing salt for centuries; Maya history indicates that they produced the valuable mineral and used it as an important trade item throughout Mesoamerica. Deposits in the water also inadvertently produce the brilliant colors of flamingos that nest in estuaries nearby! If you're interested in seeing what salt is like before it comes out of your shaker, check at the factory office. People will either refer you to the hotel tours in Rio Lagartos or may offer you a personal tour of the premises. To get to Las Coloradas, go E on the crossroads one km S of Rio Lagartos. Travel about 14 km, till you cross the only high bridge across the river; continue another 2 km and you'll be in the small village.

You can travel by bus from Rio Lagartos but the only real reason to come to Las Coloradas is to see the flamingos—and the bus schedule pretty well rules that out. From Rio Lagartos buses leave daily at 1100 and 2000, returning at 1300 and 0500. The road has a reasonable amount of traffic, so hitching is possible from the crossroad near Rio Lagartos. If there's a boat from the hotel going out to watch flamingos, you can usually join them if there's room. Check the schedule. There's little to see at Las Coloradas except maybe a hot little-league baseball game played right near the road to the canals. There's a refreshment stand, but no cafe or other facilities.

SAN FELIPE

You like small villages on the sea? Visit San Felipe, a fishing town 12 km W of Rio Lagartos. The small settlement offers few amenities but provides a relaxed and friendly atmosphere especially in the off season. During the busy months of spring and summer, the town fills up with campers; but during the rest of the year not many out-of-towners can be seen. Make sure you have *pesos* with you because you won't find a bank or post office, the closest being in Rio Lagartos.

The town doesn't have a hotel, but if you find yourself unable to leave and are without camping equipment, ask at **La Herradura** grocery store (one block from the pier) about house or room rentals around town for very little money. These are not really designed for tourists, contain limited furnishings, and may be in need of a broom. There's a cinema **(Cinema Morufo)**, a city hall (across from the cinema), and a good little restaurant called the **Restaurant El Payaso**, Calle 8 #55, open almost daily 0730-1830. Serving mostly seafood (great *ceviche*), prices are moderate and there's a bathroom for customers.

Camping

Most visitors who plan to stay over bring camping equipment and cross the estuary to Rio Lagartos Peninsula to set up their tents. In busy times, this wide flat area with tall shade trees near the tip of Point Holohit becomes a regular tent city. For a ride across the estuary, ask around at the small cement pier in San Felipe; a fisherman is always willing to haul you and your gear for about P300. Tell him when you want to be picked up. If you're visiting for the day without any gear, you can swim out from the pier to a close islet for a lazy afternoon. Most of these mangrove islets and sandbars in the estuary are wonderful for birdwatching and a little isolated contemplation surrounded by the soothing sea.

Getting There

San Felipe can be reached by bus from Tizimin. If you're driving, fill up your gas tank before you leave Rio Lagartos or Tizimin since there's no gas station till you get back. Highway 295 meets an intersection one km S of Rio Lagartos; turn L (W) onto a single-lane paved road. When you come to a well-marked fork, take the road on the R, go past the cemetery on the edge of town and into San Felipe. Here, the road dead-ends on the main street which parallels the waterfront. This last section of road is one lane with turn-outs every km in case you meet traffic coming in the opposite direction. The rule of thumb seems to be that outgoing vehicles closest to a turn-out pull over to allow incoming vehicles to pass.

flamingos at
San Felipe

SOUTH OF MERIDA

UXMAL

Located 80 km S of Merida (one-hour drive) in a range of low hills covered with brush, Uxmal is believed to be the hub of a district of about 160 sq. km, encompassing many sites, including Kabah, Sayil, Labna, and Xlapak. The Maya word Uxmal (oosh-MAHL) means "Thrice Built," referring to the number of times this ceremonial center was rebuilt—in fact, it's believed that Uxmal was built 5 times. In many instances structures were superimposed over existing buildings, built almost entirely in the "Puuc" style of pure Maya design. Puuc indicates the "hill" style of construction (because of the location). The work at Uxmal was begun in the 6th and 7th centuries, the Classic Period. It is characterized by delicately carved pieces of stone worked mosaic style into delicate designs and rich facades. Still in place after a thousand years, some of the sapodilla-tree lintels, the cross pieces over doorways and windows, were removed by John L. Stephens, taken to the U.S., and (tragically) destroyed in a fire along with many other priceless pieces. Many consider Uxmal to be the most ornate and complete complex yet found on the Peninsula.

History
There are varied historical claims about this Classic site. Some believe that it was founded by Maya from Guatemala Peten in the 6th century. Others contend that it dates back even further, perhaps to the Pre-Classic Period. By the time the Spaniards arrived it had been abandoned. An account of an early visit was given by Father Lopez de Cogulludo who explored the ruins in the 16th C., long after the Indians had abandoned the site. Without any facts to go on, he referred to the Quadrangle of the Nuns (Las Monjas) as the dwelling of the Maya "Vestal Virgins," who kept the "Sacred Fire." This comment demonstrates the beliefs the first Spaniards held about the evil of the Maya cult, based on some of the sacrificial rites they observed, no doubt. Cogulludo was followed by Jean-Fredric de Waldeck in 1836

who published a handsomely illustrated folio showing the structures of Uxmal peeking over thick brush. He compared them with the ruins of Pompeii. Only a few years later, the famous duo, John L. Stephens and Frederick Catherwood, began their well-documented journey through the Peninsula in 1841. In the interim, the Indians must have cleared the fields around Uxmal to plant corn, since Stephen's comments indicated "that emerging from the woods they came unexpectedly on a large open field strewn with mounds of ruins and vast buildings on terraces and pyramidal structures grand and in good preservation—" shown beautifully by Catherwood's sketches.

Frans Blom

The first real excavations began in 1929 led by the noted Danish archaeologist Frans Blom. Blom was involved in many archaeological digs in the Maya hinterland, and his wife still lives among the Chiapas Indians today, carrying on her own work with the Indians she has come to love and crusade for—trying to save their Chiapas rainforest as well as their culture. Since Frans Blom, many other archaeologists have worked with the Mexican government at Uxmal; the result is a fine reconstructed site open for the enjoyment of the public. Much more will one day be excavated, and who knows what exciting finds will be discovered! But for now the small area (700 by 800 m) of Uxmal presents some of the finest examples of pure Maya design, without Toltec influence, to be seen.

Precious Water

Unlike most Maya centers in Yucatan, Uxmal was not built around a *cenote,* since there are none in this arid part of the Peninsula. Rain water was collected by man-made installations of *chaltunes* (cisterns), built into the ground, sometimes right inside a house or under a patio. Another method for saving water was the use of *aguadas* (holes in the ground lined with a watertight plaster substance). Because of the almost total absence of surface lakes or rivers on the Peninsula, the collection of water has been of prime importance for the survival of the Maya. Most of their religious ceremonies and idols were devoted to the worship of Chaac, the rain god. The constant threat of drought inspired people to build great centers of worship, with hundreds of carvings and mosaics representing him and his prominent long hooked nose.

THE TEMPLES OF UXMAL

House Of The Magician

This "pyramid" is the tallest on the grounds,

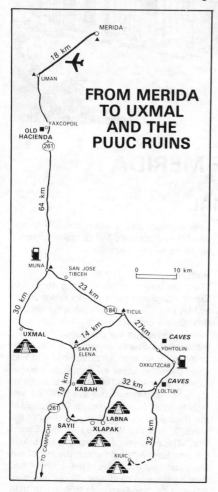

FROM MERIDA TO UXMAL AND THE PUUC RUINS

MERIDA

18 km

UMAN

YAXCOPOIL
OLD
HACIENDA
(261)

64 km

MUNA
SAN JOSE
TIBCEH

0   10 km

30 km

23 km

(184) TICUL

UXMAL

14 km

27 km

CAVES

SANTA
ELENA

YOHTOLIN

OXKUTZCAB

19 km

KABAH

32 km

CAVES
LOLTUN

(261)

SAYIL

LABNA

XLAPAK

32 km

TO CAMPECHE

KIUIC

In order to obtain water during the dry season, the Indians built this steep ladder into Bolonchen cave.

you'll be able to see the entire site of Uxmal and the surrounding brush-covered Puuc hills.

Nunnery
The Nunnery, NW of the House of the Magician, is a courtyard covering an area of 60 by 45 m, bounded on each side by a series of buildings constructed on platforms of varying heights and during different periods of time. The buildings, which contain numerous small rooms, inspired the Spaniards to name it after the nunneries in Spain.

House of the Turtles
A path leads S from the Nunnery to the **House of the Turtles**. This simple structure is 6½ by 30 m. The lower half is very plain, but the upper part is decorated with a frieze of columns and a cornice above that has a series of turtles along its facade. The turtle played an important part in Maya mythology.

Governor's Palace
Just S of the House of the Turtles is the **Governor's Palace**, considered by some to be the finest example of prehispanic architecture in Mesoamerica. It sits on a large platform and measures almost 100 m long, 12 m across and 8½ m high. With 11 entrances, the lower facade is plain, but the upper section is a continuous series of ornate carvings and mosaics of geometrical shapes and Chaac masks. Two arrow-shaped corbel arches add to the delicate design of this extraordinary building. A double-headed jaguar in front of the Palace (presumed to be a throne) was first found by John Stephens in 1841.

The Great Pyramid
Another large structure is the **Great Pyramid** (30 m high), originally terraced with 9 levels and a temple on the top. According to early explorers, at one time 4 small structures sat on each of the 4 sides of the top platform described as "palace-like." The top story is decorated in typical Puuc fashion with ornate carvings and stonework denoting flowers, masks, and geometric patterns.

Others
Walking through the grounds you'll find many

rising 38 m—shaped in a distinctive elliptical form rather than a true pyramid. The W staircase, facing the nunnery and quad, is extremely steep (60-degree angle). Before you begin your climb do some leg stretches to loosen your muscles! Under this W stairway you can see parts of the first temple built on the site; a date on a door lintel is A.D. 569. On the E facade, the stairway has a broader slant, and though still a steep incline, isn't nearly so hard on the legs. In the upper part of the E staircase you can enter an inner chamber which is **Temple 2**. **Temple 3** consists of nothing more than a small shrine at the rear of Temple 2. Climbing the W stairway brings you to **Temple 4** and an elaborate Chaac mask with an open mouth large enough for a man to pass through. **Temple 5** dates back to the 9th C. and is reached by climbing the E stairway. From this viewpoint

Uxmal's Nunnery

other structures and a ball park. Visit: the **Dovecote, Temple of the Old Woman** and **Phallic Collection, Temple of the Phallus,** other small structures, and as yet unexcavated mounds. You can pick up a guide (or he'll try to pick you up) at the entrance of the ruins. If you feel a need for this service, be sure you agree on the fee before you begin your tour. Also something to remember: every guide will give you his own version of the history of the ruins, part family legend (if you're lucky) and part fairy tale. And lets face it, no one *really* knows the history of this obscure culture shrouded by the centuries. Many good books are available on the archaeological ruins of the larger sites

(see "Booklist"). Grounds are open from 0800-1700, admission P40.

PRACTICALITIES

Uxmal is not a city; don't expect services of any kind. There are a few hotels with restaurants, and nothing else close by. To do justice to this fascinating antiquity plan at least a full day to explore thoroughly. Because Merida is only an hour away, it's easy to make this a day trip by or car. Or continue on and spend the night in Ticul, 65 km and one hour farther.

Uxmal's Adivino
Pyramid

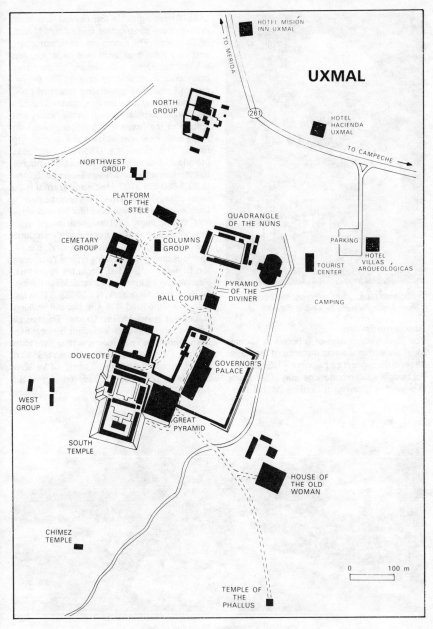

UXMAL

HOTEL MISIÓN INN UXMAL

TO MERIDA

261

HOTEL HACIENDA UXMAL

TO CAMPECHE

NORTH GROUP

NORTHWEST GROUP

PLATFORM OF THE STELE

QUADRANGLE OF THE NUNS

PARKING

CEMETARY GROUP

COLUMNS GROUP

HOTEL VILLAS ARQUEOLÓGICAS

TOURIST CENTER

BALL COURT

PYRAMID OF THE DIVINER

CAMPING

DOVECOTE

GOVERNOR'S PALACE

WEST GROUP

GREAT PYRAMID

SOUTH TEMPLE

HOUSE OF THE OLD WOMAN

CHIMEZ TEMPLE

0   100 m

TEMPLE OF THE PHALLUS

Hacienda Uxmal patio welcomes day-trippers to have lunch, followed by a dip in the pool.

Accommodations

You have your choice of 3 hotels at Uxmal. Most are within walking distance of the ruins. All are in the same price category — US$40-50 d. For budget accommodations, stay in Merida or (if driving or hitching) in Ticul (see p. 141.)

Villa Arqeologico is the newest and most deluxe of the three hotels, owned by a branch of Club Med. The rooms are small, attractive, and very functional, with twin beds, a/c, and private bathroom with shower. Both floors open onto a tropical courtyard. The flower-covered patio has a sparkling (shallow) pool, outside bar and table service, covered cabana area, and a complete library on the history and culture of the Maya. Elegant French cooking along with local specialties in the large dining room. The rates are US$48 d, includes breakfast; dinners average about US$5 pp. For more information and reservations tel. (in the U.S.) 1-800-528-3100. **Hacienda Uxmal** is an older colonial-style hotel. For years it's been a favorite of visitors with beautiful tile walkways and floors, large old-fashioned rooms with heavy carved furniture, tropical garden around the swimming pool, gift shop, and bar. A spacious dining room serves typical Yucatecan food. Rates: US$53 d, includes breakfast. Reservation information address: Maya Caribe, 14 W 95th St, New York, NY 10025. A little farther down the road (1½ km) but still walking distance is **Hotel Mision Uxmal**. This has all the modern amenities including a pool, bar, dining room, and nice rooms with private bath and a/c. Credit cards accepted, rates US$40 d including lunch. Mailing address: 14 W 95th St., New York, NY 10025, tel. (in U.S.) 1-800-223-4084.

campground between Muna and Uxmal

(2nd show) at the ruins overlooking the Quad of the Nunnery. Escorted tours to the shows are available from Merida. If you've never seen one of these shows, check it out. It's mood-altering to sit under the stars in the warm darkness surrounded by stark stone remnants and listen to Hollywood voices and a symphony orchestra echo in stereo from temple to temple, narrating the (so-called) history of the Maya while colored lights flash dramatically on first one and then another of these stark structures. Sometimes Mother Nature adds her own drama: the rumble of thunder from a distant storm, or jagged streaks of luminous light in the black sky. The already eerie temples reflect a supernatural glow evoking the memory of the Maya, their mysterious beginnings and still unsolved disappearance. Admission is P500; buy tickets either at hotels in Uxmal, in Merida at Government Tourist Centers, or any travel agency.

woodcarver of Yucatan

Food
If touring the ruins for the day, all 3 hotel dining rooms welcome visitors for lunch. Expect to pay about P2000-P3500. Bring your swim suit for an after-lunch dip — great for cooling down before you return to the ruins for the next go-around. Close by there are no other cafes for lunch; cold drinks are available at the entrance to the ruins. If driving, take the road back toward Merida (Hwy. 261), 18 km N to Muna, or 11 km S to Santa Elena, where there are small cafes in the villages and a few on the road. Another alternative is to bring your lunch (remember it gets carried up and down the pyramids with you).

Entertainment
Every evening a **Sound and Light Show** is presented in Spanish (1st show) and English

little girl getting early training

Shopping

On the outside of the entrance to the Uxmal site are Maya women and their clotheslines hung with *huipiles* for sale. Their prices can be much better than in gift shops; frequently they're made by the saleslady or someone in her family. Some dresses are machine-embroidered or made of polyester, though many are still handmade on white cotton with bright embroidery thread. Be sure you get what you want. Ask if the colors are fast and how to care for it. The *huipiles* worn by Maya women always look snow white with brilliant colors.

The only other shopping at Uxmal is at the small gift shops adjoining the hotels near the ruins. Most of them sell the usual curios, clothing, tobacco, postage stamps, and post cards. The exception is the **Villa Arqeologico Hotel** next to the ruins where high-quality Maya pottery art depicting the ancient idols is displayed. You can find reproductions in many places, but unlike these, most are not of the best quality and have very little detail. Here, the prices reflect the excellent workmanship.

Getting There

Buses leave Merida's main bus station (Calle 69 #544) daily at 0600, 0700, 0900, 1200, 1500, 1700. Allow an hour for the trip (79 km). Fare is P400; ask to be dropped off at the ruins and check on times the bus returns to Merida. To catch a return bus to Merida, stay on the highway near the ruins — 2nd-class buses will stop if you wave, 1st-class buses will not; after 2000 only 1st-class buses pass Uxmal. The bus from Merida continues on from Uxmal to Kabah and Campeche. Buses to Uxmal leave Campeche from the ADO station (Gobernadores 289).

The highway (261) from Merida to Campeche City passes the Uxmal ruins, and is a good road. From Merida the drive takes about one hour, from Campeche allow 2½ hours (175 km SW). Travel agencies in Merida have tours available to visit the ruins at Uxmal. Check with the government tourist office at Teatro Peones on Calle 61 in downtown Merida.

VICINITY OF UXMAL

Muna

From Uxmal traveling N, Hwy. 261 passes through the rustic city of Muna. Lovers of 17th C. churches might like to look at the large Franciscan church. In the late afternoon sun, the facade with its lacy belfries glows a mellow gold, almost hiding the decay that adds to its appeal. Early in the morning on the edge of the plaza women sell small quantities of fresh fruits and vegetables. Opposite the plaza, a series of open stalls sells cold drinks and Yucatecan snacks including good *panuchos* (mini burrito-types); for the big appetite, go for the *tortas* or tamales. Yaxcopoil, a turn-of-the-century hacienda, is located on Hwy. 261 between Merida and Uxmal. You can stroll through for a taste of the past.

PUUC RUINS

An entire day could be spent making a loop from Uxmal to the Maya ruins of Kabah, Sayil, Xlapak, Labna, through the village of Oxkutz-

cab to see the caves of Loltun (see "Oxkutzcab" p. 139), and Mani. For the most part these are small sites and easy to see or photograph quickly, but the ornate Puuc design is well worth the time and effort.

Kabah

Located on Hwy. 261, 19 km S of Uxmal, Kabah was constructed in A.D. 850-900. Structures are on both sides of the highway. The most ornate building is the **Codz-Pop**, dedicated to the rain god, Chaac. This temple is 45 m long and 6 m high. Part of the original rooftop comb (at one time 3 m high), with its uneven rectangular openings, can still be seen. The entire W facade is a series of 250 masks with the typical elongated, curved nose, some almost a complete circle. This is Puuc architecture with a busy Chenes influence. The Chenes design, a name given by archaeologists to the heavy and ornate style, was added onto the existing structures. The beige, rust, brown, and gray come from the oxides in the earth that engulfed the building for so many years. Small pits on each mask are said to have been used to burn incense or oil; Codz-Pop must have shone like a Chinese lantern from great distances throughout the rolling countryside. The inside of the building is 2 parallel series of 5 rooms each.

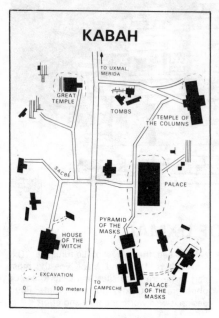

The Arch
West of the road is the impressive **Arch of Kabah**. It is presumed that this arch marks the end of a ceremonial *sacbe* built by the Maya from Uxmal to Kabah. A few more structures have been partially restored—look for the **Great Temple, Western Quadrangle, Temple of the Columns**.

Sayil
A short distance brings you to a side road to Oxkutzcab (Hwy. 184); follow this road to **Sayil**. Several hundred known structures at Sayil illustrate a progression of structures techniques from the earliest, unornamented building to the more recent ornate **Palace** constructed in A.D. 730 (carbon tested). The Palace is a large impressive structure, over 60

m long, with 3 levels creating 2 terraces, again showing the outstanding architectural talents of the Classic Period. The second level is decorated with Greek-style columns and a multitude of rich carvings including the ever-present rain god and one distinctive portrayal of a descending god (an upside-down figure also referred to as the bee god). By A.D. 800 this site was abandoned.

Because of the lack of rainfall in this area, *chaltunes* are found everywhere, including the sites of the ceremonial centers. One example of a *chaltune* that will hold up to 7,000 gallons of water can be seen at the NW corner of the Palace. Other structures to visit at this site include the fast-decaying **Temple Mirador** (on a path going S from the Palace), the monument of a human phallic figure beyond it, and the **Palace With the Heads**.

Xlapak
Six km farther on the same road (E of Sayil) is the **Xlapak** turnoff. Though this Puuc site is small, do stop to see the restored building with

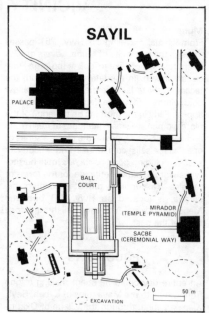

ruin at Kabah

its curious carvings: tiers of masks, curled Chaac noses, collonettes, and geometric stepped frets. It's easy to pick out the light-colored areas of restoration compared to the darker weathered stones that were covered with bushes and soil oxides for so many years. The word Xlapak in Maya means "Old Walls."

Labna

Another Maya arch of great beauty is at **Labna**, located 3 km beyond Xlapak. More correctly the arch should be referred to as a portal vault. Be sure to examine the NE side of this structure to see 2 outstanding representations of thatched Maya huts, one on each side of the portal. This arch is one of the largest and most ornate built by the Maya; the passageway measures 3 by 6 m.

The Palace

This Puuc-style structure was built at the end of the Classic Period, about A.D. 850. The elaborate multi-room pyramid sits on an immense platform 165 m long, and the structure is 135 m long by 20 m high. A *chaltune* is built into the second story of the Palace and, according to archaeologist George Andrews, at least 60 *chaltunes* have been located in the Labna area, indicating a population of about 3,000 residents within the city.

El Mirador

A stark square building with a roof comb—or more accurately, a flying facade—graces the top of a tall pyramid. The comb on the small temple was originally decorated with a carved seated figure and a series of death heads. The carvings were still in place in the 1840s when John Stephens traveled through the Peninsula. The elements and time continue to wreak their destruction on the ancient structures of the Maya.

Mani

This small town, located N of Ticul, was the scene of early surrender by the Xius (prominent Maya rulers with descendants still living in the state of Yucatan). Montejo the Elder quickly took over and by the mid-1500s a huge church/monastery complex was completed in only 7 months by 6,000 slaves under the direction of Fray Juan de Merida. He also designed and built similar buildings at Izamal and Valladolid.

the grand Palace of Sayil

Historians believe it was in Mani that Friar Diego de Landa denounced the books held in reverence by the Maya. These, the first books

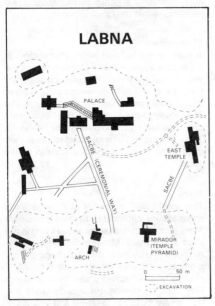

LABNA

PALACE

EAST TEMPLE

SACBE (CEREMONIAL WAY)

SACBE

MIRADOR (TEMPLE PYRAMID)

ARCH

0   50 m

EXCAVATION

produced in N. America, were hand-lettered on fig bark carefully worked until it was thin and pliable, then coated with a thin white plaster sizing and screen folded. According to Landa they were filled with vile superstitions and lies of the devil. Although it's not certain, most believe that it was Mani where the books, called **Codices**, were confiscated by the friar and his Christian followers and burned. Since that time, only 4 more have been found, and the most recent (1977) is doubted to be genuine. The remaining 3 are in museums in Dresden, Paris, and Madrid. Replicas can be seen at the Anthropological Museum in Mexico City. The destruction of the Codices was a monumental tragedy not only for the Maya—the loss to the world is uncalculable. Only a little progress toward learning the mysterious glyphs has been made; who knows—the destroyed books may have been the lost key to their language, their history, and their mystery. It is hoped that other Codices exist and will someday turn up, perhaps in an as yet unexcavated tomb. Many villages still practice the ancient rituals of their ancestors and appoint keepers of the sacred records. However, these people have learned from the experiences of their ancestors and tell no outsiders of their task.

OXKUTZCAB

This small village is known by outsiders because of its proximity to the caves of Loltun. The town itself is ordinary, but the people are friendly and appear semi-prosperous. Land in the area is fertile, and most mornings farmers and their families from outlying areas come to the produce market to sell large quantities of fruits and vegetables by the crate—unusual for most small-town markets. Approaching Oxkutzcab you travel through acres of healthy tall corn fields, giving you the same feeling you would have in a farm town near Kansas City, Missouri. Suddenly you're surrounded by citrus groves, banana trees, and coconut palms. Then you remember—you're in the tropics!

Tricyclettes

A large Franciscan church faces a barren plaza with a strange gazebo in the center and ugly cement benches. A graceful arched building along one side of the plaza is the government center. While looking around you find more examples of stark 16th C. Spanish-influenced architecture. Be careful crossing the streets— you might get run down in the bicycle traffic or overtaken by its 3-wheeled cousin *(tricyclette)* seen in many small towns all over the Peninsula. Similar to an Indonesian *becak,* it has a more utilitarian look and no overhead protection. But the result is the same: providing cheap transportation for the family, with dad pedaling in the back, mom and the kids sitting up front. When not filled with family it's used for hauling anything from a crate of live chickens to a modern TV set. Oxkutzcab's morning streets bustle with people coming to market, big and little trucks parked hither and yon unloading crates of healthy fresh produce. At 1300 all of this activity quiets down and with commerce completed, folks pack up and go home.

LOLTUN CAVES

Seven km SE of Oxkutzcab, Loltun's underground caverns are the largest known

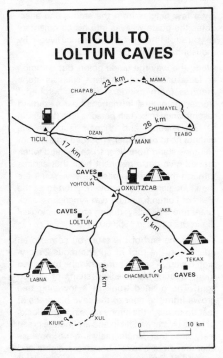

TICUL TO LOLTUN CAVES

caves in Yucatan. In addition to being a fabulous natural phenomenon, Loltun is an important archaeological find. Loltun means "Rock Flower" in Maya and in the caves are carvings of small flowers. Hieroglyphic inscriptions on the walls are said to be 2,000-2,500 years old. Throughout are *chaltunes* placed strategically under the dripping roof to catch water. This saved water was called "virgin water," important in ceremonies that Maya priests directed to the rain god.

A Guided Walk

No one is allowed to visit the caverns without a guide and for good reason. Loltun is immense, and it would be very easy to get lost in the meanderings from grotto to grotto, up and down, for 2 hours, in total darkness. (Select caverns have been wired for light and are turned on and off by the guide as the group moves through.) If you understand Spanish you'll enjoy a few giggles from the stories and anecdotes the guide weaves into his commentary as you stroll through chambers once lived in by thousands of Maya Indians.

Along the way the guide points out common artifacts used by the Indians such as stone *metates* (corn grinders) in the "kitchen." Numerous natural formations bear a startling resemblance to certain persons (like the Virgin of Guadaloupe) and animals (such as the distinct head of an open-mouthed tiger). Giant columns stand from floor to ceiling and when tapped give out a resonant hum that echoes through the darkened passageway. You'll see the stone carved head now referred to as the Head of Loltun found by two Americans, Jack Grant and Bill Dailey, during an archaeological dig in the caves in 1959-60.

Toward the end of the tour you come to an opening in the roof of an enormous 2-story-high cavern. The sun pours into the blackened room creating dust-flecked shafts of golden light. The gnarled trunk of a towering tree grows from the floor of the cave hundreds of feet up through the sunny opening, and flocks of birds twitter and flit in and around the green leafy vines that dangle freely into the immense chamber from above—breathless sights and sounds of nature not soon to be forgotten. Don't miss Loltun Caves.

Practicalities
Wear walking shoes in the caves. For the most part it's an easy 2-km walk; however, it's dark, damp, and in a few places the paths between chambers are steep, rocky, and slippery. Buy your tickets (P250) at the office next to clean restrooms (no restrooms in the caves). Tours begin daily at 0900, 1130, and 1330. Have P400 for the guide at the end of the trip (he'll ask for it). Lectures are usually given in Spanish only, but ask when you buy your ticket for an English-speaking guide; you might get lucky.

If you arrive early or need lunch or a cold drink after walking through the caves, stop at **Restaurant Guerrero**, a small cafe next to the cave exit. The owner is friendly, the beer is cold, the food is tasty and moderately priced: *poc chuc* (barbecued pork filet) or *filete venado*

(venison filet) including bean soup and hand-made tortillas are P800.

TICUL

A busy small city, Ticul has a population of 20,000. Almost everyone is on a bicycle, motorcycle, or is pushing 3-wheel carts. Here is the pottery center of the Peninsula, with ceramics for sale in many small shops lining the streets. Signs extolling *fabricas* (factories) tell of the good value of visiting and buying pottery direct from the potter—complete with location directions. It's well worth a visit to one of these small *fabricas* to watch the artist at work. The raw clay used to manufacture urns, platters, bowls, and tea pots is found at the caves of Loltun just outside of Oxkutzcab (17 km SE on

Ticul is the pottery center of the Peninsula. On the west side of town one factory specializes in oversized reproductions of traditional Maya art.

Hwy. 184, then S 7 km to Loltun on Yuc. 31). A small factory on the W side of town specializes in unglazed terracotta reproductions of classic Maya art. From the highway it's easy to spot, with very large (about 2-m-tall) miniatures of pyramids and idols.

Sights

An elaborate high-domed 18th C. cathedral faces the plaza; next to it is a Franciscan monastery built 200 years earlier. Visit the popular marketplace in Ticul — the earlier in the morning the better — which has a good choice of fresh produce with some unusual fruits. In July and Aug. try the *guaya*. This fruit grows on trees in clusters, and from a distance resembles green grapes, but on closer examination they're much larger, with the same texture, size, and color of the outer green skin of a walnut. Crack the skin and eat the refreshing sweet jelly around a seed — tasty! Ticul, an agricultural center, is a good place to find some cheap produce prices for good quality fresh food including meat — with few tourists around.

Ticul woman bargaining on market day

Accommodations

Rather than stay at Uxmal, which has no low-priced accommodations, many budget travelers find Ticul a good spot to overnight while visiting the Maya ruins on the "loop." The **Hotel San Miguel** is clean and cheap, with rooms for P800 s, P1200 d, P1500 t; P75 for an extra person in the room. **Motel Cerro Inn** (on the outskirts W of town) is a rustic motel with private bathrooms, lots of cooling shade trees, ceiling fans, swimming pool, and large outdoor restaurant. Rooms are P1800 d. For reservations or RV information write to Motel Cerro Inn, Ticul, Yucatan, Mexico. There's room for a few RVs on the motel premises if self-contained (no hookups available). The owner is friendly and will make arrangements to accommodate RV caravans downtown, providing water and a small generator for about US$2.50 per day per RV. Another small hotel, **Conchita**, is located on Calle 21 #199, tel. 2-00-29.

Food

The open-air restaurant at the **Cerro Inn** serves good, simple food at reasonable prices. The cafe is open for breakfast, (good *huevos rancheros* for P350), lunch *(comida corrida,* P450), and dinner (fried chicken plate, P650). In town near the Hotel San Miguel is the **Cafeteria Y Rosticeria Margarita** and a small open market on Calle 23, near the plaza. Another nicer eating spot is the **Restaurant Los Almendros**, N of the highway on Ticul's main street. Only Maya specialties are served and this is reputedly the originator of *poc chuk,* a very popular meat dish served all over the Yucatan Peninsula; even if you're vegetarian and not interested in *poc chuc,* you'll love their homemade tortillas. Another branch of this cafe (same name) is in Merida.

Shopping

Ticul is a center for leather and pottery with ceramic and shoe shops on all the streets. In front of the cathedral, **Centro Artesano** carries locally handcrafted items. Though prices here are often the best, the shops have a better selection. If the local townspeople shout "heepie, heepie" at you, don't be alarmed. They're not expressing an opinion, they're inviting you to see their *jipi* hats, more commonly known as Panama hats. Many folks have small underground rooms (caves) in their back yards where they weave the hats and store them during the dry season so the fiber of the *jijipa* (hee-HEE-pah) plant stays soft and supple while being woven. A few local merchants carry the Panama hats but most are sold in the larger cities of Merida, Cancun, and Campeche.

Getting There

Ticul is on the loop from Uxmal that takes in the important Maya sights of Kabah, Sayil, and Labna. Located 14 km W of Mani and 86 km SE of Merida, odd truck-buses travel frequently between Muna, Ticul, and Oxkutzcab. Fare is P20.

THE STATE OF CAMPECHE

Occupying the SW section of the Yucatan Peninsula, the state of Campeche is bordered by many geographical and political areas: on the N and E by the state of Yucatan, on the NW by the Gulf of Mexico, on the SE by the state of Quintana Roo, on the SW by Tabasco, and on the S by the country of Guatemala. It covers 50,952 sq km and has a population of over 340,000. In the N, the land is dry with little visible water. However, just a few km S of the Campeche/Yucatan border, rivers begin to run, and the land becomes green and tropical. Along the Gulf coast there are several fine harbors, and just a few km inland rolling hills frequently become low jagged mountains.

Climate
Though only a few hundred km separate the northern and southern parts of the state, the two areas exhibit a vast difference in climate. The arid north has little rainfall compared to the thick lush rainforest of the southern and eastern parts of the state, which receive as much as 1500 mm (60 inches) of rain each year. With so much water in the S, abundant lakes and rivers flow into the Laguna de Terminos. The farther south, the more humid the weather.

Fauna
Campeche harbors a variety of animals including peccary, jaguars, tapirs, armadillos, ocelots, and deer; all can be seen (often close up) with a hike into the bush and a lot of patience. Bird hunting is a popular sport supported by quantities of wild duck, wild turkey, and pheasant. Other more beautiful birds for watching only include flamingos, parrots, and herons. The coastal regions along the Gulf are thick with such popular fish as barracuda, swordfish, dolphin, tuna, snapper, as well as lobster and shrimp from the tiniest to the largest.

History
Several Maya towns in various pockets of the state are believed to have been trade centers between central and southern Mexico, as well as important crossroads between the N and E

part of the Peninsula. Twenty years after the first Spaniards arrived in Campeche, it was finally conquered by Francisco de Montejo. The state's capital, also called Campeche, was founded on 4 Oct. 1540, and soon developed into the major port of the state. During the 16th and 17th centuries the city was attacked repeatedly by vicious European pirates—destroyed and rebuilt several times over a period of many years. The Spanish crown finally approved the expenditure of funds to build a magnificent wall with protective bastions. This mighty rampart of immense proportions had gates that heaved open to give sanctuary to vessels fleeing from ships flying the "skull and crossbones." Some of the wall is still standing. For years a part of the State of Yucatan, in 1863 Campeche became an independent state.

Economy

Along with all of the Peninsula, without roads or communication systems, Campeche was isolated from the development of the rest of Mexico. Only since the beginning of the 1950s has Campeche really begun to enter the 20th C. and join the outside world. Good highways have been built; logging the precious woods of the rainforest remains high in economic contributions; agriculture is starting to thrive; fishing has grown from a family industry to big business; and the greatest boon of all has been the discovery of offshore oil. With some fine archaeological sites attaining fame, tourism is also developing within the state.

ARCHAEOLOGICAL ZONES WITHIN THE STATE OF CAMPECHE

EDZNA	HOCHOB
DZIBILNOCAC	NOCUCHICH
XCALUNKIN	CALAKMUL
HORMIGUERO	BECAN
CHICANA	XPUJIL
RIO BEC	ISLA JAINA

CAMPECHE CITY AND VICINITY

Campeche, capital of the state of the same name, is a growing city with a population of 125,000. The city lies along the Gulf coast and is approximately 16 m above sea level. Campeche is a late-comer in the growth of tourism compared to Quintana Roo and Yucatan. However, in recent years the city has realized the potential of its old wall, *baluartes,* and Maya ruins, notably Edzna located 64 km from Campeche. These attractions, along with the feeling of old Spain, is drawing more tourists than ever. It has a long way to go before it's considered a tourist destination; as a result today's travelers benefit by low prices. An example: Campeche's El Presidente Hotel is the most moderately priced of the entire chain.

HISTORY

Campeche's past is steeped in lore of the sea. During prehispanic times the Campechean coast bore the title of *Ruta Maya* ("Route of the Maya"), a main artery for Maya traders on both land and sea. Ah Kin Pech was a medium-sized village on the shore of a small bay surrounded by hills. Until 20 March 1517, the Maya people had never seen a white man; on this day the first Spaniards arrived in their village. After 25 years passed—25 years of bloodshed for both the Spaniards and Indians—Maya power in Ah Kin Pech had been destroyed. Despite the difference in arms (the Spanish musket against the Indian lance), innate intelligence and a deadly determination to repel the intruders gave the Maya a cunning that persisted an entire generation.

Pirates

In 1542 the present city of Campeche was established by Montejo the Younger, whose family conquered the Indians in Merida. After the Spaniards gained control of Campeche harbor, the financial attention of Francisco Hernandez de Cordoba (appointed viceroy to Mexico by the King of Spain) and Juan de Grijalva (Spanish explorer) enabled the city to blossom. Campeche City was destined to become a jewel of Spanish colonial development. The riches of the Peninsula were regularly channeled to Spain from here in ships belonging to the Spanish king. Tales of this great treasure drew the attention of those who resented Spain's hold on the fabled riches of the New World; sea-going highwaymen were determined to get their share—and more. A crafty breed of pirates began regular attacks on ships carrying the king's gold and silver. From 1558 for almost 2 centuries, the city of Campeche was harassed, burned, and sacked by buccaneers who'd taken up permanent residence—208 km away—on the Island of Tris (today called Ciudad del Carmen).

Accounts of Campeche's wealth eventually traveled through every major port in Europe; pirates (such as Laurent Graff "Lorencillo," John Hawkins, William Parck, Diego el Mulato, Barbillas, James Jackson, and Pie de Palo "Pegleg") came all the way from England, France, Portugal, and Holland. In the 17th C. the pillaging and killing increased. On 9 Feb. 1663 the buccaneers joined forces, gathered their ships on the horizon and launched a furious attack. They completely wiped out the city, killing men, women, children—the worst massacre in the city's history!

Walled City

Finally, the Spanish crown agreed the city needed protection. A plan was formulated and quietly the work began. On 3 Jan. 1668 the cornerstone of the new walled city was laid. The "wall" that surrounded Campeche was stout stone construction, from 3 m thick to ship's height. Eight "gates" or forts in the wall were placed strategically around the city. Indeed, in an effort to make this bastion impregnable, the wall extended right into the water, with huge gates that allowed ships to pass through into the fort! Though finishing touches weren't made until 36 years later in 1704, the completion of a sturdy bastion (its counterpart unknown in the Americas) finally gave Campecheans security against their invaders that would ultimately end the era of invasion. Still, isolated attacks upon the coastal cities S of Campeche continued from the pirates' notorious base island. Finally in 1717, determined to wipe the bandits out, in a sneak attack Captain Don Alonso Felipe de Aranda routed or killed all the pirates and burned their ships. Once and for all peace reigned over the Gulf coast.

After The Pirates

The next 200 years were occupied with the business of developing a peaceful society, including the growth of an economy not dependent on the shipment of silver and gold. The initial rumblings of Mexican independence began during the first decade of the 1800s. By 1832 Mexico was free from Spanish colonial

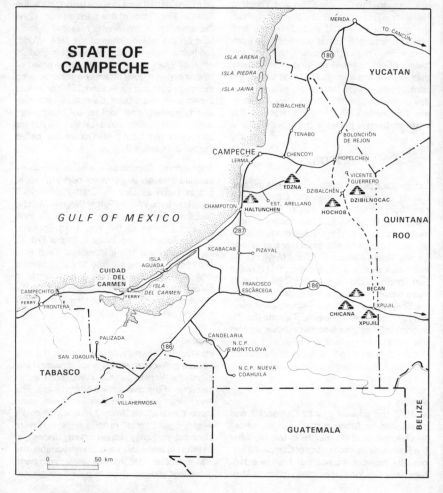

rule, but many years and many presidents passed before peace settled over the country. Campeche, though isolated from much of greater Mexico's turmoil, suffered from its own problems of development. For years Campeche was part of an alliance with Merida, but several years after the Caste War, in 1863, it seceded and became part of the Federal Republic of Mexico as an independent state.

The People

Before the Mexican revolution, Campeche City was inhabited almost exclusively by descendants of colonial Spaniards. During the early glory days after the wall was built and the pirates finally destroyed, life was good for the landowner. The Indians were slaves and suffered the same indignities as their fellows in the rest of the land. In 1813 the first moves were made to abolish slavery. Campeche settled in-

to an era of humble existence that saw few economic changes for many years.

The main industries were fishing and logging. The fishing trade helped the economy, but it was a local business until it began exporting fish to the U.S. and other countries in the 20th century. Even after tourists began visiting Mexico in the 1950s and '60s, the Peninsula was still not commonly considered a destination on visitors' itineraries.

Oil

Only after oil production began in earnest in the 1970s did Campecheans start living above the poverty level. All along the Gulf coast the oil industry grows. And if the value of a barrel of crude quits its volatile swings, Mexico should benefit by its enormous quantities of "black gold" still untouched.

SIGHTS

Central Plaza

Located near the sea, the central plaza is bordered by Calles 8, 10, 55, and 57. This charming spot provides a resting place between walking tours around the city. Renovated in 1985, contemporary wrought-iron fences and benches have been installed. Though Campeche is endowed with the charm of 1700s' architecture, the city fathers seem determined to add the cold glitz of outerspace shapes, plastic, and glass. But even with its rather odd modern gazebo in the middle, the square's feeling of antiquity is overwhelming. The central plaza is bordered on one side by **Cathedral Concepcion**, the oldest Christian church on the Yucatan, constructed from 1540-1705. On Calle 10, the Plaza faces **Los Portales**, another aging building with a graceful facade and arcaded passageways. Sunday concerts are held in the plaza on alternate weeks. (Check with the Office of Tourism on Av. Ruiz Cortines facing the sea for dates.) Incongruous or not, the plaza is still the heart of the city: families gather, friends meet, and children play. The scene is reminiscent of eveningtime in small cities in Spain. In case you're wondering, the square glass building near the waterfront with the colorful mosaic is the **Palacio de Gobier-**

no. The concrete building next to it that somewhat resembles a flying saucer is **Congressional Hall.**

Forts

Many remnants of the fortifications around the city remain more or less intact. Though neglected for years, even partially destroyed to make way for trolley tracks, the remaining ramparts have managed to survive modern architects and violent storms, leaving a wonderful old-world ambience to Campeche. What was formerly the sea wall and ship's yard within the gate were filled in some years back for a wide avenue and new buildings on a modern waterfront. You can visit 7 of 8 original forts: **San Francisco, Soledad, Santiago, Santa Rosa, San Pedro, San Juan,** and **San Carlos,** now used as a variety of public buildings. Beneath some of them remains a labyrinth of passageways that at one time connected with various houses in the city and were used by women and children to elude kidnappers during attacks by ferocious buccaneers. If you have a guide, ask about the tunnels; some will take you to the few that are open, though most have been sealed for years.

Fort San Miguel/Museum of Archaeology

A trip to this museum, formerly **Fort San Miguel**, located 2.5 km W of town, puts you right into the past, to 18th C. construction including moat and drawbridge. One can feel the terror that motivated inhabitants to build such sturdy protection—so sturdy that it has survived 200 years. Today in the fort, Campechean artifacts are displayed along with pre-Columbian pottery. Don't miss the exhibit of the wooden contraption used to deform the heads of newborn infants, giving them the deep sloping forehead considered beautiful by the ancient Maya. To get to the museum, follow the coastal road S until you come to the large statue of a man with a raised arm, a work titled "The Resurgence of Campeche."

At one time the old city was surrounded by a protective wall.

Fort Soledad

Now the **Campeche Museum of History**, this is the largest of the forts on the city's seaward side. The displays are reminders of the battles that took place during the siege of the pirates. From that time you'll find sextants, arms, ship figureheads, and other memorabilia. Open 0900-1400, 1500-2000, Tues. to Sat; 0900-1300 Sun.; closed Monday. See the Maya fountain close by. Easy to find near the waterfront on Calle 8 across from the central plaza; small entry fee.

Fort Santiago

Here you'll find the **Jardin Botanico Xmuch Haltum**, a small garden with many species of plants native to the arid plains in the N and the green jungle of the wet southern region. This walled garden is a short but worthwhile trip. **Fort Santiago** is located on Av. 16 de

lofty guard house of old Spanish fort

Septiembre near the waterfront. As well as enjoying the garden, each of these ancient gates is a wonder of architecture which shouldn't be missed.

Museo de Armas

On the SW corner of Circuito Baluartes, in the former *baluarte* called **San Carlos**, is a museum displaying the variety and types of arms used by the Spaniards while conquering the Americas. Small admission fee; Calles 8 and 65.

Church of San Jose

This first lighthouse in Campeche was raised in 1864. The original part of the structure, **The Church of San Jose**, was built by Jesuits in 1700; the adjacent building, a Jesuit college, was constructed in 1756. The church, impressive with its quixotic tile facade, is now half museum and half gift shop. History of the building is as varied as the city of Campeche: from church to army post to warehouse to gift shop-museum. The paintings on display represent a striking contrast: 2 giant religious murals are placed next to a modern artist's violent portrayal of what was wreaked upon the Maya Indians in the name of God.

detail of beautiful tilework of the former Church of San Jose

Campeche city streets are a mix of the old and the new.

PRACTICALITIES

ACCOMMODATIONS

In a city the size of Campeche, one might expect a larger number of hostelries. Though not as many as expected, there's still a good selection in each of the 3 categories, with a YH and a trailer park to boot.

Budget

The **CREA Youth Hostel** (IYHF) is very clean and offers segregated dorms with bunk beds, P650 pp. The well laid-out grounds are neatly kept and roomy, with a swimming pool, ball park, and cafeteria (acceptable food at budget prices). Breakfast is served 0730-0930, lunch 1400-1600, dinner 1930-2130. To get to the YH from the center of town, take the bus marked "Campeche Lerma" going S along the coastal highway to the corner of Melgar. If you're so inclined, it's about a 20-min. walk from the central plaza.

Another good value for your *peso* is **Hotel Castlemar**, located in an old colonial building 3 blocks S of the plaza. A relaxing patio with ornate tile provides a quiet place to visit or read. The large rooms have ceiling fan, private bathroom, and hammock hooks; if you're lucky and have a choice, ask for a front room with a balcony. The management is friendly and willing to answer questions. P1200 s, P1600 d; located on Calle 61 #2, between Calles 8 and 10. Check out 2 other budget hotels: **Hotel Campeche**, a generic inn, is clean with reasonable prices, P1000 s, P1550 d, located on Calle 57 between 8 and 10; and **Hotel Roma** is reasonably clean, some rooms have bathrooms, all have fans and hammock hooks, unexciting but cheap; P1100 s, P1500 d; on Calle 10 #254 between 59 and 61, tel. 6-38-97.

Moderate

In the colonial setting of a 3-story mansion, the **Hotel America** offers clean rooms, nicely furnished with typical touches of the era, including tile bathrooms, marble floors, and ceiling fans; P2100 s, P2500 d; located on Calle 10 #152, tel. 6-45-88.

In a modern setting, friendly, family-run **Hotel Lopez** has clean rooms simply furnished, ceiling fans, a/c (available for P500 extra), bathrooms, and central courtyard. Rates P2500 s, P3000 d; P3500. Located 3 blocks from the central plaza at Calle 12 #189, between 63 and 65, tel. 6-33-44/6-30-21.

Also centrally located near the plaza, **Hotel Mexico** offers clean rooms with bathrooms and ceiling fans. Not all rooms have windows, but all open onto an agreeable courtyard; there's a lounging area on the 2nd floor. The management is congenial, helpful, and provides drinking water. P2500 s, P3000 d; on Calle 10 #329 between 59-61.

Luxury

El Presidente overlooks the sea, and has nicely appointed rooms, a/c, coffee shop (open all day) and dining room, bar, disco, and 2 swimming pools. Non-guests can swim in the pools without charge. US$29 d, reservations needed in December. On Av. Ruiz Cortinez #51, tel. 6-22-33/6-00-31.

Hotel Baluartes fronts the promenade that runs along the water across the street from El Presidente. It's clean, has well-furnished rooms, swimming pool (non-guests can swim for a small charge), sidewalk cafe, bar, dining room and banquet facilities. P6600 s, P7200 d, P8000 t, including tax. Located on Av. Ruiz Cortines, tel. 6-39-11.

Toward the S end of town across the street from the waterfront, the Moorish-style **Hotel Alhambra** is the newest (opened 1985) of the 3 luxury hotels. Away from the hustle and bustle of town, it offers clean rooms, private bathrooms, a bar and restaurant. This is very popular with Mexican families during summer vacation. P5500 s, P6000 d, P6800 t, plus tax. Located on Av. Resurgimiento 85, tel. 6-68-00/6-68-22.

Trailers And Campsites

With complete hookups for trailers and RVs, the **Campeche Trailer Park** is a countrified spot eight km SW of the central plaza near the small community of Samula. The bathrooms are clean with hot showers, the managers speak some English, soft drinks and cold beer are for sale; P1500 for 2. Turn from the ocean road onto Melgar and follow the signs. Address is Apto Postal 241, Campeche, Campeche, Mexico.

FOOD AND ENTERTAINMENT

Seafood is naturally the culinary highlight of this Gulf coast city. The price for shrimp and prawns by the kg is less than half what you pay at your fish market back home. These delicacies are a favorite restaurant item, whether at a fancy hotel dining room or one of many small cafes around town. And when advertised as "giant," that's what they are! You can get delicious and generous shrimp cocktails in the smaller cafes away from the waterfront and larger hotels from P400 to P800. Cafes serve generous *comida corrida;* you have no choice of selection, though it usually includes fried fish—guaranteed fresh—and the price is right (about P450). Also, a growing number of fast food-type cafes sell *tortas,* or if you yearn for a hamburger try the **Pinkus** cafes (Parke Pinkus on Campeche-Hampolol, or Pinkus Burger on Av. Francisco I. Madero). For real budget food,

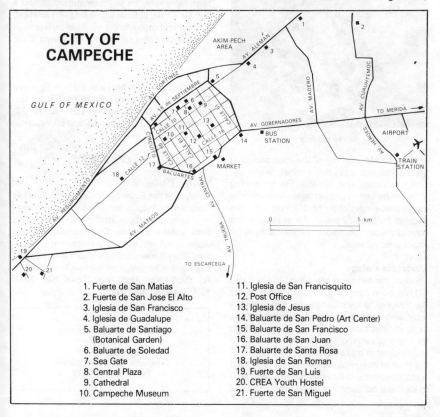

CITY OF CAMPECHE

GULF OF MEXICO

TO MERIDA
AIRPORT
TRAIN STATION
TO ESCARCEGA

1. Fuerte de San Matias
2. Fuerte de San Jose El Alto
3. Iglesia de San Francisco
4. Iglesia de Guadalupe
5. Baluarte de Santiago (Botanical Garden)
6. Baluarte de Soledad
7. Sea Gate
8. Central Plaza
9. Cathedral
10. Campeche Museum
11. Iglesia de San Francisquito
12. Post Office
13. Iglesia de Jesus
14. Baluarte de San Pedro (Art Center)
15. Baluarte de San Francisco
16. Baluarte de San Juan
17. Baluarte de Santa Rosa
18. Iglesia de San Roman
19. Fuerte de San Luis
20. CREA Youth Hostel
21. Fuerte de San Miguel

the marketplace

as in most Mexican cities, the food stands in the marketplace serve *tipico tortas,* beans, tortillas, *panuchos,* and tamales. For something different try barbecued venison—a Campeche marketplace specialty. Fruit lovers—try the unusual fruits you'll see at the markets or the buys of the season. Avocados (for instance) for about a nickel each.

Moderate Cafes

Though the **Miramar** restaurant (Calle 8 and 61) has been operating for many years, it has the flavor of today's Campeche, and is always busy with visitors and residents alike putting away excellent seafood. The **303 Club** is a treat for a special evening. Located in an old colonial building, what makes this restaurant special is the truth of its surroundings. It's obvious that it wasn't created (a la Disneyland) and decorated to look like old Spain; what you see is the real

thing cared for and maintained over a very long period of time. The dining area is a series of 14 cozy rooms, each seating 8-16 people, many on the 2nd floor. The menu is very "old continental," with unexpected extras such as pate before dinner and a fresh basket of rolls and croissants brought with each course. Naturally, seafood is highlighted, but you can find other tasty offerings, even a spaghetti dinner (a bargain at P600), steaks, veal cutlets, rich desserts and wonderful sangria, served in white linen elegance.

Discos

For night music the hotel discos are the best bet for adults—**El Ancla** at the Hotel El Presidente, and **El Olones** at Hotel Baluartes. Both have lively music, dramatic lights, and a bar. **La Copa**, at Calle 8 (behind El Presidente), is noisy and caters to the younger teen crowd. Close by, another hot spot is the **Maya**, Calle 59.

Cinema

Four theaters offer Mexican films in Spanish: **De la Cruz**, Calle 8 between 51 and 53; **Jardin**, Calle 12 and Bravo; **Salem**, Calle 12 and 57; **Teatro**, Calle 12 between 51 and 53.

SERVICES

Tourist Office

Located at the Plaza Moch-Couoh on Av. Ruiz Cortines is a helpful tourist information center. You'il find at least one staff member at all times who speaks English. They hand out good street maps and hotel and restaurant information. They'll make local calls for reservations if you have a language problem. Open Mon. to Fri. 0900-1300, 1500-1800. Open Sat. 0900-1300; tel. 6-60-68/6-67-67.

```
Federal Dept. Of Tourism
Av. Ruiz Cortines
Plaza Moch-Couch
Campeche, Campeche, Mexico.
Tel. (9 19 81) 6-38-47
```

Banks

Though Campeche appears to have banks everywhere, not all of them cash traveler's cheques or exchange foreign currency. The two mentioned below give good service: **Banamex** located on Calle 10 #15 is open Mon. to Fri. 0900-1300, tel. 6-52-52; **Bancomer** on Calle 59 #2A (across from Baluarte de Soledad on Av. 16 de Septiembre) is open Mon. to Fri., 0900-1300 tel. 6-21-44.

Postal Service

Edificio Federal at Av. 16 de Septiembre and Av. Ruiz Cortines is open for both telegraph and postal business, selling stamps, accepting outgoing mail including registered mail, 0800-1900, Mon. to Fri.; 0800-1300 Sat.; Sun. for stamps only 0800-1400; tel. 6-43-90. Telegraph service is in the same building as the post office; go to the right as you enter the building. Open to send telegrams Mon. to Sat. 0800-2000, Sun. 0900-1300; for money orders Mon. to Fri., 0900-1730, Sat. and Sun. 0900-1200.

Medical

For medical emergencies ask the hotel to refer you to an English-speaking doctor, or call **Seguro Social**, tel. 6-18-55; located on Lopez Mateos on the S side of the city.

Laundry

There's a laundromat on the S end of the *malecon* called **Lavamatic**.

Emergency Numbers

Fire Dept.—tel. 6-23-09. Policia—tel. 6-23-29. Red Cross—tel. 6-06-66/6-52-02.

GETTING THERE

Campeche is centrally located on the Gulf coast, 252 km SW of Merida and 444 km NE of Villahermosa (across the Tabasco border). On the main highway, Campeche is a natural stopover for the trip between these two capitals.

By Plane

Campeche connects by air to some cities in Mexico. Check with Mexicana Airlines located on Campo Aero and Calle 10, #365; tel. 6-18-93. Though small, the airport is modern and services good. Two km NE of the city, taxis meet most flights and charge P500 to the town center. Another option is the bus; walk 100 m down the service road (Aviacion) to Av. Nacozari. Turn R (W) and wait for a bus marked "China-Campeche." Wave your arm; he'll stop and take you downtown for P20.

By Train

The train station is 2 km NE of town center on Av. Heroes de Nacozari; taxi fare is P400 from downtown. The bus marked "China" passes in front of the station and can be caught at the market or Av. 16 de Septiembre downtown, P20. The state tourist office (see above) has the most recent schedules, prices, and information. Trains to central Mexico or Merida run daily. Get to the station at least an hour early to buy tickets and recheck departure time. If you want a *dormitorio*, make reservations at least one day in advance.

By Bus

Four blocks NE of the city on Gobernadores #289 between Calle 47 and Calle Chile, the bus station houses both 1st- and 2nd-class buses. The **ADO** (1st-class) terminal has a restaurant, waiting room, and baggage check-in facing Gobernadores; the 2nd-class terminal is on the opposite side (enter through 1st-class or Calle Chile). ADO offers more frequent service to Ciudad del Carmen, Villahermosa, and Merida. Check the schedule at the terminal for departure times to the Caribbean coast, Chetumal, Mexico City, and all other destinations throughout Mexico. The 2nd-class bus makes frequent trips to nearby archaeological zones; to Edzna daily at 0800 and 1430; and to Dzibalchen, near the sites of Dzibilnocac and Hochob; figure 2 hours OW (P400) at 0800, 1600, and 1900. You'll see the countryside, with frequent stops made in small towns along the way.

By Car

Two good highways link Merida and Campeche: Hwy. 180 *via corta* (the short route), and

TAXI STANDS

Taxi stands are located at the intersections of:

Calle 55 and Circuito, close to market.
Calles 8 and 55, left of cathedral.
Gobernadores and Chile, close to bus terminal.
Costa Rica and Circuitos Baluartes
Central and Circuito Baluartes.
Or order up a cab by calling tel. 6-23-66/6-52-30.

Hwy. 260 *via larga* (the long route). If you're making a RT to or from Merida, try both roads to see more of the countryside (traveling time is almost the same both ways: 2-3 hours). Hwy. 180 runs S parallel to the coast, and crosses a bridge which brings you to Isla del Carmen; to continue S you must travel on a series of ferries from Isla del Carmen to the mainland; staying on Hwy. 180 ultimately brings you to the state of Tabasco. To Chetumal (Caribbean coast) it's 421 km from Campeche; N to Cancun (Caribbean coast), it's 514 km.

GETTING AROUND

The old city located within the ramparts of the ancient wall is well laid out, and once you figure out the numbering system for the 40 square blocks, walking is a piece of cake! The streets that run E to W, perpendicular to the sea, are numbered odd from 51 on the N to 65 on the south. Streets running N to S are even-numbered, beginning with Calle 8 on the W through Calle 18 on the E (see city map). Most of the more popular sights and services are located within these ancient boundaries, set off by the 7 remaining forts built by Spanish settlers. This old part of the city is surrounded by Circuito Baluartes on 3 sides, and on Av. 16 de Septiembre on the seaward side. The city outside the wall is creeping ever outward toward the mountains, N and S, up and down the coast. Campeche has a good bus system covering the entire city, in and out of the wall; the fare is P20 to go anyplace in town. Bus stops are located on most corners or, as is so convenient in Mexico, they'll stop most anyplace. Remember that in Campeche W is always toward the water and E is inland.

Car Rentals

Getting around within the city is quite simple either on foot or by bus. But if you wish to visit the outlying areas at your leisure, a car rental is recommended. Prices fluctuate daily with the floating *peso,* so shop around for your best buy (see "Car Rental Info," p. 63). Try **Hertz**, Prolongacion Calle 59, Edificio Belmar, tel. 6-48-55; **Autos y Camionetas de Renta**, Calle 57 #1 in Hotel Cuauhtemoc, tel. 6-34-67; and **Easy Rent a Car**, Hotel Baluartes.

NORTH OF CAMPECHE

ISLA JAINA

Burial Grounds Of The Elite

North of Campeche City, close off the coast, lies the Island of Jaina which has the largest known Maya burial ground on the Yucatan Peninsula. According to archaeologist Sylvanus Morley, who discovered the impressive site in 1943, Jaina was used for burial ceremonies for the Maya elite since A.D. 652.

Statues found on Isla Jaina at burial sites show anatomical realism and minute details indicative of everyday living. This man is wearing a false nose piece which was considered a sign of class.

The most important and powerful dead were carried in long and colorful processions great distances from all over Central America to the small island. Bodies were interred in burial jars in a crouching position, with a statue resting on the folded arms. Some were found with a jade stone in the mouth; the skin was often stained red and then wrapped either in a straw mat or white cloth. Plates with food, jewelry, weapons, tools, and other precious items to accompany them to the other world were placed on their heads.

In 1950 more than 150 skeletal remains were discovered along the banks of Jaina rivers. The clay burial offerings (beautifully crafted figurines, some with moveable arms and legs) found on the island have given us detailed information about the customs of dress, religion, working and living habits of the Maya. The clay figures have been compared to statues found in other ancient civilizations such as China, Greece, and Persia.

Climbing the Pyramids

The ancient Maya outdid themselves again in developing this offshore island. Jaina's low elevation was raised by building platforms made of *sascab* (limestone material) brought from the mainland in canoes. This material covered the brittle coral of the island and allowed the Jaina Indians to build two imposing pyramids, **Zacpool** and **Sayasol**, as well as altars and other ceremonial structures on the island.

If you decide to climb to the top of these structures to see the magnificent view, use caution; the steps are narrow and steep. There are several ways to climb a pyramid. Some sites have such a steep slant that a chain or rope has been attached from top to bottom to hang onto as you climb the steps in an upright position—good idea, use it! However, many pyramids don't offer this thoughtful assist, such as those on Jaina. Since the structures are so steep, try walking a zig-zag pattern, putting each foot sideways on each step and walking diagonally across the staircase, then

*a ball player with protective
leather padding*

making a "switchback" in the opposite direction till you reach the top. Or—some experienced climbers suggest—an easy (and acceptable) way is to use both hands and feet in a crawling position straight up—don't look down!

Transport
There's no public transportation to Jaina. If you would like to visit the island ask at your hotel or a travel agency in Campeche for information about escorted tour groups. The trip takes about 4 hours, about P2000 depending on the type of boat.

HECELCHAKAN

Around 75 km N of Campeche on Hwy. 180 going toward Merida, make a stop at Hecelchakan's **Museo Arqueologico del Camino Real**. Here are displayed some fine examples of Jaina burial art. Hecelchakan is a small city; the museum is easy to find near the center of town N of the church. Also, the next time you visit Mexico City, go to the Anthropological Museum at Chapultepec Park to see a superb exhibit of .Maya art, including the best of the Jaina graves.

Services
If you're driving, there's a large modern **Pemex** gas station as you approach Hecelchakan. This station is one of the first of many that Pemex plans to install all over Mexico. The new service for visitors includes a representative of the Dept. of Tourism to answer questions about the area in several languages and hand out maps and brochures, including Green Angel information. Best of all, each station is scheduled to have a clean modern restroom.

EAST OF CAMPECHE

EDZNA

As you approach Edzna on the road from Cayal (about 60 km SE of Campeche), a tall pyramid rising from thick vegetation on the valley floor is visible from quite a distance. The site covers an area of 6 sq. km in the midst of a wide valley of cultivated land side by side with scrub forest bordered on two sides by a low range of mountains. This Maya city is off the beaten track, but easy to get to from Campeche.

The Temple Of Five Stories
People lived at this site as early as 600 B.C., and the existing structures are dated from around 300 B.C. to A.D. 200. The city grew and prospered for 7 centuries until A.D. 900 when it (along with many other Classic centers) was suddenly deserted for reasons yet undiscovered. The largest structure is on the E side of a large open area called **Plaza Central**. This 5-story pyramid has an open comb on top, seen on only some Maya structures in different areas to add the image of more height and bring the temple closer to the heavens. At one time this comb was covered with ornate stucco carvings and the rest of the stones of the building were coated with smooth stucco and painted brilliant colors. Over the centuries the elements have worn away the stucco coat, exposing rough stones beneath.

Edzna in Maya means "House of Grimaces"; the name comes from the masks that decorate

the comb of **The Temple of Five Stories.**
This structure sits on a base that measures 60
by 58 m and is 31 m tall. There are 4 levels of living quarters (used by Maya priests) with a
shrine and altar on the highest level and the
roof comb on top of that. Under the first floor
stairway is a corbel-vaulted tunnel that leads to
an inner chamber. The architecture is simple
compared to the ornate facades of the Puucs
only a couple hundred km down the road.

Surrounding Temples

At Edzna you can't help but be impressed with
the elegant planning of each center. The
buildings are gracefully placed around open
plazas and platforms, blending nicely with
nature. It must have been the Beverly Hills of its
day. On the W side of the plaza is the restored
Temple of the Moon "(Paal u'na"). On the two
corners of the plaza stand the **Southwestern**

Temple and the **Northwestern Temple,** with
the sweat bath next door. Another plaza surrounded by structures not yet excavated (or
previously excavated and overgrown again) is
called **Grupo del Central Ceremonial.** Here
beneath the vegetation you'll see the **Great
Acropolis, Great House, Platform of the
Knives,** and **Southern Temple.** Part of Edzna
is below sea level but the Maya, with their incredible engineering skills, solved the drainage
problem by building a complex system of
underground canals and holding basins.

In the 1920s the American Sylvanus Morley
and Mexican archaeologist Enrique Juan
Palacios studied the glyphs; those on the stairs
of the Temple of Five Stories are still in
remarkably good condition. More work was
done in the 1940s by the Palenque specialists
Alberto Ruz l'Huillier and Raul Abreu. Eventual-

Unimaginatively named Temple of Five Stories sits on Plaza Central.

ly the remainder of this lost city will be excavated and studied. Edzna is open from 0800 to 0500, admission P40.

Getting There

If you're driving from Campeche, take 180 E to Chencoyil, then go N on 261 to Cayal where you turn R and continue to the Edzna site. From Campeche, about 60 km, it's a one-hour drive. From the bus station in Campeche a 2nd-class bus leaves twice daily at 0800 and 1430. Unless you have great faith in your hitchhiking skills, forget the 1430 trip since the only return bus passes the ruins between 1130 and 1200. Allow 1½ hours for the trip. Campeche hotels will line you up with an escorted tour to the ruins, or check with any one of the travel agencies in the city.

According to legend, Maya captives were bent backwards over a stone altar, making it anatomically easy for the priest to swiftly remove the heart of the sacrificial victim and offer it still beating to their gods.

carved glyphs on step fronts on Edzna's tallest pyramid

SOUTH OF CAMPECHE

LERMA

Seven km S, just before reaching Lerma on 180 from Campeche, a sign points to a dirt road that's marked PLAYA BONITA. You'll find a *balneario* that is advertised as *the nicest* beach in or around Campeche. Though without the white sand and gorgeous blue sea of the Caribbean, the beach has sand, showers, lockers, dressing rooms, *palapa* sun shelters, and a large pavilion for food, drink, and music. This is a popular spot for Mexican vacationers during the summer *temporada.* Lovely homes line the shore. Just past Playa Bonita is Lerma. This small industrial city is really a suburb of Campeche, a fishing town that grew up along with now large shipyards, fish processing plants, and harbors filled with numerous commercial boats. Lerma is one of the main centers for exporting fish, a large part of the Campechean economy.

SEYBAPLAYA

Thirty-three km S of Campeche (on Hwy. 180), the small town of Seybaplaya has occupied this choice spot on the Gulf coast long enough to have been victimized by pirates — without a protective rampart. This small fishing village is an ideal place for artists and photographers. The waterfront is lined with posts where fishermen tie up their boats; at mid-day every post has a resident pelican that poses statue-like with wings extended, drying in the sun. You'll also see fishermen mending nets, drying them in neat rows along the beach, or unloading fish from open *lanchas.* These broad open boats with at least a 40-hp outboard motor hold 4 working men and their equipment. If you'd like to buy fresh fish, halfway down the coastal road across from the waterfront is a public market (large green building). The center of town is definitely not for swimming, with remnants of dead fish and the workings of a fleet of

boats. However, at the extreme N end of the bay is a dirt road to a bit of isolated beach called **Balneario Payucan** that's good for a cooling swim. At the junction of Seybaplaya and Hwy. 180 to Campeche, an open-air restaurant called **Veracruz** sits on the water's edge; the cafe serves great red snapper. Other than a couple more eating spots there's little else to see. Take the 2nd-class bus from Campeche to Seybaplaya, two RT daily.

Fuerte de San Miguel is located high on a hill overlooking the bay, ready to blast pirates out of the water.

drying nets along the Gulf coast

SIHO PLAYA

If driving from Campeche S on 180 toward Isla del Carmen, a few km before you reach Champoton is **Hotel Siho Playa**, a relaxing spot on the water to spend a lazy afternoon and an overnight—or more. The original structure was an old hacienda, part of a large sugar plantation. Remodeled and added to some years back, it's a favorite with Mexican families. The rooms are clean, with two double beds, a/c, and private bathroom with shower. A dining room overlooks the sea, and the garden is bordered with grass, which a gardener expertly trims with a curved machete. There's a large swimming pool, and a sandy beach area for sunbathing or watching a continuous show of gliding man-o-wars and pelicans diving for their dinner. A stone quay jutting into the water is commonly covered with sunbathing iguanas of all sizes. For the more energetic there's a tennis court and arrangements can be made for hunting and fishing. In summer months it's comparatively quiet with few guests and limited staff. The disco/bar closes down, with

no outside service by the pool, and it isn't unusual for a lightning storm to knock out the electricity (even without power the cooks manage to prepare an outstanding fresh fish dinner). All of which makes this an extremely attractive destination for anyone that revels in a low-key atmosphere. In Campeche check with the Tourist Office on Plaza Moch Couoh (near Hotel Baluartes facing the sea) and they'll make reservations for you at Siho—during the winter you may need them. Room rates are P4700 s, P5175 d.

CHAMPOTON

Dating from prehispanic days, this waterfront town is spread out on the banks of the Rio Champoton with a small lagoon at the mouth of the river. Because of its proximity to Guatemala it played an important role in the cultural exchange between Guatemala, Yucatan, and central Mexico. Earliest history places the Toltecs and then the Maya in Champoton, followed by the Spaniards in 1517. On the S side of the city you can still see the remnants of a fort built in 1719 to defend against violent pirate attacks. Today the small town is home to an ever-growing fishing fleet and a certain amount of fallout from the oil industry. In fact, all along the coast between Siho and Isla del Carmen, you'll see much more evidence of successful oil business than you really want to.

For The Sportsman

Another attraction of Champoton is hunting and fishing. Its location in the middle of thick jungle makes it an ideal spot to find such exotic animals as pecarry, brocket and white-tailed deer, jaguar, ocelot, jaguarundi, and puma. Bird hunters might find ocellated turkey, royal pheasant, crested guan, scaled pigeon, ducks, morning and white-wing dove, and *chachlaca.* Fishing enthusiasts claim this is the place to catch the biggest tarpon and snook.

The easiest way to hunt in this jungle area is with a guide that knows the ropes; several are available. Recommended is the Sansores family. For fishing and birds they offer Snooks Inn, 14 a/c rooms with a swimming pool and modern conveniences located in Champoton. For big-game hunting they have 3 jungle camps S of Campeche, (about 64 km from the Guatemalan Peten). The camps are primitive but the staff makes you very comfortable; the food is good (and plenty) with purified water and ice. For further information and brochures write to Jose Sansores, **Hotel Castlemar**, Campeche, Campeche, Mexico. Or telephone in Mexico, (981) 6-55-38/6-23-56. Start writing at least 6 months in advance which allows time for an exchange of mail and documents necessary to obtain gun permits and licenses.

Accommodations

Most of the hotels in Champoton are simple and in the budget class.

Food And Services

The restaurants are simple and—you guessed it—fish is usually the star on the menu. However, during certain times of the year you'll find wild game specialties such as *venado* and *pato.* Another local favorite along the Gulf coast is *pan de cazon* (hammerhead shark). Though there are several banks, for exchanging currency go to the **Banco del Atlantico**, open Mon. to Fri. from 0900-1230.

Transport

Both the coastal road (261) and Hwy. 180 at this point go right through Champoton. If traveling by bus from Campeche (check at the Campeche bus station on Gobernadores #289), both 1st- and 2nd-class buses pass through Champoton on their way to Ciudad del Carmen. The highway is usually busy with all kinds of traffic if you're hitching.

ISLA DEL CARMEN

This sandbar/island has been occupied since the earliest Maya fisherman. In 1558 it was taken over by a band of pirates that chose this spot as their lair. Within striking distance of the port at Campeche City, the pirates attacked the ships time after time, killing the sailors and stealing the cargo of silver and gold on its way to the Spanish king. Called the Island of Tris at that time, the pirates maintained their stronghold until 1717 when they were finally killed or driven out by the army. Today the 38-km-long island is inhabited by 80,000 people, mostly at Ciudad del Carmen (located at the SW end), the only city on the island. Formerly most of the townspeople were fishermen and coconut farmers; today new

CHAMPOTON HOTELS

Hotel Snook Inn	Calle 30 no. 1	8-00-88/8-00-18
Hotel Geminis	Calle 30 no. 10	8-00-08
Hotel D'Venecia	Calle 38	8-01-45
Hotel Imperial	Calle 30 no. 38	8-00-10
Hotel Champoton	Calle 28 no. 38	8-01-25

demensions have been added—the oil industry, a thriving shipbuilding community, fish-processing plants, and a prosperous shrimp fleet that grows yearly.

Sights

Ciudad del Carmen is not considered a tourist town, but for people with a curiosity about the oil and fishing industry and how it is developing in Mexico, this is a good spot to explore. Wander around the dock E of the ferry landing and you'll see shrimp-processing plants and one of the major fleets of shrimp boats on the Mexican Gulf—another good place for picture taking. At the **Liceo Carmelita** there's a small archaeological museum with some locally found artifacts on display. The central plaza presents free band concerts on Thurs. and Sun. evenings.

Water Sports

Although water sports are advertised (waterskiing, sailing, and swimming), by far the biggest attraction is fishing. Carmen is a crescent-shaped island creating a large lagoon (Laguna de Terminos) between it and the mainland. The lagoon is a combination of fresh and salt water; the blend makes for delectable-tasting fish! Fishing charters are available for deep-sea sport, or just 15 min. from the city are island streams where you can find snook, *corbina,* and *mojarra.* Swimming is best at either **El Playon** or **Playa Benjamin**. The resorts advertise snorkeling; however, once you've sampled the clear Caribbean water, Carmen's water will never satisfy you.

Fiesta

The people of Ciudad del Carmen take part in a yearly festival on 15-31 July, paying homage to their patron saint, the Virgen del Carmen, with a great celebration. Everyone on the island participates in this lively celebration. If you like dancing, fireworks, and partying people, try to get there early for a room, or make reservations for this busy time.

Food And Entertainment

It's not difficult to find a cafe to fit your budget. The nicer hotels have the better dining rooms with a more varied menu. Of course, shrimp and prawns are featured and are very sweet! The public market on Calle 39 and 20 is the usual source of quick and inexpensive tacos, tamales, *tortas,* and fried fish. Supermarkets have a fair selection of basics most of the time, and there are bakeries and *tortillerias.* Most of the nicer bars are in the hotels; however, you'll find a couple of active discos along the avenues.

CIUDAD DEL CARMEN DISCOS

El Corsario	Hotel Lili-Re	2-05-88
Pioneros	Aeropuerto	
Alfa Centaury	Hotel Lino's	2-17-65
El Granero	Hotel Los Andes	2-23-89
Umma Guma Disco	Lopez Mateos	
Disco Flamboyanes		
Privado	Calle 47 & 26	2-10-82

ISLA DE CARMEN HOTELS

Casa de Huespedes Carmen	Calle 20 no. 142	2-00-56
Hotel Villa del Mar	Calle 20 x 33 no. 45	2-04-12
Autel 35	Calle 35 no. 406	2-19-40
Hotel Zacarias	Calle 24 no. 58	2-01-21
Hotel Linos	Calle 31 no. 132	2-07-88
Hotel Lli-Re	Calle 32 no. 23	2-05-88
Isla del Carmen	Calle 20A no. 9	2-23-50
Hotel del Parque	Calle 33 no. 1	2-30-46
Hotel Lossandes	Periferico	2-23-89

Services

Travel agencies include Ixtoc on Calle 35 & 30 and Turismo Bahamita on Calle 28 #150, tel. 2-15-00. **Car rentals** are available at Auto Rentas del Carmen, Calle 33 #21, tel. 2-23-76 and Auto Panamericana, Calle 22, tel. 2-23-26. The municipal **police** can be reached at tel. 2-02-05, the regional **hospital** at tel. 2-03-06. You'll see many banks; go to **Banpais** or **Banco del Atlantico** for currency exchange. **ADO** bus station is located on Calle 24 #48; a taxi stand is located at the bus station, tel. 2-03-01.

Getting There

With the active oil and fish industry at Ciudad del Carmen, the airport becomes more efficient each day. Several airlines now service the island.

Reaching Isla del Carmen on Hwy. 180 from Campeche takes about 3 hours. From Champoton the road is narrow and a little hilly, often with lots of truck traffic. The new bridge *Puente de la Unidad* ("Bridge of Unity"), longest in Mexico (3.25 km), connects the mainland with Isla del Carmen. Buses run frequently from Campeche to del Carmen; check schedules at the bus station in Campeche on Gobernadores #289. For ongoing trips S, N, or E, check in Ciudad del Carmen at the ADO 1st-class bus station (on Calle 24 #48). The 2nd-class station is walking distance from the central plaza.

To Tabasco

Anyone continuing on to Villahermosa should be prepared for a long day—start early. From Ciudad del Carmen a series of ferry crossings ultimately brings you to the town of Frontera, the border town between the states of Campeche and Tabasco. Be prepared for a wait at each dock, and try to arrange to complete the entire trip in daylight. For a faster route to Tabasco, drive from Champoton S on Hwy. 287 which joins 186 at Francisco Escarcega, where you have the choice of traveling E to Chetumal in the state of Quintana Roo, or SW toward Villahermosa in the state of Tabasco. This route takes you inland, eliminating Ciudad del Carmen and the ferry crossings through the estuaries.

AIRLINES SERVING ISLA DEL CARMEN

Mexicana Airlines	Calle 22 x 37	2-11-71
Aero-Campeche	Calle 22 no. 182	2-09-98
Aviatur	Calle 26 x 29-A	2-01-30

ESCARCEGA

Escarcega is growing from a grubby little railroad stop (where you formerly thought twice before stepping off the train) to a neat respectable village of 10,000. While far from being a tourist town, many hunters and adventurers pass through each year on their way to exploring the surrounding jungle. It's also becoming an important crossroad connecting the Yucatan with the rest of the world, especially since the oil boom hit this part of the Peninsula. As the outsiders come, the services increase.

Accommodations

Escarcega lies 149 km S of Campeche, and is most often used as a gas stop on the way to Chetumal (270 km) and the E coast of the Peninsula. Merida is 355 km N, and Villahermosa is 297 km SW. If you find it necessary to overnight, expect very simple hotels in the budget class.

Food And Services

The cafe at the **Hotel Maria Isabel,** though simple, serves the best meals in town. Several other small cafes around are adequate. The **market** (beginning on Calle 31 on the corner of the plaza) has ample food supplies. There's a **Bancomer** on Calle 31 #26 for currency ex-

---

ESCARCEGA HOTELS

Akim Pech	Ascarcega-Villahermosa Rd.	
Bertha Leticia	Calle 29 no. 28	4-00-11
EL Yucateco	Hector Perez Martinez no. 42.	
Escarcega	Justo Sierra no. 86	4-01-87
Maria Isabel	Justo Sierra no. 127	4-00-45
San Luis	Calle 28	

change. The **long-distance telephone** is found at Perez Martinez 30, open 0800-1300 and 1600-2000 daily. **Post office** is on Calle 28-A. The **Social Security Hospital** can be reached by tel. 4-01-92. The **police** can be reached at tel. 4-00-39.

Transport

Escarcega is located at the junction of Hwys. 186 and 261. The town is 1½ km W of the highway. If driving follow the signs into town. If traveling by bus most of the services are downtown and accessible on foot, though it's easy to flag down a taxi. The **ADO Bus Station** is at the intersection of Hwy. 261 and Justo Sierra. The **2nd-class** bus station is on Justo Sierra and Calle 31. The **Caribe** bus station (for buses E to the Caribbean coast) is on Hector Perez Martines 3 blocks W of the plaza. The **train station** is ½ km up the tracks, N of Mendez. Two trains pass through daily headed for Campeche and Merida and 2 in the opposite direction toward Coatzacoalcos and Mexico City.

ARCHAEOLOGICAL SITES NEAR ESCARCEGA

Chicana

Roughly 145 km E of Escarcega is Chicana. The turnoff is ½ km from the ruins. An elaborate serpent mask frames the entry of the main palace called **House of the Serpent Mouth**—in comparatively good repair. Several hundred m into the bush is another structure built at the same time, though not as well preserved. Throughout the area are small and large ruins, none of which have been restored.

But if you're curious to compare the subtle differences of design and architecture of the ancient Maya throughout the Peninsula, it's worth a day's visit to this group.

Becan

On the main highway another 2½ km is the turnoff to Becan. You'll see an unusual waterless moat, 15 m wide and 4½ m deep, that surrounds the entire site. It's believed this protective-style construction indicates warring factions occupied this part of the Peninsula during the 2nd century. A few buildings have been excavated but show little or no restoration. The surrounding forest hugs the perimeter of the site, and wildlife roams freely through the once-regal ruins.

Xpujil

Six km E of Becan are 3 towers. Pass through the small village of Xpujil, then continue on to this classic example of Rio Bec architecture: the remains of 3 false towers overlooking miles of jungle. On the back side of the central tower check out what's left of 2 huge inlaid masks. If you're in a vehicle that can handle a primitive jeep road, Rio Bec can be reached by taking the road S of the gas station near Xpujil.

This is also an ideal place for birdwatching in thick jungle with little or no tourist traffic. Don't forget bug repellent! If you're traveling by bus to Chetumal, check with the tourist office or a travel agency for bus trips to these sites. Though not restored, these ruins will give you an indication of what the archaeologists find when they first stumble upon an isolated site. You will have renewed wonder at how they manage to put together a pile of stones and end up with such impressive structures.

THE STATE OF CHIAPAS

The most southeasterly state of Mexico, Chiapas is bordered in the W by Oaxaca and Veracruz, in the N by Tabasco and Campeche, and in the E by Guatemala. It covers 74,415 sq km and has a population of 1,932,000. A large part of Chiapas lies in thick rainforest with innumerable lakes, rivers, and waterfalls throughout the hilly region. The rugged mountains of the Sierra Madre del Sur average 1,500 m and some peaks are as high as 3,000 m. One of the few volcanos of this region is atop the 3,000-m peak of Tacana, overlooking Mexico's southern Pacific coast and the city of Tapachula. This bustling business center is a popular stopover to or from Guatemala—complete with smog.

Climate

Chiapas, deep in the tropics, is continuously hot and humid, especially during the rainy season, May to October. Rainfall can be as high as 4,000 mm (160 inches) in the mountains, somewhat less in the lowlands. Occasional hurricanes from the Gulf and the Caribbean pass over southern Mexico—but infrequently.

History

The earliest inhabitants of the Chiapas area are presumed to be the Olmecs. Following them, the Maya settled in during the Pre-Classic Period, and left their mark during the Classic Age when they created their most outstanding structures. After years of fighting, the Spaniards assumed control of the area in 1530, and as in all of their conquests, subjugated the Indians. When made bishop in 1544, Bartolome de las Casas began to implement changes for the better. He tried to abolish slavery, and managed to convince the Spanish crown to provide legal protection for the Indians throughout the New World. Although marginally successful, it was a first step. Bishop de las Casas is held in great respect by the Indians of the area. Through the years, until Mexico's independence in 1823, Chiapas was under the legal jurisdiction of the Spanish in Guatemala. Repeated Indian risings against the Spanish colonialists and the Republic continued through the years until 1911; the last was by the Tzotzil and Tzeltzal tribes. Chiapas has plodded along, mostly hidden from the world in its rainforests. Along with an increase in tourism, mining silver, gold, and copper, oil is bringing new money into the state.

Only now is the outside world beginning to effect modern changes in the state; some tribes of Indians still remain virtually isolated in the mountains (mostly by choice). The tribes of the Tzotzil, Zoque, Tzeltal, Chol, and Lacandon, though shrinking in numbers, still speak their own language and practice the traditions of the ancient past.

Economy
For many years the chief industry was harvesting and exporting timber. Today, add cocoa beans, coffee, and most importantly, oil. Tourism is making strides in the state: Chiapas offers some of the finest Maya stone cities on the Peninsula. Oil money is providing the base to build roads, extend advertising, and improve facilities for tourists—but slowly!

ARCHAEOLOGICAL SIGHTS IN CHIAPAS

PALENQUE	BONAMPAK
YAXCHILAN	CHIAPA DE CORZO
CHINKULTIC	TONINA
IZAPA	

HETZMEK

The Maya woman took the infant, maybe 6 months old, and spoke slowly and reverently to him in a Maya dialect as she placed a gold bracelet on each tiny wrist. The young mother and father watched the "godmother" intently as she introduced the infant to his future. On a table between them lay a book, a coin, a weeding blade, a gun, and scissors. *"Koten, Antonio Cuitok, ten kin mentik hetzmek tech*—Come, Antonio Cuitok, I make the *hetzmek* for you." She went on, "I give you all these things to hold; so that you learn them when you grow up." She picked up the book from the table, a Catholic Missal, and read several prayers from it, then placed it in the baby's tiny hands. "I give you this book so that you will learn to read." Then the blade—"...that you will learn to farm"—the gun, etc., until all the items were given and explained.

Then the godmother placed the baby astride her left hip, a signal that he'd passed from infancy to babyhood. She then circled the table counter-clockwise 9 times. Though the godmother was dressed in a beautiful white *huipil*, embroidered with bright flowers, the baby was dressed in 20th C. style: a blue nylon romper suit.

The ceremony was complete, the baby's future now assured. The 9 lords of the night would protect him—with some help from the Christian Church; the bracelets pledged good health during his first 2 years.

In each community, *hetzmek* is carried out in a slightly different manner. Some must call in a friend from another village because no one at home remembers all of it. Though the ceremony might differ from village to village, the child is always shown his potential future and placed astride the hip for the first time on this day. Who knows how many hundreds or thousands of years the ceremony has been repeated or when the Christian components became part of it? But its powerful roots signify the continuation of the Maya people.

PALENQUE AND VICINITY

Palenque is a *do-not-miss* attraction on any itinerary of Maya ruins. The setting, on a lush green shelf at the edge of the Sierra de Chiapas rainforest, adds to the serenity of this noble compound of ornate carvings and graceful design. Located in the W part of the Peninsula about 150 km SE of Villahermosa, the structures are continually being excavated and restored. It may be several lifetimes before all of the still-buried ruins are revealed. But those structures that have been freed from the jungle offer a mysterious, awe-inspiring vision of great pomp and opulence. Experts say some 8-11 km of unexcavated buildings surround the present site.

In a recent breakthrough scholars have been able to decipher enough of the many glyphs to construct a reasonable geneology of the Palenque kings, over a roughly 300-year period, from the rule of Chaacal I (A.D. 501) to the demise of Kuk (A.D. 783). But it was during the reign of Lord Shield Pacal and his son, Chan-Bahlum (A.D. 615-701), that Palenque grew from a minor site to an important ceremonial center. Again we see the brilliance of the Classic Period (with beautiful sculpture, unusual life-size carvings, and innovative architectural design). These buildings are outstanding even within the context of comparable sites of the same period constructed throughout the Peninsula.

Passed By
Somehow the *conquistadores* missed Palenque completely, although Cortez passed within 35-45 km of the site. By that time, however, Palenque had been long abandoned. The earliest recorded comments on Palenque were made by a Spanish army captain, Antonio del Rio, who passed through in March 1785. He drew maps and plans and was highly criticized by archaeologist J. Eric Thompson for "bulldozing" the ruins. Captain del Rio broadcast wild and fantasy-like assumptions about

the beginnings of the Maya. After visits by a few other laymen who took home strange drawings, it wasn't long before the people in Europe envisioned Palenque as the lost city of Atlantis or part of Egyptian dynasties. When Americans John Loyd Stephens and Frederic Catherwood wrote about the site and drew outstanding realistic reproductions in the mid-1800s, a true picture of Palenque began to emerge.

Palenque's one-of-a kind 4-story building

Everywhere on the grounds you'll see reminders of the great leader Lord Shield Pacal. Carvings of him and his family, as well as some of the finest examples of Maya funerary art, are found in many of the structures. Palenque is renowned for its extraordinary stucco bas-relief sculpture. Rather than work in smaller figures, typical of most art everywhere, the Palencanos created figures often as tall as 3 m.

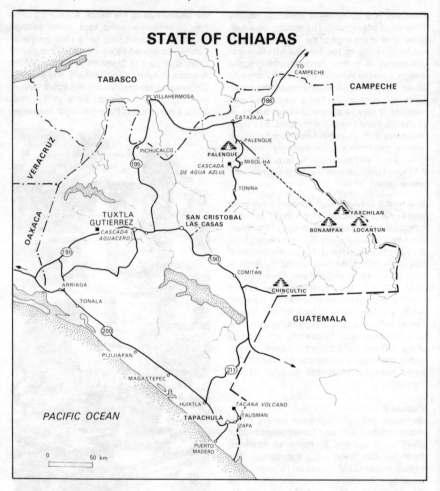

STATE OF CHIAPAS

Temple of the Inscriptions at Palenque's archaeological zone

SIGHTS

TEMPLE OF THE INSCRIPTIONS

After walking through the entrance and past Temple XII (also called Temple of the Skull—look for the carved skull on the lower right corner) and XIII on the right side of the road, you'll come to **Temple of the Inscriptions.** This 24-m-high pyramid kept a secret hidden within its depths for over a thousand years, until 1952. At the top of the 8-stepped pyramid is the Temple, where magnificent tablets of glyphs tell the ancestral history of the Palenque rulers. The rear gallery is divided into 3 chambers. Here, cleverly hidden under a stone slab floor of the center chamber, Mexican archaeologist Alberto Ruz L'Huillier (in 1949) first uncovered a stairway filled with rubble. After 3 years of excavating the steep passageway, he made a great discovery.

Untouched Crypt
At the foot of the stairs another sealed passage was found, in front of which were clay dishes filled with red pigment, jade earplugs, beads, a large oblong pearl, and the skeletons of 6 sacrificial victims. When the final large stone door was removed, L'Huillier experienced the lifetime dream of every archaeologist in the profession: before him was the untouched crypt of the much-revered ruler, Lord Shield Pacal. On June 15, 1952 after 3 years of hard work, L'Huillier entered the small room for the first time. The centerpiece of the chamber is the sarcophagus topped by a flat, 4-m, 5-ton slab of stone. The magnificent slab is beautifully carved with the figure of Pacal in death surrounded by monsters, serpents, sun and shell signs, and many more glyphs that recount death and its passage. The walls of the chamber are decorated with various gods, from which scientists have deduced a tremendous amount about the Palencanos' theology.

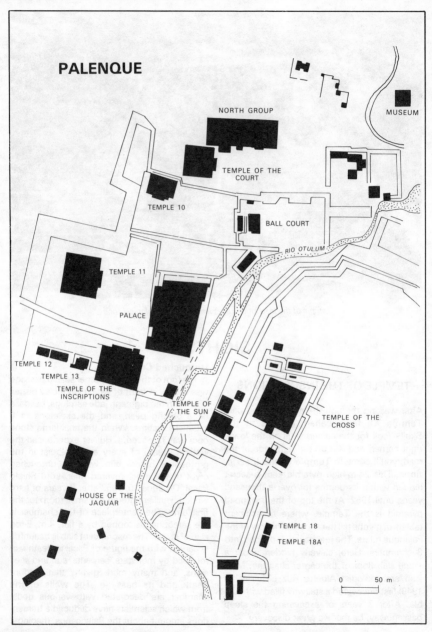

PALENQUE

NORTH GROUP

MUSEUM

TEMPLE OF THE
COURT

TEMPLE 10

BALL COURT

RIO OTULUM

TEMPLE 11

PALACE

TEMPLE 12

TEMPLE 13

TEMPLE OF THE
INSCRIPTIONS

TEMPLE OF
THE SUN

TEMPLE OF THE
CROSS

HOUSE OF THE
JAGUAR

TEMPLE 18

TEMPLE 18A

0   50 m

Further Discovery

Working slowly to preserve everything in its pristine state, L'Huillier didn't open the lid of the sarcophagus for 6 months. It took a week of difficult work in the stifling, dust-choked room to finally lift the 5-ton slab. On Nov. 28, 1952 the scientists had their first peek into the sepulchre. In the large rectangular cement sarcophagus they found another body-shaped sarcophagus (a first in Maya history), within which were Pacal's skeleton, with precious jewelry and special accoutrements to accompany him on his journey into the next world. A jade mosaic mask covered the face, under which his own teeth had been painted red. The mask was exhibited at the Anthropological Museum in Mexico City until Dec. 24, 1985 when it was stolen along with several other precious historical artifacts. It is estimated the man was taller than the average Maya of the time. A disagreement between scientists stemming from different methods of deciphering the number-glyphs has given him a choice of ages at death. Some say he was 80-100 years

into the tomb

old, while others say he was only 60 at the most. We may never know for sure.

This excavation began a new concept in Maya archaeology. It was formerly believed that the pyramids had served a single function, as a base for temples brought closer to the heavens. But now it's possible that other pyramids were used as crypts for revered leaders. All of this bears a resemblance to the culture and beliefs of the Egyptians, and imaginative students of history have tried to link the two cultures, so far unsuccessfully.

The Climb

The Temple of the Inscriptions is probably the most difficult climb at Palenque, but don't let that stop you. To reach the Temple, you walk up 69 very steep steps. Take it slow! At the top, while catching your breath, study the fine panels and carvings in the Temple, then begin your trip down the stairs into the depths of the pyramid. Occasionally the lights of the abrupt stairway leading down into the crypt are off; check with the ticket-taker before you make the climb. The steps can be slippery, and without light it's pitch black! An iron gate

sarcophagus of Lord Shield Pacal

Palenque's Palace dominates the entire site with stately beauty.

allows you to view the burial chamber without entering the room (a flashlight helps). The magnificent carved slab is suspended several centimeters above the sarcophagus.

The stairway passage is wide, unlike the pyramid of Cheops in Egypt where all visitors must go up and down a single-file claustrophobic ramp. The climb from the Temple back to ground level can be made down the steps (a little shorter) on the back side, where you'll find a path through the forest and up a hill to the small moss-covered **Temple of the Foliated Cross** that seems to be in imminent danger of takeover by the thick jungle once again.

OTHER SIGHTS

The Palace

Palenque's **Palace** is one of the most unique structures on the Yucatan Peninsula. Located to the R and across from the Temple of the Inscriptions, the Palace occupies the unusually large space of a city block. The eye is caught immediately by the 4-story tower, another rarity of the Classic Maya. It's believed that the tower was constructed to give a good view of the winter solstice (Dec. 22) when the sun appears to drop directly into the Temple of the Inscriptions. It was also used to make astronomical calculations—an important part of their daily lives. A dominating structure, larger-than-life panels are still clearly recognizable thoughout the site; various glyphs which line steps and walls give an insight into the life of the Maya during the reign of Pacal. The Palace sits on a platform 10 m high, and labyrinth underground passageways and tunnels can be explored. While wandering you'll discover more than 10 buildings and several courtyards on different levels, and discoveries continue to be made today.

More Temples

The restored buildings cover a fairly small area, making it easy to investigate each structure. Other buildings to look for are the **Temple of the Cross, Temple of the Sun, Temple of the Count, Temple XIV,** and the **North Group.** Many still have distinct carved tablets within. Visit the **ballpark,** where today you're apt to see a vigorous baseball game going on, with the steps of a once-sacred temple serving as bleachers! Near the N group of buildings (turn L as you enter the grounds), a small **museum** displays a selection of artifacts found on the Palenque site; small admission fee. Near here is a stream ideal for a refreshing dip. The small structure sitting kitty corner from the Temple of the Inscriptions entrance is a memorial to Alberto Ruz L'Huillier.

SANTO DOMINGO

The community of Santo Domingo, often referred to as Palenque, is 8 km from the archaeological site. The small town bulges at its seams with the influx of tourists interested in the Palenque ruins. Hotels, cafes, curio shops, a large shady plaza, and a tourist information office help make the traveler feel welcome. Note, however, that the Indians living in the surrounding rainforest, who come colorfully dressed to Santo Domingo for supplies, mostly don't like to have their pictures taken. If you wish to take a photo, *ask* first; some of the locals used to seeing travelers might agree (with a tip). However, if you persist after their efforts to hide, cover their face, or turn their back, don't be surprised if one of the Indians grabs your camera and throws it over the nearest precipice. This is a strong religious belief (albeit changing); respect it.

Economy

The town itself has matured over the past 10 years from a dirt-road village to an amiable small city. Much of the surrounding area has been cleared of trees and jungle (to the consternation of ecologists who believe it's blasphemous to cut a tree) and converted to cattle-grazing land. Some of the small farms are growing into large agricultural complexes. Fine mahogany forests have been destroyed

THE TUMPLINE

Like the deity of his Maya ancestors, this man carries his heavy load with the help of a tumpline around his forehead.

by outside lumber companies which have bought the timber rights from local Indians. Many say this will ultimately destroy the lush rainforest and the culture of the Indians that has survived in this isolated world for centuries.

Tourism is beginning to take hold as the biggest money-maker for the city. In Santo Domingo, you'll find most services necessary for a few day's stay. The largest numbers of visitors come in tour buses and pass through quickly, but Palenque also has become a gathering

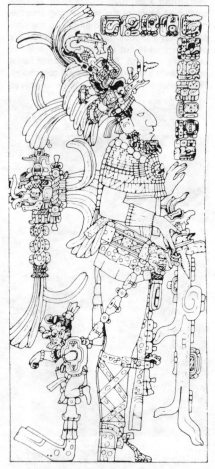

panel in Temple of the Cross

place for backpackers from all over the world. And psilocybin seekers. The wise pilgrim will ask fellow travelers rather than locals about the mushroom trade, since the government has offered good rewards to be informed of 'shroom activity.

ACCOMMODATIONS

Budget
For such a small town it's amazing how many hotels are scattered about. Most are simple inns in the budget category. The **Hotel Regional** offers small rooms with overhead fans, reasonably clean with tile floors, and have private toilets. Rates: P1100 s, P1400 d. Located on Aldama and Juarez. **Hotel Vaca Vieja**, on a side street that parallels Av. Hidalgo, is a little gem for the money. Extremely clean, each room has a private bathroom, overhead fan, tile floors; an open skylight down the middle of the upper corridor lets in light and moisture that nurture lovely plants which add a nice touch to the simple hotel. On the main floor the small dining room serves excellent food and is very reasonable. Rates: P1350 s, P1700 d, P2000 t, 5 de Mayo #42; tel. 5-03-88.

The **Hotel Palenque** is near the Plaza. The rooms are simple and clean, with choice of fan or a/c. And if a swimming pool is important, you'll find one surrounded by a small garden. Rates: P1600 s, P1950 d, P2200 t, add P300 for a/c. Located at 5 de Mayo and Jimenez; tel. 5-01-03/5-01-88.

Several other budget hotels in town include the **Hotel Avenida**, Calle 20 de Noviembre, tel. 5-01-16, P1600 d; **Casa de Huespedes Leon**, Av. Hidalgo, P1000 s or d; and the **Hotel Misol-Ha**, Av. Juarez, #12, tel. 5-00-92, P1200 d.

Moderate
Hotel de las Ruinas is 1½ km E of the ruins. This clean modern-style motel surrounds a swimming pool and has private bathrooms, ceiling fans, and outdoor dining room. Rates: P2500 d. On the main highway coming into town (about one km N of the plaza) you'll see **Hotel Tulija**. The rooms are simple, there's a/c, private bath, swimming pool, and a/c din-

airy open-sided dining room at Hotel Chan Kah, Palenque

ing room. Rates: P2600 d. Other moderate hotels in Santo Domingo are the **Hotel Casa de Pacal**, Av. Juarez, #10, P2200 d; and **Hotel La Canada**, one km S of the plaza, tel. 5-00-20, P2200 d.

A Cut Above

None of the hotels in Palenque is really deluxe, but a few have rooms a cut above average, or are sensationally located. The following fall into that group. Approximately 2.2 km SW of town on the road to Agua Azul is the **Hotel Nututum** in a lush green setting on the Rio Chacamax. The rooms are modern, with fans or a/c, some with kitchen facilities, waterfall baths, swimming in the river, and an outdoor dining room that overlooks the water and jungle. A small gift shop sells cards, T-shirts, suntan lotion, and a few sundries. Nighttime entertainment is presented during the high season. Rates: P4000 d, suites available; tel. 5-01-00.

If you're a birdwatcher (or not), you'll enjoy **Hotel Chan-Kah**. Here a series of roomy

cabanas with large open porches are perched on the edge of an arm of a river in the midst of thick jungle. The rooms are well kept, fan cooled, with decorative stone-lined bathrooms and lots of privacy. An attractive *palapa*-roofed building houses the reception desk, lounge area, and dining room, with jungle vines dangling exotically down the open sides. The food is very good; cocktails are served. From your front porch, you can see many exotic creatures of this jungle. Guests have claimed to spot the elusive quetzal bird with its rich blue green plumage, once common in the area and used by Maya royalty for their headpieces. The owner, Roberto Romano, speaks English, is a font of information about Palenque, and can usually be found at mealtimes in the dining room. In answer to the oft-asked question about drinking the water (which comes from a spring behind the Temple of the Inscriptions at the ruins), Senor Romano passes out a little card that explains it this way: "This water endowed the men who lived thousands of years ago on this site with the capability of a superior mind and who by drinking it brought to light the zero and discovered the infinite." However, if you still have doubts, ask for bottled water. Rates: P5500 d. The hotel is located about 3 km E of the ruins. For reservations write to Hotel Chan-Kah, Apto. Postal 26, Palenque, Chiapas, Mexico.

RVs And Camping

Several places are open to campers and RVs in Palenque. The **Mayabel** is located about 2.2 km E of the ruins. It's a grassy area with trees and space for either tents or camping vehicles; hammock huts and hammocks are available but it's suggested you travel with your own hammock and mosquito netting (found easily at any marketplace). Toilet and shower facilities are fairly clean. The *senora* in the office will keep valuables while you're out sightseeing. Rates: P250 pp. Mailing address, Apto. Postal 20, Palenque, Chiapas, Mexico. The **La Canada Trailer Park** is about one km N of the central plaza. This shady park has water and electrical hookups for 20 camping vehicles; tent campers welcome. P300 pp.

FOOD AND SERVICES

Palenque has many small cafes. Most of the prices are reasonable, but for really budget prices go to the marketplace; this is also a good place to pick up the fixings for picnics, or to eat a reasonably priced *comida corrida*. The hotel dining room at the **Hotel Vaca Vieja** serves quality food in clean surroundings for few *pesos*. If you want something fancier, try the dining rooms at the **Nututum** or the **Chan-Kah**, both out of town. At least 2 bakeries make delicious breads and pastries.

Services

The **bank** cashes traveler's cheques between 0900-1200. The **long-distance telephone of-**

State Tourist Office Of Chiapas
la Av. Pte 1482
Tuxtla Gutierrez, Chiapas, Mexico
Tel. (9 16 61) 2-07-32

fice is located in the ADO bus station (24 Av. Hidalgo), open Mon. to Sat. from 0800-1400 and 1630-2000. When calling collect (always cheaper) have your name, the city, state, and number you want written down and be prepared for a long wait: there's only one operator and one line out of the village! Close to the ADO station (28 Av. Hidalgo), is a 24-hour **medical clinic**; they speak Spanish only.

TRANSPORT

By Train

Getting to Palenque is a matter of choosing among a variety of transportation. The train, at one time the only way to go, is a marvelous sightseeing expedition and very economical. From Merida it's an overnight trip (sleeping cars available), and the route takes you through beautiful jungle with rushing rivers and waterfalls. This train, which travels between Merida and Mexico City, stops at Palenque twice daily, morning and evening; check at departure points for current prices and schedules.

By Bus

Buses to Palenque arrive frequently from a number of cities. From Mexico City, twice daily (14 hours). From Merida, twice daily (7 hours). From Villahermosa (2½ hours) twice daily on ADO, and on the 2nd-class bus more frequently. In Palenque the 2nd-class bus station is on Calle 20 de Noviembre, and the ADO 1st-class station is on Av. Hidalgo, 3 blocks N of the central plaza.

By Car

This is a good drive; the road from Villahermosa is in excellent condition, and it takes about 2 hours to cover the 150 km. Drive 114 km on Hwy. 186 to Cataja, then take the road to the R another 27 km to the village of Palenque. From there it's 9 km to the ruins site. The road from San Cristobal de las Casas is still primitive and rocky in spots. You can make it in most vehicles, but expect a rough trip. If flying, it's convenient to fly into Villahermosa, pick up a reserved rental car at the airport, and continue on to Palenque.

By Air
A small landing strip is serviced by air taxi from Villahermosa, Tenosique, San Cristobal, and Tuxtla Gutierrez.

Getting Around
The town itself is small and can easily be covered on foot. If you're staying at one of the hotels out of town, it's a different matter: you can either grab a taxi or hitch. Taxis are reasonable and easy to flag down in the village. There's daily bus service from the village to the ruins.

VICINITY OF PALENQUE

Misol-Ha
The lush rainforest around Palenque has an unbeatable combination of tall trees, thick tropical plantlife, beautiful waterfalls, and rushing streams. Don't leave Palenque without first exploring the surrounding areas! Taking the Ocosingo road for 20 km, a side road goes off to the R leading to a breathtaking waterfall, Misol-Ha (means "Waterfall" in Maya). The falls plunge from a height of 30 m into a large shimmery pool, perfect for a cooling swim.

AGUA AZUL

When returning to the main Ocosingo road, continue on farther another 50 km to a side road that turns off to the R for 4 km to Agua Azul—in Maya Yax-Ha ("Blue Water"). The road is rocky and potholed in parts. As you climb up into the mountains you'll see the locals (including youngsters) making their way to small villages carrying large loads of wood,

giant plants in
Misoul Ha
rainforest

sweet potatoes, full hands of bananas, all carried on their backs with a tumpline around the head. *Milpas* are cut out of the thick forest; small huts, mostly with tin roofs (undoubtedly because of the heavy rains) are grouped here and there. As you climb higher the view below is dazzling with brooks and rivers cutting across the green valley floor.

Agua Azul has more than 500 cascades crashing onto a limestone bed. The water boils and whirls, flows and ebbs, all a luxuriant blue. Calm pools provide good swimming and a

large grassy area (that fills with people when tour buses arrive) for flaking out and picnicking. Camping is permitted for a small fee at the site; in fact campers will meet many fellow backpackers from all over the world, especially Europeans. You might even see kayakers taking a wild ride down the cascades after toting their kayaks up into this wild jungle! The hike upstream, following the cascades over rickety bridges and into a small village above, takes plenty of time; start out early.

At the site there's a small cafe (expensive), no

Chiapas fruit vendors at Agua Azul. Some of these young women speak no Spanish, only Tzeltzal. Photographers take note — they have strong religious beliefs.

just a few of dozens of cascades at Agua Azul

stores, plus many Lacandone Indians who arrive daily with truckloads of kids (mostly girls)
dressed in dirty flowered dresses selling fruit,
and *not* accepting "no" to their sales pitch. The
adults as well as the children do not like their
pictures taken, so ask first. These Indians present a very intimidating attitude, totally unlike
those found in the N part of the Peninsula.
Many speak no Spanish, only their own dialect
which can be Tzeltal or Tzotzil. The women all
dress alike wearing identically colored skirts,
sashes and white blouses.

Getting There

From Palenque you can catch a bus that brings
you ¾ of the way to Agua Azul to a 4-km,
1 ½ -hour walk on a steep treacherous climb the
rest of the way to the cascades. A backpack
gets very heavy; many backpackers make this
a day trip. If that's your choice, get an early
start in order to spend a good part of the day at
this beautiful site. You may get lucky and hitch
a ride, but don't count on it. Allow enough time
to arrive at either end of your trek before dark.

BONAMPAK

Among the brightest stars in the galaxy of excavated ceremonial centers is Bonampak, about 160 km SE of Palenque near the Guatemalan border. Unfortunately, since its discovery by the outside world, it has lost some of its luster and is not considered by all a must-see site. However, Bonampak reinforces the hope that uncountable archaeological treasures still wait to be uncovered in the dense jungles and rainforests of Mesoamerica.

DISCOVERY

The story goes that in 1946 a young American conscientious objector, Charles Carlos Frey, took refuge in the jungles of E. Chiapas in a small village called El Cedro. He soon became a familiar figure wandering the paths around the village and ultimately met Kayon, one of 250 remaining Indians from the Lacandon *caribal* (village) located between the Lacanha and Usumacinta rivers. A warm friendship grew between the two men, and Frey began to learn

the language of the Indian. The American was accepted so completely by the tribe that Kayon offered him one of his 5 wives. This small group of Indians lived isolated in the rainforest, still practicing polygamy and worshipping the ancient gods. Eventually, Kayon led Frey deep into the thick forest and shared the knowledge of a secret ceremonial center of his ancestors. Frey found 9 structures and *stelae* scattered around the overgrown site. But the greatest discovery was the brilliantly colored frescoes in Building 1.

Breaking The News
Apparently this discovery was too much for Frey to keep to himself, and he told Mexican federal authorites of the magnificent find. At first his news was not met with too much enthusiasm, probably because getting there was a treacherous trip through some of nature's worst hazards, as well as trespassing on the land of aggressive xenophobic Indians. But, with the help of another American, John Bourne, Frey managed to pique the interest of several Mexican archaeologists; over the next few years several scientific expeditions were made to Bonampak. In 1949, Frey also personally organized an expedition of Mexican artists, archaeologists, architects, photographers, and chemists, sponsored by the Mexican National Institute of Fine Arts. This trip would pave the way for future scientific research, but it ended in tragedy. Carlos Frey lost his life attempting to rescue an engraver, Franco Lazaro Gomez, when their canoe overturned in the rampaging water of the Lacanha River. Perhaps the initial tragedy was the breach of trust between 2 friends. None of this stopped other scientists from studying the site. Once a trip for adventurers *only*, roads—though still not the best—are being built and improved each year.

Murals
The most exciting finds at Bonampak were the murals found in the **Temple of the Frescoes**. After removing hundreds of years of thick

1. carved Maya art at the Anthropological Museum in Mexico City; 2. display of popular art, Merida;
3. dramatic Maya mask in Mexico City museum; 4. old world detail from turn-of-the-century
architecture, Panamerican Hotel, Merida; 5. Mother's monument in Merida park;
6. tribute to the first Euro-american family at Akumal

1.Palenque temple; 2. Temple of the Seven Dolls at Dzibilchaltun

brush and grasping vines that had engulfed the building, 3 rooms were found to contain brilliantly colored murals depicting a broad view of life during the era. The paintings covered all 4 walls in each chamber. Almost from floor level and continuing around the room without interruption was a parade of people that caused great excitement among scientists and artists alike. The panels bring into view a cross section of the past with servants, rulers, musicians, soldiers at war, children, women, victims of sacrifice—a chaos of people—two dimensional and all life size. The colors used were deep siennas, Venetian reds, and brilliant emerald greens, while unpainted lime was left white and outlined in black giving added brilliance to the scenes.

Restorations

To see the paintings it was neccesary to scrape off the accumulation of centuries of limestone. The walls were then washed with kerosene, which temporarily brought out the brilliant colors; sadly, however, this was a mistake. The kerosene weakened the adhesion and contributed to the murals' deterioration. Today, there is very little color left on the walls. Fortunately, these fine paintings were duplicated in precise color and content by the early artists. You can see replicas in several places. At Tuxtla Gutierrez' Hotel Bonampak there's a large-scale reproduction from the central chamber; others are found in Villahermosa at the state museum; and farther away, Mexico City's Anthropological Museum has a full set of reproductions from each chamber. The murals are considered the finest example of frescoe art thus found in the Maya world.

GETTING THERE

A trip to Bonampak is an adventure. Unless you fly, you must travel over rough gravel roads in a 4WD vehicle; during the rainy season the road becomes impassable. When you arrive there are no facilities. Although most of the Indians in the area are aloof and keep their distance, there have been reports of robberies, even from locked cars. Women backpackers traveling alone should be wary of

A variety of monkeys live in the rainforest. The howler monkey may be the noisiest, especially at night. His shrieks echo from tree to tree and have kept more than one camper awake.

offers of hospitality, which have been used as a ruse for theft. Obviously, not all offers of kindness are would-be threats. Just use common sense when dealing with these Indians.

By Plane

Flying to Bonampak may be a bit expensive, but it gives you the opportunity to see the ruins (which doesn't take very long) and possibly combine the trip with a stop at Yaxchilan, a

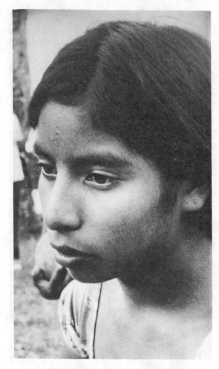

This Indian girl spoke no Spanish, only Tzeltal.

larger, more architectually important site. Trips can be arranged in small air-taxis from Villahermosa, Tenosique, Palenque, and San Cristobal de las Casas. The flight averages about US$400 for a 4- or 5-passenger plane, so if you're traveling in a group it saves a few *pesos*.

By Car
Ask at the State Tourist Office across from the main plaza in Palenque about an on-again off-again jeep trip that takes around 8 hours. if driving your own car, continue on the road from the Palenque ruins. Be prepared for a rough road the last half; if it's raining expect a muddy mire. Four-wheel drive vehicles are available for rent in Palenque and San Cristobal de las Casas. Chains should be carried at all times and bring an extra tank of gas. The only other way to get there is the way of the Indians: walking. From Palenque it's 160 km through thick rainforest.

Safety Tips
When traveling through the rainforest it's wise to carry a few extra necessities: a flashlight, a sharp knife (preferably a machete that will handle sturdy vines), extra batteries, a strong bug repellent. Wearing long, lightweight cotton pants (no jeans) helps to ward off insects. If you're sleeping in a hammock bring good mosquito netting (some dangerous flying critters out there thrive on fresh blood and can cause severe problems). Before you leave home ask your doctor about malaria pills (some malaria medication must be taken in advance of exposure), and check with the state department for a list of any other tropical diseases that might be ravaging the locals (hepatitis, etc.). Remember the other usuals: bring water and your own victuals. If this seems a little drastic, remember what Mom used to say, a stitch in time saves you know what!

THE STATE OF TABASCO

Technically, only three states make up the Yucatan Peninsula: Campeche, Yucatan, and Quintana Roo. However, to provide a continuity for anyone studying the Maya culture it would be a mistake not to include the classic past of the Olmec culture, which flourished in the nearby jungles and hills of what is today the Mexican state of Tabasco.

Geographically, there's a vast difference between Tabasco and its northern neighbors. In Tabasco the land is flat near the sea, then swells into gentle hills as it nears the border of Chiapas. Water is everywhere: swampy marshland, lakes, and 2 large navigable rivers (Usumacinta and Grijalva). The soil is rich and fertile, with so few rocks that the Olmecs had to travel many miles to find the material to carve their colossal heads. Much of the land is covered with thick rainforest, rich stands of coconut, healthy banana groves, and cacao plantations. The state occupies 25,337 sq km; the population is 1,065,000. Most of the inhabitants are mestizo and Chontal Indians,

with the greatest density of people in and around the capital, Villahermosa.

Climate
Tabasco is tropical—hot, humid, more sticky than its neighbors in the north. Most of the approximately 1,500 mm (60 inches) of yearly rainfall occurs between May and October.

History
This was first the land of the Olmecs, predecessors of the Chontal Maya that followed. In has been determined that the Olmecs preceded all others; their society is considered the mother culture of Mesoamerica. The Olmecs flourished from about 1200-400 B.C., the first progressive society in the Americas. More than likely they were the first to begin carving in stone and building ceremonial centers.

For the most part, their centers had been long deserted by the time the Spanish first stepped on Maya land. Arriving on the coast of Tabasco in 1519, Cortez faced his first battle with the Maya on the Gulf coast and established a city called Santa Maria de la Victoria in honor of his initial victory. But it was short-lived, as the Indians fought it out for 20 years more before Francisco de Montejo really gained control of the land. As the Peninsula developed and the riches of the New World began flowing from the Gulf ports to Spain, pirates attacked often enough to make living on the coast a day-to-day gamble. In 1596 the city was moved inland and renamed Villahermosa de San Juan Bautista.

Life went on with little agitation. An oblivion settled over the colony until the 1821 break from Spain, which was followed by chaos in the rush for positions of leadership. Internal conflict continued until 1863's invasion by the French. This act was the catalyst that finally brought Tabascans together, and the French were ungraciously ousted from their lands.

The age of President Porfirio Diaz (1876-1911) was the longest period of peace in Mexico in its first 100 years of independence. But though modernization and economic advances began throughout most of the country, Tabasco and the other southern states barely felt this wave of progress. Outside foreign capital was welcome; British and U.S. oil industries saw the potential and the seed of Tabasco's future growth was planted. The country mopped up after the bloody revolution (1910-1920) and began putting its economic life together. Nationalization of foreign industry slowed things down, but ultimately the government-sponsored Pemex oil company brought Tabasco into the 20th century.

Economy

If you haven't been to Tabasco for 10 years or more, you'll be surprised at the changes that have taken place since the introduction of oil into the state's economy. A side effect is the upsurge of agriculture with the introduction of modern machinery and improved methods, enabling the state to become a viable world-class producer of the excellent Tabasco banana and cocoa bean products.

Signs of money are everywhere. The state is growing into a center for culture as well as for big business. The people are swept up in this new-found wealth, and most of Tabasco's inhabitants are benefitting with better paying jobs, improved housing, upgraded roads, and a higher standard of living. The cities are now trying to attract tourists with modern hotels, restaurants, and an advertising campaign extolling the archaeological attractions available in Tabasco.

TABASCO ARCHAEOLIGICAL ZONES

LA VENTA	SAN MIGUEL
COMALCALCO	JONUTA
EL TORTUGUERO	

VILLAHERMOSA
AND VICINITY

The Olmecs, oldest culture of Mexico, left a rich history; travelers interested in the ancient past should not leave the Yucatan Peninsula without a visit to Tabasco's capital, Villahermosa. Two archaeological sites are Comalcalco, the largest and most important Maya site in Tabasco, and La Venta.

Today, Villahermosa combines the sophisticated look of a big city with the friendly atmosphere of a small town (population of close to 500,000). You can't help but notice a happy independent feeling among the Villahermosans. The cafes, parks, and shops are alive with chattering bustling people who seem content with their present lifestyle and proud of their ancient heritage. Walking the streets of Villahermosa you notice an abundance of museums, public buildings, schools, and doctor's offices. Perhaps in their growing sophistication Villahermosans have switched from the ancient *curanderas* (healers), *brujas* (witches), and *espiritualistas* (spiritualists) to more modern medicine.

SIGHTS

La Venta Park

The original site of the Olmec's art was in **La Venta**, just off the Gulf coast 127 km W of Villahermosa near the border of Veracruz. Although the ruins were known and first investigated by Frans Blom in 1925, if it weren't for the intrusion of the Pemex oildrills, an entire ceremonial center of the Olmec Indians might still be an obscure footnote in ancient history. With oil development in the region threatening to destroy the site, the entire complex was moved to the outskirts of Villahermosa and today occupies a park laid out in the precise configuration of the site as found by petroleum engineers when draining an unlikely marsh. Called **Parque-Museo La Venta** (a must-see!), you'll find the colossal heads and unusual sculptures not found anyplace else on the Peninsula.

sculpture at La Venta Park outdoor museum

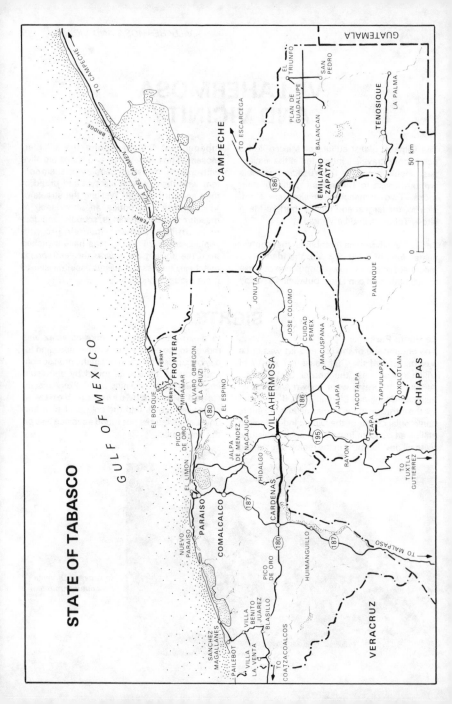

STATE OF TABASCO

La Venta Park Museum

The park is a combination outdoor museum and wildlife preserve, with small animals running freely and others in cages or, as in the case of the crocodiles, within their own muddy moat. The complex was conceived by Carlos Pellicer Camara, poet and much-revered Tabasco statesman. A self-guided tour (brochures with explanations are available at the entrance for a small fee) leads you by way of concrete footprints through the trees and tropical foliage past 5 giant heads more than 2 m tall and weighing over 15 tons each. No one has yet figured out how the Olmecs (without the wheel) managed to move these giant basalt heads and altars weighing up to 30 tons, since the raw material comes from an area almost 100 km distant.

The park, 3 km from the center of Villahermosa, is located on the lovely **Laguna de las Il-**

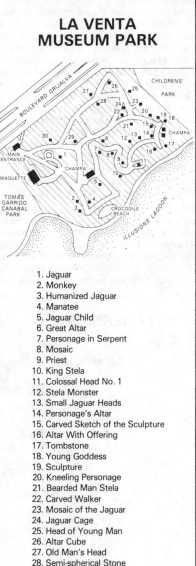

1. Jaguar
2. Monkey
3. Humanized Jaguar
4. Manatee
5. Jaguar Child
6. Great Altar
7. Personage in Serpent
8. Mosaic
9. Priest
10. King Stela
11. Colossal Head No. 1
12. Stela Monster
13. Small Jaguar Heads
14. Personage's Altar
15. Carved Sketch of the Sculpture
16. Altar With Offering
17. Tombstone
18. Young Goddess
19. Sculpture
20. Kneeling Personage
21. Bearded Man Stela
22. Carved Walker
23. Mosaic of the Jaguar
24. Jaguar Cage
25. Head of Young Man
26. Altar Cube
27. Old Man's Head
28. Semi-spherical Stone
29. Altar for Infantile Sacrifices
30. Owl's Stone

priest, La Venta Park

lusiones. A relaxing resting place, its high-flying jet of water shoots rainbow crystals toward the hot mid-day sun. The Olmec culture left a diverse collection of carvings at La Venta ("Market Place"). Along with the giant carved heads wearing war helmets and facial features displaying thick down-turned lips (that are supposed to typify the jaguar), other more delicate carvings are scattered here and there. Dwarfs coming out of doorways, or framed within structures, along with a mammoth altar and an arrangement of stone pillars called the **Jaguar's Cage,** are part of this outstanding collection. You'll see stone carvings of animals, including the unusual manatee, along with *stelae* depicting various unique scenes such as the bearded man, all placed in appropriate settings.

The park also houses a children's playground, cafe, and bookstore. Every evening except Wed., a good **Sound and Light Show** is presented at 1900, 2010, and 2115 for a small fee. The park is open daily except Wed. from 0830-1700, small admission fee. La Venta Park is located at the intersection of Boulevard Gri-

jalva and Paseo Tabasco. From Madero near the center, buses marked TABASCO 2000, CIRCUITO 1, FOVISTE, and PARQUE LINDA VISTA go to La Venta (ask the driver when you board). Taxis are reasonable and easy to flag down. After visiting the park if you're still in the mood to explore, from La Venta it's an enjoyable walk along a busy boulevard (Paseo Tabasco) to 2 more parks, Tabasco 2000 and Parque La Choco.

Tabasco 2000

This series of new buildings is developing into an impressive cultural center. It includes a modern **Palacio Municipal,** a convention center with facilities for large groups, often presenting plays and other entertainment, and a planetarium that offers permanent exhibits and occasional special shows. If you haven't time to see a scheduled evening show (Tues., Fri., Sat., and Sun.), stop by for a tour of the building. The planetarium exhibits (in Spanish) depict the environment and energy of Tabasco — it's worth a visit. Lovely fountains

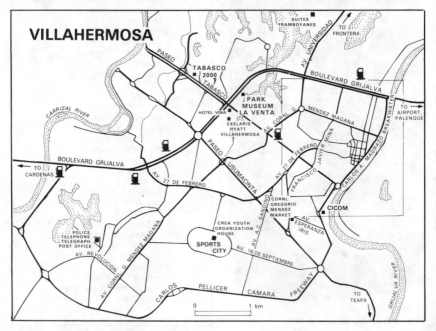

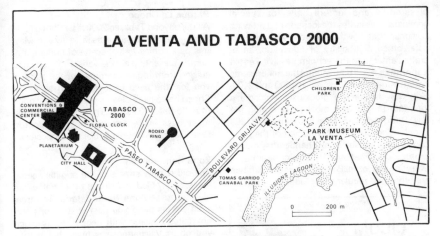

LA VENTA AND TABASCO 2000

and walkways make a pleasant stroll. Whether you want to shop or not, stop in and take a look at Tabasco's most modern shopping mall, the Tabasco 2000 commercial center. This mall is unusual in this part of Mexico with its polished marble floors and glass-enclosed shops that carry everything from well-stocked camera equipment to the latest in fashions and the newest of electrical appliances that are becoming a way of life in the growing metropolis.

CICOM

Another well laid-out complex of interest to the visitor along the Grijalva River is CICOM (Centro de Investigaciones de las Culturas Olmeca Y Maya), an investigation center for the Olmec and Maya cultures. One of the main attractions is the **Museo Regional de Antropologia Carlos Pellicer Camara**, a well-designed museum dedicated to Carlos Pellicer Camara. Documentation of the history of Tabasco and the Olmec, Toltec, and Maya cultures is beautifully presented throughout 4 floors. You'll see Olmec and Maya pottery, clay figurines, stone carvings, and delicate pieces of jade, along with explanatory photos showing the sites where they were discovered. One exhibit is devoted to Carlos Pellicer Camara and his life. This poet, also an anthropologist, is much respected by Villahermosans and is remembered and honored in many ways throughout the city.

On the grounds of the CICOM complex is a complete and efficient installation dedicated to the study of the ancient cultures including offices, laboratory, workshops, auditorium,

CICOM museum has artifacts such as this exhibit which shows bodies buried in large clay pots in a fetal position.

classrooms and lecture halls for special seminars. This is also the location of a growing business center with an Aeromexico office, a cafe, office of Ministry of Education, handcrafts center, and the very impressive **Teatro Esperanza Iris**. This beautiful theater presents entertainment Wed. to Sat. at 1900 and 2130. However, people are graciously welcome a look into the building most times during the day. Designed as an opera house, it seats 1300 people. The **Casa de Artes**, part of the complex, offers classes in art, handcrafts, music, drama, classical and folkloric dancing — everyone welcome. Performances and exhibits are presented regularly by students.

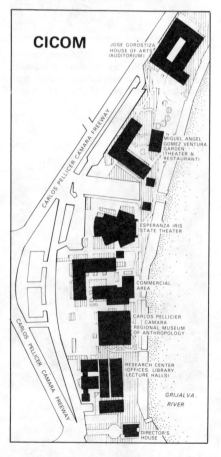

CICOM

JOSE GOROSTIZA HOUSE OF ARTS (AUDITORIUM)

CARLOS PELLICER CAMARA FREEWAY

MIGUEL ANGEL GOMEZ VENTURA GARDEN (THEATER & RESTAURANT)

ESPERANZA IRIS STATE THEATER

COMMERCIAL AREA

CARLOS PELLICIER CAMARA REGIONAL MUSEUM OF ANTHROPOLOGY

CARLOS PELLICER CAMARA FREEWAY

RESEARCH CENTER (OFFICES, LIBRARY, LECTURE HALLS)

GRIJALVA RIVER

DIRECTOR'S HOUSE

Parque La Choco

A little beyond Tabasco 2000 is La Choco Park. During Villahermosa's artisan festival in May, this park comes to life, scene of hundreds of booths presenting a wide variety of crafts and cuisine from regions throughout the state. If you feel the need of a refreshing swim, La Choco has a large clean swimming pool open Mon. to Sat. 0700-2100. There's a fee and you must pass inspection by the pool doctor. Check with the Tourist Office for particulars.

Zona Remodelada

The old narrow streets of the original central areas, nicely tiled and closed off to traffic, are referred to as **Zona Remodelada**. The tree-lined streets bring you past small shops and tiny cafes bustling with people. Every place you go in Villahermosa is busy, but with a friendly laid-back atmosphere.

Deportivo Recreativo

This is really an impressive lay-out! Blocks and blocks devoted to sports of all kinds are located S of the main part of Villahermosa. Here Tabascans take part in baseball, basketball, aerobics, football, tennis, volleyball, soccer, and swimming. There's a huge playground and even (what looks like) a resident circus for the children. The grounds are well landscaped with monuments, fountains, and wide walkways. There's a large CREA building (youth organization house, daytime use only) where many activities are planned for Villahermosa's young people. The city fathers are to be commended for creating such a fine sports complex open to everyone for a small token fee. No doubt oil money had something to do with this.

Museum of Popular Art

This small museum displays the culture of the people of more recent history, between the time of the Spanish occupation and the discovery of oil. A changing exhibit introduces you to whatever custom is taking place at the time of year you happen to visit. For example, between Oct. 31 and Nov. 15, you'll see typical displays as they appear in homes to commemorate *El Dia de Muerte* ("Day of the Dead," in the U.S. known as All Souls Day, the

Wash tubs like the one pictured have been in use for hundreds of years.

day after Halloween). Skeletons are dressed with an article of the deceased's clothing and set on a shrine in a prominent place in the home. Also at the shrine favorite foods are arranged along with candles and a religious picture or symbol. According to belief, eternity opens its doors during this time and the deceased are allowed a visit to enjoy some earthly pleasures. Cemeteries overflow with visitors, and cart vendors do a thriving business selling skeleton and skull candies, flowers, and soft drinks. It's not a gloomy time, just a melancholy holiday celebrated all over Mexico, which the people take very seriously. After the cataclysmic earthquake hit Mexico City in Sept. 1985, the cemeteries were more crowded the following Nov. than they'd ever been.

A Spanish-speaking guide takes you through the very small museum. Thatched huts of the rural areas are recreated. In detail you'll see how the cooking is done, how food in baskets is hung from the ceiling in the huts made of tall smooth sapling trees placed close together with a *palapa* roof. There's little furniture in these humble homes, but they accommodate many hammocks. A movable bathtub has its place in the corner of the room. Waist-high slanted wash tubs on stands (still commonly seen outdoors on wash day in rural areas all over the Peninsula) show the fine art of scrubbing clothes by hand without breaking the back. On the premises of the museum is a small shop selling typical handcrafts, and a library and bookstore.

Marketplace

Visit the marketplace in Villahermosa for an introduction to some exotic foodstuffs. Besides small stalls displaying mounds of herbs and spices with piquant aromas and colors of ochre, sienna, saffron, and rust, there are rows of dewy fresh vegetables and fruits, game animals not usually seen on the grocery store back home. Right out of the jungle, hanging up front waiting to be bought and skinned if you wish, are iguanas, peccary, pheasant, paskenkly; there's also ordinary chicken, beef, pork, and fresh fish.

PRACTICALITIES

ACCOMMODATIONS

Budget

The best selection of budget hotels is on Madero or in the Zona Remodelada. Inconve- niently, both the ADO 1st-class and 2nd-class bus stations are about a 20- to 30-min. walk to these areas. Luckily taxis are easy to find and economical. Overnight camping and trailer parking is located at the Sports City complex, also a considerable distance from the bus

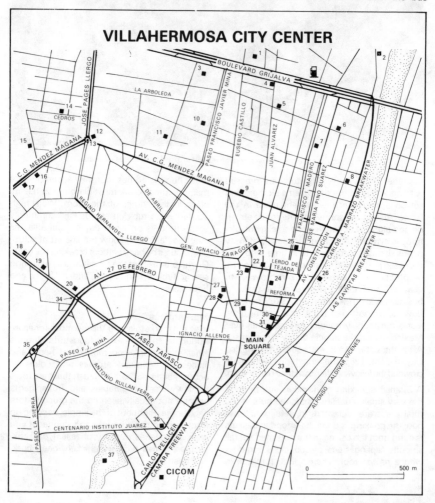

VILLAHERMOSA CITY CENTER

depots. Keep in mind that Villahermosa is a busy city and the best-value rooms are taken quickly, which makes room-hunting a first priority upon arrival.

The **Hotel Providencia** is spartan, squeaky clean, with small rooms. On Constitucion 216, it's between Reforma and Lerda, 6½ blocks S of Fuentes; rates P1000 s or d; tel. 2-82-62. Near Parque Benito Juarez, you'll find the **Hotel San Francisco**. This hotel is clean, has a/c, comfortable rooms (some with balconies), elevator, and is a 10-min. walk to the center of town, located on Madero 604, 4 blocks S of Fuentes; P1400 s, P1600 d; tel. 2-31-98. Off a quiet walkway, the **Hotel Caballero** is an adequate stopover. The rooms are moderate size with shared bath, fans, and purified water. Located at Lerdo 303 6 blocks S of Fuentes, P1100 s, P1400 d; tel. 2-14-55.

Other Budget Hotels
Hotel Balboa, Hermanos Bastar Zozaya 505, tel. 2-45-50.
Hotel La Paz, Madero 923, tel. 2-33-62.
Posada Bariloche, Pino Suarez 311, no phone.
Hotel Frisa, Constitucion 1025, tel. 2-29-59.
Hotel San Rafael, Constitucion 232, tel. 2-01-66.

Moderate
These hotels are all near city center. The **Hotel Manzur** is comfortable with clean rooms, a/c, dining room, cocktail lounge, travel agency and car rental. Madero 422, P5000 d; tel. 2-24-99

Other Moderate Hotels
Hotel Maria Dolores, Aldama and Reforma, tel. 2-22-11.
Hotel Choco's, Constitucion and Lino Merino, 2-94-44.
Hotel Miraflores, Reforma 304, tel. 2-00-22.
Plaza Independencia, Independencia 123, tel. 2-12-99.
Suites Chalet Izumac, Malecon las Gaviotas, no phone.
Suites San Angel, Jose Pages Llergo 108, tel. 2-51-44/2-55-75.

Luxury
Since Villahermosa is growing fast, more and better hotels are being added all the time. One of the best, **Hotel Villahermosa Viva,** is nicely furnished, a/c, with room service, restaurant, coffee shop, disco, large swimming pool and patio area, sauna, tennis court, and car rental. Located at Paseo Tabasco and Grijalva, **Tabasco 2000 Hotel** is the newest in Villahermosa and offers the most modern accommodations in the city. The rooms are spacious, and well furnished, deluxe bathrooms, room

---

VILLAHERMOSA CITY CENTER

1. Bus Depot
2. Port Capt. of Grijalva River
3. Maya Tabasco
4. Kansas Steak House
5. Tabasco I and II Cinema
6. Jose Maria Pino Suarez Market
7. Galan Cinema
8. Choco's Hotel
9. Di Bari Pizzeria
10. ADO Buses
11. Pemex Hospital
12. Suites San Angel
13. Young Men Heroes Monument and Plaza
14. Country Steak House
15. Cuauhtemoc Park and Monument
16. Sahara Compound (Disco, Restaurant Alhambra, Snack Bar Mezquita and Oasis Bar)
17. Chez Monette Restaurant
18. Lions Club
19. Manuele Mestre Ghigliazza Park and Monument
20. Cathedral
21. Hotel San Francisco
22. Tourist Information Booth
23. Post and Telegraph Central Offices
24. Telephone Central Office
25. Manuel R. Mora Library
26. Capitan Beulo Floating Restaurant Ship
27. Jose Marti Library
28. House of Culture
29. Government Palace
30. Mexicana Airlines
31. Superior Cinema
32. Hotel Plaza Independencia, Restaurant, Bar, Car Rental
33. Flag Monument
34. Mendez Magana Monument & Plaza
35. City Clock Fountain and Plaza
36. Suarez Cinema
37. Recreation Park "Laguna de la Polvora"

service, beautiful dining room, bar, disco, swimming pool, along with every service you need. Located just in front of the Tabasco 2000 shopping mall, tel. 2-55-55. Several other luxury hotels near Illusion lagoon include the **Exelaris Hyatt,** Av. Juarez 106, tel. 2-81-03/2-08-88; **Cencali,** Juarez and Paseo Tabasco, tel. 2-60-00; **Maya Tabasco,** Blvd. Grijalva, one km NW of town, tel. 2-11-11.

FOOD

You can get as exotic with your food as you wish in Villahermosa. A few cafes specialize in pre-Columbian recipes. For instance: how about cooked turtle in green sauce, or *tamales de chipilin, pejelagarto* (lizard meat), or *chirmol de congrejo* (a spicy rabbit stew), *mondongo en ajiaco* (tripe and vegetables), or just plain iguana stew? For a drink that's native to the area, try *pozole* (made of corn and raw cacao beans); *cacawada* is another tasty drink, (cacao beans mixed with water and sweetened), though it doesn't taste anything like chocolate. Before roasting, the flesh around the beans has a tart fruity flavor—very refreshing.

Restaurants
Choosing a restaurant can be tough since there's a large selection. For the budget traveler the food around the bus station is nothing to write home about. As usual the cheapest meals are available at the market, off Pino Suarez near Zozaya. Lots of Conasupo supermarkets are scattered throughout the city. Here's are a few good, economical restaurants: **Tacos El Rodeo,** Calle Hidalgo; **Rico Mae Tacos,** Madero between Zaragoza and Mendez; **Restaurant Gemenis II** (good wild game, seasonal wild pig, pheasant, mountain lion) across from Rico Mae Tacos. **Cafe Su Casa,** look for the Cabal sign at the intersection of Suarez, Madero, Reforma; and **DiBari Pizzeria,** Mendez 712.

Though more costly, if you have the yen for a good steak try either the **Kansas Grill,** Alvarez 803, or **Country Steak House,** Cedro 209. **Old Canyon** at Tabasco 2000 is worth a trip to take a look, like stepping into an old Hollywood western, cowboys and all. A change of pace from Latin food is **La Pagoda,** Ninos Heroes 167, or **McTavish Pub** (at Garcia and Madrazo). And if you like window-shopping, you'll find many more cafes serving *tipico* cuisine all over the city.

Capitan Beulo, Villahermosa's floating restaurant

Sea Fare

For something a little special, take a lunch or dinner cruise along the Grijalva River on board the small restaurant-ship *Capitan Buelo*. The lunch trip is a breezy tour with a peek into life on the busy river. The food is nicely served, fresh fish the specialty. If you order the shrimp cocktail, don't be surprised when it's served to you "naked" — they bring many bottles of interesting condiments and fresh lime, all meant to be added by the diner. The shrimp is so fresh and sweet it's delicious *au natural*.

At night, the small ship takes on a sparkling dimension. For the most part you sail along black banks, so your attention turns to the linen decor, the food, or perhaps a special companion to share the stars reflecting on the quiet river. This is not a cheap dinner, but with the boat excursion included it's good value. The trip is made daily except Mon. at 1330, 1530, and 2100; catch the floating restaurant at the pier on the Madrazo Breakwater at the foot of Lerdo de Tejada. During winter's high season reservations are suggested, tel. 2-31-71/ 2-49-97.

ENTERTAINMENT

Villahermosa sports a variety of nightspots, mostly in the hotels scattered around town. Some are small and cozy, others are wild and vibrate with music into the wee hours. Some are just for dancing, others also have floorshows. Look them over, try them *all* for fun!

Tabasco 2000

The Tabasco 2000 **planetarium** puts on impressive Onmimax 70 documentaries. Shows are presented Tues. to Fri., 1800 and 2000; Sat. and Sun. at 1700, 1830, and 2000. The planetarium is next to the Municipal Palacio in the Tabasco 2000 Complex. Also check for events that might be taking place in the **Teatro Esperana Iris**; call the tourist office, tel. 2-31-71.

> Dept. of Tourism
> Malecon Y Ignacio Zaragoza
> Villahermosa, Tabasco, Mexico
> Tel. (9 19 31) 1-31-71

SPECIAL EVENTS

EXPOTAB Annual fair

During the second half of April, this fun event brings the town alive. Decorated folkloric floats, art exhibits, food booths, livestock judging, dances, cockfights, and the election of the Flower Queen make April a good time to visit if you like lots of activity.

Nautical Marathon

Something different in May is an internationally acclaimed marathon on the Usumacinta River. Four categories of boats cover a distance

---

VILLAHERMOSA NIGHTCLUBS

Show Bar El Candil Hotel Choco's Constitucion and Lino Merino	tel. 2-94-44.
Bar La Covacha Hotel Maria Dolores Aldama 404	tel. 2-22-11.
Lobby Bar Flamboyan Hotel Exelaris Hyatt Juarez 106	tel. 2-84-33.
Bar Fandango Hotel Villahermosa Viva Paseo Tabasco	tel. 2-55-55.
Bar Las Garzas Hotel Plaza Independencia Independencia 123	tel. 2-12-99.
Bar Miraflores Hotel Miraflores Reforma 304	tel. 2-00-22.
Bar Miragua Hotel Manzur Madero 422	tel. 2-24-99.
Estudio '8' Discotheque Sheik Hotel Maya Tabasco Mendez 505	tel. 2-11-11.
Discotheque La Troje Hotel Villahermosa Viva Paseo Tabasco	tel. 2-55-55.

Yearly boat-racing event brings racers from all over Mexico and Central America.

of 600 km from Tenosique to Villahermosa over 4 days. Participants come from all over Mexico and bordering countries to this big event. Cash prizes are awarded and everyone has a good time. For more information call the State Tourism Office at 2-31-71, or write to Carlos Izundegui Rullan, Director of Tourism, N. 101-A Zaragoza, Villahermosa, Tabasco, Mexico.

GETTING THERE

Considered a gateway to central Mexico, Villahermosa is easily reached by many means. A fine transportation network connects with Mexico City, Chiapas, Guatemala, the Quintana Roo coast, and the rest of the Yucatan Peninsula.

By Plane
Villahermosa has a busy modern international airport. Flights arrive daily from many cities in Mexico as well as connecting international flights from Madrid, Paris, London, Rome, the U.S., and several points in the Orient. You can make direct flights to Mexico City, Oaxaca, Merida, Tuxtla Gutierrez, and other large cities, as well as to special destinations in small air-taxis: Bonampak, Ciudad del Carmen, Emiliano Zapata, and Palenque. Both **Mexicana Airlines** (Madero 109, tel. 2-27-15/2-11-69) and **Aeromexico** (in the CICOM Complex, tel. 2-69-91) fly in and out of Villahermosa.

When you arrive at the international airport (tel. 2-43-86), you have the choice of a taxi or combi service to your hotel or the center of town. It's at least a 45-min. walk to town center. There are numerous auto rentals within the a/c air terminal plus a coffee shop, restaurant, and several gift shops. The staff at the state tourist information booth located in the terminal is very helpful, provides detailed city maps, and someone almost always speaks English along with several other languages.

By Train
To link up with the national train service you must travel 58 km to Teapa.

By Bus

Buses from all over Mexico arrive frequently. The **ADO** 1st-class bus station is located at Mino and Merino, in the NE section of the city; tel. 2-14-46. The 2nd-class bus station, called **Central de Autobuses de Tabasco,** is on Grijalva. Both stations are very busy; you can find transportation to anyplace in Mexico from these 2 spots.

By Car

Highways into Villahermosa are easy driving from both N and south. From Campeche and points E take Hwy. 186. From Campeche along the coastal route take Hwy. 180. From Veracruz along the coast take Hwy. 180 east. From San Cristobal de las Casas and points S take Hwy. 190. These all converge in Villahermosa.

VICINITY OF VILLAHERMOSA

RUINS OF COMALCALCO

A beautiful pastoral site of green rolling hills and plains, Comalcalco is a 55-km drive NW of Villahermosa. Built in the Classical Period between A.D. 200-700, its distinct architectural design is different from the sites in the N part of the Peninsula. Because of a lack of stone, the building method was to compact earth and clay creating high platforms. Next, kilned bricks for the structures, walkways, and domes were held together with mortar made from ground oyster shells. The entire facade was then faced with stucco, which was often molded into beautiful ornamentation: glyphs, masks, human and animal figures, religious symbols, and high polychromed reliefs. Most of the artwork is barely visible now after centuries of exposure to the elements. The stucco surface is almost totally gone, exposing the bricks that so closely resemble those made today. **Note!** The bricks are fragile and it is not permitted to climb on the pyramids — watch for signs that say *NO SUBIR!*

Several mounds are now bare of any structure;

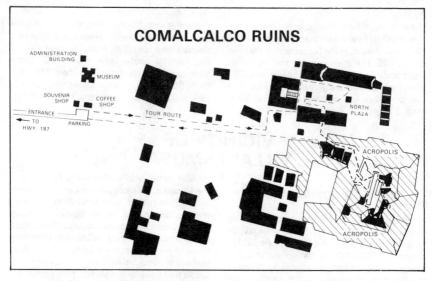

COMALCALCO RUINS

ADMINISTRATION BUILDING

MUSEUM

SOUVENIR SHOP   COFFEE SHOP

ENTRANCE
— TO
HWY. 187   PARKING

TOUR ROUTE

NORTH PLAZA

ACROPOLIS

ACROPOLIS

Comalcalco's kilned-brick construction is evident here.

at one time the original structures were built of wood and have long since deteriorated. **Temple Number 1**, the immense structure on the L as you walk from the entrance, has the best remaining example of the stucco high relief that once covered most of the structures. Today these valuable remnants of history are covered with glass and have been roofed over to deter any further deterioration. The facial features of these figures are unique, with thick strangely shaped lips, somewhat resembling the colossal heads in La Venta, yet vastly different in style. The Palenque site in Chiapas flourished at the same time as the Chontal Maya here in Comalcalco, and artifacts indicate there was communication and trading between the 2 sites. At the entrance to the ruins is a small museum, a gift/book shop (that doesn't have much to sell), and a snack stand; admission to the site is P40 and it's open from 0800-1700.

The walk up a hill to the **Palace** reveals a lovely view of the green countryside below and mounds scattered here and there but not yet excavated. From the top of the hill you'll see healthy cattle, unknown to the Maya Indian, living in the shadows of the ancient structures.

The entomologist might enjoy observing a giant beetle often seen in the trees near the buildings at the entrance. The insect is the size of a man's hand and about 3 inches thick, shiny black in color, and apparently common in this rural part of the state.

While wandering you'll discover a sunken courtyard, many halves of the traditional corbel arch, and the remains of small display niches all through the structures. The Chontal Maya were as talented and creative as the rest of the Maya throughout Mesoamerica.

Getting There

You can reach Comalcalco from the Villahermosa ADO 1st-class bus station on Mino and Merino. Buses depart at 1230, 1730, and 2030; check with the driver for return trip information. If driving take Hwy. 180 W from Villahermosa to the city of Cardenas, and when you come to the junction with Hwys. 187 and 180, continue on 187 to Comalcalco. Just beyond the ruins is cacao bean country. A chocolate factory (ask at the Comalcalco gift shop) gives a tour if it's the right time of year, (harvest season usually begins around Oct. 15, but the weather determines the exact date and when the factory begins operating).

Day Trip

A good day trip is the visit to Comalcalco, then continuing through the small city of Paraiso, with a stop at Puerto Ceiba on the coast of the river, perfect for marvelous scenery and a

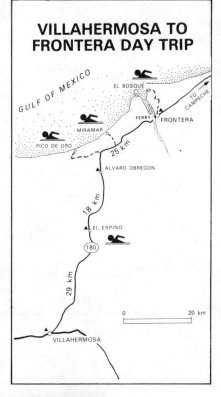

VILLAHERMOSA TO FRONTERA DAY TRIP

Comacalco stucco carving shows unique style of the Chontal Maya.

DAY TRIP TO THE COAST

lunch stop of fresh fish and shrimp in an outdoor cafe on the edge of the river. Making a loop on your return trip to Villahermosa by way of one of several different highways (watch for signs marked VILLAHERMOSA) gives a pleasant change of landscape.

Allow a full day with an early start for this trip. You'll travel through small towns with colorful churches painted in bright blues and yellows, very atypical. Dense groves of trees — coconut, banana and cacao — are thick along the highway. Tabasco is the largest producer of bananas in Mexico, especially in this immediate area. With lots of banana stands along the way you can pick up either a large hand or just a few for an energy snack — very cheaply. You'll see coconut being worked all along here in preparation for copra. And if you have never seen the cacao bean grow, make a point of looking for a cacao plantation. This area is loaded with them, small family affairs that welcome visitors. The bean looks much like a pale greenish-yellow ridged squash about the size of an elongated cantaloupe. It grows not only on the branches of the tree, but strangely from the trunk also.

THE STATE OF QUINTANA ROO

The state of Quintana Roo is bordered by Campeche and Yucatan states on the W, Belize and Guatemala on the S, and the Caribbean coast on the east. Quintana Roo occupies 50,350 sq km and has a population of almost 140,000. Mostly flat, this long isolated state is covered with tropical forest and boasts the most beautiful white-sand beaches on the Peninsula. Several islands lie offshore, and a magnificent 250-km reef runs parallel to the Quintana Roo coast from the tip of Isla Mujeres to the Bay of Honduras, whose undersea life provides a world-class attraction. Chetumal, the capital of the state, borders Belize, formerly known as British Honduras. From Chetumal it's possible to drive to Belize City, largest town in the small country.

Climate

Quintana Roo has a tropical climate and during the summer months becomes hot and humid; the farther S, the more humidity is felt. The major portion of rain falls between May and Oct.; cooling trade winds, which blow most of the time, make it pleasant during the dry season, but also contribute to higher rainfall than the northern part of the Peninsula. Annual rainfall averages 1,553 mm (61 inches).

History

This stretched-out coastal region was ignored by Mexico longer than the rest of the Peninsula because of its dense jungle and notorious Chan Santa Cruz Indians. When defeated by the Spanish, many Maya took refuge in this coastal territory, keeping would-be intruders easily at bay with their xenophobic reputation until the beginning of the 20th century. The only real Spanish settlement, Bacalar, on the S end of the state, was destroyed twice, once by pirates and again during the Caste War by rioting Maya. Quintana Roo was held as a territory of the Republic for 73 years, then admitted as the 30th state to the United Mexican States in 1974. Not until the 1970s were highways built, when Mexico finally realized that Quintana Roo possesses all the elements of one of the most beautiful resort areas in the entire world.

Economy
Until recently the economy of this lost territory amounted to very little. For a few years the chicle boom brought a flurry of activity centered around the harbor of Isla Cozumel. Native hardwood trees have always been in demand; coconuts and fishing were the only other natural resources that added to the economy—but none on a large scale. Today the face of Quintana Roo is changing. Tourism is its number one attraction with the development of an offshore sandbar, Cancun, into a million-dollar resort.

ARCHAEOLOGICAL ZONES IN QUINTANA ROO	
TULUM	XELHA
COBA	KOHUNLICH

WILD CANARIES

Early one morning while getting ready for thirsty sun worshippers in a still-deserted patio, a bartender was delighted to show two birdwatchers how a trickle of condensed milk in the bottom of an ashtray immediately attracted hundreds of wild brown and yellow *canarios*. With the first thick drops out of the can the tiny birds swooped in from every tree and bush in and around the patio until the bar was covered. It had taken on life with hundreds of happy, chortling creatures queueing up for a turn at the tray, obviously in milky heaven.

ISLA DE COZUMEL

INTRODUCTION

Cozumel ("Land of the Swallow") is a Caribbean island surrounded by water the color of imperial jade. Edged with stretches of white sand and craggy castles of black limestone and coral, its 64-km shoreline is continuously washed by an inquisitive restless sea. The island (47 km long and 15 km wide) is the largest of the three off the E coast of the Peninsula, the others being Isla Mujeres and Contoy. Lying 19 km offshore, Cozumel was a sacred mecca for Maya noblewomen who traveled in large dugout canoes to worship Ixchel, the goddess of fertility.

A calm sea on the lee (W) side of the island makes it ideal for swimming, diving, waterskiing, windsurfing, beachcombing, or relaxing in the sun. It's also the developed side, where clusters of buildings in the town of San Miguel house 50,000 residents and visitors. Offices, shops, banks, markets, hotels, restaurants, and two docks are all concentrated in this small seaside town. The E coast is another world, with few people and little activity, but dotted with isolated coves and bays, some with placid water, others with spectacular surf crashing on the beach and spraying mist on passing windshields. Clear water and the proximity of at least 20 live reefs make snorkeling a must, even for the neophyte. Exploring the Maya ruins in the overgrown interior of the island is an adventure by motorcycle, bike, car, or foot. The people of Cozumel, in their quiet way, are accepting and friendly to the growing number of visitors who come each year. Although Cozumel, with its lively discos and steady influx of divers, is more upbeat then Isla Mujeres, it still lacks the jet-set feeling of Cancun.

Climate
The climate is warm year-round. The heaviest rains begin in June and last through Oct. (average 80 F). Rain falls almost every day, but the usual afternoon shower is brief and the ground absorbs moisture quickly, so any travel interruption is minimal. During wet months, expect high humidity. November through May is generally balmy, with lower humidity and an occasional cool evening (average 78 F).

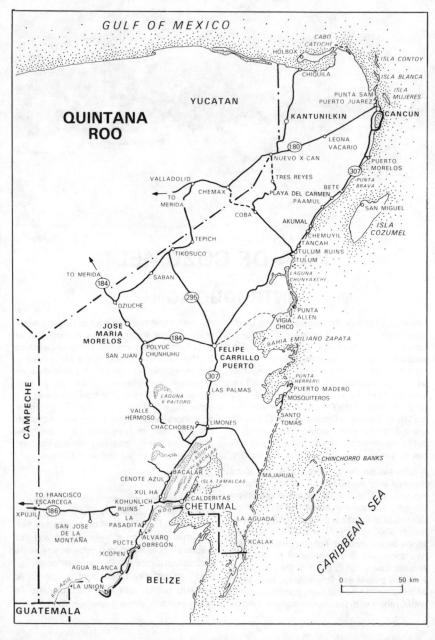

FLORA AND FAUNA

Birds

In 1925, Ludlow Griscom from the American Museum of Natural History was one of the first ornithologists to discover Cozumel's varied and concentrated birdlife. Since then, Cozumel has been considered a prime birding site in the Western world, since outside of town, civilization has not intruded into natural habitat. Except for the network of above-ground plastic water lines paralleling graded roads, the tangled brush, tall trees, and occasional abandoned hut all assure protected nesting grounds for these exotic winged creatures. If you enjoy watching birds, then getting up very early and trekking into one of several swampy areas on the island is worth the effort. One such place is located close to town behind the Sol Caribe Hotel. Here, at dawn, you're likely to see flocks of small multi-hued parrots, blue warblers, macaws, spindly-legged white egrets, and hear a glee club of sounds echoing through the trees and across the murky water. Another marshy area that attracts fowl is just S of the junction where the cross-island road meets the E shore; and if you have a car, a large swamp lies parallel to the coast behind the Celerain Lighthouse.

Other Animals

Lizards and iguana skitter through the jungles; armadillos, deer, small foxes, and coati also call the Cozumel jungle their home. The iguana, more visible than the others because of its size and large population, is often seen sunning atop rocks along the E shore, or even in the middle of the warm paved road that parallels the beach. Though the iguana is described as timid and said to move slowly, the traveler with a camera has to be lightning-fast to capture it (on film) before it slips quickly into its underground burrow or up the nearest tree once an outsider is spotted. The secret is not to be seen by the wary creature. (Photographers — keep trying, it can be done!) The iguana found in Cozumel commonly has shades of dark green, can grow up to 2 m long including its black-banded tail, and has a comb-like crest of scales down the middle of its back. Varicolored species are found on the Yucatan mainland.

Hummingbirds are seen everywhere in the Yucatan bush. The tiny bird was an important part of Maya art and religion.

Plantlife

Cozumel was never known for its agriculture, partly because of the shortage of water. However, during the early 1900s, chicle sap was gathered from numerous *zapote* trees which grow wild in the interior; *zapote* also produces a delicious red-fleshed fruit. Evidence of

an abandoned hut can be seen now and then where a farmer once tried to eke a living from the thin, rocky soil. Coconut palms grow thick near the sea and it's not unusual to see a sprouted coconut bobbing up and down in the surf. Many coconut trees take root that way, but if grown too close to the sea, they produce

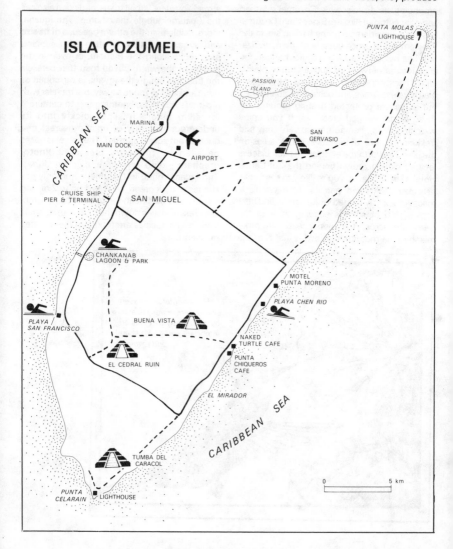

ISLA COZUMEL

PUNTA MOLAS
LIGHTHOUSE

PASSION
ISLAND

CARIBBEAN SEA

MARINA

MAIN DOCK

AIRPORT

SAN
GERVASIO

CRUISE SHIP
PIER & TERMINAL

SAN MIGUEL

CHANKANAB
LAGOON & PARK

MOTEL
PUNTA MORENO

PLAYA CHEN RIO

PLAYA
SAN FRANCISCO

BUENA VISTA

NAKED
TURTLE CAFE

PUNTA
CHIQUEROS
CAFE

EL CEDRAL RUIN

EL MIRADOR

CARIBBEAN SEA

TUMBA DEL
CARACOL

0   5 km

PUNTA
CELARAIN   LIGHTHOUSE

poor-tasting fruit. Take a stroll through the cool botanical garden at **Chankanab National Park** where hundreds of tropical plants found on the island have been planted and labeled with botanical names. A small entry fee (P100) gives access for the day to the lagoon and beach.

Marinelife

Brilliantly colored fish, from tiny 2-inch silver bait fish traveling in cloud-like schools to the grim thick-lipped grouper, lurk in and around graceful, asymmetrical formations of coral reminiscent of their names: cabbage, fan, and elk. You'll see rainbow-hued parrot fish, yellow- and black-striped sergeant majors, French angelfish, yellow-tailed damsel fish, and shy silver-pink squirrel fish with their big sensitive eyes. In shallow coves, daring Bermuda grubs come up out of the water to eat from your hand; watch the teeth!

HISTORY

Earliest Maya And Spanish

Cozumel's history consists of alternating bursts of unique activity and years of obscurity. During the Post-Classic Period, Cozumel was not only a sacred island but an important trading center. Artifacts, especially pottery remnants of the female figure made in distant parts of Mesoamerica, were left by women who traveled from all over the Peninsula to worship Ixchel at shrines scattered throughout the jungle. Afer that era the island existed undisturbed until 1517, when it was briefly visited by Juan de Grijalva, who traveled from Cuba on a slave-hunting expedition. He was soon followed by Spaniard Hernan Cortez, who embarked on his history-changing course in 1518. Cortez used Cozumel as a staging area for his ships when he launched his successful assault on mainland Indians. It was here that Cortez first heard of Geronimo de Aguilar, a Spanish shipwreck survivor of several years before. Aguilar had been living as a slave with his Indian captors; when he heard of Cortez's arrival, one story claims that he swam 19 km from the mainland to meet him. Because of Aguilar's fluency in the Maya tongue, he became a valuable accomplice in Cortez's takeover of the Indians. Francisco de Montejo also used Cozumel as a base in his war on the mainland. With the influx of Spaniards and accompanying diseases the Maya all but disappeared. By 1570 the population had dropped to less than 300.

Pirates And Chicle

The sparsely inhabited island led a placid existence until the late 1600s when it became a

D.LASICH

refuge for bandits of the sea. Pirates such as Jean Lafitte and Henry Morgan favored the safe harbors of Cozumel, especially during violent storms. The buccaneers frequently filled their water casks at Chankanab Lagoon and created general havoc with their heavy drinking and violent fights, disrupting life within the small population of Indians and Spanish. In 1843 the island of Cozumel was totally abandoned, when refugees from the Caste War began to resettle it.

Cozumel again became a center of activity when the chewing gum industry began to grow in the U.S. For centuries, the Maya had been satisfying their thirst by chewing raw sap from the *zapote* tree that grows on Cozumel and most of Central America. In the early 1900s, the developed world was introduced to this new sweet, bringing an economic boom to the Quintana Roo coast. New shipping routes included Cozumel, one of the best harbors along the coast suitable for large ships. A few big companies made their fortunes on the nickel-pack of chewing gum, while the Indians who cut their way through the rugged jungle to tap the trees managed only subsistence. Because of these companies, however, obscure but magnificent jungle-covered ruins hidden deep in the forests were discovered, fascinating the outsiders. This was the beginning of a large-scale interest in the Maya ruins by outsiders that continues into the present. At one time the only route to Cozumel was by ship from the Gulf of Mexico port of Progreso. Cozumel's shipping income dwindled gradually as airstrips and air freight became common on the Peninsula. In addition, synthetics replaced Central America's hard-to-get chicle and is now used almost exclusively in the manufacture of chewing gum.

WW II And Cousteau

In 1942, as part of their defense network guarding the American continent, the U.S. government made an agreement to protect the coastline of Mexico. The American Army Corps of Engineers built an airstrip on Cozumel where the Allies also maintained a submarine base. After the war, the island returned to relative obscurity until 1961, when a TV documentary produced by oceanographer Jacques Cousteau introduced the magnificent underwater world that exists in and around its live reefs. Since 1974 statehood, Quintana Roo (including Cozumel) has enjoyed (or suffered) a rebirth into the world of tourism. But while the government is trying hard to develop its beautiful Caribbean coast, Cozumel itself will never grow into a highrise city. Why? Because the water supply won't support an enormous increase of people, and everything needs to be shipped across the 19-km stretch that separates it from the mainland. So the historical "Land of the Swallow" may be about as developed as it's going to get—unless the Mexican computer that created Cancun has another brainstorm!

SAN MIGUEL

Cozumel has only one city: San Miguel. And though it's no longer a sleepy fishing village, it still has a relaxed, unhurried atmosphere, a good selection of restaurants from budget to gourmet, and hotels in every price range. Grocery stores, curio shops, banks, a post office, and anything else you might need are available. The main street, known either as Malecon ("Seawall") or Av. Melgar, depending on which map you're studying, extends 14 blocks along the waterfront. The main dock is at the foot of Av. Juarez, in the center of town. Plaza del Sol, the large central plaza, boasts modern civic buildings and an imposing statue of the late Mexican president Benito Juarez. In spring, masses of orange *flamboyane* (poinciana) flowers bloom on the surrounding shade trees where local townspeople gather for festivals, religious celebrations, or friendly chats. Cafes and gift shops line the N side of the plaza. The billfish tournament is held every year in May, bringing fishing enthusiasts from all over, especially boaters from the U.S. who cross the Gulf of Mexico to take part in the popular event.

ACCOMMODATIONS

Budget
Older hotels in the center of San Miguel are less expensive and within walking distance of cafes, discos, shops, and the sea-front promenade. A wide variety of rooms is available: some small and sparsely furnished; others expansive with heavy colonial decor, central courtyards, restaurants, and comfortable gathering places to meet fellow travelers.

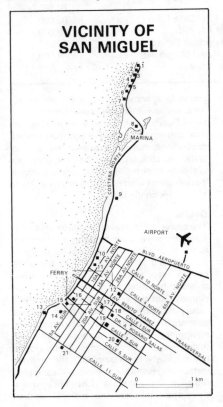

VICINITY OF SAN MIGUEL

VICINITY OF SAN MIGUEL

1. Mayan Plaza Hotel
2. El Cozumeleno Hotel
3. Cabanas del Caribe Hotel
4. Playa Azul Hotel
5. Cozumel Caribe Hotel
6. Cantarrel Hotel
7. Mara Hotel
8. Club Nautico de Cozumel
9. Condumel Condos
10. Los Portales Restaurant
11. Pizza Rolandi
12. Gonzalo de J. Rosado Library
13. El Hipopotamo Disco
14. Post and Telegraph Office
15. Aqua Safari Diving
16. Maya Cozumel Hotel
17. Benito Juarez Municipal Market
18. Lions Club
19. Javier Rojo Gomez Baseball Park
20. Children's Park
21. Health Center (S.S.A)

SAN MIGUEL BUDGET HOTELS

	Tel.	Address	Rates From-
Aguilar	2-03-07	Av. 5 Sur #98	P4,400
Antillano	2-03-96	Av. 5 Sur	P4,000
Bahia	2-02-09	Av. Rafael Melgar 25	
Capitan Candela	2-01-79	Calle 2	
El Pirata	2-00-51	Av. 5 Sur #3	P4,500
Flores	2-01-64	Av. 5 Sur #72	
El Marques	2-05-37	Av. 5 Sur #12	P4,125
Lopez	2-01-08	S side of plaza	P5,775
Malibu-Dorado	2-03-15		
Mary Carmen	2-05-81	Av. 5 Sur #4	P6,600
Maya Cozumel	2-00-11	Av. 5 Sur	P4,200
Meson del Peregrino	2-02-44	Av. Juarez & Av. 25 N	
Meson San Miguel	2-02-33	N side of plaza	P6,600
Paraiso Caribe	2-07-40		P4,830
Pepita	2-00-98	Av. 15 & Calle 1 Sur	P3,000
Posada Cozumel	2-03-14	Calle 4 N #50	P3,500
Suites Elizabeth	2-03-30	Calle Adolfo Salas 3	P4,880
Vista del Mar	2-05-45	Av. Rafael Melgar #45	P4,500
Yoli	2-00-24	Calle 1 Sur	

Many hotels offer an economical junior suite with cooking facilities and private bath, a great bargain for families or small groups. Most have ceiling fans; some are a/c. With few exceptions, higher winter rates prevail from the middle of Dec. through Easter week, and reservations are recommended. Rates quoted are for a double room during high season and can fluctuate; add 15% tax. Since the *peso* continues to change (almost daily), check prices on arrival if reservations aren't made in advance. There are no YHs on the island.

Deluxe
The newer, more modern hotels located on or across the street from the water are N and S of town. Most of these fit the deluxe category. Sand hauled from the E side of the island covers razor-sharp coral and limestone, creating beautiful white beaches for their patrons (and the public). The hotels offer a variety of lures to get you out of town: spacious palm-shaded grounds, beach activities, diving equipment, charming outdoor patios and thatch-roofed bars, swimming pools, tennis courts, lively entertainment, and modern restaurants, with tour services and car rentals right on the premises. Cozumel's under-developed bus service makes (almost)

DELUXE HOTELS

NORTH OF TOWN

Cabana del Caribe	2-00-72	P10,800
Cozumel Caribe	2-01-00	Club Med-Type-Resort.
Cantarell	2-01-44	P9,900
El Cozumeleno	2-00-50	P16,500
Mara	2-03-00	P12,180
Mayan Plaza	2-04-11	P19,775
Playa Azul	2-01-99	P10,400

SOUTH OF TOWN

Barracuda	2-00-02	P9,030
Galapago Inn	2-06-63	P15,400
La Ceiba	2-03-79	US$55
El Presidente	2-03-22	P12,100
Sol Caribe	2-07-00	P18,500
Villablanca	2-07-30	P13,340

hourly trips to the hotel zone; fare is P100. Taxis charge about P400 from town to the hotel zones (1-4 passengers).

Condominiums

Condos have not taken over the Cozumel shoreline...yet! If you wish to stay at a small, intimate, well laid-out condo, try the **Condumel**, a 20-min. walk N of town. Condumel has its own beach and swimming dock where iguanas sunbathe with the visitors. The condos all have one bedroom with a king-size bed, living room with sleeper sofa, roomy modern marble bathroom with tub and shower, and well-equipped kitchen ready for the cook. A few basic food items, including beer and purified water, are chilling in the fridge in case you don't want to go shopping right away. Fans and the offshore breezes usually keep your rooms cool, but there's also a/c if you want it cooler. Maid and laundry service are available. Just ask, and you can borrow fins, mask, and snorkel to use while there. Rates for up to 5 people, US$80 per night Dec. to June 1; US$65 per night June 2 to Dec. 15. The 5th person sleeps in a hammock. For reservations write to Bill Horn, P.O Box 142, Cozumel, Quintana Roo, Mexico; or call in Mexico (987) 2-08-92.

Bill also manages Aqua Safari dive shop and will arrange diving trips and equipment.

Out-Of-Town Hotels

The only budget motel on the windward (E) shore is **Punta Morena,** set on a low rise with spartan accommodations: cooking facilities, electricity that goes off when the generator quits at 2200 (public power is on its way), an open-air restaurant, bar, and a beguiling view of the rough coast. A few sleepy monkeys tethered to the trees constitute an advertised "zoo" on the path to a beach with miles of shore to explore; P2000 d.

Camping

Cozumel has no campgrounds with facilities. However, hidden coves and isolated beaches on the E side of the island let the outdoorsman enjoy roughing it. Bring everything needed to camp, including water. Don't expect even a tiny *tienda* to buy forgotten items.

FOOD

San Miguel has a variety of ways to spotlight mealtime. Fast-food stands and restaurants

Condumel—modern condominiums on the beach north of town in Cozumel.

Punta Morena motel, one of the few businesses on the backside of the island

abound and fit all budgets. Seafood is exquisite and fresh. Yucatecan specialties simply must be tasted! *Camarrones con ajo* (shrimp with garlic), *caracol* (conch), and tangy *ceviche* (fish or conch marinated in lime, vinegar, chopped onions, tomatos and cilantro) are all tasty treats. *Huachinango Veracruz* (red snapper cooked with tomatoes, green pepper, onions and spices) is a popular fish caught off the reef year-round; eating it a few hours after being caught makes a good fish dinner perfect. Fresh seafood at its best is sold in most cafes.

Moderate Cafes

Las Tortugas, Av. 10 between Av. Juarez and 2 Calle Norte, serves authentic Mexican specialties from 1900. **Pepe's,** ½ block S of the plaza on 5 Av. Sur, noted for its relaxed atmosphere and reasonable prices, has been popular for 20 years. **El Portal,** a simple cafe facing the waterfront, serves good family-style food. A sturdy breakfast of ham, eggs, beans, and toast costs P400. Open for breakfast, lunch, and dinner. Be sure you peruse the old photos on restaurant walls, which date back to the days of Cozumel's chicle boom.

Have dinner and a drink at **Costa Brava,** located on Av. Melgar across from the navy buildings on the waterfront. The food and prices are very good. A simple breakfast begins at P200, set lunch P500, Mexican platter for P550, and you can indulge in usually high-priced shrimp, crab, or lobster dinners at reasonable prices. If the chef has had a good night, he treats his customers to a glass of Xtabentum, spicy liquer made in Yucatan.

Italian

If you're ready for something different, try the Swiss-Italian specialties at **Pizza Rolandi** on Melgar 22. Good pizza, lasagna, calzone, and salads, beer and great sangria. The outdoor patio/dining room is a pleasant place to be on a balmy Caribbean evening; indoor dining available in case of rain.

Mexican Entrees

For the zany crowd, **Carlos and Charlie and Jimmy's Kitchen,** N of the plaza on Av. Melgar, tel. 2-01-91, is a lively restaurant that specializes in fun. Any respectable beer drinker owes it to himself to witness the beer drinking contests held nightly. Sounds like a place to drink and not eat? Surprisingly, the terrific food includes good Mexican entrees. Open nightly. For a leisurely lunch in a tropical atmosphere, **Las Gaviotas,** out of town past the Hotel Playa Azul, sits right over a blue silk sea. A thatched roof over the patio protects diners from the hot sun. *Mole* lovers, try the enchiladas. Excellent Mexican club sandwiches with fresh turkey, (no plastic pressed stuff—yet!). The view of clear water and bright-hued parrot fish waiting

1. Temple of a Thousand Columns, Chichen Itza; 2. Tulum; 3. Yamil lum'um, Cancun;
4. Temple of the Inscriptions, Palenque; 5. El Mirador, Labna

1. Isla Mujeres sunset; 2. Agua Azul; 3. Cozumel sunset; 4. Akumal beach

for a handout helps make this a pleasant lunch spot. On Friday attend a traditional Mexican dinner-show.

More Expensive

The **Acuario Restaurant**, ½ km S of town on Av. Melgar S at Av. 11 (1200-2400), serves elegant fish and lobster dinners with cocktail service. Walls are uniquely lined with huge aquariums filled with tropical fish, including a few brightly colored eels. Open tanks outside have even larger denizens of the sea (sharks and giant turtles) on display. If you happen to be in the neighborhood around 1400, stop by for a drink and watch the handler feed the fish. It's a bit scary — seeing sharp shark teeth in action! **Morgan's**, on the N side of the plaza, is an elegant/casual restaurant serving a continental menu along with typical fish and Mexican entrees. You can spend from some to a lot. A special treat is crepes suzettes with a spectacular flaming show (and they taste terrific!). Mexican music starts about 1900, followed by a rhythmic Argentinan group including an expert on the S. American flute — don't miss it! For two people expect to pay anywhere from P3000 to as much as P10,000 for a good dinner including crepes, a drink, tax, tip, and entertainment — worth the splurge!

Hotel Restaurants

On Wed. and Sat. at 2000, the **El Presidente** and **Sol Caribe** hotels present a Mexican buffet and folkloric entertainment (about US$12) offering literally dozens of tasty dishes. Reservations can be made through most hotels.

Street Vendors And Markets

During spring and summer, street vendors offer mangos on a stick, peeled and artistically carved to resemble flowers, P100 each with your choice of lime or chili powder garnish, or both! A good selection of grocery stores, fruit vendors, and two bakeries make it easy to eat on the run. Nothing tastes better than a crusty hot *bolillo* (hard roll) fresh from the oven; a bargain at P30 each. The bakeries (one a block N of the main plaza at 2 Calle Norte in the Banco Serfin Plaza, and the other on the corner of 3 Calle and 10 Ave. Sur) sell a variety of pastries and cookies. The *tortilleria* makes corn tortillas all day; buy a kg for only P50 hot off the grill.

The **Central Comercial**, on Av. Juarez facing the plaza, and **Comercial Caribe** on Juarez closer to the waterfront, are grocery stores stocking a wide variety of canned goods, fresh produce, notions, alcholic drinks. Expect American-made products to cost more. Looking for plain Mexican ground coffee in Cozumel markets is frustrating. Instant coffee and coffee grounds with sugar added you can find. If you're desperate, American brands are available (at inflated prices) at PAMA on Av. Melgar.

Morgan's Restaurant

OTHER SAN MIGUEL RESTAURANTS

Grip's, at Calle Adolfo Salas, on Melgar, tel. 2-0213.
La Langosta, 5 blocks S of plaza on Melgar.
Soberanis, 3½ blocks S of plaza on Melgar.
El Ranchito, ½ block S of plaza on Melgar.
El Foco, 1½ blocks S of plaza on 5 Av. Sur.

ENTERTAINMENT

Discos are popular in Cozumel. At night, the town jumps with lively music, as energetic people meet and mingle. Dancing continues till morning at **Scaramouche** (Av. Melgar), **Grips** (Seafront/10 Norte), and **Neptuno** (Av. Melgar/11th). **El Presidente, Mayan Plaza,**

Best food show in town is at Morgan's, where waiters make a tasty flaming dessert.

Sol Caribe, La Ceiba and the **Mara** have music at cocktail hour and often during dinner. For a quiet evening of camaraderie and exercise for the brain, go to **El Encuentro**, where San Miguel's chess and domino enthusiasts enjoy challenging visitors; Calle 1 Sur and Av. 10 Sur, restaurant, open daily from 0800.

Fiestas
For typical Mexican entertainment, the **Forum** (one block from the aquarium on Av. Circumvalacion) presents a fiesta each night at 2200: P3500 admission includes 2 drinks, and a Mexican ballet with mariachis and marimba music. Check with your hotel or the Office of Tourism for reservations and time.

Cinemas
Cinema Cozumel is on Av. Melgar at 4 Calle Norte; **Cine Cecilio Borgues** is on Av. Juarez and Av. 35; showtime 2115 at both. U.S. films are sometimes shown with original soundtrack and Spanish subtitles, but most are Spanish-language films.

The Plaza
On Sunday evenings local citizens meet in the central plaza. Only a few women still wear the lovely white *huipiles.* Men in their best white hats look crisp and cool in the typical *guayerba* with its tailored pleats. Families (sometimes 3 generations) gather in the plaza to hear Latin rhythms and the tunes of the day presented by local musicians. The charming white gazebo takes on a modern look with the addition of powerful speakers placed around the park. Children, dressed as miniatures of their parents, run, play, and chatter in front of the live band. It's hard to say who does the best business—the balloon man or the cotton-candy vendor. This is a nice place to spend an evening, under the stars, meeting the friendly folk of Cozumel.

SHOPPING

You can buy almost anything you want in Cozumel. Gift shops are scattered all over town. You'll see black coral jewelry, pottery of all kinds, typical Mexican clothing and shoes. A few trendy fashion houses carry the latest

downtown Cozumel

sportswear, T-shirts, and elegant jewelry. One of the nicer gift shops, **La Concha**, displays traditional folk art from all over Mesoamerica including beautiful Guatemalan weavings in flamboyant colors; on Av. 5 Sur #141 near the plaza, tel. 2-1270. A small shop that sells a conglomeration of unique souvenirs and artwork is **Antiques and Artifacts** on Av. 10 between Juarez and Calle 1: you'll find Cuban cigars, old coins, wierd sculpture, Xtabentum (in fact they give you a taste of this Yucatecan liqueur to introduce you to it before you buy or not), artwork from strange to talented, and good English-language books. The gift shops of some hotels also carry a limited selection of English-language reading material. **La Belle Ondine**, on Melgar at 4 Calle Norte, has an unpredictable selection and also sells maps of the coastal area.

SERVICES

The 4 banks in town—**Bancomer, Banpais, Banco del Atlantico** (all on the main plaza), and **Banco Serfin** (2 Calle N)—exchange dollars or traveler's cheques between 1000-1230. **Long-distance phone office** is on Calle 1 on the S side of the plaza, open 0800-1300, 1600-2100. Long-distance calls can be made from many hotels as well. Calling collect will save only part of the added tax. **Post office** is on Calle 7 and Melgar, open 0900-1300 and 1500-1800 Mon. to Fri.; the **telegraph office** in the same building is open Mon. to Fri. 0900-2030, Sat. and Sun. 0900-1300. **Office of Tourism** (booth in plaza) is a font of information, usually manned by someone who speaks English. A complete list of hotels in every price bracket is available, along with maps of the island and any general info you might need; tel. 2-14-98.

State Tourist Office of Quintana Roo
Alvaro Obregon #457
Chetumal, Quintana Roo

For **taxi** service it's usually a matter of standing on the sidewalk and waving your arm; or wait on Av. Melgar at the foot of the downtown dock—taxis queue along the sidewalk on the waterfront. The taxi office is on 2 Calle Norte, tel. 2-02-36/2-00-41, and any hotel will call a taxi. The closest **U.S. Consular Office** is in Cancun, tel. 3-10-15. Cozumel has one **gas station**, 5 blocks from downtown at Av. Juarez and Av. 30, open 0700-2400 daily. Cozumel has government-sponsored **Green Angel** motorist assistance. If your car should break down on the coastal highway, stay with it until they come by to give you gas, parts, or whatever help you need to get you on your way. The Green Angels cruise only on paved roads during daylight hours. Laundry can be left at **Lavanderia Manana,** Av. Circumvalacion #101. Charge is by the kg, open 0700-2000 Mon. to Sat., usually one-day service. Pick up service on request, tel. 2-06-30.

Camera Shops
Several camera stores in town sell film, rent underwater cameras, and have one-hour color-print processing service. **Aquascene** is next to the La Ceiba Hotel; tel. 2-03-79 ext. 102. **The Flash Camera Shop** is in Discover Cozumel Dive Shop (weather reports available here), tel. 2-02-80/2-03-97.

Medical And Pharmacies
In the event of medical emergency, contact your hotel receptionist for an English-speaking doctor. **Hospital y Centro de Salud,** a small clinic with a doctor on duty, is open 24 hours a day, Av. Circumvalacion, tel. 2-10-81. One pharmacy, **Los Portales,** is located on Calle 11 Sur; tel. 2-07-41. Another is in Centro Comercial, on the N side of the plaza. **Farmacia Joaquin** is on the plaza in front of the clock tower; open 0900-1300 and 1700-2100; tel. 2-01-25. If still in need of help, call the American Consular Office in Cancun: tel. 3-10-15. Dr. Manuel Marin-Foucher Lewis is located at Adolfo Rosado Salas 260; tel. 2-09-12/2-09-49. Three dentists are listed in Cozumel's Blue Guide: Z. Mariles, tel. 2-05-07, T. Hernandez, tel. 2-06-56, and Escartin, tel. 2-03-85.

GETTING THERE

By Boat
Passenger ferries come and go from the downtown dock in San Miguel; car ferries use the **International Pier** across from the Sol Caribe Hotel where cruise ships dock. If crossing with a car, arrive 1½ hours early and be prepared with exact change and your car license number when you approach the ticket window...or you may lose your place in line and possibly on the often-crowded ferry.

By Air
Air travel from various points on the Peninsula is becoming more common: from Merida to Cozumel (Aero Caribe, US$22 OW); from Playa del Carmen (Aero Caribe, P2200 pp OW); schedules change with the season. The airport is approx. 3 km from downtown San Miguel. Taxis and minibuses meet incoming planes. Taxi fare to town is P500 pp in a collective taxi (a van) and will take you to your hotel. When departing, an airport-use tax is collected in

EMERGENCY PHONES

Police	2-00-92	Red Cross	2-10-58
Fire Dept.	2-08-00	Ambulance	2-06-39
Hospital	2-01-40	Clinic (24 hrs)	2-10-81

DOWNTOWN SAN MIGUEL

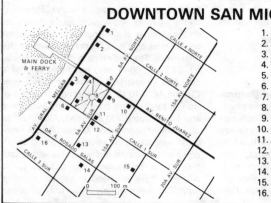

1. Port Captain
2. Mexicana Airlines
3. Las Palmeras Restaurant
4. Tourist Information Booth
5. Meson de San Miguel Hotel
6. Lopez Hotel
7. Young Heroes Monument
8. Benito Juarez Park
9. Convention Center
10. San Miguel Archangel Church
11. Arts and Crafts Market
12. El Pirate Hotel
13. Suites Colonial Hotel
14. Telephone Office
15. Bungalows Pepita
16. Pepe's Grill

COZUMEL BY FERRY

Boat	From	Departure	To	Fare
Passenger ferry	Playa del Carmen	0600-1200 1800	San Miguel Dock	P230 pp OW
Car ferry	Puerto Morelos	Call for Times	International Dock	P1,000 car OW
Car ferry	Puerto Morelos	Call for Times	International Dock	P150 pp OW

pesos only. This tax applies to all international Mexican airports, so check on arrival how many *pesos* are needed in order to leave and hold them back from the moneychanger at departure—most won't take dollars. Change your money in town, as banks and some shops give the best exchange rates, with hotels giving the worst. There are small duty-free shops with a limited number of gifts but a good selection of reading materials, especially English-language pictorial books about the area. The airport has a dining room upstairs and on the ground level a coffee bar opens for snacks, but usually not before the earliest flights.

GETTING AROUND

Travelers, especially backpackers, should be aware that no bus service exists outside of the immediate area of San Miguel. Several different transport options exist for exploring the outlying areas of the island—which everyone should do! Avenida Juarez begins in downtown San Miguel at the dock and cuts across the middle of the island (16 km), then circles the S end. The road around the N end of the island isn't paved. Walking the flat terrain is easy, but distances are long. Bicycles and 125cc motorcycles are available to rent at several shops in town. Taxis will take you anywhere on the island and are available by the day; agree on price before your tour begins. Traveling with a local cabbie is often a real bonus since the drivers know the island and its hidden corners better than most (other!) guidebooks. A last option is car rental, which means total freedom to explore. Tour buses go to a few ruins. In the city of San Miguel the roads are laid out in a grid pattern with the even-numbered *calles* to the N of the town

AIRLINES SERVING COZUMEL

From	Frequency	Airline	Cozumel Phone	
San Francisco	Daily	United	2-08-77	Airport
		Mexicana	2-02-63	Airport
		Continental	2-05-76	Airport
Los Angeles	Daily	United	2-08-77	Airport
		Continental	2-05-76	Airport
		Aeromexico	2-02-51	Downtown
			2-05-26	Airport
Chicago	2 Wkly.	United	2-04-68	Airport
Houston	10 Wkly.	Aeromexico	2-02-51	Downtown
Miami	Daily	Mexicana	2-02-63	

Sailing across the Gulf of Mexico is a challenge for American boaters.

plaza, odd-numbered *calles* to the S; numbered *avenidas* run parallel to the coast.

Bikes, Motorcycles, Car Rentals

All of downtown San Miguel is easily reached on foot. For those staying at the beachfront hotels out of town, good and reasonable taxi service operates to and from town, P400 OW for 4 passengers. Cozumel has a limited bus service to the hotel zones. The 70 km of paved island roads are flat and easily explored on bikes (rented at **Ruben's**, S side of the plaza, tel. 2-01-44, for about US$6 per day). Motor-bikes and 125 cc motorcycles rent for about US$20 daily.

Cars

Car rentals run approximately $30 daily, plus tax and insurance.

BIKE RENTALS

Hotel Aguilar, 5 Av. Sur #22, tel. 2-0307.
Hotel Lopez, S side of plaza, tel. 2-0108.
JB Motoscooter, 2 Calle Norte.
Pancho's, 2 Calle and 5 Norte, tel. 2-0204.
Renta de Motos El Dorado, 5 Av. Sur.
Rentadora Caribe, 3 Calle Sur, tel. 2-0961.
Reuben's, S side of plaza and at the cruise ship terminal. Tel. 2-0144, hotel delivery.

CAR RENTALS

Hotel Aguilar, 5 Av. Sur #22, tel. 2-0307.
Avis, Hotel Presidente, tel. 2-0389 and airport, tel. 2-0903.
Budget, 5 Av. Norte, tel. 2-0009 and airport, 2-0903.
Cozumel Maya Rent, tel. 2-0655
Hotel Cozumeleno, tel. 2-0344.
Hertz, Hotel Cozumel Caribe, tel. 2-0100.
Rent un Carro, Adolfo Salas 2, tel. 2-0111.

AROUND THE ISLAND

ARCHAEOLOGY

Nine Maya sites are scattered across the island. A few are difficult to reach, and only the hardy hiker will want to make the attempt. Most ruins on the island are of the "oratorio" type: small square buildings, low to the ground, with short doors that led early Spaniards to believe the places were once inhabited by dwarfs. **El Cedral** is the exception; though a small temple, major ceremonies were probably held on this site. The story goes that a large Maya city was destroyed when the U.S. Army Corps of Engineers built an airstrip in dense jungle (now the location of the new Cozumel airport).

El Cedral
Several of the ruins are easily reached by car or motorbike. Just beyond San Francisco Beach on the main highway leaving town, a paved road takes off to the left and ends in 3½ km at **El Cedral.** Small and not enormously impressive, this is the oldest Mayan structure on the island. Amazingly, it still bears a few traces of the paint and stucco of the original Mayan

artist. But the deterioration indicates that hundreds of years have passed it by. A tree grows from its roof with thick exposed roots interminably tangled in and around stones of the ancient structure. Fat iguanas with bold black stripes tracing their mid-section guard the deserted, mold-covered rock structure; sounds of cows blend with the songs of countless birds and the resonant buzz of exotic unseen insects. Located in what is now a small farm settlement, and used as a jail in the 1800s, El Cedral is presumed to have been a major site. Right next to it is a rustic, modern-day stucco church painted vivid green. Go inside and take a look at 2 crosses draped with finely embroidered lace mantles—a typical mixture of Christianity and ancient cult.

Aguada Grande
Another ruin that's difficult to reach is **Aguada Grande.** After crossing the island (Av. Juarez) to the beach, turn L on the dirt road and travel 21 km to another dirt road going inland; it's about a 1½-km hike to the site. This is ¾ km from the northern tip of the island and the **Puntas Molas** lighthouse and **El Real** (30½ km

Modern-day Catholic church next to El Cedral ruin. A continuing mixture of faiths shows up on the altar with linen bibs.

from San Miguel). If walking, the beach along here is difficult because of a rocky shoreline and you make better time on the dirt road. At about km 12, prepare for one of the most beautiful beaches on the island.

San Gervasio

This is a well-preserved and recently reconstructed group of several structures. Travel E on Av. Juarez, then left (N) on a dirt road (look for SAN GERVASIO sign) for approx. 10 km until it dead ends at the entrance to the site. The silence of these antiquities looming in the midst of dense brush with only birds singing in the tall trees overwhelms the visitor with an aura of what it was like centuries ago when only the Maya visited. San Gervasio has a snack bar for cold drinks and is open 0800-1700, small entry fee.

WEST SHORE BEACHES

Chankanab Lagoon

Chankanab, located 9 km S of San Miguel, is a national park. A small natural aquarium is surrounded by a botanical garden of 352 species of tropical and sub-tropical plants from 22 countries, as well as those endemic to Cozumel. The lagoon contains more than 60 species of fish, crustaceans, turtles, and in-

tricately designed coral formations. This is a wonderful shady park to spend hours watching underwater activity from the side of the lagoon through transparent water. The lagoon is shallow, and until recently swimmers could go from the lagoon to Chankanab Bay (on the sea) through underwater tunnels (that have collapsed and no longer assure safe passage). Now it's *no swimming*. Don't bring your crumbs and stale tortillas: caretakers frown on anyone feeding fish in Chankanab Lagoon. Without the former opening to the sea the biologists must work at protecting life in the small area. Save food offerings for your short walk from the lagoon to the bay, where hundreds of fish will churn water along the shore to get a scrap of anything.

Chankanab Bay

This is a popular beach for sunbathers, swimmers, divers and snorkelers to explore limestone shoreline caves. Showy sea creatures have no fear of humans invading their domain. For adventurous scuba divers, the coral reef close offshore is 2-16-m deep. A sunken boat, rusty anchors, coral-crusted cannons, and an antiquated religious statue all make for eerie sightseeing among the fish. A well-equipped dive shop is located here for rentals, air, sales, and certification instruction. Several gift shops, a snack stand, and a restaurant are all conveniently located near the beach where shade *palapas,* freshwater showers, dressing rooms, and lockers are all included in the small entrance fee of P100. This is a national park open 0900-1700 daily; when you pay your fee the attendant gives you a short list of restrictions.

San Francisco Beach
Four km S of Chankanab is **Playa Maya**, a small, calm swimming area on a narrow strip of sand. A snack stand is open daily. Following the main road past Chankanab (14 km from town), you'll come to **Playa San Francisco** on the right. This 3½ km of busy beach has 2 open-air restaurants, dressing rooms, bar, gift shops, volleyball net, wooden chaise lounges, and snorkeling equipment rental (P1500 per day). During the week, it's relatively quiet, but during busy seasons and on weekends is inundated with tourists, many brought by bus from cruise ships that anchor in the downtown harbor. San Francisco is also a popular Sunday destination for local citizens. Fresh fish and Mexican specialties are served to the accompaniment of loud, live music, romping kids,

and chattering adults. The bay is usually filled with dive boats attracted to nearby San Francisco Reef (see p. 226).

Isla de Passion
This tiny island in Abrigo Bay has secluded beaches and a rocky shoreline good for underwater exploring (no cafes, restrooms, or any other facilities). A good snorkeling beach, it's often the destination of Robinson Crusoe picnic trips or chartered fishing trips.

WINDWARD BEACHES

Northern
From San Francisco Beach around the southern end of the island are many beaches. Some are good for swimming; some are dangerous for swimming but great for beachcombing. Add sunning, camping, and birdwatching to provide more than enough reason to visit the shore from **Punta Molas** at the N tip to **Punta Sur** at the south. To visit beaches on the E shore, N of the island-crossing highway, take either a motorcycle or

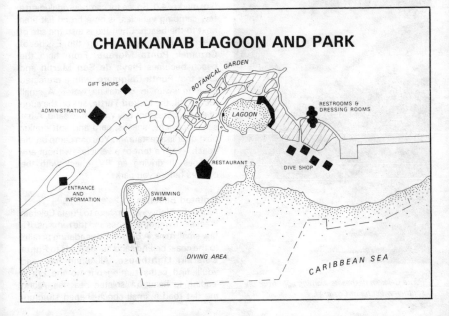

CHANKANAB LAGOON AND PARK

Punta Celerain flashes its warning light from the southernmost tip of Cozumel.

4WD for the unpaved sandy road. If you rent a jeep for this trip, make sure that the 4WD hasn't been disengaged by the rental agency. Because of its condition, the 24½-km road is seldom used, and few people see these beautiful beaches. If you decide to hike along this coast, you'll make better time in many areas on the road than on the rocky shore in between sandy areas. The first 2 beaches, **Santa Cecilia** and **Playa Bonita**, are good beachcombing spots, and **Playa Bonita** is a good camping beach (no facilities). For the real adventurer, the "Brown Map of Cozumel" shows trails from this dirt road to various little-known Maya ruins, abandoned *cenotes,* and caves. This kind of jungle trek requires carrying all essentials. From the Maya site at **Castillo Real** to the N, no more sandy beaches come before the lighthouse on Punta Molas. Many ships have sunk along this violent shore: cannons and anchors are occasionally found to prove the legends.

Chen Rio

At the end of the cross-island highway turn right (S), and the first beach is called **Chen Rio** (km marker 42). Space for campers, including a few camping vehicles, is on a broad flat area next to the beach. Chen Rio is also the site of the only motel/restaurant on the E side of Cozumel: **Punta Morena.** From here the beach becomes **Playa de San Martin** and after that **Punta Chiquiero**, with a protected cove to swim in crystalline water. A small restaurant, the **Naked Turtle**, sits on the edge of a lovely crescent bay with white sand. A bar serves *ceviche,* snacks, hard and soft drinks; next door is a restaurant. You can camp on the beach—with a tent or a vehicle—without any facilities. If driving an RV, check with the owners before you park.

Isolated Beaches

Along the highway from here to Punta Celerain is access to many beaches and the remains of a few small ruins. A dirt road meandering parallel to the coast behind sand dunes leads to **Punta Celerain Lighthouse.** All along this road you'll find paths turning out (to the L), all leading to beautiful isolated beaches. Along the dirt road a small conch-shaped structure

Lighthouse prism reflects light far away.

has been restored (and looks almost *too* new). According to the legend it was built between A.D. 1200-1400, used as a ceremonial center and a navigational guide by the Maya. Behind this small building, a dirt path over a sand dune goes to another great beach for swimming, sunbathing and beachcombing.

Punta Celerain

This lighthouse is 4 km from the main road. From a distance it appears white, tall, and regal; up close it needs a paint job. Next to the lighthouse is a small army base with soldiers on guard. An exciting spot, it's well worth the detour to wander around the point where a strong surf crashes over the irregular black limestone shore in great clouds of misty surf, spraying tall geisers through jagged blow holes. The family at the lighthouse is friendly, and usually you'll run into them on the grounds, either doing their laundry or cooking. Ask to climb to the top for a spectacular 360-degree picture of the island; don't forget your camera and wear comfortable walking shoes. The view one way is a long strip of white sand with a lacy scalloped edge of turquoise waves, the other way you'll see red marshy swamps in the middle of green scrub jungle; beyond it all — unending sea. On Sun. the lighthouse keeper sells cold drinks and fried fish.

Back on the paved road just as it rounds the curve and turns N, a large sign warns of the consequence of taking turtle eggs. There's a stiff fine for this since the turtle is a protected species; they come to shore here in large numbers during the summer and lay their eggs (see ''Turtles,'' p. 9). You'll often find a soldier (with tent) standing guard over the sign. However, this coastal watch keeps tabs on the boating activity between Cozumel and the Yucatan coast; boatloads of illegal drugs are frequently picked up along here. A return to the paved highway continues through the hotel zone and on into downtown San Miguel.

Punta Celerain

WATER SPORTS

Snorkeling and diving are the most popular outdoor activities on Cozumel. If you can swim, but haven't tried snorkeling, Cozumel is the finest place to begin. It's easy to find a fascinating marine environment close by without too much swimming or boating; in many cases you need only step from your hotel. Along the lee side of the island, almost all beaches are ideal sites. Practice with a snorkel and mask: sit in shallow, calm surf with your face under water, and breath through the snorkel that protrudes above the surface of the water. (Or use your bathtub to learn before leaving home.) Once accustomed to breathing with the tube, the rest is simple. Wear fins which make it easier to maneuver in the water. A few easy-to-reach snorkeling sites include: Chankanab Bay and San Francisco Beach, El Presidente Hotel beach, Hotel Cozumel Caribe beach, La Ceiba Beach (underwater plane wreck).

Scuba Diving
If you've always wanted to learn to scuba dive, here's the place to do it. A multitude of dive shops and instructors offer certification, or instruction sufficient for one dive. Thousands of people come to Cozumel because of the surrounding reefs. Fairly simple dives for the neophyte are on offshore fringing reefs. Caves and crevices line the shore, and coral heads rise to within 3 m of the surface. Some divers prefer wall diving, while others find night diving more exciting. Certain reefs are for only the most experienced diver. Boat reservations must be made in advance. Diving is an exciting sport, and the clear waters around Cozumel allow outstanding photos; underwater camera rentals are available at some dive shops (see p. 228).

DIVE SPOTS

Plane Wreck
The average non-diver wouldn't think of a wrecked plane as a reef. However, if it sits on the bottom of the sea it serves as a reef by affording schools of fish shady hiding places on the white sandy bottom. A 40-passenger Convair airliner (engines removed) reposes upside down after being purposely sunk in 1977 for the Mexican movie production of "Survive II."

The water's clarity allows a clear view of the submerged wreck, located 100 m off the La Ceiba Hotel pier. Beyond the wreck are huge coral heads in 14 m of water. At the plane wreck, a 120-m trail has been marked with underwater signs which point out the various types of marinelife on La Ceiba reef. The visibility is up to 30 m, and the average depth is 9-17 meters. A pillar of coral is an impressive sight and multi-colored sponge are outstanding here.

Paraiso Reef

Around 200 m off the beach just S of the International Dock (between El Presidente and the dock), **North Paraiso Reef** can be reached either by boat or from the beach. It averages 9-17 m deep and is a site of impressive star and brain coral, and sea fans. The S end of the reef, farther offshore and located S of the International Dock, is alive with churning reef life. This is a good spot for night diving.

Chankanab Caves And Reef

For easy-access diving, go to **Chankanab Lagoon**. A series of 3 caves on the shoreline provides a unique experience. Along the shore, steps are carved from coral for easy entry into water that surges into large underground caverns. Within seconds, you're in the first cave filled with hundreds of fish of all varieties. Striped grunt, snapper, sergeant majors, and butterfly fish are found in all 3 caves. Dives average 5-12 m.

A boat is needed to dive Chankanab Reef, several hundred m offshore S of Chankanab Lagoon (sometimes referred to as Outer Chankanab Reef). There's good night diving here, in depths of 8-15 m where basket starfish hang out with octopus and jail-striped morays. At the drop-off, stunning coral heads are at a maximum depth of 10 m; in some spots coral is within 3 m of the surface. Coral heads are covered with gorgonians and sea fans; striped grunt and mahogany snapper slowly cruise around the base. This is a good location for snorkelers and beginning divers.

Tormentos Reef

This is a medium-depth reef with innumerable coral heads in 8-12 m of water above a sandy bottom. The heads are decorated with fans, gorgonians, and sponges. With little current, you can get excellent photos. Along the sandy bottom are great numbers of invertebrates: flamingo tongue shell, arrowcrab, black crinoid, coral shrimp, and sea cucumber. When the current is going N, the farthest section of the reef drops to 21½ m where you'll see deep-sea fans, lobsters, and immense groupers.

Yocab Reef

One km S of Punta Tormentos, **Yocab Reef** is fairly close to shore, shallow (good for beginners), and alive with such beauties as queen angelfish, star, brain coral, sponge, and seawhip. The coral reef is about 120 m long,

Chankanab Lagoon

with an average depth of 9 m and coral rising from the floor about 3 meters. When there's current it can be 2 or 3 knots.

Tunich Reef

A half km S of Yocab — directly out from Punta Tunich — this deeper reef (15-24 m) has about 1½ knots current or more, and when it's stronger you could be swept right along to Cuba! It's loaded with intricately textured corals and the water activity attracts manta rays, jewfish, and barracuda; a good reef to spot shy moray eels.

San Francisco Reef

Another popular reef is located one km off San Francisco Beach. The abbreviated (½ -km) coral runs parallel to shore; this is a boat dive into a site teeming with reef fish of many varieties and brilliant colors. Depths average 17-19 m.

Santa Rosa Wall

This sensational drop-off, which begins at 22 m and just keeps going to the black bottom of the Caribbean, really gives you the feeling of the depth. Strong currents make this a drift-dive, a site for experienced divers only (watch your depth gauge). You'll discover tunnels and caves, translucent sponge, stony overhangs, queen, French, and gray angelfish, white trigger fish, and many big groupers.

Paso del Cedral

This flat reef with 22-m garden-like valleys is a good wall dive. In some places the top of the reef begins 15½ m from the surface. Good sea life includes angel fish, lobster, and the thick-lipped grouper.

Palancar Reef

The reef most associated with Cozumel Island is actually a 5-km series of varying coral formations about 1 ½ km offshore. Each of these formations offers a different thrill. Some slope, and some drop off dramatically into winding ravines, deep canyons, passageways, through archways and tunnels with formations 15 m tall all teeming with reef life. Startling coral pinnacles rise to 25 m from the sloping wall. Much deeper at the S end, the top of the reef begins at 27 meters. **Horseshoe,** considered by some to be the best diving in the Caribbean, is a series of coral heads which form a horseshoe curve at the top of the drop-off. The visibility of 66-86 m, plus a solid bronze, 4-m-tall, submerged modernistic sculpture of Christ, make this a dramatic photo area. The statue, created especially for the occasion, was sunk on 3 May 1985 with great pomp and ceremony and the presence of Ramon Bravo, well-known Mexican diver. The much-discussed reef is well worth its good press.

San Francisco beach on Sunday afternoon has more local visitors than tourists.

Cozumel reefs make it a favorite diver's destination.

Colombia Reef

Several km S of Palancar, Colombia Reef is a deep-dive area, with the top of the reef climbing from 25-30 m. This is the same environment as Palancar, with canyons and ravines; here the diver may encounter giant turtles and huge groupers hiding beneath deep overhangs of coral. Seasonally, when the water cools down, you'll see spotted eagle rays (water temperature averages 74 degrees in winter and 82 degrees in summer). This reef is best for experienced divers, as there's usually a current with visibility of 50-66 m.

Maracaibo Reef

At the southern tip of the island, this is an exhilarating experience. Restricted to the experienced only, **Maracaibo** is considered by most to be the ultimate challenge of all the reefs mentioned. At the deepest section, the top of the wall begins at 37 m; the shallow area—23 m. Unlike many other reefs, coral formations here are immense. Be prepared for strong currents and for who-knows-what

pelagic species of marinelife, including shark. Dive boats do not stop here on their regular trips and advance reservations are required for this dive.

Other Good Diving Areas

Not shown on most maps are **Cardona Reef, La Francesa Reef, Barracuda Reef,** and parallel to Barracuda, **San Juan**—for *experienced divers only;* currents can be as much as 6 knots. In that kind of current a face mask could be ripped off with the wrong move. The faster the current, the clearer the water and the more oxygen, definitely a specialty dive (somewhat like a roller-coaster!). Check with Aqua Safari for more information, including length of time to reach these reefs; 3 hours in a slow boat, an hour in Aqua Safari's fast boats. Reservations necessary. A handy scaled map-guide with water depths around the island (and other reef information) is called "Chart of the Reefs of Cozumel Mexico," put out by Ric Hajovsky and available at his unique shop called Antiques & Artifacts, as well as most dive shops.

DIVE TRIPS

Unless you have your own boat, many of the reef sites mentioned may be arranged through one of the many dive shops in town, the boatmen's co-op, or by some of the hotels that have their own equipment and divemaster. All equipment is provided, and sometimes lunch and drinks. Prices vary, so shop around. For beginners, scuba lessons for certification or a resort course for one-day dives are available at most of the same shops. Be sure to check the qualifications and track record of the dive shop and divemaster you choose. A few are outstanding, most are good.

Also, shop around for your needs and level of

COZUMEL DIVE SHOPS

Aqua Safari, S of the plaza, on Melecon at 5 Calle Sur, tel. 2-01-01/2-06-61. For more info (including hotel reservations): Box 41, Cozumel, Quintana Roo, Mexico.

Aventuras Tropicales, Malecon N of the plaza, tel. 2-03-93.

Blue Angel Scuba School, Villablanca Hotel, tel. 2-07-30.

Bonanza Boat Trips, N of the plaza on 2 Calle Norte, tel. 2-05-63.

Caribbean Divers, Hotels Cantarell, Mayan Plaza, and Cabana del Caribe.

Deportes Acuaticos, 4 blocks N of the plaza on Calle 8 short distance from the Malecon, tel. 2-06-40. Underwater cameras available.

Discover Cozumel, S of the plaza on the Malecon; also at Chankanab Lagoon, tel. 2-02-80.

Fantasia Marina, S of town, in front of Hotel Sol Caribe, tel. 2-07-25.

La Ceiba, S of town, at Hotel La Ceiba, tel. 2-03-79.

SCUBA Cozumel, S of the plaza on Malecon, tel. 2-06-27; also at the Galapago Inn, 2 km S of town, tel. 2-08-53.

Sociedad Cooperativa, tel. 2-00-80.

Viajes y Deportes del Caribe, S of town, at the Hotel El Presidente, tel. 2-03-22.

---

diving. **Aqua Safari** has an excellent reputation for safety, experience, good equipment, and happy divers who return year after year. Aqua owns 2 large fiberglass boats geared for 16-18 divers each with platforms for easy entry and exit. The boats leave from in front of the dive shop (addresses below) at 0930, returning at 1600, daily except Sun., Christmas, and New Year's Day. A typical dive-day consists of 2 dives on different reefs with a stop at the beach for a seafood lunch. The first dive is usually about 19-25 m, the second dive about 13 meters. The exact location is determined by the divemaster on each boat according to the weather conditions, currents, divers' requests and experience. The fee is US$30 plus 20% tax. This includes 2 tanks, weights and belt, backpack, dive guide, lunch and refreshments. Additional gear may be rented: regulator with pressure gauge, US$5, horsecollar B.C., US$5, tanks for beach diving, US$6 (includes weights, belt, and backpack), mask, snorkel and fins US$4. They have a few lights available for night diving but suggest that you bring your own. During the winter months water temperature drops slightly and it's suggested you bring a wet suit top. Aqua Safari store hours are 0800-1300 and 1600-1830.

For a quickie morning dive, **Blue Angel Divers,** with a 6-diver capacity, is back by 1330. The boat is fast and comfortable with easy entrance and exit. Ricardo Madrigal, a divemaster who caters only to advanced divers, can be reached by phone (tel. 2-15-78); he supplies tanks, weights, and belts—*only*. All other scuba equipment must be supplied by the diver. Ricardo first checks your ability, and when satisfied you're in the expert class makes specialty trips to the mainland for diving and camping or trips to the Barracuda and San Juan reefs in his Bertrim twin-engined boat. All scuba divers must show certification card before going on boats or renting tanks.

Notice To Divers

Since 1980, a refuge for the protection of marine flora and fauna on the W coast of Cozumel from the shore up to and including the Drop-Off (El Cantil) makes it illegal to fish or to remove any marine artifacts including coral

Aqua Safari, just one of several well-equipped dive shops in Cozumel

from the area. So, scuba divers and snorkelers, take only pictures. This piece of nature has not been damaged and has in fact grown richer with the care and pride of Cozumel divers in recent years.

OTHER WATER ACTIVITIES

Glass-Bottom Boat Tours

For the non-diver, glass-bottom boats provide a close-up view of Cozumel's flamboyant underwater society. Small boats cruise along the lee side of the coast and bigger motorized launches travel farther out to the larger reefs. Prices vary accordingly. Ask at your hotel or one of the dive shops. From US$2-$4 pp. Another popular cruise is the "Robinson Crusoe," which also varies in size and type. One boat is even designed to look like a pirate ship out of the 1600s. Destinations vary, though usually along the lee side, with a guarantee of a white beach for good swimming. Often the boats go to Isla Passion where you can swim, sunbathe, or snorkel while the crew dives for and cooks lobster or fish over an open fire for your lunch. Depending on how extensive the lunch, prices start at P5000.

motorsailer used as a dive boat

Charter Boats
Customized boat trips can be arranged through Bill Horn at **Aqua Safari** (tel. 2-01-01) for crossing the channel to Tulum for a day of sightseeing at the Maya ruins; return trip at your leisure. Trips to Cancun and Isla Mujeres or some other mainland destination can also be arranged.

Fishing
Cozumel boasts good deep-sea fishing year-round. Red snapper, tuna, barracuda, dolphin, wahoo, bonito, king mackerel, and tarpon are especially plentiful March through July, also high season for marlin and sailfish. Hire a boat and guide for the day at the downtown dock. Small boats, including tackle, bait and guide, cost US$130 to US$160 a day: boats 30-35 feet go for US$210-US$400 a day; larger boats rent for US$500 full day, US$300 ½ day. Arrangements can be made at the boatmen's co-op (tel. 2-00-80), Pancho's (tel. 2-02-04), or call Club Nautico de Cozumel at Marina Puerto De Abrigo Banco Playa, mailing address Box 341, Cozumel, Q. Roo, Mexico; tel. 2-01-18/2-01-24.

Miscellaneous
Instruction and equipment for windsurfing and waterskiing can be rented at **Pancho's**—2 blocks NE of the plaza, corner of 2 Calle and 10 Av. N., tel. 2-0204. At the Hotel Presidente, S of town, **Viajes y Deportes del Caribe** offers boat rentals (small and large fishing boats, ski boats, sail boats and motorboats). Windsurfing instruction and sail boards are also available.

CANCUN

By now everyone knows the story of a wise Mexican computer that in 1967 chose a small, swampy finger of land in an isolated part of the Mexican Caribbean and said "Let There Be Tourists." And so it happened — Cancun resort was born. Designing Cancun — an island shaped like a "7", with a bridge at both ends connecting the mainland — from the ground up began in 1968: new infrastructure, modern electrical plants, pure water from the tap, paved tree-lined avenues, buildings which fit into the landscape (reincarnated Mayas could almost mistake some of them for new pyramids). When the first hotels opened their doors in 1972, the visitors began coming and haven't stopped since. For some, the name "Yucatan" conjures immediate images of sugar-fine sand, a pallet-blue sea, and the word Cancun surrounded by flashing dollar signs. Think again! The beaches *are* stunning, the water *is* enticing, but it *doesn't* take lots of money to enjoy Cancun. The reality is there's something to fit every pocket; the best of both worlds — you just have to look a little harder for the less-expensive world.

At one end of the bridge is the "island' (the hotel zone where the most elegant hotels are located); on the other end — Cancun city (where new moderately priced hotels continue to be built). Hotels in the city serve up the flavor of Yucatan in the moderate P8000 to P10,000 category and offer easy access to crowded sidewalk cafes (good for meeting people), romantic dinners, hot discos, intimate bistros, cinemas, buses, and a multitude of shops to explore — all within a few km of the beach and lagoon. But if you need a shot of luxury, Hotel Row is the place to get it. Here, the most modern hostelries on the Yucatan Peninsula provide a vacation in a sunny tropical setting. There's glamour, excitement, excellent service, great entertainment, lavish rooms, epicurean delights, and the surroundings bombard the senses with nature's simple beauty.

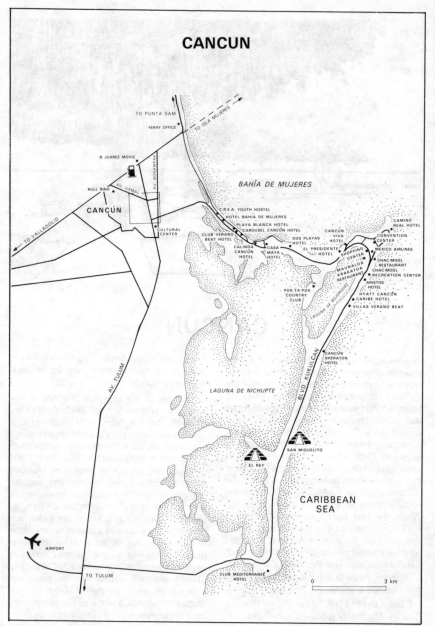

CANCUN

TO PUNTA SAM

FERRY OFFICE

TO ISLA MUJERES

B. JUAREZ MOVIE

AV. UXMAL

AV. BONAMPAK

BULL RING

CANCÚN

TO VALLADOLID

CULTURAL CENTER

BAHÍA DE MUJERES

C.R.E.A. YOUTH HOSTEL
HOTEL BAHIA DE MUJERES
PLAYA BLANCA HOTEL
CAROUSEL CANCÓN HOTEL
CLUB VERANO BEAT HOTEL
CALINDA CANCÚN HOTEL
CASA MAYA HOTEL
DOS PLAYAS HOTEL
EL PRESIDENTE HOTEL

CANCÚN VIVA HOTEL

CAMINO REAL HOTEL

CONVENTION CENTER

MEXICO AIRLINES

SHOPPING CENTER
MAUNALOA RESTAURANT
KRAKATOA RESTAURANT

CHAC MOOL RESTAURANT
CHAC MOOL RECREATION CENTER

ARISTOS HOTEL

HYATT CANCÚN
CARIBE HOTEL

VILLAS VERANO BEAT

POK TA POK COUNTRY CLUB

LAGUNA DE BOJORQUEZ

AV. TULUM

LAGUNA DE NICHUPTE

BLVD. KUKULCAN

CANCÚN SHERATON HOTEL

SAN MIGUELITO

EL REY

CARIBBEAN SEA

AIRPORT

TO TULUM

CLUB MEDITERRANEE HOTEL

0   3 km

SIGHTS

Archaeological Zones

Cancun has little to offer the archaeology buff by comparison to the large sites at Uxmal and Palenque. But surprisingly, structures built on this narrow strip of land have contributed important information to our knowledge about the people that lived here hundreds of years ago. Remnants of 2 sites, **Del Rey** on the S end of the "island" (close to Club Med), and *Yamil Lu'um* ("Hilly Land") next to the Sheraton Hotel, are both worth a look; Yamil Lu'um is also on the highest point of mostly flat Cancun. The 2 small temples (15 m high) were probably used as watchtower and lighthouse along this navigational route. Between 400-700 years old, they were first noted by 2 intrepid American explorers, John L. Stephens and Frederick Catherwood.

Museum of Anthropology

Located in the Convention Center (see "city map"), the museum houses Maya artifacts found on Cancun and other parts of the Peninsula. Though small, it graphically answers some questions about the everyday life of the Maya Indian. For example, a display of misshapen skulls has an explanation of how the Maya formed the heads of infants to conform to their idea of beauty. The museum is open from 1000-1400 and 1700-2000 daily; small entrance fee.

Scenic Spots

All of Cancun is scenic. But the most scenic beaches are on the seaward side of the island, extending 21 km, parallel to Paseo Kukulcan. Walking along the coast is rated a 5-star activity, and it's free (all beaches in Mexico are public). The panorama is capricious — the color of the sea changes subtly throughout the day from pale aqua at dawn to deep turquoise at noon to cerulean blue under the blazing afternoon sun to pink-splashed purple during the silent sunset.

Nichupte Lagoon

This large lagoon that parallels Paseo Kukulcan is a combination of sweet water fed by underground springs and salt water that enters from 2 openings to the sea. In certain areas where the water is still and swampy, mangroves provide hiding places for the cayman, little brother of large crocodilians found on other parts of the Peninsula. Birdlife is plentiful with a treasure trove of over 200 cataloged species including heron, egret, osprey, screaming parrots, and parakeets; the sooty tern returns here to nest each year. The best way to see the lagoon and its wildlife is by boat. One of the many travel agents or your hotel can arrange a boat and guide who knows his way around. Along the N end of the lagoon the marinas bustle with activity, and the trim greens of the Pok Ta Pok golf course extend out over the water. Nichupte is a favorite for waterskiing, sailing (Sunfish and Hobiecat rent-

Modern hotels line the shore with an ancient Maya structure in the foreground.

als), and sailboarding. Restaurants from exotic to generic are open all day, with a variety of shopping centers offering something for everybody. The arts and crafts center offers those who find bargaining stimulating a chance to practice the art. For the more timid who may be used to paying the marked price, there are also shops which have become very Americanized.

Aviary
For a closer look at some of the more exotic birds, bring your camera and visit the aviary located on the grounds of the Mauna Loa Complex near the Convention Center. Housed in *palapa*-roofed cages are colorful large or small parrots, the now-rare oscillated turkey (at one time it roamed the Peninsula in great numbers), the exotic long twin-tailed mot-mot, along with some of the small animals that usually live in the bush.

BEACHES

Note!
The water on the ocean side of Cancun can be hazardous. Pay particular attention to warning signs, and if in doubt, don't swim. Each year a few people drown off the beaches of Cancun because of a lack of respect for the power of this beautiful sea.

Bus To The Beach
Cancun is one big beach, or more accurately, a series of breathtaking beaches laid end to end and around corners and curves. It's simple to reach any beach by bus; the route begins in downtown Cancun, making a circuit along Paseo Kukulcan, through the hotel zone, past the Convention Center, to the last stop at the Sheraton Hotel. Bus stops are frequent and marked with blue signs that say *PARADA*. However, most drivers will stop for a waving arm almost anywhere (if there's room). Bus fare is P40 to anyplace.

Beginning Snorkelers
These beaches are for relaxing and soaking up the sun. The sandy sea-floor along here doesn't provide hiding places for the kind of sealife which prefers cool caves and rocky crevices. (Don't despair, there are a number of reefs in the area with rich marinelife to explore.) But for beginners (including children), this is a great place to learn to snorkel — and sun-loving fish like tanned beauties and burnt-back beach nappers will provide the thrill of accomplishment when viewed for the first time through the glass.

Lifeguards
The hotels on the island all have beaches with various activities; some provide *palapa* sun shelters, volleyball courts, aerobic classes, bars, restaurants, showers, restrooms and towels for their guests, and most importantly, lifeguards. Everyone is free to use the 60-foot strip of sand along the sea on any part of Cancun; signs indicating this are prominently posted everywhere by Sectur, the Ministry of Tourism. Visitors staying in the city have been known to spend their entire vacation (on their own towels) under the eye of a hotel lifeguard.

parasailing on Cancun beaches

WATER SAFETY

The usual precautions apply: don't swim alone in isolated places, and take small children to calm surf areas, especially if there isn't a lifeguard. Familiarize yourself with the beach before splashing into the surf. Most of the beaches are posted with surf condition signs; (in Spanish) they specify the condition each day with a colored flag. Red is high surf or undertow—DANGEROUS; yellow is medium high surf—USE WITH CAUTION; green is CALM. While swimming, if you feel yourself being pulled out to sea, don't panic, and don't wear yourself out trying to swim to shore. Instead, swim parallel to the beach in either direction, and usually after swimming 3 or 4 m you'll be out of the undertow—then swim to shore.

Common-sense protection with sun-screen lotions, broad brimmed hats, and dark glasses are suggested for anyone still walking around in winter-whites (skin). Familiar brands of American sun-screen lotions are available at all pharmacies and many hotel gift shops—but will cost much less in the States.

The Surf

There isn't a beach suitable for surfboarding anywhere on Cancun. For the most part it's a placid sea ideal for swimming. After leaving the city, the first stretch of beach from the YH to Hotel Cancun Viva provides calm water and is also protected from strong currents and dangerous surf. The water at the lagoon is usually calm, but not as clear as the sea. Along the lagoon side you'll find many marinas and headquarters for water activities. On the E (the Caribbean or windward side) from Punta Cancun to Punta Nizuc the surf can be as high as 3 feet, and at certain times you'll encounter an undertow. If you don't see a water-condition sign, ask at the concession stand—or *don't* swim. The calmest and most protected beaches (on the windward side) face Bahia Mujeres on the N end of the island.

Public Beaches

Don't expect lifeguards or showers; some have snack stands and good parking areas. **Playa Linda** is close to the city (10 min. by bus), located on Paseo Kukulcan near the Nichupte bridge; it's a large, fairly isolated beach. Bring a picnic and drinking water; there are no snack stands or restrooms; the water is clear, shallow, and calm. Two km farther on the road is **Playa Tortuga**, easily spotted by a sign that reads PLAYA RECREATIVA. The water is crystal clear, calm, deep, and on the beach is a *palapa*-covered snack bar.

Around the point beyond the Convention Center is **Playa Chacmool**. This stunning beach displays the vibrant colors that make the Caribbean famous. You can walk out to sea 14 m in shallow water before it begins to drop off. Check the tide conditions on a sign just S of the beach cafe—the water can be changeable here, and at times gets rough. South of the Sheraton Hotel, just beyond the entrance, look for a narrow dirt path that wanders through the brush. What remains of Cancun's undeveloped beach is available from this point to Punta Nizuc. This, too, is included in the master plan of the island and will ultimately be fully developed, but for now—enjoy; no facilities available.

WATER SPORTS

The Reefs

One of the most popular reefs, despite its shallow depths, is **Chital,** located a short distance N of Hotel El Presidente on the island. The reef is made up of 2 sections, both about 20 m wide. Expect a one-knot current, and clear visibility up to 33 m. **Cuevones Reef,** about 3 km N of Punta Cancun, is just what its name tells us in Spanish, "Small Caves." Here the body of the reef is comprised of elk-horn, rock, and brain coral. The series of caves varies in size from the largest (a 5-m cavern) to the smallest (2 m), all at a depth of about 10 m. With an amazing 45-m visibility, divers find themselves surrounded by large schools of reef fish, groupers, amberjack, and the ever-lurking predators, barracudas. **Manchones Reef** is a shallow reef closer to Isla Mujeres (3 km S) than to Cancun (8 km NE). Its 10-m depth, 60-m visibility, lack of current, and abundant sealife make it an ideal learning reef for beginning scuba divers.

Snorkeling

The experienced snorkeler will want to observe the beauty of the reefs which are mainly made up of a variety of uniquely shaped and textured elk-horn, rock, and brain coral. In the immediate vicinity the most popular snorkeling areas are Chital, Cuevones, and Manchones reefs. These reefs are home to large populations of reef fish including blue chromis and barracuda. Chital, 2 km N of the island, is good snorkling with depths between 2-5 m. Cuevones and Manchones reefs are between Cancun and Isla Mujeres with depths 10-15 m. Usually dive boats will take snorkelers along (room permitting) on scuba trips. Tour boats leaving daily for Garrafon Beach on Isla Mujeres carry snorkeling equipment. Garrafon is a logical spot for beginners and intermediates. Non-divers, bring dry bread to feed the little critters. They'll jump from the water and eat out of your hand—watch the fingers! Snorkeling equipment is available for rent at all the marinas and some of the hotels.

Scuba Diving

For the experienced scuba diver, Cancun would be second choice; Cozumel is unquestionably *numero uno!* For dive spots, however, none of the Caribbean is dull. An abundance of rich sea life surrounds each of the reefs; though around Cancun they're somewhat shallow, the beauty and excitement of the scenery are still dramatic (for scuba certification, see p. 242). At **Punta Nizuc** (next to Club Med), experienced divers can explore the starting point of the Belize barrier reef that runs S 250 km parallel to the Yucatan coast to the Gulf of Honduras. This reef is the 5th largest reef in the world. Great Barrier Reef, Australia (1600 km); New Caledonia's barrier reef (550 km); Great Sea Reef, Vanua Levu, Fiji (260 km); Belize's barrier reef (250 km); Louisiade Archipelago PNG barrier reef (200 km).

Windsurfing

For anyone who doesn't know, a windsurfer (also known as a sailboard) is comprised of a surfboard with a sail on a mast attached to the board by a swivel joint. This is controlled by a standing passenger who manipulates the sail with a wishbone tiller. It's a great wind-powered sport; in a brisk wind the sail billows and this surfboard-cum-sailboat takes its sailor on an exhilarating ride skimming across the waves at mind-boggling speeds. Lessons are available at most of the marinas or the Internationl Windsurfer Sailing School at Playa Tortuga, tel. 4-20-23. Usually 6 hours of lessons give you a good start. Sailboards are available to rent at many of the hotels and the marinas.

Sailboats

If your idea of a ride in the wind is a deck under foot and a tiller in hand, Hobiecat and Sunfish rentals are available at a few hotels and most of the marinas. These small catamarans will give you a good fast ride if the wind is up. Negotiate for the fee you prefer to pay (remember, you're in Mexico)—sometimes you can get a better daily rate instead of the hourly rate as posted.

Waterskiing

Most waterskiers prefer Nichupte Lagoon, although skiers are seen on calm days in Bahia de Mujeres N of the island. Equipment and instruction information are available from the marinas.

Jetskiing And Parasailing

One of the new speed thrills on the lagoon is jetskiing, obtained on a small motorized sled that will slowly circle around the driver should he or she fall off (rentals available at most marinas). Parasailing is popular at most beaches. The sailor, strapped into a colorful parachute, is pulled high over the sand and surf by a speed boat; after about 10 minutes of "flying" he is gently deposited back on land with the help of two catchers. Once in awhile the rider gets wet when he is inadvertently dropped in the bay—usually to the guffaws of the beach crowd.

FISHING

Deep-Sea Fishing

Fishermen come to Cancun for what is considered some of the finest game fishing in the world. Charters are available and easily arranged with a day or two advance reservation. For information on half- and whole-day trips, call the marinas or check with your hotel. On full-day trips you can cap off the afternoon with a fish barbecue on the beach (ask the captain in advance). One of the most exciting game fish, the sailfish, runs from March to mid-July, bonito and dolphin from May to early July, wahoo and kingfish from May to Sept., and barracuda, red snapper, bluefin, grouper and mackeral are plentiful all year.

Shore Fishing

Once you find a place to fish from shore, you'll catch plenty. Try fishing in the lagoon off the Nichupte bridge. By now you're spoiled, used to seeing the crystal-clear water of the Caribbean; well, the water is not as clear, but the fish are down there. Expect needlefish or a possible

barracuda, and rumor has it that an occasional shark takes a wrong turn at the bridge and finds itself in the lagoon. Contrary to universal belief—shark is good eating.

TOUR BOATS

Organized Boat Trips

Many tour boats are available for a variety of trips, most going to nearby Isla Mujeres: glass-bottom boats slowly drift above flamboyant undersea gardens, or on a musical cruise you can dance your way over to the small island. These often include snorkeling, and the necessary equipment is furnished. The *Manta, Don Diego, Cancun 5-0,* and *Aqua-Quin* are motorized trimarans going to Isla Mujeres daily; reservations required. Prices start at P5000, some include drinks and lunch. For further info check with the marinas.

The *Fiesta Maya* is a party boat with a snack bar, boutique, glass-bottom viewing, a live band, dancing, and 2 free drinks. The boat leaves the Fiesta Maya pier on the N shore of the lagoon across from El Presidente Hotel. During the 4-hour cruise, it stops at Garrafon Beach for snorkeling (small fee charged for equipment rental); departs 1000 daily except Mon., tel. 3-03-89. To get information on trips that explore the lagoon, visit the Del Rey ruins, or take sightseers to close-by reefs, ask at your hotel or call one of the marinas.

Self-Guided Tours

If you prefer to investigate Garrafon Beach on your own, it's easy and cheap. On Av. Tulum catch the city bus marked Ruta 1-A (P40) to Puerto Juarez (runs every 15 min.). Take the passenger ferry to Isla Mujeres (P150), and from here if you want to spend your day diving, take a taxi to Garrafon Beach (about P400 for up to 4 passengers), or it's a 5-km walk. Garrafon admission is P100, snorkeling equipment rents for P1500 (per day). A snack stand serves light lunch and cold drinks. If there's time before the last ferry back to Cancun take a look at the town of Isla Mujeres.

OTHER SPORTS

The **Pok Ta Pok Club de Golf** has tennis courts and a well-kept 18-hole golf course designed by Robert Trent Jones. The golf club is a great sports center with a pro shop, swimming pool, marina, restaurant, bar, and even its own small restored Maya ruin. Arrangements to play golf or tennis at the club can be made through your hotel. Many of the hotels on the island also have tennis courts, some with night lighting for a small fee.

PRACTICALITIES

ACCOMMODATIONS

Youth Hostel
The best bargain in Cancun is the **CREA Youth Hostel** on Paseo Kukulcan next to Club Verano Beat. Located in the hotel zone, the YH has a beach, swimming pool, bar, disco, dining room serving inexpensive food, and 650 bunk beds in women's and men's dorms. Rates are P900 pp (bedding included).

Budget
Budget hotels are located in bustling downtown Cancun. The biggest drawback to this location is the absence of beach; but blue sea and white sand are accessible in short order by bus: P40 every 15 minutes. These hotels, though simple, are clean, offer a/c and hot water. Rates begin at approximately P4500. Try **Hotel Rivemar**, Av. Tulum, tel. 4-17-08; and **Hotel Hacienda**, Av. Sun Yax Chen, tel. 4-12-08; **Hotel Tulum**, Av. Tulum, tel. 4-13-55

Moderate
Though sometimes crowded, these hotels are good bargains. The Yucatecan ambience pervades and each has a helpful staff willing to answer questions about the city. The hotels have private baths, a/c, hot water, swimming pool, phone in room, bar, and restaurant. The rates run from P8000 d. Check out **Hotel Plaza**

Yamil Lu'um—one of several small Maya ruins at Cancun near the Sheraton Hotel.

Caribe, corner of Av. Uxmal, tel. 4-13-77; **Hotel Cancun Handall,** Av. Tulum, tel. 4-19-47; **Hotel Plaza del Sol,** Av. Yaxchilan, tel. 4-38-88.

Deluxe

Every hotel on the "island" or hotel zone fits into this category. All offer a swimming pool (sometimes 2) and good beaches; an assortment of restaurants, bars, and nightlife; beach activities and gardens; travel, tour, and car agencies; laundry and room service. In fact, a tourist could conceivably find everything under one roof. Rates on the island begin at P19,000. The **Cancun Sheraton,** one of the first hotels built on the island, provides excellent service, each room having a view of either the sea or the lagoon. If you're on a honeymoon, inquire about a suite, each with a built-in jacuzzi on its private terrace. Try the Gaviota dining room, one of 3 on the grounds, for an elegant, romantic dinner served with a backdrop of fine piano music. The continental-style food is delicious, beautifully served, and expensive, with a good wine list. After the quiet dinner if you're ready for live action, try the Sheraton disco, Tabano's, which comes to life at 2100; tel. 3-19-88.

The **Fiesta Americana** is a colorful, well-appointed, relaxing hotel with fine restaurants, bars, and services; tel. 3-14-00.

The **Hotel Krystal** bubbles with charm, has large comfortable rooms, servi-bar in each room — you're charged on your bill (about triple the average price) for what you use: liquor, beer, soft drinks, candy, nuts. Employees go out of their way to make you feel welcome, and every imaginable service is available; tel. 3-11-33. A **Club Med** is located very close to Punta Nizuc in the hotel zone. Reservations in advance.

Condominiums

Cancun is sprouting condos everywhere you look. While one wonders when the building will end, they provide some of the best bargains in town for families or small groups. For as low as US$130 a night, a family of 5 can stay in lovely surroundings, near the beach, with a pool, cooking facilities, often 2

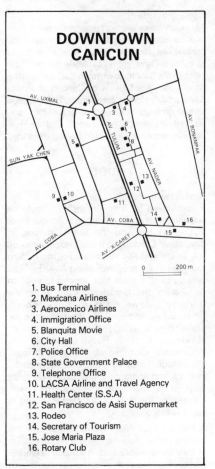

DOWNTOWN CANCUN

0   200 m

1. Bus Terminal
2. Mexicana Airlines
3. Aeromexico Airlines
4. Immigration Office
5. Blanquita Movie
6. City Hall
7. Police Office
8. State Government Palace
9. Telephone Office
10. LACSA Airline and Travel Agency
11. Health Center (S.S.A)
12. San Francisco de Asisi Supermarket
13. Rodeo
14. Secretary of Tourism
15. Jose Maria Plaza
16. Rotary Club

bathrooms, and daily maid service. The prices can soar much higher. Travel agents can help find them or you can write direct to the managers. If you're daring, your best buys come if you just arrive on the scene without reservations, go from condo to condo, and negotiate the price of one that isn't reserved. However, you run a certain risk of not finding what you want, especially during the winter. The following company rents condos from the U.S.: Luxury Villas of Cancun, 1-800-531-7211, Box 18225, San Antonio, Texas.

Campgrounds

Although there are no campgrounds on Cancun, travelers in RVs can park overnight in the parking lot next to **Playa Linda** at Paseo Kukulcan. There are no facilities, but you'll be close to the beach, downtown Cancun, and the hotel zone. Eight km N of Cancun at **Punta Sam**, a fairly decent campground offers clean simple grounds in a coconut grove, tent rentals, hot showers, a nice beach, and an inexpensive restaurant all within busing distance.

FOOD

Restaurants

If you stayed for 3 or 4 months, it might be possible to sample each of the fine restaurants in Cancun city and the island—maybe. In downtown Cancun are many budget cafes on Av. Tulum and Av. Yaxchilan. For more *tipico* food and ambience, walk along Av. Yaxchilan until you find a place that appeals to you. On Av. Tulum and Uxmal are many resort-like touristy sidewalk cafes—busy, noisy, Americanish, and fun! For the epicurean explorer, there's Swiss, French, Chinese, Italian, Mexican, Arabic, Polynesian, Texan, Yucatecan, Continental; there's Fastfood, Simplefood, Fancyfood, Seafood; Homemade, Rushed, and Romantic food. Hamburgers, hot dogs, tacos, and *tortas*. This is gourmet headquarters for the state of Quintana Roo, and all you have to do is look!

A curious food fact—Mexico is one of the leading coffee producers of the world. In spite of this, most restaurants in Mexico serve instant coffee. However, on a few Cancun menus you can find an old traditional favorite, *cafe de olla* (coffee cooked and served in a small earthen mug). Remember, in Mexico it's considered an insult for a waiter to submit a bill before it's requested; when you're ready to pay, say *"la cuenta, por favor."*

Groceries

Mercado Municipal, 6 blocks N of the bus station on Av. Tulum, is well supplied, sells everything. Come early for the best selection of fresh produce and meat. **Javier Rojo Gomez,** behind the post office on Sun Yax Chen, is a smaller version of Mercado Municipal. **Super Carniceria Cancun,** Av. Sun Yax Chen 52, sells familiar American-style cuts of meat. **San Francisco de Asisi Super Market** (on Tulum) is a modern well-stocked market designed for one-stop shopping (somewhat novel in Yucatan): butcher case, bakery counter, along with row upon row of groceries, liquor, electric appliances, even clothes. Another supermarket a trifle smaller down Av. Tulum just past the *glorieta* (traffic circle) is the **Glorietta Supermarket.**

Bakeries

Indulge yourself in fine Mexican pastries and crusty *bolillos* at the Panificadora Covadonga on Av. Tulum, a few hundred meters N of Av. Uxmal. Another smaller bakery is Los Globos on Tulipanes just W of Av. Tulum.

ENTERTAINMENT

Nightlife

Cancun offers a marvelous choice of nighttime entertainment. It's easy to dance the night away at any one of a number of inviting places. Most of the hotels on the island have discos in motion until the early hours of morning. Some *cantinas* offer live bands ranging from jazz to popular marimba to reggae. Many of the touristy hotels offer Mexican "fiestas" weekly, including *tipico* dinners with traditional dances and colorful costumes. The auditorium at the **Convention Center** regularly presents the Ballet Folklorico de Naucalpan and a tasty dinner (P5500 pp), and often brings in other special shows. The **Lone Star Bar** in

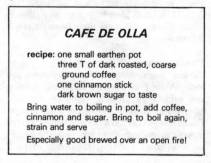

CAFE DE OLLA

recipe: one small earthen pot
three T of dark roasted, coarse
ground coffee
one cinnamon stick
dark brown sugar to taste

Bring water to boiling in pot, add coffee, cinnamon and sugar. Bring to boil again, strain and serve

Especially good brewed over an open fire!

downtown's Hotel Maria de Lourdes advertises they "speak Texan," has great down-home country-western music, and is busy at happy hour when they serve a free margarita (2000-2200, Sun., Tues., and Thurs.). **The Mine Co.** disco next to the YH on Paseo Kululcan charges a small cover. The **Mauna Loa** at the Convention Center presents 2 Polynesian floor shows nightly, but after 2300 the place transforms into a hot disco.

For zany fun with wild and comedic waiters as well as exceptionally good food (try the Mexican combination plate with *carne asada*), you can't beat **Carlos 'N Charlie's**, Paseo Kukulcan. For more romantic live music try **La Cantina** in Cancun 1900 at the Convention Center. And for a serene romantic spot to begin or end an evening, watch Cancun's sensational sunset or glittering stars in **La Palapa**, a mellow bar in a thatched-roof pavilion on the end of its own pier over the lagoon at Hotel Club Lagoon Caribe, Paseo Kukulcan. La Palapa serves snacks, exotic drinks, and has live music and dancing from 2130-0130.

Cinema

Unlike most Peninsula cities, the majority of films shown in Cancun are usually American made with Spanish subtitles. Expect the bill to change every 3 or 4 days. **Cines Cancun**, Av. Xcaret #112, tel. 4-16-46 and **Cine Royal**, Av. Tulum provide a cultural experience. Some of the larger hotels have their own movie theaters and large-screen TV.

SERVICES

Dive Certification

Cancun has a good selection of dive shops; check with the marinas for recommendations. Before a diver can rent equipment, it's necessary to show a certified divers card. If not certified, resort courses (for one dive accompanied by the divemaster) and certification classes (around 40 hours) are offered. For class info call **Mundo Marina**, PADI tel. 3-05-54, **Neptune**, NAUI 3-07-22, **Aqua Tours**, 3-02-07.

Medical Information

Most hotels in Cancun can provide the name of a doctor that speaks English. For medical assistance in dire emergency, call 3-01-63 or the American Consular office, 4-16-38.

Post Office And Telegrams

The post office is W of Av. Tulum on Av. Sun Yax Chen; open 0900-1200 and 1500-1700 Mon. to Sat., tel. 4-14-18. Telegraph office, tel. 4-15-29.

Consulates

American consular agent, tel. 4-16-38.

Tourist Information

One info center is downtown on Av. Tulum next to Ki-Huic shopping mall, another is at El Parian convention center in the hotel zone, tel. 4-33-40. The informed staffs are bilingual, cheery, and genuinely helpful. Ask for maps, brochures, prices, schedules, or directions. Chamber of Commerce is also a good source of information; tel. 4-12-01.

Immigration

Remember that you must turn in your Mexican visitors card when you leave the country. If you should lose it, need an extension, or have any questions, call Mexican Immigration, tel. 4-28-92 and at the airport, tel. 4-29-92.

Book Stores

Don Quixote Bookstore in downtown Cancun on Tulum (one block S of Tulipanes) carries a limited supply of English-language books—both fiction and non-fiction. Most of the island hotel gift shops sell American magazines as well as a supply of paperback novels, Spanish-English dictionaries, and several English-language newspapers: *The News* (published in Mexico City), *Miami Herald,* and *New York Times Weekly Review.*

EMERGENCY NUMBERS

Police	tel. 4-19-13
Fire Dept.	tel. 4-12-02
Air-Vac Medical Life Service	
Houston, Texas	tel. (713) 961-4050

GETTING THERE

Airport
Quintana Roo's busiest airport is 20 km S of Cancun. Along with everything else around this infant city, the airport is new and shiny, and continues to grow and add to its facilities each season. Visitors from many cities in the U.S. arrive daily on Mexicana, Aeromexico, United, Continental, Lacsa, and Eastern airlines. Aerocaribe and Aerocozumel bring passengers on daily flights from Isla Cozumel. Car rentals, taxis, and yellow-and-white combis are available at the airport to bring you to town or the island (hotel zone). Remember to reconfirm your flight 24 hours in advance and be at the airport an hour before your scheduled departure.

By Bus
From Merida and Chetumal, buses make frequent trips daily, linking smaller villages to Cancun enroute. The bus terminal is located in downtown Cancun on Av. Tulum. Call or go to the terminal for complete schedules — they're apt to change. For other bus info see "Transport" in Merida, p. 98.)

Car Rentals
Car rentals are available from Mexican and American agencies at the Merida airport, Cancun airport, and many hotels in both cities. Remember there is a hefty drop-off fee in a city other than the origination point. The 320-km, 4-hour drive from Merida is on a good highway (180), through henequen-dotted countryside, historic villages, and aged archaeological ruins. From Chetumal (307), it's 343 km (4 hours), along a well-maintained highway through thick jungle parallel to the Caribbean coast.

AIRLINES SERVING CANCUN

Airline	Offices	Telephone	Arrivals	Departures
American	Airport	4-29-47 4-26-51	Dallas	Dallas
Aerocaribe	Av. Tulum at Uxmal	4-12-31 4-13-64	Cozumel Chetumal Isla Muj. Chichen Itza	Cozumel Chetumal Isla Muj. Chichen Itza
Aeromexico	Av. Tulum at Uxmal	4-27-28 4-26-39	Houston Mexico Merida L.A. Monterrey	Houston Mexico Merida Monterrey L.A.
Aerocozumel	Airport	4-25-62	Cozumel	Cozumel
Continental	Airport	4-25-40	L.A. Houston	L.A. Houston Denver
Eastern	Airport	4-28-70	New Orleans	New Orleans
LACSA	Av. Yaxchilan 5	4-12-76	Guatemala New Orleans	New Orleans San Jose
Mexicana	Av. Coba	4-12-65 4-11-54	Mexico Miami Dallas Philadelphia	Mexico Miami Dallas Philadelphia
United	Airport	4-28-58 4-25-28	Chicago	Chicago

ISLA MUJERES

Climbed enough pyramids? Need a respite from the brain-boggling Maya technology? Then hop the ferry and spend a few hedonistic days on relaxing Isla Mujeres. This finger-shaped island lying off the E coast of the Yucatan Peninsula is 8 km long and 400 m at its widest point. After resting up a day or two on the most convenient Isla Mujeres beach, jump back into your explorations with a walk through the Fortress Mundaca and a visit to the marine biology station — devoted to the study of the large turtle.

Though the overflow of tourists from Cancun and Cozumel is beginning to be noticeable, few stay for very long — the island is relatively quiet. But for some adventurers, Isla Mujeres has it all. Snorkeling is outstanding, especially teeming Garrafon Beach; slow moving, the absence of jet setters isn't missed by anyone, including the easy-going populace. The small town smiles at backpackers, and travelers from budget to deluxe can easily find suitable lodgings. Isla Mujeres has a large naval base, with many ships in its harbor. By the way — the Mex-ican Navy doesn't like people photographing the base, ships, or crewmen on duty. If you're struck with the urge to film *everything*...ask someone in charge first. Fishing has always been the prime industry on the island, with turtle and lobster the local specialties. Today the turtle is protected; only certain times of the year may they be hunted. The eggs are *never* to be taken and stiff fines are given those that break this law.

History

One legend tells us that the name Isla Mujeres ("Island of Women") comes from the buccaneers who stowed their female captives here while conducting their nefarious business on the high seas. Another more prosaic (and probably the correct) version describes the large number of female-shaped clay idols found on the island when the Spaniards arrived. Archaeologists presume the island was a stopover for the Maya Indians on their pilgrimages to Cozumel to worship Ixchel, female goddess of fertility and an important deity to Maya women.

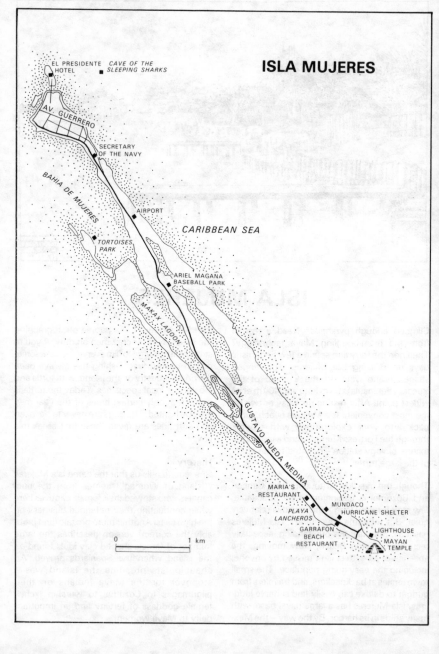

ISLA MUJERES

EL PRESIDENTE HOTEL
CAVE OF THE SLEEPING SHARKS
AV. GUERRERO
SECRETARY OF THE NAVY
BAHIA DE MUJERES
AIRPORT
CARIBBEAN SEA
TORTOISES PARK
ARIEL MAGANA BASEBALL PARK
MAKAX LAGOON
AV. GUSTAVO RUEDA MEDINA
MARIA'S RESTAURANT
PLAYA LANCHEROS
MUNDACO
HURRICANE SHELTER
GARRAFON BEACH RESTAURANT
LIGHTHOUSE
MAYAN TEMPLE

0   1 km

SIGHTS

The city is 10 blocks long and 5 blocks wide. Calle Hidalgo, the main street, is where the central plaza, city hall, police station, cinema, *farmacia,* and large supermarket are located. Most streets are really only walkways, with no vehicles allowed (although they frequently squeeze by anyway). The ferry terminal is 3 blocks from the plaza; if you're traveling light, you can walk to most of the hotels when you get off the ferry.

GARRAFON NATIONAL PARK

The best snorkeling is 5 km out of town at **Garrafon Beach,** with a close-in coral reef that's a great spot for beginners. This beach has little swell and is only one m deep for about 5 m offshore, after which the bottom drops off abruptly to 6 m. The brazen fish—which aptly describes Bermuda grubs—gaze at you eye to eye through your mask; if you have food they'll follow you almost onto shore. In fact, feeding the fish here with stale bread or tortillas makes for good pictures—the fish literally jump out of the water to grab the treat, so watch your fingers! Swim past the reef and you'll see beautiful angel fish that seem to enjoy hanging

around a coral-encrusted anchor and a couple of antiquated ship's cannons. For the non-snorkeler, there're *palapa* sun shelters and beach chairs on the sand—that is until boats loaded with tourists arrive from Cancun (about 1000). After that the beach gets crowded and loses its "Robinson Crusoe" ambience. The purist who prefers to snorkel with the fish in a private sea better get there early. The ticket taker doesn't arrive until 0800 but even earlier someone can usually let you in.

Amenities

Built into the steep cliff which backs the beach are a dive shop (snorkel, mask, and fins for P900 a day), a seafood cafe, lockers, showers and changing rooms (P200). Garrafon is a national park, open from 0800-1700; P200 pp admission. Taxi fare (up to 4 passengers) from town to Garrafon is P600, from Hotel El Presidente at the N tip of the island is P800. Finally, coral outcroppings along this beach add much to the beauty of Garrafon, but it can be razor sharp and dangerous. Even the coral that isn't dangerous should be avoided—don't walk on it or scratch your initials into it. It took millions of years to establish, and it's unthinking to kill it for a moment's pleasure.

Garafon Beach is a snorkeler's paradise.

MAYA RUINS

A short distance past Garrafon at the S tip of the island on a cliff overlooking the sea is what's left of an ancient Maya temple used as a coastal observation post. To get there, continue on the main road from Garrafon until you can see the lighthouse road going off to the R, then take a well-traveled dirt path to your left. These ruins were first seen and described by Francisco Hernandez de Cordoba in 1517. In addition to being a temple of worship to Ixchel, goddess of fertility, the slits in the walls of the temple facing the 4 cardinal points were used for sophisticated astronomical observations — part of Maya daily life. Two of the walls of the Maya structure are gone; they slid into the sea along with the corroding cliff. Today, the lighthouse keeper looks after the small temple, and makes colorful hammocks, fresh fish *ceviche*, and handmade black coral jewelry. A friendly guy, he's more than happy to let you try out the hammock, will answer all questions (if asked in Spanish), and loves to pose for the camera. This is a magnificent spot to see both the open sea and surf on the windward side of the island, and peaceful Mujeres Bay. If traveling by taxi, ask the driver to wait while you look around. Or let him go — you can walk back to Garrafon Beach and catch a taxi to town (till 1700). The walk all the way to town is long and sweaty — figure about 2 hours.

FORT MUNDACA

To make a visit to Fort Mundaca meaningful, dwell on a touching local legend from the mid-1800s. It tells of a swashbuckling slave-trading pirate, Fermin Mundaca de Marehaja, who fell in love with a young woman on Isla Mujeres, Prisca Gomez, also called *Triguena* ("The Brunette"). In some versions she was a visitor from Spain, in others she was from the island. After 10 years of plying the seas buying and selling slaves, he retired to the land to ap-

pease her, unsuccessfully. Coincidentally, pirates were slowly being put out of business by the British navy right about then. He built a lavish estate to woo her further, but to no avail. She married another Mujeres man and ultimately moved to Merida and the high life, leaving the heartsick slave trader behind to live only with his memories of the past. If you're a romantic, you'll feel a haunting melancholy while strolling in the once-gracious gardens of this deserted, almost destroyed estate. Mundaca lived the remainder of his lonely life on the island and left behind this inscription on his tombstone — *"como ere yo fui; como soy tu seras"* ("like you are I was; like I am you will be"). Fate can be fickle — and perhaps just.

To get to Fort Mundaca from downtown, follow the signs that say HURRICANE SHELTER, then take the dirt path going to the L 4½ km from town. Just before the Mundaca turnoff, there's a dirt road to the right (at 4 km) that takes you to a small center for marine biology studies (mainly lobster and the white turtle). This is not an official museum; however, visitors are welcome during work hours where you will see dry and preserved specimens of local sea life.

BEACHES

The closest beach to downtown is **Playa Norte**, on the N edge of town, the lee side of the island. Here you can relax in the sun and swim in a blue sea calm as a lake. In this shallow water you can wade for 35 m and still be only waist deep. At the W end of the beach are *palapa* cafes selling lunch, with both soft and hard beverages.

Four km S toward Garrafon on the main road out of town is **Playa Lancheros**. Several giant turtles swim around a large sea-pen and submit to being ridden by small children, as long as they can stay seated on the slippery-backed animal. Clean white beaches attract sun-worshippers, and a large *palapa* cafe sells fried fish, snacks, drinks, and fresh fruit. Live music begins in the afternoon.

WATER SPORTS

Snorkeling And Scuba Diving

The snorkeler has many choice locations to choose from: **Garrafon** is considered the best, and the E end of **Playa Norte** has visibility up to 33 m near the wooden pier, though on occasion the sea gets choppy here, clouding the water. The windward side of the island is good for snorkeling, except when the sea is rough: don't snorkel or even swim on the windward side, or risk being hurled against the sharp rock. Besides cutting you up, an open wound caused by coral laceration often becomes infected in this humid tropical climate. The dive shops on the island sponsor trips to nearby

The Yucatecan boatmen keep a sharp watch for the reef between Isla Mujeres and Isla Contoy. Hundreds of ships over the past 400 years have been wrecked on the reef that runs parallel to the Quintana Roo coast to the bay of Honduras.

reefs for snorkeling and scuba diving. A lot of press has been devoted to Isla Mujeres' **Sleeping Shark Caves**. Ask at the dive shop for detailed information. Although some divemasters will throw you in among the sluggish though dangerous fish, others feel that it isn't a smart dive. Bill Horn, experienced diver/owner of Aqua Safari dive shop on Isla Cozumel, warns there's always danger when you put yourself into a small area with a wild creature. In a cave, even if a large fish isn't trying to attack, the swish of a powerful tail could easily send you crashing against a wall. Reasons given for the shark's somnambulant state vary with the teller: salinity content of the water, or low carbon dioxide. Between Cancun and Isla Mujeres, experienced divers will find excitement diving **Chital, Cuevones, La Bandera**, and **Manchones** reefs, (see "Reefs" in Index). Diving equipment can be rented at **Mexico Divers** at 2 locations — Av. Rueda Medina and Garrafon Park; or at **El Canon**, Av. Rueda Medina, tel. 2-00-60.

Fishing

Deep-sea fishing trips can be arranged through any of the marinas. Spring is the best time to catch the big ones: marlin and sailfish. The rest of the year you can bring in good strings of grouper, barracuda, tuna, and red snapper. **Mexico Divers** (Av. Rueda Medina), just left of the boat dock, offers a day-long deep-sea fishing trip, which includes bait, tackle, and lunch. The **Boatmen's Cooperative** is helpful with questions about destinations, fishing trips, and boat rentals, tel. 2-00-86.

Robinson Crusoe Trip

If you enjoy group trips, the Robinson Crusoe boat trip includes snorkeling for a few hours at Garrafon Beach, a visit to the turtle pens, a cruise to Manchones Reef, and a *tikin chik* feed of fresh fish, caught by the crew and cooked over an open fire on a hidden beach somewhere along the Mujeres coast. Fee is about P3000. For more information ask at the Boatmen's Cooperative, tel. 2-00-86, or your hotel.

Dockage Facilities

The marinas in Isla Mujeres are getting more sophisticated with many services available. **Pemex Marina** in the bay offers electricity, water, diesel, gasoline, and mechanic service; tel. 2-00-86. At the navy base dock you'll find a mechanic and electronic service; tel. 2-01-96. The **Marina de la Laguna Makax** offers only docking facilities. For boating emergencies call either by radio using the word *"Neptuno"* for the Coast Guard, or on VHF channel 16 or band 2182. Gasoline for cars and boats is at Av. Rueda Medina, tel. 2-00-86.

Boat Regattas

Sailors from the southern U.S. have the opportunity to take part in sailing regattas each year. Organized by the Club de Yates of Isla Mujeres and started in 1968, many participants come in April from St. Petersburg, Florida. Each 2 years in the spring a group sails to the island from Galveston, Texas. This is a challenging trip for the adventurous navigator. For more info and dates contact Club de Yates de Isla Mujeres, Av. Rueda Medina, tel. 2-01-88/2-01-73; in Cancun tel. 4-23-71.

PRACTICALITIES

ACCOMMODATIONS

A surprising number of hotels are on this miniscule island. Most of them are small, simple, family-run inns downtown near the oceanfront. None can really be considered luxury class, but some offer more services than others. Since most are clustered downtown, it's simple to shop (on foot) until you find the one that suits you.

Budget

An independent youth hostel, **Poc-Na** is easy to reach on foot. From the boat dock walk 2 blocks to the L, then 3 blocks to the right. The hostel offers clean attractive sleeping space: either a bare bunkbed or hammock hooks. This is a gathering place, especially for European travelers accustomed to staying in YHs; however, if you must rent a hammock, sheets, pillow, towel, or anything else, the price begins to lose its bargain-luster and soon you're paying hotel prices. It offers a comfortable courtyard and garden with room to read or play checkers, plus a laundry, and a cafeteria serving good inexpensive food. P700 pp per space. 50 Matamoros, tel. 2-00-90.

Xul-ha is a small plain inn. The rooms—clean, with 2 double beds—are kept reasonably cool with cross ventilation. Turn L from the boat dock and walk 4 blocks, turn R (onto Lopez Mateos) and walk 2 blocks to Hidalgo. Rates vary according to number of people in your group, usually P2000 d. Av; Miguel Hidalgo N. #33, tel. 2-00-76.

Osorio is a spotlessly clean hotel with large rooms, hot and cold water, twin or double beds, private bath, fans, and window screens. Right over the street, the rooms can be noisy. From the boat dock turn L and walk 1 ½ blocks, then R (onto Madero), across from Hotel Martinez. P2500 d; Av. Madero #15, tel. 2-00-18.

Run by a long-time Isla Mujeres family, **Hotel Martinez** offers clean, quiet double rooms, with good cross ventilation. House rules require you to be in by 2200 and no one can leave before 0630. Follow directions to Osorio and cross the street; Av. Madero #14, tel. 2-01-54.

Moderate

The following 2 hotels are clean, with a pleasant staff and charming surroundings that make them stand out from the others in this category. From the boat dock turn L for 2 blocks, then right for a half block to **Hotel Berney**. This 3-story hotel is built around a patio and small pool, with restaurant and bar. The rooms are simple (though colorful), clean, and have purified tap water. P5000 d, a/c rooms slightly higher; on Av. Abasolo #3, tel. 2-00-26.

Close to the central plaza on the windward shore is **Hotel Rocamar**, a 3-story hotel with balconies overlooking the often wild sea. From the boat dock: one block to the R, and 2 blocks inland. The hotel provides lounge chairs for sunning on the beach; swimming can be treacherous here. Clean rooms, hot and cold water, restaurant, friendly staff. Rates P5800 d; Av. Nicolas Bravo, tel. 2-01-01.

First-Class

Posada del Mar is a multi-storied modern a/c hotel. Carpeted rooms overlook the waterfront with swimming either in the sea or its own pool. A *palapa* dining room, bar, and snack pavilion adjoin the pool. From the boat dock turn L and walk 4 blocks. Rates P8400; Av. Rueda Medina, #15-A, tel. 2-01-98.

On the northernmost tip of the island, the modern **El Presidente Hotel** lies on a shallow lagoon. It has a lovely white beach next to a swimming pool with swim-up bar, outdoor dining, a/c, coffee shop, clean plain rooms, tile bathrooms (with giant bath towels, typical of the El Presidente chain), and a friendly helpful staff. Gift shop, tobacco shop, and snorkeling equipment for rent. Credit cards accepted, P9100 d; tel. 2-01-22.

FOOD AND ENTERTAINMENT

As always, seafood is the highlight of most restaurant menus on Isla Mujeres; the fish is caught right in the front yard. Around town are dozens of indoor and outdoor cafes, simple and informal, plus a number of small fast-food places selling *tortas,* tacos, and fried fish.

Bucanero

On Hidalgo, this large outdoor cafe serves good seafood and Yucatecan specialties for breakfast, lunch, and dinner. Prices are reasonable—a breakfast of bacon, eggs, beans, and toast for P450. An excellent fried-fish dinner with cole slaw and rice for P790, and if you like chicken *chiliquiles,* this is the place, P690.

Sergios

On Guerrero, this is a combination cafe, bar, and art gallery with an open-air 2nd-story dining room. The food is tasty (though the servings are rather small); try the chicken tacos (3 for P350). The lobster is good and a bargain at P1990. At cocktail hour (1800-2000) drinks are two for one. The owner/artist Sergio and his wife Maureen (from Chicago) are friendly and willing to answer questions in English about the island. They have a second business on the beach near the dock, a small *palapa* cafe called **Lili's,** which serves hot dogs, french fries, good *ceviche,* and more.

Ciro's

On Matamoros and Guerrero. A fancier restaurant with glass-topped tables, in the evening light reflects from old-fashioned glass

---

ISLA MUJERES ACCOMMODATIONS

The following lists more hotels in order of ascending price:

Cabanas	Av. Carlos Lazo no. 1	2-01-79
El Caracol	Av. Matamoros no. 5	2-01-50
Caribe Maya	Av. Madero no. 9	2-01-90
Carmelina	Av. Guerrero no. 9	2-00-06
El Zorro	Av. Guerrero no. 7	2-01-49
Isla Mujeres	Av. Miguel Hidalgo no. 3	
Las Palmas	Av. Guerrero no. 20	
El Marcianito	Av. Abasolo no. 10	2-01-11
Margarita	Av. Rueda Medina N no. 9	2-01-46
Maria de los Angeles	Juarez no. 35	
Maria Jose	Av. Madero no. 27	2-01-30
Posada San Jorge	Juarez no. 29-A N	
Rocas del Caribe	Av. Madero no. 2	2-00-11
Vistalmar	Av. Rueda Medina	2-00-96
Cielito Lindo	Av. Rueda Medina no. 78	

lamps mounted on the walls. The clean, modern, fan-cooled, open-sided dining room serves all day. Good food, moderate prices, well-stocked bar, and choice seafood. Excellent shrimp-in-garlic dinner—P950. Good bargain breakfast; bacon and eggs with toast and black beans, P250. Special omelette with ham, bacon, and cheese is P350.

Maria's Kan-Kin Restaurant Francaise

If your palate yearns for something continental, get a taxi and have an elegant lunch at **Maria's** (close to Garrafon Beach). She serves in a *palapa* dining room overlooking the Caribbean. A small seawater tank holds live lobsters from which you can take your pick. The sophisticated menu offers curries, snails, and rabbit, and her prices are accordingly more expensive. Closed Sunday. A good meal for two with a cocktail can average P10,000-12,000.

Other Cafes

Many more food places include pool-side barbecues at the **El Presidente**, **Gomar's** colorful Mexican patio, **Michoacan** where you can buy *carnitas asada* by the kg (a bargain!), and be sure you try the *licuados* (liquified fruit in sweetened water and ice) at a small open

stand across from the playground.

Markets

However, if you prefer to cook your own, the ***mercado municipal*** opens every morning till around noon; it has a fair selection, considering everything must come from the mainland. There are 2 well-stocked supermarkets— including liquor and toiletries. **Mirtita** (Juarez #14, tel. 2-01-27) is open 0600-1200 and 1600-1800. Larger **Super Bertino** (Morelos #5, tel. 2-01-57) is on the plaza, open 0700-2100. **Panaderia La Reina** makes great *pan blanco* and *pan dulce,* open 0600-1200 and 1600-1800.

Entertainment

Isla Mujeres has few nightspots. The discos seem to fade in and out of business. However, one survivor, at the **Restaurant Villa del Mar** (near the main dock), attracts a nightly group. Other evening activities boil down to: the movies (on Morelos near the plaza), ball games in the plaza, an occasional boxing match, dancing in the plaza during special fiestas, listening to the military band that comes to the navy base, or (the most common) visiting in the plaza on a bench or sitting by the sea and watching the stars reflect off the water.

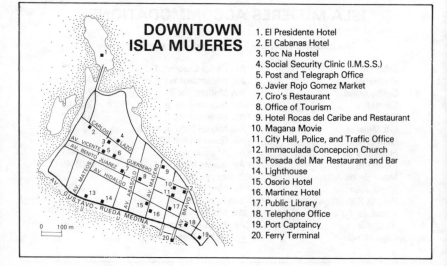

DOWNTOWN ISLA MUJERES

1. El Presidente Hotel
2. El Cabanas Hotel
3. Poc Na Hostel
4. Social Security Clinic (I.M.S.S.)
5. Post and Telegraph Office
6. Javier Rojo Gomez Market
7. Ciro's Restaurant
8. Office of Tourism
9. Hotel Rocas del Caribe and Restaurant
10. Magana Movie
11. City Hall, Police, and Traffic Office
12. Immaculada Concepcion Church
13. Posada del Mar Restaurant and Bar
14. Lighthouse
15. Osorio Hotel
16. Martinez Hotel
17. Public Library
18. Telephone Office
19. Port Captaincy
20. Ferry Terminal

Pick out your own lobster at Maria's Restaurant on Isla Mujeres' southern coast.

SERVICES

A well-stocked **drugstore** is on Calle Juarez #2. A limited selection of **newspapers** and **magazines** can be found on the corner of Juarez and Bravo. Check at the **photo studio** for film. Two **banks** in town will change money daily except Sat. and Sun.: Bank Atlantico (Av. Juarez #5) between 1030-1200; Banpais (Av. Juarez #3) between 0930-1330. The **post office** (Av. Guerrero #15) is open 0800-1300 and 1500-1800 on weekdays, and on Sat. from 0900-1200. General delivery will accept your mail and hold it for 10 days before returning it. Addresses should read: your

name, Lista de Correos, Isla Mujeres, Quintana Roo, Mexico. The **telegraph office** next to the post office (Av. Guerrero #13) is open from 0900-2030 and 0900-1200 on Sat., Sun., and holidays; money orders and telegrams will be held for 10 days only. Address to your name, Lista de Telegrafos, Isla Mujeres, Quintana Roo, Mexico. A **long-distance phone** office is on the corner of Juarez and Bravo, open 0800-1200 and 1500-2000. Ask about the service charge on collect calls. A call to Cancun is P100.

Gift Shops
This small town has many, many gift shops. Most carry the same things; one worth browsing through is **El Paso** on Rueda Medina across from the waterfront. Anyone interested in colorful cloth will find a large selection of Guatemalan weavings often hard to locate even in larger cities because of the current mood between the Mexican and Guatemalan governments.

Medical
Centro de Salud (health center) is located at Calle Guerrero on the plaza. Emergency service 24 hours daily, open for regular visits 0800-2000; tel. 2-01-17.

USEFUL PHONE NUMBERS

City Hall . . . . tel. 2-00-98
Police Station . . . . tel. 2-00-82
Immigration . . . . tel. 2-01-89
Chamber of Commerce
Av. Juarez #17 . . . . tel. 2-01-32
Office of Tourism
Av. Guerrero #8 . . . . tel. 2-01-88.

passenger ferry from Cancun to Isla Mujeres

GETTING THERE

A passenger ferry from the Puerto Juarez dock located a few km N of Cancun makes trips almost hourly throughout the day at 0500-1800, one hour, P150. Check the schedule since it changes often. A car ferry leaves Punta Sam (5 km S of Puerto Juarez) daily, but you really need a good reason to bring a car to this short island with narrow, one-way streets. RVs can travel on the ferry, and there are places to park (no hookups) on a sandy beach. The trip on the ferry from Punta Sam is slightly longer; fare is P400 for vehicles. Arrive at the ferry dock an hour before departure time to secure a place in line; tickets go on sale 30 min. in advance. For those traveling the Peninsula by bus, it's easier to make ongoing connections in Puerto Juarez than in Punta Sam. A landing strip on Isla Mujeres is used mostly by the Mexican Navy, but will accommodate private planes; a current rumor is that the airport is being lengthened for use by large passenger planes. For airport info, tel. 2-01-96.

GETTING AROUND

Mujeres is small and mostly flat, making it easy to walk the 8-km length. Other options include taxi, bicycle, motorcycle, or the municipal bus. You can walk everywhere; also, a tour around the island in a taxi and back to your hotel costs around P2000 and takes an hour, including stops to watch the lighthouse keeper making hammocks, see the Maya temple on the S tip, and the turtles at Playa Lancheros.

By Bicycle

Bicycle rentals are available at: **Arrendadora Maria Jose** on Madero #16, tel. 2-01-30; **Arrendadora Carmelina** on Av. Guerrero #6; and **Arrendadora de Bicicletas Ernesto** on Av. Juarez #25. Rental fee of P150 an hour is standard.

By Motorcycle

Most of the bikes on the island are new and come with standard or automatic shift for the same rate. Be sure to check the bike for damage before you take responsibility. Beware of narrow one-way streets and numerous children darting back and forth. Rates are fairly standardized in most of the *rentadoras* at P500 hourly—all requiring a deposit of P5000. It's quite simple to rent, no minimum age and no driver's license required at any of the following: **Gomez Castillo** (Av. Bravo and Hidalgo, tel. 2-01-42); **Moto Servicio Joaquin** (Av. Juarez 7-B, tel. 2-00-68); or **Ciros** (Av. Matamoros #11, tel. 2-01-02).

By Taxi
Taxis are many, easy to get, and the fares are reasonable. To go anyplace downtown the fare is P600. At the taxi stand on Av. Rueda Medina (tel. 2-00-66) all fares are posted; open 0600-2300.

By Bus
The municipal bus operates 0600-2100 daily; P40 pp. It runs from Posada del Mar on Av. Rueda Medina to Colonia Salinas (a small community of homes facing the windward side of the island); departures every half hour.

VICINITY OF ISLA MUJERES

Contoy
From Isla Mujeres, take a one- or 2-day trip to Contoy, an island 24 km N of Mujeres. The small bit of land (2½ by ½ km) is a national bird sanctuary. Outside of wayward flamingos, heron, brown pelicans, the magnificent frigatebird, olivaceous cormorants, and a couple of humans at the Biology Station, you'll find only a lush isolated island—the kind of place

around which fantasies are spun. From a tall viewing tower (about 3 stories of steps) open to the public, you can see most of the island. Under a shady arcade there's an information display with lighted photos of numerous birds, including full details of each specimen. A white beach close by provides a refreshing swim with delicate tropical fish. Often you'll swim amid large schools of young trumpetfish,

Barbecuing fresh-caught fish on the beach is a delicious Yucatan art.

almost transparent as they glide through the water sucking up small fish and shrimp. Tiny flying fish in groups of 10-30 or more skim the surface as they flee large predators. A day at Contoy is well worth the money.

Getting To Contoy

Among others, trips are provided by Richard Gaitan aboard his 10-m sailboat the *Providencia*. The 2-day trip is well worth the P10,000, which includes all meals (mostly fresh-caught fish, liquor extra), snorkeling equipment, a cruise around the island, and time for hiking and exploring. Bring your own sleeping bag for the beach, and don't forget sunscreen, bug repellent, and mosquito netting. The boat anchors close to shore near some excellent bird-watching sites (bring your camera and Fielding's *Mexico Bird Guide*). Rick can be contacted at the Cooperativa in town.

Other boatmen offer a one-day trip (P6500) departing 0800 and returning 1730. These cruises typically include a stop at the reef to snorkel (equipment provided), fishing off the end of the boat enroute (if you wish), a light breakfast snack on the way of *pan dulce* and fresh fruit, and a delicious lunch of *tikin chik*, along with Spanish rice, and green salad. Soda and beer are extra. The captain often treats his passengers to a lime/salt/tequilla drink on the return trip. Most of the boats are motor sailors, usually motoring N to Contoy and raising the sail for the trip back to Isla Mujeres. Don't expect the boats to be luxurious or too comfortable (wooden benches), but look forward to meeting about 15 people from various parts of the world. Check at the marinas, or at Dive Mexico for Contoy trips. Signs giving full information are seen literally all over town, or contact the Cooperativa, tel. 2-00-86.

SECLUDED BEACHES OF
THE QUINTANA ROO COAST

Anyone looking for isolation can find it on Quintana Roo's Caribbean coast between Cancun and Boca Paila. Along this 153-km stretch are dozens of fine beaches, some with facilities for camping, several with modest cabanas, and a few with more deluxe accommodations. Others offer nothing but nature's gifts: the sun, white sand and blue sea—free! Often the only way to spot the entrance to these beaches is by noting the km count on small highway signs that begin at Chetumal and end at Cancun (360 km). To get to some of them you must leave Hwy. 307 at the Tulum turnoff and continue on the uneven, potholed road that parallels the sea. This road ends at Punta Allen, an isolated bit of paradise with little more than a lobstering village, but what a place to forget about civilization for a while!

PUERTO MORELOS

Port City—Km 328
On the northern Caribbean coast, Puerto Morelos is 17 km S of Cancun. It has limited accommodations and few attractions to detain ordinary tourists. Its only claim to fame is the one vehicle ferry to Cozumel. But more and more people are beginning to notice Puerto Morelos' peaceful mood, lack of tourists, and easy access to the sea. As with some of the other towns on the Caribbean coast, divers are bringing low-key attention to this small town using it as a base to explore the rich coastline. Puerto Morelos is also the coastal headquarters of CIQR (Centro de Investigationes de Quintana Roo), an ecological organization sponsored by the Mexican government, the UN, and other environmental groups dedicated to maintaining the ecosystem of the Quintana Roo coast.

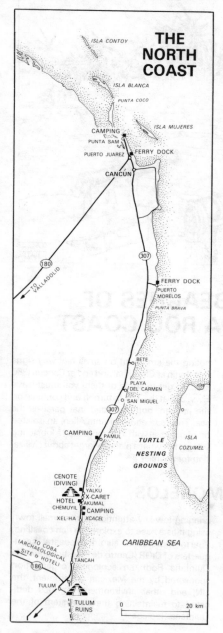

THE NORTH COAST

Canoe Harbor

In prehispanic times this was a departure point for Maya women making pilgrimage trips in large dugout canoes to the sacred island of Cozumel to worship Ixchel, goddess of fertility. Remnants of Maya structures decay near the highway and throughout the jungle; though small ruins, they're not considered insignificant, but there isn't enough money to investigate and restore them. The descendants of Indians in these parts occasionally find artifacts dating to pre-Columbian times, which sadly are often sold to private collectors, and their archaeological value is never measured. If caught with the genuine article, whether a pottery shard you may have picked up at one of the ruins or a piece bought from a local, you will be fined and your treasure will be taken from you. Remember that old American saying, *Caveat Emptor!*

SIGHTS AND SPORTS

A short walk through town reveals a central plaza, shops, a cantina, and nearby military base. Puerto Morelos' most spectacular attraction is its reef that begins 20 km N of town. Directly in front of Puerto Morelos, 550 m off shore, the reef takes on gargantuan dimensions—between 20 and 30 m wide. For the scuba diver and snorkeler this reef is a dream come true, with dozens of caverns alive with coral and fish of every description.

Snorkeling

Snorkeling is best done on the inland side of the reef where the depth is about 3 m. Equipment is available from Ojo de Agua Dive Shop and arrangements can be made for a ½-day trip to the reef. Snorkelers can expect water clarity up to 25 m along the reef.

Scuba Diving

The reef has been a menace to ships for centuries. Early records date losses from the 16th century. Many wrecks have become curiosities for today's divers who come from great distances to explore the Quintana Roo coast. Puerto Morelos can provide the most experienced diver with exciting destinations, in-

Puerto Morelos car ferry sails to Isla Cuzumel six days a week.

cluding a wrecked Spanish galleon with coral-crusted cannons—clearly visible from the surface 5 m above. Looking for another kind of excitement? Sleeping Sharks Caves are 8 km E of Puerto Morelos. An intriguing cavern but, yes, the sharks still claim proprietorship. Scuba trips, tanks and other equipment are available at Ojo de Agua Dive Shop, Box 1281, Suc. "A", Merida, Yucatan, Mexico.

Fishing
A never-ending variety of fish provides good hunting for sportsmen. On-shore fishing is only fair off the pier, but if you're interested in deep-sea fishing, boats and tackle are available at the Ojo de Agua Dive Shop. Reservations necessary.

ACCOMMODATIONS

Budget
The **Posada Amor** is spartan, a small (6-room), friendly, family-run hotel with ceiling fans, shared baths, and hot water, P1500 d. Hammock space available, P150 pp, and limited tent space, P100 pp.

Moderate
La Ceiba Beach Hotel, just N of town, is modern, and has a casual tropical atmosphere with ragged palm trees scattered about cabanas on the beach. Each room is equipped with a refrigerator, private terrace, (some) king-size beds, along with a swimming pool, rustic bar (decorated with paintings by the talented manager), good food, windsurfing, waterskiing, but most especially this entire complex is geared for the convenience of the diver. The owner is Pancho Morales, a well-known diver and owner of the La Ceiba Hotel in Cozumel where divers also get special treatment. Non-divers are welcome! Usual rate is P12,000, but if you're a diver, write for "dive package" info: Apto Postal 1252, Cancun, 77500 Quintana Roo, Mexico. In the U.S. tel. 800-621-6830.

Almost Deluxe
Hotel Playa Ojo de Agua is located N of town center. Also catering to the needs of divers, they have on the premises a well-supplied dive shop and close by a private dock plus a bar, dining room, swimming pool, and beautiful beach. Private cabanas available. Each room has a ceiling fan, hot water, and all 3 meals are included for US$70 d. Special rates for divers. Address: Nery Vada, Apto Postal 299, Cancun, Quintana Roo, Mexico.

FOOD AND SERVICES

Restaurants
Several small budget cafes serving typical Mexican and good seafood circle the main continued on page 260

QUEEN CONCH

A popular easy-to-catch food beautifully packaged—that's the *problem* with the queen conch (conk). For generations inhabitants of the Caribbean nations have been capturing the conch for their sustenance. The land available for farming on some islands is scant, and the people (who are poor) have depended on the sea—especially the conch—to feed their families. Even Columbus was impressed with the beauty of the peach-colored shell, taking one back to Europe with him on his return voyage.

In the 1970s the locals discovered a new means of making cash: export conch meat to the U.S., and use its shell as a cash byproduct sold to throngs of tourists looking for local souvenirs. An easy way to make money—except for one thing: soon there will be no more conch! In recent years the first signs of overfishing has become evident: smaller-sized conch being taken, and fishermen finding it necessary to go farther afield to get a profitable catch.

It takes 3-5 years for this sea snail to grow from larvae stage to market size. It also takes about that long for planktonic conch larvae carried into fished-out areas by the currents to replenish themselves. What's worse, the conch is easy to catch; large (up to 390-cm shell length) and heavy (about 3 kg), the mollusk moves slowly and lives in shallow crystalline water where it's easy to spot. All of these attributes are contributing to the demise of the conch.

Biologists working with various governments are trying to impose new restrictions that include closed seasons, minimum size of capture, total numbers taken by the entire fishing industry each year, limited numbers per fishermen, types of gear that can be used, and most important—the cessation of exportation. Along with these legal limitations, technology is lending a hand. Research has begun, and several mariculture centers are now experimenting with the queen conch (raising animals in a protected environment until

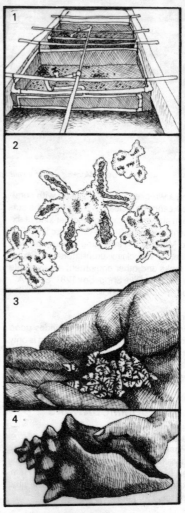

1. *These tanks hold juvenile queen conch.*
2. *conch larvae stage*
3. *From these tiny shells...*
4. *...grow these beautiful large mollusks.*

large enough for market or to juvenile size to be released into the wild).

A new research center at Puerto Morelos (on Yucatan's eastern coast, in Quintana Roo) is in operation and recently released its first group of juvenile conchs to supplement wild stock. This is not always successful. One group of larvae survive, and

then the next 10 will not—for no clear-cut reason. In the wild, conch has man to contend with, but it also has underwater predators: lobsters, crabs, sharks, turtles, and the ray.

The conch is not an endangered species yet—but it must be protected for the people that depend on it for life.

FISHING INDUSTRY MANAGEMENT IN QUINTANA ROO

David Miller, associate professor of geography at State University at Cortland has been very active in the mariculture of the state of Quintana Roo since 1979. David spent two years doing research and living with fishermen in small villages along the Caribbean coast while gathering material for his book, *The Development of the Fishing Industry in Quintana Roo.* The biogeographer now spends summers and college breaks working with people from several organizations all interested in the local dynamics of the Quintana Roo fishing industry as well as the biosphere of the area.

These concerns include the revival of the queen conch at Puerto Morelos, lobster habitats at Punta Allen, and the giant turtle along the Caribbean coast.

The lobster-management plan is working very successfully; the local fishermen have learned the importance of adhering to fishing seasons, and have taken responsibility to police illegal fishing within their community. This alone has helped to eliminate the sale of lobster on the black market which in turn will preserve Quintana Roo's lobster industry.

As with all projects of this nature, funding is always inadequate. Though these particular scientific experiments are performed in Mexico, the results will help every fisherman and country that depends on the sea for its livelihood (not to mention seafood lovers) around the world. It's a worthwhile

David Miller

project. For more information on how to help, contact:

Director de Estacion Dept. de Pesca
Puerto Morelos, Quintana Roo
Mexico

continued from page 257
plaza. The **Posada Amor Restaurant** can usually be depended on for outstanding *mole poblano* and other regional dishes at moderate prices. **La Ceiba Beach Hotel** and **Hotel Playa Ojo de Agua** both serve good seafood, but prices are a shade higher than other restaurants in town.

Markets

Puerto Morelos is one of 2 small cities you'll find between Cancun and Punta Allen. Local markets carry fresh fruit and vegetables, plus a limited selection of sundries. Supplies of basic food items can be sketchy and intermittent. If camping or backpacking, it's advisable to stock up on in Cancun.

Services

Puerto Morelos has one of the few **gas stations** along this route (also at Tulum, and Puerto Felipe Carillo). If driving, be advised to top off your tank whenever you find a gas station. Besides being few and far between, stations frequently run out of gas, so get it wherever and whenever possible. If you run out near the coast and can find a dive shop, they're usually willing to help out with a couple of gallons of outboard motor gasoline. Though laced with oil, it might get you to a gas station without doing irreversible damage to your car. Also, many rural towns have a supply of gas in 5-gallon drums even though you don't see a sign or a gas pump. Ask at the local store. *Larga-*

distancia telephone service is found just S of the military camp, open 0800-1300 and 1600-1930 daily. The **bank** is open to cash traveler's cheques from 0930-1300, Mon. to Saturday.

TRANSPORT

Getting There

Buses from N and S stop at Puerto Morelos frequently. From Cancun it's a 45-min. drive; from Chetumal 5 hours. Hitching is reasonably easy from the larger towns (Chetumal, Cancun, Puerto Felipe Carillo, Playa del Carmen): try for your ride on Hwy. 307 where the service roads enter the towns.

Vehicle Ferry

The vehicle ferry to Cozumel departs Puerto Morelos 0800 daily except Monday. Check the schedule the night before in case it changes. Be at the dock by 0500 to get in the passenger-car line. It also expedites things to have the car's license number and correct change ready. The ticket office is open 0600-0700; passenger fare P150, motorcycle P200, car P850—ask for prices for larger vehicles. The trip takes 2 hours and can be a rough crossing so put on your elastic cuffs if you tend to get seasick (see "Health," p. 71). For those with sea-legs (and stomachs), light snacks are sold on the passenger deck. The return trip leaves Cozumel at 1300.

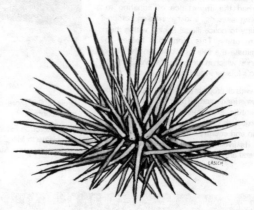

Stay away from the black spiny sea urchin; it's dangerous.

PUNTA BETE — KM 298

As recently as 1965 there were no tourists along this coast. At that time Quintana Roo was only a federal territory. There wasn't even a road to this fine white-powdered beach. Family groups, mostly descendants of the Chan Santa Cruz Indians, tended their small *cocals* (coconut farms). These miniature coconut plantations were self sufficient. Together a family worked enough coconuts each year to earn spending money from the resulting copra. The custom continues today. We saw one man wrestle 70-kg bags of fresh coconuts (a harvest representing several months' labor) onto a bus to Merida (3 hours each way), sell them in a public market, and come home with about US$50!

Punta Bete, a 4-km stretch of beach, is a complete tropical fantasy — swaying palms hovering along the edge of pure white sand with gentle waves running blue crystal across the shore. Swimming is perfect in the calm sea, and 10-20 m offshore the rocky bottom makes a perfect snorkeling area.

ACCOMMODATIONS AND FOOD

Along the 4-km stretch are several places to stay in a variety of price ranges. Each of them (depending on your travel style) is ideal.

Budget
Xcalacoco (SHKAH-lah-co-co) **Campground** can be a social experience if you wish. However, it's still large enough to lose yourself in your own little coconut grove, hammock slung between 2 palms (close enough to the sea that the breezes blow the mosquitos away, but be prepared with bug repellent and mosquito netting anyway). On the grounds are clean bathrooms and showers, separate *palapas* for socializing — or for cover in case of an unexpected shower. The pure water supply comes from nearby wells (boil it anyway); fires are not allowed, so if you're cooking bring a backpacking stove. To camp on the beach the rate is P300 pp; a few cabanas rent for about

P1500 d: individual bathrooms, no electricity, not the best bargain unless you feel the need for a bed.

Moderate
Cabanas Marlin Azul is a secluded, well-appointed little resort close to Xcalacoco. Opening onto the beach are 15 cabins with private bathrooms, beds, electricity, hot and cold water, ceiling fans, and a wonderful bay. The small restaurant, though tiny and limited in its menu selection, serves outstanding fresh seafood and the prices are moderate. Room rate is P5000 d. **Note!** Before shedding your shoes to hike along this beach, look it over. Often in front of the hotel sharp little bits of coral hide in the sand. When swimming beware of the sharp limestone in the shallow areas; if you

Cabanas Marlin Azul at Punta Bete Beach

RVs can park on most beaches along the Quintana Roo coast.

have diving booties they are ideal in this area.

Luxury Campout

Kai Luum Camptel offers a lazy man's campout. In the tradition of the British safari, it's camping with a touch of class. Though there's no electricity, modern tents on the beach have large comfortable beds, communal hot and cold showers and clean toilets very close by, and daily maid service. Each tent is shaded by a shaggy *palapa* roof strung with a hammock facing the sea for lazy afternoons. The restaurant is one of the great attractions at Kai Luum—the food is outstanding. Prepared by Maya cooks, the menu is overseen by owner Arnold Bilgore who happens to have a gourmet touch and plans something new and unusual (sometimes continental) every day. The dining room is a large *palapa* structure on the beach, where dinner is served under the sparkling light of hundreds of candles. Arnold jokes that next to the church, Kai Luum is the biggest buyer of candles in Mexico. The bar is at one end of the dining room: each person makes and keeps track of his own drinks with a numbered pegboard. The whole feeling of the resort is much like the honor system at the bar—relaxed, intimate, friendly. The restaurant attracts travelers from other resorts in the area, and if you're one of them, reservations are necessary. There are no telephones, so if you aren't staying at Kai Luum you must drop by and make

them in advance. At night the dirt road from the highway is very dark. Three persons maximum in each tent, rates include breakfast and dinner, US$28.50 d, lunch runs around US$4. For accommodation reservations write to Camptel Ventures, Inc., Box 2664, Evergreen, Colorado 80439, tel. 1-800-538-6802.

Deluxe

Cabanas Lafitte has been around for many years, and it is as well known for its charming managers, Jorge Fuentes and family, as it is for its fine service, wonderful beach location, good food, swimming pool, and pleasant game room. All provide a serene backdrop for welcome camaraderie among the people that return year after year from distant parts of the globe. The stucco cabanas have double and king-sized beds, hot water, ceiling fans, private bath, and along with daily maid service, each room is provided with a handmade reed broom to help keep the sand out. A full dive shop on the premises has a good selection of equipment available to rent, including sailboards. The management provides (to guests) free transport in its skiff to Lafitte Reef, an exciting snorkeling destination. Here, a lazy day of floating on the clear sea surface will bring you face to face with blue chromis, angel fish, rock beauties, and often the ugly grouper—a great place to use your underwater camera. Fishing is another satisfying sport, since you'll always come away with a tasty dinner that the restaurant chef is happy to prepare from your catch. Hands off the large handsome turtles you may see and don't expect to find turtle soup or conch *ceviche* on the menu. The management makes it clear that they support the need to preserve these endangered species. And speaking of species, every afternoon between 1700-1800 a flock of small colorful parrots flies over the dining *palapa;* they're unmistakable with their awkward wing movements and peculiar squawk.

Each week the hotel staff and guests get together and have a *fiesta*—not the impersonal version that you see at the big clubs, but the type of good time that a family has at a Mexican birthday party where everyone takes part. The waiters demonstrate rhythmic dance skills balancing filled glasses on their heads, then try to teach anyone else that wants to give it a try—it's not easy! A zesty smorgasbord of typical food is served. It's a down-home party,

Maya style. During high season it's best to have reservations. Rates include breakfast and dinner, US$50 d. Reservation address the same as preceding, Camptel Ventures.

TRANSPORT

Getting There

If arriving by plane in Cancun, taxis are available; arrange your price before you get in the cab. Figure approximately US$25 (up to 5 passengers). From Playa del Carmen (a ferry arrival point from Cozumel), taxi fare is less. Car rentals are available at Cancun Airport, which is a straight shot on Hwy. 307; look for the large sign on the left side of the road that says CAPITAN LAFITTE. Hikers can look forward to 6½ km of shoreline between Xcalacoco (southernmost point of Punta Bete) and the next town, Playa del Carmen.

PLAYA DEL CARMEN — KM 287

For years there was but one reason to go to the small village of Playa del Carmen—the Cozumel Island ferry dock. Thousands of people pass through here each year on their way to or from Cozumel, a popular island 19.2 km off the Quintana Roo coast. Now, however, Playa del Carmen is taking on a personality of its own. Nature did its part by endowing the small town with a broad beach, which is still uncluttered by highrises or a busy tourist strip. With several modest hotels, a few restaurants, campgrounds on the ocean, several dive shops, and a busy bus terminal, this slow-moving fishing village is becoming a "destination" to consider while traveling along the Caribbean coast. The swimming is a pleasure, and its proximity to attractions such as Tulum, Xelha, Cancun, and coastal Hwy. 307 makes it a convenient stopover. For lovers of early morning walks along the water, Carmen's long beach is perfect to stroll for hours, often without seeing another soul. If you enjoy watching crabs scurry about, feeding breakfast crumbs to the fish, or catching fluttering sea birds in your camera lens—then early morning on the beach at Playa del Carmen is just the place for you.

SIGHTS

By far the nicest thing to do in Playa del Carmen is to enjoy the people and the sparkling Caribbean. Walk through the village. Once out of the downtown area the streets are potholed and bumpy—its lack of sophistication is appealing. Buy a fresh donut from the bakery man who wanders through town each morning with a large tray of still-warm goodies on his head ready for the incoming ferry. The milkman no longer delivers milk from large cans strapped to his donkey's back; now he travels the streets in a dilapidated station wagon known by the village ladies who bring their jars and pots to be filled. The number of small curio shops and cantinas is growing, and there's a movie theater, but it's still a long way from being a tourist resort.

While investigating the village you'll be escorted by children, dogs, little black pigs, and even turkeys. The cool early hours are best for walking the beach. Warm afternoons invite snoozing in the sand or watching the magnificent man-o-war frigatebird make silent circles above you hoping to find another bird with a fish in his beak (to rob). Since you're here, take a tip from the sun-worshipping Maya (with sunscreen of course), who once lived on this very spot. One learns fast to enjoy lazy activities, such as people watching, easy from the comfortable wooden deck of the *palapa* bar of the Playacar Hotel (located above the beach next to the wharf).

Ferries from Cozumel come and go all day; in addition, luxury cruise ships anchor close by in the bay, and tenders bring tourists to shore. The ship passengers have a choice of lounging on the beach hosted by one of the hotels, or escorted immediately to large modern buses parked near the ferry dock, then whisked off to the more famous sights of Xelha and Tulum. Playa del Carmen has two faces: a busy touristy beach when the ship is in port; the rest of the time, it remains its calm, small-village self.

Outdoor Activities
Sailboards are available for rent or lessons at the **Cueva Pargo Hotel** dive shop (N of the dock on the beach), P1200 an hour. A little steep, but talk to Huacho, owner of the dive shop—he'll negotiate. This part of the coast generally has a 5-8 mile breeze with a gentle

swell, giving you a good sailboard ride. Though swimming is wonderful and the water clean, it's not crystalline directly in front of Playa del Carmen; a short distance N or S of the wharf are great reefs with clear water and active undersea life for snorkeling. The best fishing is offshore; ferry traffic discourages most fish around the wharf. The **Molcas Hotel** offers deep-sea fishing, a 5-hour trip, bait and tackle provided. **Cueva Pargo Dive Shop** takes diving and fishing groups, provides equipment; fees are negotiable.

ACCOMMODATIONS

Camping
Playa del Carmen is growing up. Thanks to frequent bus service it's a backpacker's gateway to Quintana Roo. Many come here, stay a few days on the beach, then begin their exploration of the rest of the coast. From the ferry dock, a 5-min. walk N on the first street that parallels the sea brings you to 2 campsites: **La Ruina** and **Brisa del Mar**. They're small, and in the high season can be extremely noisy and crowded. If you have a choice, stay at La Ruina—it's usually cleaner. Its facilities include a cold water shower, restroom, and room for about 6 small pickup campers, P1200 per

The ferry travels between Cozumel and Playa del Carmen several times each day—fare is about P300.

This relaxed family enjoys living out of their camper on the beach for several months each year.

vehicle. For P700 pp you can pitch a tent on the beach, or hang a hammock in a *palapa*-covered building. Sound floats throughout, and if a light is turned on it floods everyone's space. The fee is P500 pp; hammocks provided for a small deposit. The Brisa del Mar is ill kept, with a primitive shower — often without water. Neither place can be recommended very highly. A few blocks N, past town, there are great stretches of quiet deserted beaches for peaceful camping if you can do without facilities.

Budget Hotels
One block from the plaza, on the main road coming into town from Hwy. 307, **Posada Lilly** is reasonably clean with hot shower and ceiling fans, P3500 d.

Moderate Hotels
Xaman Ha (formerly Christine's Bungalows) is an unexpected surprise. Located behind a white wrought-iron fence between a dentist's office and a gift shop across from the park 2 doors up from Mascaras restaurant and the beach, once through the gates you'll find yourself in a small tropical garden with 3 small *palapa* bungalows. Two are furnished with double beds, mosquito netting, extremely clean community shower and toilet within a few feet; the 3rd bungalow is large enough to accommodate a family. Prices are US$10 d, discounts for longer than a few days. You can always just show up and take your chances, but for reservations send a 2-day deposit to Christine de Cajina (an American married to the local Mexican doctor), Box 1434, Cancun, Quintana Roo, Mexico. Since there's no mail delivery along this coast and people must travel to Cancun to pick it up, allow a couple of months for RT letters.

Another quaint place to stay is **Cueva Pargo Hotel**, also owned by a young American woman and her Mexican (diver) husband. Details (like toilet paper) are always tended to. The shared bathrooms are extremely clean. Available are 9 rooms (US$20 daily), 2 houses that sleep 4 in beds and 2 in hammocks (US$50 daily), and a beach house that sleeps 6 (US$80 daily). The unique airy house, with everything you need to live the good life, opens onto the beach with fully equipped kitchen, shower, living room, and loft. Large jugs of pure water, ceiling fans, and even a decorative stained-glass window add a special touch. Discounts for long term. Rates are open for negotiation in the off season (between May 1 and Nov. 1); ideal for a family or a group. On the premises the owners, JoAnne and Huacho Corrales, operate the **Sailorman Pub** with meals served in a beachy *palapa* hut. Not particularly cheap, but the food is good and the surroundings amiable. Huacho also operates a dive shop on the premises and guests of the hotel are offered free diving and windsurfing lessons. Another attraction is a trip aboard their large sailboat; half-day cruise begins at US$25, refreshments are served, and you're part of the crew. If you've never sailed before, not to worry, they teach you all about it and it's fun! If that trip suits you, they also have a full-day expedition including several hours sailing N to Punta Moroma for snorkeling, spinnaker sailing, lunch and drinks provided; US$35 for the expedition. Reservations are suggested, and a minimum of 6 persons is needed before the boat sails. For those interested in larger adventures, the Corrales take overnight trips to the cays off Belize, Chinchorrow Reef, or your choice—write to Cueva Pargo, Box 552, Cancun, Q. Roo, Mexico.

Another Robinson Crusoe-type hotel is the **Blue Parrot Inn**, on the beach N of town. It's a whimsical stucco tower-like structure with *palapa* roof, tile floors, spotlessly clean shared bathrooms, lots of hot water, one or 2 double beds in each room, an ice chest filled with soda and beer purified water is available and a romantic dining room sits atop a 2nd-story terrace overlooking the beautiful palm-dotted beach and azure sea. For a midnight swim you need only step out your front door. Each room has a view of the water, and just a short walk on the white sand (N) you can watch the fishermen throw their nets or return in their open launches with the morning catch. No radios, TV, or telephones—the edge of civilization but only a 10-min. walk to town. Room rates begin at US$10 depending on the size of

the room and the time of year, credit cards accepted. For more information write to Blue Parrot Inn, Box 1258, Cancun, Q. Roo, Mexico.

Closer to town, **Cabanas Nuevo Amanecer** offer private baths, double beds, and *palapa*

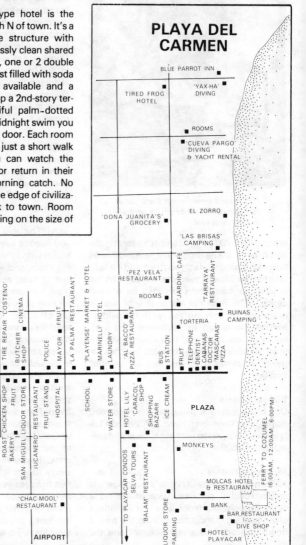

roofs for US$15-20. Clean and pleasant. For reservations write to Arlene King, Apto Postal 1056, Cancun, Mexico.

Almost Luxury-Class
Los Molcas Hotel is close to the ferry dock and the beach. It has nicely decorated, a/c, spacious rooms with private bath, swimming pool, dining room, terrace dining, and 3 bars. Also free ferry trips to Cozumel, tours to Chichen Itza, Tulum, and Coba, diving equipment, and laundry service. Rates are P11,000 s, P12,600 d, P14,000 t, plus 15% tax. For reservations write to Turismo Aviomar, SA, Calle 60 No. 469, Merida, Yuc., Mexico; tel. 1-66-20.

Across the street next to the Banco Atlantico on the beach is the **Playacar Hotel**. New yet designed to look old, some rooms have an ocean view, furnished in dark colonial wood furniture, private bath, and a/c; there's a large dining room, and comfortable outdoor *palapa* bar with a view of the beach, the sea, and the ferry dock. Rates begin at US$35. For more info and reservations call from the U.S. 1-800-223-4084, or write to Cancun Mexico Playacar Reservation Center, Box 396, Cancun, Quintana Roo, Mexico 77500.

Luxury
Next to the Playacar Hotel are **Villas and Condominiums Playacar**. These are privately owned condos, rented by a reservation center when not being used by their owners. They're beautifully designed in a convenient location either right on the beach or a short walk away. A 5-min. stroll from town, they have one to 3 bedrooms, kitchen, washer and dryer, fully furnished — great for families or groups. Prices begin at US$50 per night for a one bedroom depending on time of year, location, and size. All plus 15% tax. For more information write to Villas and Condominiums Playacar, Box 396, Cancun, Quintana Roo, 77500 Mexico.

FOOD

Around the central plaza several small cafes serve a variety of good inexpensive Mexican (and Italian) food. The **Molcas Hotel** serves several delicious Oriental dishes, a welcome change after *tipico* food for a month or so. If you want to stick with the typical Yucatecan food or are looking for good fresh seafood, try **Dona Juanitas** on the main road close to Hwy. 307. Two fishermen sons provide only the freshest catch, and prices are quite reasonable: dinners begin at P700. Behind Dona Juanitas (way back in a *palapa* hut with sapling walls) is a wonderful bakery where the *panaderos* bake their tasty doughs in a wood-burning stone oven, the only light in the room filtering in from between the saplings; a hole in the *palapa* roof lets the smoke escape. Generous *pan dulces* come out of the oven at about 1400 — though this isn't the sales room, buy them warm and fresh for P25 each! They also make a variety of breads, sold at the downtown market.

Hotel Playacar, though not cheap, serves good meals. Their open deck is perfect for dining or drinking while watching the waterfront. Try their fresh coconut custard and flan; happy hour offers two-for-one drinks. **Chac Mool** restaurant is clean and serves great Yucatecan food, moderately priced; about P700 for an average dinner and P400 for a hearty breakfast. **El Jardin** is a small open cafe on the corner, one block inland from Las Ruinas campgrounds. The cafe serves good breakfast and quick lunch, open from 0700 to 1200 only.

Two good Italian restaurants in town both serve pizza. **Al Bacco** is 2 blocks off the beach just up from El Jardin. Straight from Rome, one of the owners, Pasquale, serves some unexpected gourmet dishes such as *escallopes limon* (thin slices of beef sauted in lemon). The portions are very generous, served with a small salad, vegetables, and homemade bread. The other Italian restaurant is **Mascaras** on the first block off the beach across from the plaza. Their pizza and pasta are excellent. Try the spinach canneloni — marvelous! Be sure to take a close look at the brick wood-burning oven where most everything is baked. Mascaras makes the best fresh limeade in town; ask for *limonada,* served in large bulbous glasses with lots of purified ice. You can also get *big* margaritas, and cold Yucatecan Leon Negra *cerveza*.

Groceries

Several small grocery stores around the plaza and on the main street coming into town have an ample supply of fruit, vegetables, and basics. A good variety of meat is available at the butcher shop, and there's a *rosticeria* selling fresh roasted chicken. Nearby is the purified ice shop, a drugstore, and bakery. Liquor is sold across from the Molcas Hotel and several other locations in town.

ENTERTAINMENT AND SERVICES

The cinema is usually open on the weekends with Spanish-language films. Dona Juanitas cafe becomes a disco later on in the evening with videos. As usual people gather at the plaza and poke around the gift shops. Sitting on the end of the pier and watching the stars is *muy bueno* on the Caribbean; when you tire of that, a before-bed drink on the Playacar Hotel deck comes with lots of travelers to talk to.

Services

If going to Isla Cozumel for the day, you can park your car at the **military camp** a block from downtown for a small fee. **Banco del Atlantico** will cash traveler's cheques (commission) 1000-1230, Mon. to Fri.; located next to the ferry dock. ***Larga-distancia*** phone service is located across the plaza next to the vegetable stand, open daily from 0800-1300, 1500-2000. There are now 3 phone lines into Playa del Carmen, easing the waiting time. Two **hardware** stores will help you out with twine or a knife blade. Both a **doctor** and a **dentist** are in town. While there's not a post office (yet), the **Office of the Delegacion** will forward mail and sell postage stamps; located on the main road going out of town on the right side of the street.

GETTING THERE

By Air

Carmen's small airstrip (5 blocks S of the main plaza) is open from 0700-1700. Most of the flights go to and from Isla Cozumel (P2200 OW). Reservations are not necessary, but if convenient drop by the airport and make them in advance. Otherwise, arrive at the airport an hour before you wish to fly. The first flight leaves Playa del Carmen at 0720, then every 2 hours thereafter. If business dictates, more flights are added.

By Bus

Three bus lines provide this small town with

As regular as clockwork, the donut man shows up to meet the ferry every morning with a fresh tray of donuts.

Playa del Carmen beachfront

the best bus transportation on the coast. From Merida via Cancun (5 hours), three 1st-class and seven 2nd-class buses arrive daily. Buses arrive frequently from Chetumal and other points south. Playa del Carmen is an ideal base for many attractions along the Quintana Roo coast. Buses N to Cancun's bright life travel the 65 km in 50 minutes. On the bus S to Chetumal ask the driver to drop you off at the turnoff to Tulum, to Xelha Lagoon National Park entry road, or one of the small beaches S along the coast. Ask what time his schedule brings him back since you must be on the highway waiting to return to Carmen.

By Ferry

Five RT each day from Playa del Carmen to Cozumel, P340 OW. The ferry crossing is usually a breeze. The calm sea does flex its muscles once in awhile, however, making it difficult to berth the boat snugly against the dock. When this happens, hefty crewmen literally swing each passenger over the side into the capable hands of 4 other strong-armed receivers on the dock, quickly followed by your luggage. This adds a bit of adventure to your voyage, but if it isn't your forte, delay your

departure till the next day—the sea seldom stays angry for long. Young boys with imaginative homemade pushcarts or 3-wheel *tricyclettes* meet incoming ferries at the dock to carry luggage for a small fee. (See "Cozumel," p. 217, for ferry schedule.)

By Taxi

Taxis at Cancun International Airport will bring you to Playa del Carmen. If there are several passengers you can make a good deal—bargain with the driver before you start your journey. Non-metered taxis meet the incoming ferries at Playa del Carmen and are ready for long or short hauls. Again, make your deal in advance. A trip from Carmen to Tulum (with 3 passengers) can be about P10,000 RT, depending on supply and demand and the time of year. If you're interested in finding a good diving spot, tell the taxi driver. He may share with you his favorite cove that you'd never find on your own, and might even join you for a swim.

Hitching

Because of the ferry traffic, this is a good place to try for a hitch going N or south.

PAMUL — KM 274

Another small beach that deserves exploring is Pamul. If you're a natural packrat, you'll like the beachcombing here: shells, coral, and sometimes interesting flotsam from ships far from Yucatan shores. This is not one of the wide white beaches so common along the coast; in places it's steep and rocky. The water is crystal clear and it's fascinating to examine life within the shallow tidepools made by rocks and limestone that parallel the shore. Snorkel-

GIANT TURTLES AND THE INDIANS

At one time the giant turtle was plentiful and an important addition to the Indian diet. The turtle was captured by turning it over (no easy matter at 90-100 kg) when it came on shore to lay its eggs. The eggs already laid in a hole on the beach were gathered, and then the family all took part in processing this nourishing game. First, the parchment-like bag of unlaid eggs was removed from the body, then the undeveloped eggs (looking like small hard-boiled egg yolks). After that, the meat of the turtle was cut into strips to be dried in the sun. The orange-colored fat was put in calabash containers and saved for soups and stews, adding rich nutrients and considered an important medicine. They wasted nothing.

Today the turtle can be hunted at designated times of the year only. CIQR, a protective organization along with the government, keeps a sharp lookout along the coast for egg poachers during the laying season. Turtle-egg farms are being developed to insure the survival of this ancient mariner. The poacher of the '80s travels the entire coast, and each beach is hit night after night; the turtle can lay as many as 200 eggs in an individual nest or "clutch." One beach may be the instinctual home for hundreds of turtles (at one time thousands) that return to the site of their own hatching each year. Turtles can live to be a hundred years old, which means they can lay a lot of eggs in their lifetime. But as the poachers steal the eggs on a wholesale basis, the species could eventually be wiped out entirely. If caught, poachers are fined and can be jailed. However, they've already done the damage, and when released usually return to their lucrative habits. A ready market for these eggs exist in most Mexican marketplaces of superstitious men who believe they give magical sexual power.

The survival of the giant sea turtle lies within the education of the people—both locals and visitors. Shoppers will see many sea turtle products offered for sale: turtle oil, tortoise shell combs, bracelets, rings, buttons, carvings, and veneer inlaid on furniture and jewelry boxes, plus small stuffed, polished hatchling paper weights. It is against the law to bring these products into the U.S. and other countries. If discovered they will be confiscated; however, if they were ignored by the tourists before the vendor made his dollar, the market would dry up and this would be a step toward preserving these lumbering beasts.

Pamul's trailer park has full hookups and electricity.

ing is better the closer you get to the reef 120 m offshore. The sea bottom drops off to about 8 m and its colorful underwater life can absorb you for hours.

Beach

The S end of Pamul's beach is sandy, but the shallow water along here harbors the prickly sea urchin—look before you step, or wear shoes while you're wading. If you are self-contained with your own compressor and equipment, the Quintana Roo coast offers miles and miles of pristine dive spots, and the waters near Pamul are especially ideal for scuba diving. Fishermen and divers along this coast are a jovial group, always ready for a beach party, potluck style, when the fishing is good—especially during lobster season (July 15 through March 15).

Turtles

If it's a bright moonlit night in July or Aug., you may be treated to the unique sight of seeing large lumbering turtles coming ashore and laying thousands of eggs in the sand. If you're there a few weeks later it's even more exciting to watch the tiny (about 8 cm in diameter) hatchlings make their way down the beach to begin life in the sea. Much has been written about protecting the turtles of the Caribbean from man, but nature in the form of egg-eating animals provides its own threat to the endangered species. On the beach of Pamul, more than half the eggs are scratched up from the sand and eaten by a variety of small animals that live in the surrounding jungle.

Practicalities

You have a choice of the small hotel (8 rooms) on the beach, or the campsite at the S end of the hotel. The hotel would be considered spartan, but does have electricity between sunset and 2200, hot and cold water, communal bathroom and toilet, P5000 d. The campsite has room for 15 RVs. All spots have electricity and water, 5 have sewerage, and you can use the shower and toilet in the hotel. Fee is P1200-plus, depending on the number of people in the party. Tent camping is permitted for P700 for 2 persons including use of toilet and shower. A small cafe next to the hotel is run by the family that owns the hotel and usually offers fresh-caught seafood plus other typical dishes at reasonable prices; full lunch and dinner for about P800 each. A small *cenote* nearby provides water for Pamul; do boil it for drinking. Otherwise, bottled water can be bought from the hotel manager.

AKUMAL — KM 255

Akumal Bay is a crescent of intensely white sand along the blue Caribbean. This quiet beach, edged with hundreds of wind-bent coconut trees, is home to a medium-sized resort that survives nicely without telephones, TVs, or bustling activity. The traveler desiring the tropical essence of Yucatan *and* a dash of the good life will appreciate Akumal. Compared to Cancun it could not be described as luxury class, but it does offer a good range of hotel rooms, dining, and activities.

The barrier reef that runs parallel to the Quintana Roo coast protects the lagoon from the open sea and creates desirable swimming and snorkeling. Proximity to the reef and easy access to the unspoiled treasures of the Caribbean make it a gathering place for divers from all over the world. For the archaeology buff, Akumal is 10 km from Tulum, one of the few walled Maya sites located on the edge of the sea. From Tulum, it's another 5 km to Xelha, a natural saltwater aquarium where divers (even amateurs) snorkel or scuba among surrealistic limestone formations that give the eerie impression of swimming through an ancient sunken city. In Maya, Akumal means "Place of the Turtle," and from prehistoric times, the giant green turtle has come ashore in summer to lay its eggs in the warm Caribbean sands.

Flora

Akumal is surrounded by jungle and thick coconut groves. In March, bright red bromeliads bloom high in the trees, reaching for a sun that's rapidly hidden by fast-growing vines and leaves. These "guest" plants that have found a home in an established tree are not parasites but rather epiphytes: they don't drain the sap of the host tree. They sustain themselves with rain, dew, and humidity with leaves that absorb moisture and organic food requirements from dust in the air, insect matter, and visiting birds. The bromelian family encompasses a wide variety of plants, including pineapple and Spanish moss. The genus seen close to Akumal is the tillandsia, and the flamered flower that blooms on the tops of so many of the trees here is only one variety of this remarkable epiphyte. While searching out bromeliads, you undoubtedly will see another epiphyte, the orchid.

History

Akumal was a small part of a sprawling coconut plantation until 1925. A *New York Times*-sponsored expedition along the then-unknown Yucatan coast stumbled on this beautiful bay. But it was another 33 years before the outside world intruded on its pristine beauty. In 1958, the nucleus of what is now CEDAM, a renowned divers' club, introduced Akumal to world-class divers. Soon

Building a very large palapa roof Maya style; no nails, just twine. The structure, now complete, is the Zasil dining room on Akumal Bay.

This airy palapa *school house is located a few meters from Akumal Bay. Children from the surrounding ranchitos attend classes half day, which leaves them free to help their parents run the farm*

the word was out. The first visitors (divers) began making their way to the unknown wilderness. At that time, the only way in to Akumal was by boat from Cozumel. A road was built in the 1960s. Since then, it has continued to grow in fame and size each year. Though more people come now, it still remains unspoiled and uncluttered. Keep your fingers crossed.

The Beach

The porous sand of the Yucatan Peninsula never gets hot enough to burn. There are km of white beach to walk, with bits of flotsam to investigate: conch shells, lacy red seaweed, an occasional coconut sprouted after soaking in the sea for months, and the ever-present crabs, all sizes and colors, popping in and out of their sandy homes. Take a walk at dawn. The sun bursts from the sea, spotlighting leaping fish as they jump at winged breakfast bugs hovering just above the surface of the water. When the sun rises higher, late sleepers stake out spots on the beach and create a colorful patchwork of beach towels on the sand. Fortunately, the beach is so large that it never gets crowded—only coveted spots under shady palms become scarce. A *palapa* bar, open until 1800, serves beer, cocolocos, pina coladas, and more. This is a friendly place to meet other travelers and swap adventure stories.

WATER ACTIVITIES

Two dive shops on the beach rent equipment, including boats and motors for scuba divers and snorkelers. Both offer a 3-day dive course for those who wish to become certified. If you just want to make one dive on the reef, instructors give a 4-hour "resort course" for about US$78, including equipment, transportation, and one escorted dive. If you decide to take this resort course, check to make sure that you will be making the dive with a divemaster on a one-to-one basis. Many come for the excitement of exploring the wreck *Mantanceros,* sunk in 1741. Although it was completely salvaged, a job that took CEDAM several years, the sea yields an occasional coin or bead from this ancient Spanish merchant ship. A good collection of memorabilia from the *Mantanceros* is on display at a small museum at Xelha, open from 0800-1700 daily, with a small entry fee charged. A multitude of dive spots is hidden in the reefs nearby, about 130 m offshore.

Snorkeling

Akumal Reef not only protects the bay from waves of the open sea, it provides calm swimming areas ideal for snorkeling. A good spot within wading distance is the rocky area on the

N end of the bay. Floating along the surface of the water and looking through your private window into the unique world below can become habit-forming along this coast. Take it slow and easy, and you won't miss anything. Search the rocks and crevices you'll drift over, even the sandy bottom, and what may look like a rocky bulge on the floor of the sea may eventually twitch an eye and turn out to be a stonefish trying to hide in the sand: hands off, he's deadly!

Fishing

World-class fishing is done farther out to sea where pescatorial game, including marlin, sailfish, and bonita, grow to enormous size. The dive shop will arrange outings including all gear, but make reservations in advance if possible.

ACCOMMODATIONS

There are limited accommodations at Akumal. If traveling off season you'll have little difficulty finding a room. However, make reservations between 1 Dec. and 15 April. No camping is permitted at Akumal, but just a few km S, good beaches are available at Xcacel (SHA-sell) and Chemuyil; some with camping facilities. The hotels at Akumal are all set on the beach, perfect for a tropical vacation.

Moderate Hotels

While Akumal cannot be considered a budget resort area, the most economical choice is **Hotel Villas Maya,** the original cottages built for the CEDAM diving club. The owners replaced the elderly thatched roofs with Western-style coverings. These roomy cabanas on the beach are spartan but clean, with private bath, tile floors, a/c and some have cooking facilities; if you're a reader the lightbulb provided is very dim. Tennis and basketball courts; US$40 d. Dive packages with some meals and room are available. Villas Maya also offers 3 lovely condos on a separate beach around the point N of Akumal Bay. Each has 2 bedrooms, 2 bathrooms, furnished kitchen, and living room with 2 sofa beds. These rent for US$115 per night for up to 6 people. For prices of dive packages and reservations contact Akutrame

Inc., Box 1976, El Paso, Texas 79950, tel. in Texas (905) 584-3552, outside of Texas toll-free 1-800-351-1622.

Deluxe

Las Casitas Akumal has light, airy condominiums nicely furnished with 2 bedrooms, 2 baths, living room, kitchen and patio, located at the N end of the beach with the bay at your front door. No heavy-duty cooking allowed, but use of the refrigerator and your own crockpot or electric skillet is permitted, daily maid service included. Walking distance to restaurants, grocery store, snack stand, dive shop, and beach bar. Up to 5 persons P23,000 plus tax, extra person P2000; P.O. Box 714, Cancun, Q.R., tel. 4-19-45 and 4-16-89. **Hotel Akumal Caribe** (also known as Ina Yana Kin), located on the S end of the beach, is a newer 2-story hotel. All rooms are simple but delightful with private bath, terrace, plus bar, restaurant, swimming pool, fishing and diving arrangements. Rates US$40 d. Make reservations through your travel agent.

OTHER PRACTICALITIES

Food

The largest of several restaurants in Akumal, **Zasil,** is on the N end of the beach next to Las Casitas, housed under an enormous traditional *palapa* roof — held together with twine, no nails or screws. Zasil has become a bit pricey (lobster dinner: P4300), but seafood is fresh, bread is homemade, and they serve 3 meals. Several times a week, a busload of tourists is brought in from cruise ships that anchor off Cozumel, Cancun, and Playa del Carmen — don't eat here then! Next to the dive shop on the beach is another good restaurant, **Lol Ha.** It's open for dinner, and the food is tasty with wonderful fresh fish. Prices are similar to Zasil's (not cheap), and service is good. If you should happen to be there on Thanksgiving, the cook prepares a turkey dinner, American style (almost), and all gringos in the area come and party well into the night using the pilgrims as a good excuse. A smaller open-air restaurant at the S end of the beach is part of the **Ina Yana Kin Hotel** complex. The food is generally good, specializing in Mexican rather than Yucatecan food. The continental breakfast is served with a large platter of fresh tropical fruit.

A **snack bar** on the beach serves the usual cold drinks, hamburgers, hot dogs, sandwiches. You'll also find an **ice cream** stand and just before the main entrance/arch to Akumal resort, a small **general store** sells a limited selection of groceries, cold drinks, liquor, sundries, fresh fruit and vegetables. If you plan on being there for any length of time and cooking, the store takes orders for chicken and meat. Attached to the store is a small fast-food window selling inexpensive tacos and *tortas;* it closes early in the evening.

Entertainment
Usually you can find one disco that's open. During high season or any time there's an appreciative audience, music continues into the wee hours. Akumal and Playa del Carmen have the only commercial nighttime entertainment between Chetumal and Cancun, though comparatively tame. Without the bright glare of city lights, however, Mother Nature provides her nightly spectacular of stars, moon, and rippling water far better than any Hollywood screen.

Shopping
Two gift shops (one next to Zasil dining room) and a large boutique (farther down the beach) sell a little of everything: typical Mayan clothing, leather sandals, shawls, postcards, pottery, original Maya art and reproductions, black coral and silver jewelry, and a good selection of informative books (in English, French, and German) about the Peninsula and Maya. Stamps are sold here; liquor is available at the market on the main entrance.

Dive shops
The dive shops have excellent equipment for rent, and they offer a good selection for sale. Rental fees vary slightly between both shops.

PER DAY RENTAL IN US$

Tank	$5
B.C.	$4
Regulator	$7
Weight belt	$2
Mask, snorkel, fins	$4
Underwater camera	$9

DIVING FEES

One person	$60
Two persons	$50

Includes: all equipment, one lecture and 45 minutes practice in the bay of Akumal.

PADI Certifications and resort courses; negotiable at the dive shop.

Escorted dive trips—morning dive trip $18, second dive afternoon trip $9. Includes: boat, tank, air, guide, weight belt and B.C.

Kayak rentals	$4/hour.
Windsurfers	$10/hour.

Services

The desk clerk will make arrangements for your **laundry** to be done by one of the women who works at the hotel; the nearest laundromat is in Cancun. The closest **bank** is 36 km N at Playa del Carmen. A convenient **gas station** is at the junction of Hwy. 307 and the Tulum ruins road, 24 km south. Another station is located in Puerto Morelos. Remember the gas stations are just that, with no mechanics. However, there's a good and reasonable mechanic in the village of Tulum on Hwy. (307). He doesn't have a sign but is easy to find (on the left side of the road going S), with many cars parked under a large metal awning; prices are reasonable.

TRANSPORT

Getting There

Buses pass the Akumal turnoff going both N and S frequently throughout the day. Ask the driver to drop you off (it's not a regular stop); from there walk about one km toward the sea. The bus from Playa del Carmen to Tulum (P500) makes the trip several times each day. Check on the time you must be on the highway to be picked up.

By Car

Traveling by car is the most convenient way to get up and down the coast. From Merida take Hwy. 180 E to Cancun and turn S on 307 (both good 2-lane highways) which passes the entrance road to Akumal. From Cancun, it's an 80-km, one-hour drive. Car rentals are available in Cancun and Merida, or if you're using public transportation and want to explore some of the dirt roads and off-the-track beaches S of Akumal for only a day, a car rental is available at the Las Casitas condominiums at the N end of Akumal. Check with the manager for all details (rentals priced just slightly higher than in Cancun). The highway is good but the side roads can be rough with potholes, though driveable.

By Taxi

Taxis will bring you to Akumal from Cancun or from the ferry docks at Playa del Carmen. Arrange the price before you start. The average fare from Carmen to Akumal is around P4000 (up to 4 passengers), depending on the season and the demand; from Cancun P7000. If you're staying in Cancun or Cozumel and are interested in a one-day tour-guided trip that stops at both Xelha and Tulum, make arrangements at a hotel.

Hitchhiking

There's not a lot of traffic on the highway. If hitchhiking, it's best to originate your ride from one of the larger cities, Cancun or Merida, or in the small towns along the highway, either Playa del Carmen or Puerto Morelos.

AVENTURAS — KM 250

This little beach resort entertains private guests: government-sponsored families from diverse locations on the Yucatan Peninsula. Here in a hostel-like recreation area children play on a small palm-shaded beach, swim in shallow water, or romp in a playground of simple equipment. Visitors are free to use the beach close by, but please check at the office for permission to use the restrooms. No camping permitted.

XCARET — KM 249

A half km off the highway hidden behind a couple of small *palapas* (occupied by the family that collects P40 for an entrance fee), are 2 small ruins. Not spectacular in themselves, they illustrate the Maya choice of ascetic (and safe) spots for lookouts and ceremonial centers. A path from the small structures leads to a cave below a large rock that shows a hidden *cenote,* but looking down you'd never know water was down there. If you want to prove it, drop a rock; ripples expose crystal clear water. Just beyond the decaying ruins is a small *caleta* (cove) reminiscent of a serene watercolor painting. Not a sandy beach here, just a dark limestone-edged lagoon filled with darting fish of brilliant colors. After you make your way across the rocks, the *caleta* eventually opens out to the sea. The whole bay is no bigger than a football field, but must be seen for its quiescent harmony.

Sacbes

Archaeologists will continue excavating this area that they feel is rich with hidden history.

Xcaret's small bay is clear and perfect for diving.

They are convinced they'll eventually find traces of a *sacbe* beginning at Coba and ending at Xcaret. The scientists conjecture this small cove was used as a protected harbor and debarkation point for Maya sailors that traveled up and down the coast in dugout canoes.

Cave Diving

Along the limestone shore it's possible to enter a water-filled cave and swim (with scuba gear) inland a considerable distance underwater. At the mouth of the cave a layer of saltwater floats over freshwater from an underground river flowing from the cave opening into the sea. Swimming farther into the cave ultimately brings you to a shaft of light coming from an opening in the roof of the cavern where you can then climb out and back into the jungle near the small ruined Maya structure. This area of the coast is dotted with similar caves and waterways.

CHEMUYIL — KM 248

The poor-man's Akumal, Chemuyil is a tranquil beach with natural attributes of powder-fine sand, turquoise sea, and crowds of shady coconut palms. The water is calm, thanks to the reef, and snorkeling and fishing attract many day visitors for a fee of P50 pp. Feel free to camp here among the trees for P300 pp. Pay at the circular *palapa* refreshment stand near the entrance of the parking lot. The stand serves small packaged sweets, donuts, coffee, juice, bananas, plus beer, tequila, and fresh seafood including lobster if the traps have lured a captive.

If you like tequila — ask the barkeep to fix a "hangover" special. First he brings out a "mystical" slice of the *zapote* tree and sets it on the counter. Then he puts a jigger on top of the wooden round. He pours tequila almost to the top, and finishes filling it with Squirt. Placing the wood round on top of the jigger he gives it three sound taps on the counter, then the bedeviled one gulps it down. Actually, the ceremony is worth the time, as long as it's *someone* else taking the cure!

Accommodations And Food

Although the barkeep does his best to control the cannibal flies that hover around the refreshment stand, if you're going to eat ask to sit in one of the small screened shelters with a round table and mushroom-shaped stools. For P1000 each, there are 2 screened *palapa* rooms with 2 hanging double beds (bedding included). Besides the beds are hammock hooks and you are free to fit as many people as you can. The *concierge* claims a record of 15!

Chemuyil can get crowded during the busy winter season. Day-trippers from Cancun drive their rental cars to this particular beach, but it never appears to be overcrowded with overnighters. Camp on the S end of the beach to avoid the day-trippers. Anyone can be a successful fisherman in this bay. It takes little more than throwing a baited hook into the surf 5 or 6 m off the beach. If you want to fish for something special, make arrangements with the owner to take you farther out to sea in his launch — this is the hunting grounds of great red snapper.

XCACEL — KM 247

The beaches just keep coming, one right after the other. Though this coast really hasn't been discovered by most of the world, some have found it and keep returning year after year. Part of the reason for coming is the fascinating people you can count on meeting: some in campers, some on cycles, some on foot. A few pack everything they can in small pickup campers and spend an entire exotic winter among Xcacel's (SHAH-sell) palms for US$50 a month total rent for a small piece of paradise. For one night, a fee of P300 provides a clean shower and toilet, no electricity, and lots of space to spread out. There's a small restaurant here, but if you're cooking bring plenty of food and water; it's a long way to the local Safeway.

Surf And Sand

The sea directly in front of the campgrounds can be rough, but only a few hundred m N, the reef shields large waves producing calm water again—great swimming, fishing, snorkeling, and scuba diving on the reef. When beachcombing, wear shoes along this strip of beach to protect from little sharp things crunched up in the sand. This is a good place to find shells, especially in front of the campgrounds after a storm. All manner of treasure can be found, from masses of dead coral (all white, now) to sea urchin shells, keyhole limpets, maybe even a hermit crab carrying an ungainly topsy-turvy shell on his back.

Hiking

If you're a hiker or birdwatcher, an old dirt road runs parallel to the shoreline from Chemuyil to Xelha, about 5 km in all. The road edges an old coconut grove now thick with jungle vegetation. Just after dawn, early birds are out in force looking for the proverbial worm, or anything else that looks tasty. If at first you don't see them, you'll surely hear them. Look for small colorful parrots, brilliant yellow orioles, or you may even see the long-tailed motmot. If you decide to hike to the mouth of Xelha National Park, figure about a 20-min.

walk each way. Bring your snorkeling gear, especially if you get there early before all the tour buses. Don't forget sunscreen and bug repellent.

The coconut crab rips the husk from the coconut with its strong claws, then drags it up the coconut tree and drops it. The shelled fruit cracks and the crab descends for a fine feast.

XELHA — KM 245

Xelha (shell-HAAH), a national park on Yucatan's E coast, is just 5 km from Akumal. Xelha's lagoon consists of fresh and salt water inhabited by rare and colorful tropical fish. Through small openings from the sea, a multi-fingered aquarium has developed through the centuries, providing a safe harbor for such exotic underwater life as the brightly hued parrot fish. As a national park, the lagoon is protected from fishing, thereby preserving these beautiful creatures for all to see. Xelha can get crowded at certain hours when tour buses bring passengers from cruise ships docked at Cancun, Cozumel, and Playa del Carmen. Come early when there are few tourists. Xelha is open from 0800 to 1700. Admission P90. **Note:** Do not wear tanning lotions or oils before jumping into the lagoon. These potions are hard on the lifespan of the fish and other marinelife.

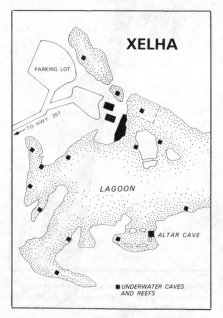

SIGHTS

Museum
At Xelha a small maritime museum is open 0800-1700 (P100). Artifacts brought from the sunken ship *Mantanceros* are seen here. There's a small collection of belt buckles, cannons, coins, guns, tableware, and various clay relics from Maya ruins on the Quintana Roo coast. The *Mantanceros* ("Our Lady of the Miracles"), a Spanish merchant ship that left Cadiz, Spain, in 1741 headed for the New World loaded with trade goods, foundered and sank on the reef 2 km N of Akumal. No one knows for certain why the *Mantanceros* sank since there were no survivors. However, the CEDAM organization spent several years salvaging it (beginning in 1958). Research shows the ship probably engaged in a violent battle with a British vessel and then drifted onto the treacherous reef now known as Punta Mantanceros. For more detailed information on the finds of the Mantanceros read *The Treasure of the Great Reef* by Arthur C. Clark. Also on display, from the British ship *Tweed* (sunk more recently), is once-elegant tableware, a gold watch, a 1905 San Francisco newspaper, even a gold denture. There are several unimpressive stone Maya idols. The museum could use a little TLC, and the exhibits are limited but well worth the price.

Snorkeling
You can stroll around the lagoon and see to the bottom through incredibly clear water. Snorkeling is allowed in marked areas, and equipment is available for rent, P1600 and a wait in a long line after the tour buses arrive. In one of many underwater caverns that punctuate the lagoon's coast, you'll see the remains of a decaying Mayan temple. There's little to authenticate its origins, but once was located on the now-submerged shoreline. Little islands, narrow waterways, and underwater

passages are marvelous to snorkel in amidst beautiful coral formations and a variety of warm-water fish.

Other Activities

The lagoon is surrounded by tropical vegetation with paths that wander around the 10 sq acres of water. Small platforms over the water provide a perfect place for the non-swimmer to study the fish and sea creatures below. It's possible to rent kayaks (P1600 per hour), a good way to explore the entire lagoon and its many waterways. There are no shallow wading areas along the shore, but you'll find frequent platforms to climb in and out of the marked areas where swimming and snorkeling are permitted. It's a temptation, and fun, to feed the fish, which is okay as long as you give them the nutritious prepared food sold in plastic bags at the entrance under the large arch.

Practicalities

Xelha has a cafe open during the day for lunch, snacks and drinks. Lovers of coconut milk can buy the whole nut from a straw-hatted vendor who deftly swings his machete, preparing the fruit to order (straws included) under the tall cooling shadows of a palm tree. Outside the entrance to Xelha, a large shop offers a variety of Yucatecan crafts, clothing, leather goods, locally carved black coral, postcards, and other local arts.

TULUM RUINS

Five km S of Akumal on Hwy. 307, a side road leads to Tulum, the largest fortified Maya site on the Q.R. coast. Tulum, meaning "Wall" in Maya, is quite small (the area enclosed by the wall measures 380 m by 165 m). It has 60 well-preserved structures that reveal the stylized Toltec influence and an impressive history. The sturdy stone wall was built 3-5 m high with an average thickness of 7 meters. Originally this site was called *Zama* ("Sunrise"). Appropriately, the sun rises directly out of the ocean over Tulum, which is perched on a cliff 12 m above the sea. The first view of this noble, then-brightly colored fortress impressed the Spaniards in Juan de Grijalva's expedition as they sailed past the Quintana Roo coast in 1518. This was their first encounter with the Indians on this new continent, and according to ship's logs, the image was awe-inspiring.

HISTORY

Tulum was part of a series of coastal forts, towns, watchtowers, and shrines established along the coast as far S as Chetumal and N past Cancun. Archaeologists place the beginnings of Tulum in the Post-Classic Period after the Maya civilization had already passed its peak and was in its Decadent stage, somewhere between A.D. 700-1000. Although a *stela* dated

A.D. 564 was found at Tulum, investigators are certain it was moved there from some other place long after it had been carved and date figures cut into it. The structures show a strong Toltec influence, such as flat roofs, plumed serpent, columns, and even pottery shapes that have definitely been established as Toltec.

Talking Cross

From 1850, Tulum was a part of the Chan Santa Cruz Indians "talking cross cult." The Spanish had taught the Indians Catholic rituals, many reminiscent of Maya ceremonies; even the cross reminded them of their tree of life. In fact, for centuries the gods had been speaking to their priests through "idols." In order to manipulate the Indians, a clever revolutionary half-caste, Jose Maria Barrera, used an Indian ventriloquist, Manuel Nahuat, to speak through the cross. It began 3 years after the end of the Caste War in the woods at a shrine with a cross near what is now known as Felipe Carrillo Puerto, but then was simply called Chan. A voice from the cross urged the Indians to take up arms again against the Mexicans. Bewildered, impressed, and never doubting, they accepted almost immediately the curious occurrence. The original cross was replaced by 3 crosses that continued to instruct the simple Indians from the holy, highly guarded site. This political-religious cult grew quickly and ruled

view from moderately priced Hotel Las Lagunas in Bacalar

Quintana Roo efficiently. The well-armed, jungle-wise Chan Santa Cruz Indians kept the Mexican government successfully out of the territory for 50 years. Even the British government in British Honduras (now known as Belize) treated this cult with respect, more out of fear of their power and their cause than diplomacy, and needing the timber trade. Around 1895 the Indians requested that the Territory of Quintana Roo be annexed by British Honduras, but the Mexican government flatly refused and sent in a new expeditionary force to reclaim Quintana Roo.

The Mexican army was doomed from the outset. They fought not only armed and elusive Indians, but constant attacks of malaria and the jungle itself. The small army managed to fight its way into the capital of Chan Santa Cruz, where they were virtually trapped for a year. The standoff continued until The Revolution in 1911, when President Porfirio Diaz resigned.

Four years later the Mexican army gave up, the capital was returned to the Indians, and they continued to rule as an independent state, an embarassment and ever-present thorn in the side of the broadening Mexican Republic. This small determined group of Indians from another time zone managed to keep their independence and culture intact while the rest of the world proceeded on to the 20th century. But, life in the jungle is tough on everyone. With famine, malaria, 90 years of fighting (and beating) the Mexican army, the Chan Santa Cruz Indian's population was reduced to 10,000. Weary, in 1935 they decided to quit the fight and were accorded the recognition given to a respected adversary. When their elderly leaders signed a peace treaty, the Chan Santa Cruz Indians agreed to *allow* Mexico to rule them.

Into The 20th Century

One of the few pure Chan Indian villages left in 1935 was Tulum, and today many residents are descendants of these independent people.

Even after signing the treaty, the Indians still maintained control of the area and outsiders were highly discouraged from traveling through. A skeleton imbedded in the cement at

MANATEE BREEDING PROGRAM

The state of Florida, under the auspices of the Miami Seaquarium and Dr. Jesse White, have begun a captive/breeding program to learn more about the habits of the manatee and try to increase its declining numbers. Several manatees have been born in captivity, and they along with others that have recuperated from injury or illness will be or have been released into Florida's Crystal River where boat traffic is restricted. They are tagged and closely observed. Florida maintains a 24-hour hotline where people report manatees in need of help for any reason. Rescues are often carried out — removing an adult male from a cramped storm drain, or rushing to Seaquarium newborns that somehow managed to get separated from their mothers and have washed ashore. These newborns are readily accepted by surrogate-mother manatees and are offered nourishment (by way of a thumb-sized teat under the front flipper) and lots of TLC. Medical aid is given to mammals that have been slashed by boat propellers. The manatee has a playful curiosity and investigates anything found in its underwater environment, many times sustaining grave injury.

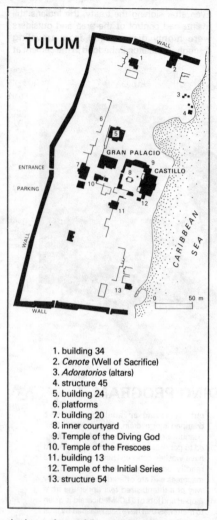

TULUM

1. building 34
2. *Cenote* (Well of Sacrifice)
3. *Adoratorios* (altars)
4. structure 45
5. building 24
6. platforms
7. building 20
8. inner courtyard
9. Temple of the Diving God
10. Temple of the Frescoes
11. building 13
12. Temple of the Initial Series
13. structure 54

the base of one of the temples at Tulum is the remains of an uninvited archaeologist, as a warning to other would-be intruders.

All of this has changed. With foresight the Mexican government in the '60s recognized the beautiful Quintana Roo coast as a potential tourist draw, and the new state has entered the 20th century. The advent of roads and airports has paved the way for the rest of the world to come visit the unique ruins of Tulum. The indigenous people welcome the tourist and what he represents, at least for now.

The thick stands of coconut trees along this part of the coast were once part of an immense coconut plantation that included Akumal and Xelha, owned by a gentleman named Don Pablo Bush. The CEDAM organization and Bush donated Xelha Lagoon to the government for use as a national park.

SIGHTS

In the **Temple of Frescoes,** looking through a metal grate, you'll see a fresco that still bears a trace of color from the ancient artist. Archaeologically, this is the most interesting building on the site. The original parts of the building were built around 1450 during the late Post-Classic Period. And as is the case with so many of the Maya structures, it was added to over the years.

Diving God

Across the compound a small *palapa* roof protects a carved descending god. This winged creature is pictured upside down, and has been described as the God of the Setting Sun by some historians. Others interpret the carving as representing the bee; honey is a commodity almost as revered on the Peninsula as maize. Because so little is known about the glyphs of the Maya, it may be many years before this and other questions can be fully answered and understood.

El Castillo

The most impressive is the large pyramid which stands on the edge of the cliff overlooking the sea. The building, in the center of the wall on the east side, was built in 3 different phases. A wide staircase leads to a 2-chambered temple on the top. Two serpent columns divide the entrance, and above the middle entrance is another carved figure of the Diving God. The climb to the top rewards you with a breathtaking bird's-eye view of the ocean, the surrounding jungle with an occasional stone ruin poking through the tight brush, and scattered clearings where small farms are beginning to grow.

Tulum's archaeological zone is open daily from 0800-1700. At 0800 few tour buses have arrived yet, making the cooler early hours a desirable time to explore and climb the aging structures. Opposite the main entrance to the site are a number of open stalls with typical tourist curios along with a growing number of small cafes selling soda pop and snacks. A fee of P50 is paid across the street from the entrance to the ruins. Parking is available directly outside the Tulum site (if not filled with tour buses) for P25.

Village Of Tulum

A few km past the road to the Tulum archaeological zone on Hwy. 307 is the pueblo of Tulum. This small village (not surprisingly) has had a delayed reaction to all the tourists that come to their famous "ruins" down the road. The town has little to offer except a few simple markets, a couple of *loncherias,* and maybe most important a couple of mechanics. You'll spot one just as you drive into town on the highway on the L side of the street. There's no sign, but a large number of cars on the property is a dead giveaway. He and his son are good, cheap, and willing to help if they can.

ACCOMMODATIONS AND FOOD

Only a few places to overnight are available in the immediate area. Follow the paved road from the parking lot along the coast; you'll come to a series of unspoiled beaches edged by thick stands of coconut trees. Between Tulum and Punta Allen there are only simple cabanas on the beach. Many don't have public power and depend on gas lanterns or small generators for part of the day; most have a good supply of cold water and some sell bottled water, but if not, boil your drinking supply. Expect simple accommodations all in the budget class. If you require deluxe rooms, your best bet is to headquarter at Akumal, 25 km north. The beach camps along the coast are open to parking an RV vehicle, though most don't have hook-ups; ask the manager if in doubt.

Temple of the Descending God

Camping

Two combination cabana/campgrounds side by side, **El Mirador** and **Santa Fe**, are on the beach immediately S of the Tulum ruins. Follow the paved road going from the parking lot (about a 12-min. walk). The cabins are tiny. Bring everything—hammock, drinking water, bug repellent, mosquito netting, food (Tulum village has a few limited markets, Santa Fe has a small cafe). If you're camping it helps to have a tent; when the wind blows it gets mighty gritty on this beach. The cabins (at both) are P300 pp and tentsites are P200 pp.

Budget

El Crucero Motel is conveniently located at the crossroads of Hwy. 307 and the Tulum ruins entrance road. It's a 10-min. walk to the ruins, and several restaurants are close. The rooms are plain, clean; P1800 s, P2500 d. In a tropical park-like setting shaded with tall palms (it's so perfect it could have been used for the movie "Hurricane"), **Chac Mool** is at the end of the paved road leading S from the Tulum parking lot. You'll enjoy cabanas, community bathrooms and showers, a dining room, bar, and a beautiful bay good for swimming and snorkeling. Run by another American/Mexican couple, both are quite helpful; US$15 d. Continue on the same road (7 km from Tulum) and on the L is a white wall (covered with colorful paintings dominated by a bright yellow submarine) that surrounds small stucco cabanas: reasonably new, very clean, well-kept grounds and usually with an abundant water supply (boil your drinking water), P2300. The owner's wife cooks meals for guests. Another clean camp, **Cabanas Tulum**, includes small cabanas with beds, bathrooms, ceiling fans, and cold water for sure (sometimes it's hot). There's a restaurant on the premises and a white beach that looks deserted most of the time; P2000 d.

Last Resort

El Paraiso Cabanas are about a km beyond the campsites. Although *paraiso* means "paradise," don't let that mislead you—El Paraiso is anything but. The cabins have uncomfortable beds, and are not clean. They advertise showers and community toilets, but neither work most of the time. Even the grounds donated by nature somehow manage to look scrubby here. P2000 per cabin or P700 pp in the hammock-hut with your own hammock.

Cafes

Restaurant El Faisan Y Venado has the most varied offerings and reasonable prices around Tulum. And though you can still order venison at this chain cafe, it's usually served in a spicy sauce and hard to recognize. This is deer country, and despite (or because of) over-hunting by the locals, venison seems to be readily available on this part of the coast. Across from the gas station is a vegetarian restaurant called **Alexandros.** The **Crucero Motel Cafe** serves simple food reasonably priced. A few fast-food stands at the *bazaar* across from the entrance to the ruins serve small tacos, *tortas,* combination plates, cold beer and soda. For more deluxe meals try the restaurants at Akumal, 25 km N of Tulum.

TRANSPORT

Getting There

Buses going N and S stop at El Crucero Motel about every 1-2 hours 0630-2030. From here you can also catch a bus to Valladolid that passes Coba at 0600 or 1200; the return bus leaves Coba at 0600 and 1600. Both 1st- and 2nd-class buses are usually crowded by the time they reach Tulum; 1st-class allows no standing. Be there in plenty of time—the buses don't wait. It's always a good idea to check with the bus driver about destination, times, and return trips.

This is a busy place, and not difficult to hitch a ride. Be practical and wait where a driver can pull off the road easily.

ROAD TO PUNTA ALLEN

If you're driving S to Punta Allen fill your gas tank at the Tulum crossroads gas station since there's not another on the coastal road to Punta Allen (57 km). Traveling N on Hwy. 307, the next gas station is in Puerto Morelos. If traveling S to Chetumal on 307 there's one in Felipe Carrillo Puerto.

BOCA PAILA

Twenty-five km S of Tulum on the Punta Allen road are the lagoons of Boca Paila. It's smooth sailing for about 6 km beyond the ruins, then the road becomes potholed and rugged. It's slow going and bumpy, but otherwise all vehicles can handle this all-weather road. Fifteen km from the Tulum parking lot is **La Villa de Boca Paila** on the left. This is a small group of modern *palapa*-roof cabanas owned individually (some by absent Americans) with a small restaurant on the grounds. La Villa is a favorite hangout for fishermen who come for bonefish; there are no other hotels close by. In

addition, the location is truly isolated, next to a large saltwater lagoon perfect for sailing (boats available to rent), diving for lobster, waterskiing, and birdwatching. Each cabana has 2 bedrooms and bathrooms, kitchen, dining area, and living room with a view of the sea. If it's busy, management will put couples (strangers) in one cabana. When making reservations specify shared or total villa, and if you want a boat for fishing or skiing. Bring your own fishing tackle and all clothing you'll need. A small gift shop on the premises sells snacks, food, soft drinks and juices. A bar serves beer, wine, and cocktails. Rates are based on modified American plan (2 meals included), US$80 d. Since there are limited accommodations, reservations are suggested: P.O. Box 159, Merida, Yucatan, Mexico.

Across The Bridge
Beyond La Villa de Boca Paila another 10 km is the Boca Paila Bridge. When you first see the bridge you may feel a little uneasy; not to worry, it only *looks* unsafe. The wooden bridge

crosses the canal that connects the lagoons with the Caribbean and since the 1970s when it was built, it has handled many cars and large vehicles. This exotic spot offers stretches of lonely beach N and S of the mouth of the lagoon crowded with tropical vegetation and coconut trees. The water, though warm and inviting, is not clear enough for snorkeling or diving. The beach is open to campers. Be sure to bring all necessities, including water.

Continuing on the road, south of the bridge is **El Retiro,** a small group of cabanas offering hammock accommodations for rent and light refreshments. It's a good stop for a cold beer on your way to Punta Allen which is another 25 km south.

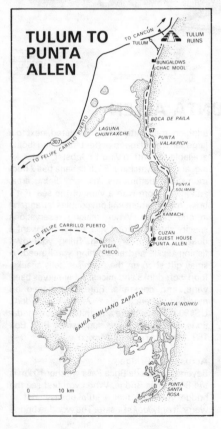

Exploring Ancient Caves
If you're traveling with a small boat (rubber raft is best) narrow canals (said to be built by the Maya) curve inland to remnants of isolated ceremonial centers—all small and none restored or even excavated. This is a trip for intrepid adventurers with sturdy muscles: in some spots the channel narrows, and you have to carry your boat overland or wade through muddy swamps. Caves are scattered about—some you can swim into, others are hidden in the countryside; glyphs still intact on the inside walls suggest the Indians may have lived in them. A guide (from Punta Allen) familiar with the area is suggested. Bring a flashlight, and walking shoes that will survive in the water.

PUNTA ALLEN

In the last century ships would occasionally drift off course onto the dangerous reef that stands just off the coast. Maya boatmen, however, expertly navigate in and out of the submerged reefs and shallow spots that lie hidden across the mouth of the bay. Punta Allen is a small fishing village on a finger of land that overlooks a large bay called Bahia de la Ascencion, considered the hottest lobster grounds in Mexico. Wildlife groups, in association with the local lobster cooperative and the Mexican equivalent of the National Science Foundation, are studying the way the Yucatecan fishermen handle the spiny crustaceans. The villagers don't use lobster traps as we know them, but instead create artificial habitats. The lobsters grow within these habitats and when they reach a determined size, the fishermen gaff them by hand. Scientists have been carrying on research here each summer since 1982 to determine if this concentration of lobster leads to overharvesting, or if protecting the habitat reduces the natural mortality rate of the open sea. Once they make their determinations perhaps they will be able to help preserve the lobster industry from being wiped out in Punta Allen as it has been in other once-rich lobster-growing areas. Over-harvesting the lobster has depleted the spiny delicacy in several areas in the Gulf of Mexico and in Baja's Todos los Santos Bay.

Sights

Punta Allen is an exotic wonderland of sea, sand, and thick jungle. The village is small and rustic, an ideal place for the artist or photographer to capture typical Yucatecan life. Snorkeling, swimming, and fishing are outstanding here. Long walks will introduce you to unusual birds and maybe even a shy animal. In fact, this is an extraordinary place for observing the nesting grounds and natural habitats of nearly 300 classes of birds identified by ornithologists.

Practicalities

The beach is free for campers; certainly the polite way is to ask permission of the local villager (whose house you'll be in front of) before setting up camp. Dispose of your trash and leave the beach clean. RVs can park on the beach; no facilities.

The **Cuzan Guest House** is a perfect resort for certain travelers. If you need modern conveniences, *don't* come to Punta Allen. But if your tastes run to low-key relaxation, sleeping in cabanas in hammocks, community bathrooms, gourmet cooking (over an open fire, yet!), and lobster for breakfast, lunch, and dinner (during the lobster season July 15 through March 15), then this is the place for you. Armando (and Sonia) will take you sailing (or motorboating) to the reef where the snorkeling is outstanding. Another popular outing is a trip to **Cayo Colibri**, a small uninhabited island off the coast where you'll see a tremendous variety of colorful and unusual birds. In the spring hundreds of man-o-war frigates hang like kites overhead, displaying the brilliant red mating pouch under their beaks that attract females. Fishing off Colibri, as well as several other uninhabited islands close by, is excellent. If you like, you'll be shown (and taught) how the locals fish for lobster in the artificial habitats with snorkel, mask, fins, and gaff. Armando will make arrangements for boating trips into the jungle if your curiosity lies in that direction.

The rates are varied depending on what you wish to do. Rooms begin at US$10-20. Breakfast and lunch are US$5, dinner US$10. For accurate prices write and describe the activities you're interested in: Cuzan Guest House, c/o Sonia Lillvik, Box 703, Cancun, Quintana Roo, Mexico. When making arrangements by mail, please allow plenty of time before your arrival date — at least 6 weeks. If you just happen to be in the neighborhood and drop in, Armando and Sonia will do everything possible to find hammock space for you.

tidy house and modern little girl in Tulum

COBA

This early Maya site covers an immense area (50 sq km) and hundreds of mounds are yet to be uncovered. Archaeologists are convinced that in time Coba will prove to be one of the largest Maya settlements on the Yucatan Peninsula. Only in recent years has the importance of Coba come to light. First explored in 1891 by Austrian archaeologist Teobert Maler, it was another 35 years before Coba was investigated by S. Morley, J. Eric Thompson, H. Pollock, and J. Charlot under the auspices of the Carnegie Institue. In 1972-75 the National Geographic Society, in conjunction with the Mexican National Institure of Anthropology and History, mapped and surveyed the entire area. A program funded by the Mexican government continues to explore and study Coba, but it is time-consuming, costly work and it will be many years before completion.

For the visitor interested in exploring, it's important to know that the distances between groupings of structures is long (in some cases 1-2 km), and they're not located in a neatly kept park such as Chichen Itza. Each group of ruins is buried in the middle of thick jungle, so come prepared with comfortable shoes, bug repellent, sunscreen, hat, and a canteen of water never hurts.

Flora and Fauna

Coba in Maya means "Water Stirred by the Wind." Close to a group of shallow lakes (Coba, Macanxoc, Xkanha, and Zalcalpu), some very marshy areas attract a large variety of birds and butterflies. The jungle around Coba is perfect for viewing toucans, herons, egrets, and the motmot. Colorful butterflies are everywhere including the large, deep-blue *morphidae* butterfly, as well as the bright yellow orange-barred sulphur. If you look on the ground, it's almost certain you'll see long lines of cutting ants. One double column carries freshly cut leaves to the burrow, and next to that another double column marches in the opposite direction (empty-jawed), returning for more. The columns can be longer than a km, and usually the work party will all be carrying the same specie of leaf or blossom (until the plant is completely stripped). The vegetation composts in their nests: mushrooms which grow on the decaying compost are an important staple of the ant's diet. The determined creatures grow up to 3 cm long. It's amazing how far they travel for food!

People

Thousands of people are believed to have lived here during the Classic Period. Though the numbers are drastically reduced, today pockets of people still maintain their archaic beliefs side by side with their Christian faith. They plant their corn with ceremony, conduct their families in the same manner as their ancestors, and many villages still appoint a calendar-keeper to keep track of the auspicious days to direct them in their daily lives. This is most common in the Coba area because of its (up to now) isolation from outsiders, and because these people have maintained a very low profile when it comes to their ancient heritage.

THE RUINS

White Roads

The most important reason to visit Coba is the archaeological remains of a city begun in A.D. 600. These structures were built near several lakes, along a refined system of *sacbeob* (plural

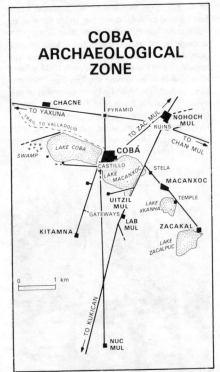

near Coba

of *sacbe*). The remains of 40 *sacbeob* have been found criss-crossing the entire Peninsula, more here than in any other location. They pass through (what were once) outlying villages and converge at Coba, which indicates it was the largest city of the era. One *sacbe* is 100 km long and travels in an almost straight line from the base of Nohoch Mul (the great pyramid) to the town of Yaxuna. Each *sacbe* was built to stringent specifications: a base of stones 1-2 m high, about 4½ m wide, and covered with white mortar. However, in Coba, some as wide as 10 m have been uncovered.

A roof has been placed over this carved stela to help preserve it from nature's constant attack.

The Pyramids

While you wander through the grounds it helps to use the map (see p. 291). When you enter, follow the dirt road a few m until you come to the sign that says GRUPO COBA directing you to the right. A short distance on the path brings you to the 2nd-highest pyramid at the site (22½ m), called **Iglesia**. From the top is a marvelous view of the surrounding jungle and Lake Macanxoc. Farther to the right (SE on a jeep trail) is a smaller pyramid called **Conjunto Las Pinturas**, so named because of the stucco paintings that once lined the walls, (minute) traces of which can still be seen on the uppermost cornice of the temple. From the summit of this structure is a dizzying view of **Nohoch Mul**, tallest pyramid on the Peninsula (42 m, a 12-story climb!). At the fork just beyond the Grupo Coba, a path to the left leads to that great temple. Watch for signs and stay on the trail.

Scientists conjecture there may be a connection between the Peten Maya (hundreds of miles S in the Guatemalan lowlands) and the Classic Maya that lived in Coba. Both groups built lofty pyramids, much taller than those found in Chichen Itza, Uxmal, or others in the N part of the Peninsula.

Undiscovered

All along the paths are mounds overgrown with vines, trees, and flowers—many of these are unexcavated ruins. More than 5000 mounds wait for the money it takes to continue excavation. Thirty-two Classic Period *stelae* (including 23 that are sculptured) have been found scattered throughout the Coba archaeological zone. For the most part they are displayed where they were discovered. One of the better preserved can be seen in front of the Nohoch Mul group. Still recognizable, it has a nobleman standing on the back of 2 slaves, dated, in Maya glyphs, 30 Nov. 780.

PRACTICALITIES

Accommodations

There's only one hotel here, the deluxe **Villa Arqueologica**, part of a chain that has placed hotels at archaeological zones (Uxmal,

Coba's Castillo is the tallest pyramid on the Peninsula.

Chichen Itza) in several parts of Mexico. Each hotel has a well-equipped library with many volumes containing history of the area and the Maya people. Run by the owners of Club Med, it has small attractive rooms, a/c, swimming pool, outdoor bar and dining, delicious French food, and a gift shop which carries quality reproductions of Maya art. It's hard to predict seasonal highs since groups from Europe are bused in all year long; reservations could be important even though the hotel is often quiet. Rates are US$48; in the U.S. for reservations call 1-800-528-3100.

Otherwise, if you find yourself stranded in Coba and need a cheap place to overnight, ask at the cafes or the bakery; usually someone will offer you hammock space.

Food

A couple of generic cafes are near Coba going toward the Villa Arqueologica. The food, though limited in choice, is typical and can be quite good, especially at **Restaurant Isabel**, where the *comida corrida* is big and cheap. Close by a tiny bakery sells good *pan dulce*, and a small store sells cold soda pop. The food at Villa Arqueologica is great, and if you bring your swim suit, you can take a dip after lunch and relax in their garden. The bar serves a terrific Planters Punch, especially when you come out of the jungle hot, sweaty, and tired from hiking and climbing the pyramids. Sandwiches cost about US$3, full meals average US$5.

Getting There

Getting to Coba is easiest by car. The roads are good and from Coba you can continue on to Valladolid, Chichen Itza, and Merida, or onto the coast highway (307) that goes S to Chetumal and N to Cancun. If traveling by bus your schedule is limited to 2 buses a day. Northbound buses depart Tulum at 0600 and 1200, stopping at Coba 0730 and 1330 before continuing on to Valladolid. Southbound bus leaves Valladolid at 0400 and 1400, stopping at Coba 0600 and 1600 on the way to Tulum and points N on Hwy. 307. When you get on and off the bus, ask the driver about the return trip and times to the ruins. Bus travelers tell of waiting at the ruins for a bus that just skips it entirely at certain times of the year. It's a 3-km walk to the highway where buses pass. You'll often run into travelers on the trail at Coba that are willing to give you a ride. Organized bus tours are available from Cancun, Cozumel, and Merida.

CHETUMAL

Chetumal, a good base for the many sights in the southern section of Quintana Roo, is also the gateway to Belize. The capital of this young state, Chetumal is without the bikini-clad, touristy crowds of the north, and presents the businesslike atmosphere of a growing metropolis. A 10-min. walk takes you from the marketplace, bus station, and most of the hotels to the waterfront. Modern sculpted monuments stand along a breezy promenade that skirts the broad crescent of bay. Also explore the back streets where worn wooden buildings still have a Central American/Caribbean look. The largest building in town — white, 3 stories, close to the waterfront — houses most of the government offices.

Wide tree-lined avenues and clean sidewalks front dozens of small variety shops. The city has been a free port for many years, and as a result, has attracted a plethora of tiny shops selling a strange conglomeration of plastic toys, small appliances, exotic perfumes (could be authentic), famous label clothes (ditto), and imported foodstuffs. Because the tax in Chetumal is only 6% instead of the usual 15, it's a popular place for Belizeans and Mexicans to shop. The population is a handsome mixture of many races including Caribe, Spanish, Maya, and English. Schools are prominently scattered around the town.

Climate
Chetumal is hot and sticky. Though sea breezes help, humidity can make the air terribly uncomfortable. High temperatures in Aug. average 100 F, in Dec. 86 F. In the last 30 years, 2 destructive hurricanes have attacked the Peninsula, and Hurricane Janet all but destroyed Chetumal in 1955. Not something to be too concerned about though — these devastating blows are infrequent. The most comfortable time to visit is the dry season from Nov. to April.

Flora and Fauna
Chetumal is noted for its hardwood trees, such as mahogany and rosewood. (Abundance of wood explains the difference in rural housing between the N and S ends of the Peninsula. Small houses in the S are built mostly of milled board, some with thatched roofs; structures with circular walls of slender saplings set close together are still common in the north.) Copious rainfall in the Chetumal area creates dense jungle with vine-covered trees, broadleafed plants, ferns, and colorful blossoms. Or-

Chetumal's imposing government building where the capital of Quintana Roo is located

chids grow liberally, attached to the tallest trees. Deer and javelina roam the forests.

SIGHTS

Calderitas Bay

On Av. Heroes, 8 km N of the city, is **Calderitas Bay**, a breezy area for picnicking, camping and RVing. The trailer park is one of the few in the state that provides complete hookups for RVs, including a dump station and clean showers, toilets and washing facilities (P800 for a large rig). Right on the water's edge, the spotless camp is in a park-like setting fringed with cooling palm trees. Amateur divers will find exotic shells; the fishing is great. Nearby public beaches have *palapa* shelters which are normally tranquil, but on holidays they're crowded with sun- and fun-seekers.

Isla Tamalcas

Tiny **Isla Tamalcas**, 2 km off the shore of Calderitas, is the home of the primitive *capybara*. This largest of all rodents can reach a length of over a meter, weigh up to 50 kg, and is found few other places in the world. The animal is covered with reddish-yellowish-brown coarse hair, resembles a small pig or large guinea pig, has partially webbed toes, and loves to swim. It's referred to by the locals as a water pig, and is a favorite food of the jaguar. Isla Tamalcas is easily accessible from Calderitas Beach.

Xcalak

Xcalak (Shka-lak), a tiny fishing village located across the bay of Chetumal, is the southernmost tip of Quintana Roo. Trekking there is an extraordinary expedition for those having a wellspring of energy and plenty of time. If you plan to stay for a few days, bring your camping gear: Xcalak doesn't have a hotel — yet, though a couple of *tiendas* sell simple food and supplies. Here is an ideal place to rent an outboard skiff and explore the coast with its many coves and bays. It's easy to strike a deal with a local fisherman to take you across the reef to breathtaking **Chinchorro Bank**, 26 km off the coast, which covers a large area (43 km N to S, 17 km E to W). Skin divers find crystal clear water

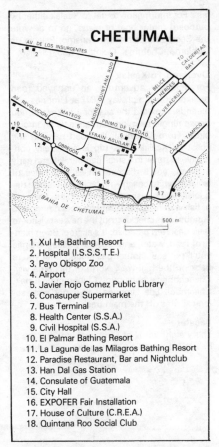

1. Xul Ha Bathing Resort
2. Hospital (I.S.S.S.T.E.)
3. Payo Obispo Zoo
4. Airport
5. Javier Rojo Gomez Public Library
6. Conasuper Supermarket
7. Bus Terminal
8. Health Center (S.S.A.)
9. Civil Hospital (S.S.A.)
10. El Palmar Bathing Resort
11. La Laguna de las Milagros Bathing Resort
12. Paradise Restaurant, Bar and Nightclub
13. Han Dal Gas Station
14. Consulate of Guatemala
15. City Hall
16. EXPOFER Fair Installation
17. House of Culture (C.R.E.A.)
18. Quintana Roo Social Club

with a huge variety of colorful fish, delicate coral, and 3 sunken ships clearly visible from above.

A 2-hour boat trip (about P2000 pp) can be arranged from Chetumal's downtown docks. Another possibility is to fly to Xcalak. Its airstrip can handle any twin-engine plane. If in your own plane, flying once over the village will bring someone to the airport to take you to town. Small planes with pilot are available to hire in Chetumal for a trip to Xcalak, about P34,000 RT for 3 or 4 people. You'll be dropped off, then picked up at an arranged time. If it's just a day trip and the pilot stays, the cost is less. For information to get to Xcalak either by outboard motor boat or plane, go to or write the Secretaria Estatal De Turismo, Palacio de Gobierno, Chetumal, Quintana Roo, Mexico.

Overland To Xcalak

For a longer adventure, an unpaved road breaks off the highway (307) at Limones and meanders toward the sea for 120 km through dense jungle teeming with animals and noisy birds. From Majahual, the road parallels the coast to Xcalak. This trip is especially conducive to travel in a small camper. Like an early explorer, you'll discover miles and miles of isolated white beach — no facilities, just the turquoise sea, transparent white crabs, a variety of fish waiting to be caught for your dinner, and curious birds checking out the newest visitor to their deserted paradise. It's all free. Bring plenty of food, water, and especially gasoline since you'll not see another gas station until you're back on the highway. North of this area visit Chacchoben, Ichpaatun, Chichmoul, Tupak, Chacmool, Los Limones — all minor archaeological sites off the main track.

Bacalar

Thirty-eight km N of Chetumal (on 307) lies a beautiful multi-hued lagoon called **Las**

Lagunas de Siete Colores ("Lagoon of Seven Colors"). Bacalar, complete with 17th C. Fort San Felipe, is a small town founded by the Spanish to protect themselves from the bands of pirates and Maya that regularly raided the area. Today, part of the fort has a small museum housing metal arms used in the 17th and 18th centuries. A small assortment of memorabilia recalls history of the area. The stone construction has been restored, and cannons are still posted along the balustrades overlooking beautiful Bacalar Lagoon. The museum is open daily except holidays, small entry fee charged.

Cenote Azul

Thirty-four km N of Chetumal (on 307) is a circular *cenote* 61 ½ m deep, 185 m cross, filled with brilliant blue water. A charming outdoor restaurant is a popular stop for visitors both for swimming and refreshment.

ACCOMMODATIONS

Although Chetumal is not considered a tourist resort, its low taxes and location on the Belize border make it a desirable marketplace for both Mexicans and Belizeans. If traveling without

view from moderately priced Hotel Las Lagunas near Chetumal

Cyclers find good roads on the Peninsula.

reservations, arrive as early in the day as possible to have your choice of hotel rooms. During the holiday season, it's wise to reserve in advance. Most of the hotels listed are within walking distance of the bus station, marketplace, downtown shops, and waterfront.

Budget
The budget traveler has a choice of several hotels, a Youth Hostel at Bacalar, or camping at Calderitas Bay. Some of the *posadas* are spartan without hot water, and few even have food available. At the following hotels, prices range from P800-1200. **Colonial**, Benjamin Hill 135, tel. 21520; **Tabasco**, Av. Zaragoza 206, tel. 22045; **America**, Othon P. Blanco 11.

Moderate
The moderate-priced hotels for the most part are friendly (some clean, some not, look before you pay), usually fan-cooled, and have hot water. Prices range from P2000 to 2500 d at: **San Jorge**, Av. Juarez 87, tel. 21065; **Maria Dolores**, Av. Alvaro Obregon 206, tel. 20508; and **Tulum**, Av. Heroes 2, tel. 20518. The following hotels are small, modern, friendly, have a/c with a restaurant, bar and evening entertainment. They range in price from P3000-4000 d: **Hotel Real Azteca**, Av. Belize 186, tel. 20720; **El Dorado Hotel**, Av. 5 de Mayo 21, tel. 20315; and **Hotel Caribe Princess**, Av. Alvaro Obregon 180, tel. 20900.

Higher Priced
Chetumal doesn't have a true luxury hotel. The **El Presidente** comes close with general cleanliness, a/c, pretty garden, and clean large swimming pool, bar with evening disco music, and a quiet dining room with a friendly staff that serves an uninspired menu; US$30 d, Av. Heroes con Chapultepec, tel. 20544. The **Hotel Continental-Caribe** *advertises* itself as luxury, has a/c, restaurant, pool, bar with evening entertainment, and though the rooms are clean the overall appearance is not. Prices range from P5000-6500. Av. Heroes 171, tel. 20441.

OTHER PRACTICALITIES

Food
It's easy to find a cafe to fit every budget in Chetumal. Those near the bus stop are reasonable—some good, others questionable. Walk down the street to Av. Alvaro Obregon for several fast-food cafes. On the same street, for seafood try **El Pez Vela**; for barbecued chicken go to **Pollos Sinaloa**. On the corner of Av. Efrain Aguilar and Revolucion is **Los Pozos**, a regional cafe serving typical Yucatecan dishes. If your taste buds yearn for good American red meat, try **Buffalo Steak**, Av. Alvaro Obregon 208. For *helado* and *postres* try **Carlena**, Av. A. Lopez Mateos 407,

or **Fonagora,** the corner of Av. Heroes con Lazaro Cardenas. The **public market** has just about everything you could need; three **Conasuper** markets can provide the rest.

Entertainment

For dancing, try one of these small discoteques: **El Elefante,** Blvd. Bahia; **Focus** at the

DOWNTOWN CHETUMAL

1. Telephone Office
2. El Presidente Restaurant
3. El Caracol Shopping Center and Fonagora (cultural center)
4. Post and Telegraph Offices
5. Conasuper Supermarket
6. Leona Vicario Cinema
7. Arts and Crafts House
8. Superfama Supermarket
9. Big Ben Hotel
10. Baroudi Hotel
11. Sergio's Pizza
12. Caribe Princess Hotel
13. Josefa Ortiz de Dominguez Gardens
14. Sagrado Corazon de Jesus Church
15. Aeromexico Airlines
16. State Government Office
17. Immigration Office
18. Fishing Club
19. El Mulle Amusement Park for Children
20. Sailor's Monument
21. State Congress

Hotel Continental, Av. Heroes 171; **Huanos Astoria,** Av. Reforma 27; **Sarawak** at Hotel El Presidente, Av. Heroes Y Chapultepec. Cinemas and theaters include: **Campestre,** Av. A. Lopez Mateos con Milan; **Avila Camacho,** Calle 22 de Enero; **Leona Vicario,** Av. Alvaro Obregon con Independencia; **Cine Juventino Rosas,** Av. Hidalgo. The larger hotels usually have a TV in the lobby; the El Presidente Hotel will provide one with your room for a small fee. There are no English subtitles. **Javier Rojo Gomez Public Library** is on Av. Efrain Aguilar.

Sports

A yearly event in Chetumal is an auto road race. Open to drivers from all over the globe, it's gaining prominence in the racing world. This event takes place in Dec. and hotel reservations should be made well in advance.

A popular sport in both Chetumal Bay and Bacalar Lagoon is windsurfing. State competitions are held in both areas yearly. What a great place to fly across the sea! Make reservations early since many others will have the same idea. For more information, write to the Secretaria de Turismo, Palacio de Gobierno 20, Piso, Chetumal, Quintana Roo, Mexico.

Services

The **post office** is on Calles 2 A. You can send a telegram from **Telegrafos Nacionales,** Av. 5 de Mayo. **Long-distance** phone calls can be made from Tico-Tico, Av. Alvaro Obregon 7, or Novedades Caribe, Av. Heroes. For any **medical** emergency, there are several hospitals and clinics. Ask at your hotel for a doctor who speaks English. One **pharmacy** is on Carmen Ochoa de Merino Y Heroes, tel. 2-01-62. Four **gasoline stations** and at least 7 mechanics are in town. Several **banks** will cash traveler's cheques Mon. to Sat. 0900-1300. First- and 2nd-class buses use the station at Av. Heroes 172. Batty Bus to Belize leaves daily from the side street next to the bus station. A visit to the **Tourism Office** is helpful; ask for their *Guia Turistica,* which lists cultural activities, monuments and murals open to the public, along with addresses of all banks and other solid information about Chetumal.

TRANSPORT

By Air

Chetumal's new airport still has only a few flights each day. An airport van provides transportation to hotels or downtown for P600 pp. When a plane is crowded, it's not unusual to have to wait as much as 45 min. for the van to make a second RT into town. Aeromexico flights arrive in the city daily from Mexico City, Merida, Cancun, Villahermosa, and Campeche.

By Bus

Buses arrive at the bus station on Av. Heroes throughout the day from Merida, Puerto Morelos, and Mexico City. With the expanding road system, bus travel is becoming more versatile and is still the most inexpensive public transportation to the Quintana Roo coast. Buses to Chetumal arrive from: Merida, P1300, 5½ hours, Mexico City, P4600, 22 hours, plus frequent trips from Cancun and Campeche.

By Car

A good paved road connects Merida, Campeche, Villahermosa, and Francisco Escarcega to Chetumal; a highway (307) links all the Quintana Roo coastal cities. There's little traffic, and gas stations are well spaced if you top off at each one. Car rentals are not yet available at the Chetumal airport. Go to El Presidente Hotel for Avis. Chetumal is a good place to rent your car since there's only a 6% tax instead of the usual 15.

Walking

For the hardy type with lots of time, walking the 347 km from Puerto Morelos to Chetumal can be high adventure. Taking at least 3 weeks (or longer if you take time to smell the flowers), this trip is only for the fit. While the main highway (307) is the most direct route, it often veers away from the beach—boring and flat with little to see except the jungle hemming in the road on both sides. An alternate route: on 307 at the turnoff to the Tulum ruins walk past the ruins then continue south. For 6 km it's a paved road, then it becomes potholed and rough, meandering along the sea. Though sometimes behind sand dunes, it's not that long a trudge to dozens of fine beaches where you might be seduced into staying a day or a month—or forever.

Some of these beaches have established campsites where you're required to pay. The

Calderitas Bay has one of the best trailer parks in all of Yucatan.

Kohunlich Temple with a palapa *roof to protect the giant masks from the weather.*

average fee, P600 pp, gets you showers, toilets, water, and lots of coconut trees on which to sling your hammock—a tropical paradise. Some have *palapa* huts (P1500 to P2500) that sleep 4-6 with your own hammocks (no beds). Rental hammocks are available (P100). A few *palapa* huts have hanging beds with mosquito netting and no windows. If hammock sleeping doesn't suit you (though the Maya believe the hammock is a gift from the gods), you'll find a couple of (almost) Western-style resorts along the way—simple cabanas with beds, communal bathrooms, and cold water only. Restaurants are sparse along this 347-km stretch, so come prepared with your own victuals and water. For the last 75 km before you come to Punta Allen, you'll find only the Boca Paila resort (not always available and El Retiro (a small group of cabanas and a cafe). At Punta Allen it's best to return inland to Felipe Carrillo

Puerto and continue on 307 for the remaining 134 km. From this small city it's fairly easy to hitch a ride to Chetumal.

Cycling
Though most of the Yucatan Peninsula is flat, and the primary arteries are in good condition, the Caribbean coast appears to be the gathering place for cyclers. For exploration off the main roads, be prepared for bumpy, irregular and hard-packed dirt surfaces which become a muddy morass when it rains. Bring spare tires and a repair kit. With a motorcycle you can travel almost any road on the Peninsula. Beware the swampy shoulders near the sea. Repairs can be a problem in some areas, and few cycle shops exist except in the larger cities.

Other Transport
There's a moderate amount of traffic on 307, so you could combine hitching on the paved road with hiking off it. Train service is available from Merida and Mexico City. Bahia de Chetumal, largest harbor on Quintana Roo's coast, is very shallow—useless as a port of call for large ships, but small local boatmen travel the coast and would probably be available for hire.

Into Belize
The Rio Hondo River forms a natural border between Quintana Roo and Belize. Chetumal is the only land link between the 2 countries, from which Belize is easily reached by Batty Buses (P300 pp) or taxi (P1000 for 2); there's rarely a problem crossing the border. Be prepared to show money and proof of citizenship. If driving you must buy insurance with Belizean dollars. Moneychangers are readily available when you cross the border, but rates are poor so get only what you need until you get to the banks in the city. U.S. citizens and those of most other countries do not need visas, only proof of citizenship; but it's advisable to carry a passport. West Germans and Austrians must have visas, obtainable (fee) in Merida. Check with your embassy before you leave home. If you plan to continue to Guatemala from Belize, visas can be obtained in Chetumal at the Guatemalan Embassy, but not in Belize City.

giant masks of Kohunlich

VICINITY OF CHETUMAL

Kohunlich

Sixty-seven km W of Chetumal on Hwy. 186, turn R and drive 8 km on a good side road to this unique Maya site. The construction continued from late Pre-Classic (about A.D. 100-200) through Classic (A.D. 600-900). Though not totally restored nor nearly as grand as Chichen Itza or Uxmal, Kohunlich is worth the trip if only to visit the exotic **Temple of the Masks** dedicated to the Maya sun god. The stone pyramid is under an unlikely thatched roof (to prevent further deterioration from the weather), and unique gigantic stucco masks stand 2-3 m tall. The Temple, though not extremely tall as pyramids go, still presents a moderate climb. Wander through the jungle site and you can find 200 structures or uncovered mounds from the same era as Palenque. Many carved *stelae* are scattered throughout the surrounding forest.

Walking through luxuriant foliage, you'll discover a green world. Note orchids in the tops of trees plus small colorful wildflowers, lacy ferns, and lizards that share cracks and crevices in moldy stone walls covered with

picnic area on the Sea of Seven Colors near Chetumal

velvety moss. The relatively unknown site attracts few tourists. The absence of trinket-sellers and soft-drink stands leaves a visitor feeling he's first to stumble on haunting masks with star-incised eyes, mustaches (or are they serpents?) and nose plugs—features different from any carvings found at other Maya sites. Even the birds hoot and squawk at your intrusion as if you're first. Like most archaeological zones, Kohunlich is fenced and opens from 0800-1700 (P40). Camping is not allowed within the grounds, but you may see a tent or two outside the entrance.

Bacalar

In the small town of Bacalar (38 km W), near the town plaza and across from an old Spanish fort is a small budget *casa de huespedes*—not fancy, but cheap (P900); a YH (P700 s), and a trailer park (P900). Close by, built into the side of a hill overlooking the colorful Bacalar Lagoon, is **Hotel Las Lagunas**, moderately priced with clean rooms which have private baths. Special touches make it an out-of-the-ordinary stopover: local shells decorate walls and ceilings, ornate fences are neatly painted in white and green. The friendly owners, Senor Carlos R. Gutierrez and his wife, can usually be found in the outdoor dining room. A small pool (filled only during high season) and outdoor bar look out across the unusually hued Lagunas de Siete Colores. A diving board and ladder make it convenient to swim in the lagoon's sometimes blue, sometimes purple, sometimes red water; fishing is permitted, and you can barbecue your catch on the grounds. P3000 s, P4000 d. A bungalow for 6 is P8000 including a kitchen with refrigerator, stove, and hammock space for 4 more persons (extra fee P300 pp). Reserve in advance during tourist season and holidays; the rest of the year there are few people around. Write: Hotel Laguna, Bacalar, Quintana Roo, Mexico. Send one night's fee and allow plenty of time for the mail to reach its destination. Close by is the **Laguna Milagros Trailer Park** with tent camping also permitted (P700 pp). Restrooms, showers, sun shelters, narrow beach, small store and open-air cafe combine to offer an exotic milieu on the edge of the lagoon.

APPENDIX

EMBASSIES AND TOURIST OFFICES

U.S. Embassy, Paseo de la Reforma, Mexico City, DF; tel. (905) 553-3333.

American Consulate in Merida, Paseo de Montejo, at Av. Colon, #453; tel. 7-70-11

In the U.S.A., Mexican Embassy, 2829 16th St. NW, Washington, DC 20009; tel: (202) 234-6000.

In Canada, Mexican Embassy, 130 Albert St., Suite 206, Ottawa, Ontario K1P 5G4; tel. (613) 233-8988.

Mexican Tourist Offices in the U.S.A.
Government tourist offices located in many of the larger cities in the U.S. can give you information on almost everything you to need to know for a trip to Mexico.

Atlanta, GA 30303	Peachtree Center, Cain Tower, Suite 1201,
Chicago, IL 60601	233 N. Michigan Ave.
Los Angeles, CA 90212	9701 Wilshire Blvd., Suite 1201,
Dallas, TX 75219	Two Turtle Creek Village
Houston, TX 77008	2707 North Loop W., Suite 450
Denver, CO 80222	425 S. Cherry,
Miami, FL 33132	100 N. Biscayne Blvd. Tower Bldg.
New York, NY 10022	405 Park Ave.

Mexican Tourist Offices In Canada

Montreal, QUE	1 Place Ville Marie H3B 3M9
Toronto, ONT	101 Richmond St. W. M5H 2E1
Vancouver, B.C.	1055 Dunsmuir St., Suite 2754, V7X 1L4

SCHOOLS AND UNIVERSITIES

Cuernavaca:
CALE
Nueva Tabachin #22,
Col. Tlaltenango
Cuernavaca, Morelos, Mexico.
President: Javier Sotelo H.

Center for Bilingual Multicultural Studies
304 San Jeronimo, Col. Tlaltenangl
P.O.Box 1520,
Cuernavaca, Morelos, Mexico
Coordinator: Santiago Olalde.

Guadalajara:
Instituto Anglo Mexicano de Cultura
Tomas V. Gomez #125
Guadalajara, Jalisco, Mexico.

Universidad de Guadalajara
Cursos de Verano e Invierno
Apdo. Postal 1-2543
Guadalajara, Jalisco, Mexico.

In Merida:
Centro de idiomas del Sureste
Calle 57-66
Merida, Yucatan, Mexico.

APPENDIX

EMBASSIES AND TOURIST OFFICES

SCHOOLS AND UNIVERSITIES

BOOKLIST

The following books provide insights to the Yucatan Peninsula and the Maya people. A few of these books are easier obtained in Mexico. Most are non-fiction, though several are fiction that are great to pop into your carry bag for a good read on the plane, or anytime you want to get into the Yucatan mood. All of them cost less in the U.S. Happy reading!

Coe, Michael D. *The Maya*. New York: Thames and Hudson, 1980. A well-illustrated, easy-to-read volume on the Maya people.

Cortes, Hernan. *Five Letters*. Gordon Press, 1977. Cortes wrote long letters to the king of Spain telling of his accomplishments and trying to justify his action in the New World.

De Landa, Bishop Diego. *Yucatan Before and After the Conquest*. New York: Dover Publications, 1978. This book, translated by William Gates from the original 1566 volume, has served as the base for all research that has taken place since. De Landa (though he also destroyed countless books of the Maya people) has given the world an insight into their culture before the conquest.

Diaz del Castillo, Bernal. *The Conquest of New Spain*. New York: Penguin Books, 1963. History straight from the adventurer's reminiscences, translated by J.M. Cohen.

Fehrenbach, T.R. *Fire and Blood: A History of Mexico*. New York: Collier Books, 1973. 3,500 years of Mexico's history told in a way to keep you reading.

Ferguson, William M. *Maya Ruins of Mexico in Color*. Norman: University of Oklahoma Press, 1977. Good reading before you go, but too bulky to carry along. Oversized with excellent drawings and illustrations of the archaeological structures of the Maya Indians.

Franz, Carl. *The People's Guide to Mexico*. New Mexico: John Muir Publications, 1972. A humorous guide filled with witty anecdotes and helpful general information for visitors to Mexico. Don't expect any specific city information, just nuts and bolts hints for traveling south of the border.

Greene, Graham. *The Power and the Glory*. New York: Penguin Books, 1977. A novel that takes place in the twenties about a priest and the anti-church movement that gripped the country at the time.

Heffern, Richard. *Secrets of the Mind-Altering Plants of Mexico*. New York: Pyramid Books. A fascinating study of many subtances used from the ancients in ritual hallucinogens to today's medicines.

Lawrence, D.H. *The Plumed Serpent*. New York: Random House, 1955. The legend of Quetzalcoatl presented in a sensual novel.

Lewbel, George S. *Diving and Snorkeling Guide to Cozumel*. New York: Pisces Books, 1984. A well-illustrated volume for divers and snorkelers going to Cozumel. The small, easily carried volume is packed with hints about different dive sites, reefs, and marinelife of Cozumel.

Nelson, Ralph. *Popul Vuh: The Great Mythological Book of the Ancient Maya*. Boston: Houghton Mifflin, 1974. An easy-to-read translation of myths handed down orally by the Quiche Maya, family to family, until written down after the Spanish conquest.

Sodi, Demetrio M. (in collaboration with Adela Fernandez.) *The Mayas.* Mexico: Panama Editorial S.A. This small pocketbook presents a fictionalized account of life among the Maya before the conquest. Easy reading for anyone who enjoys fantasizing about what life *might* have been like before recorded history in the Yucatan. This book is available in the Yucatecan states of Mexico.

Stephens, John L. *Incidents of Travel in Central America, Chiapas, and Yucatan.* 2 vols. New York: Dover Publications, 1969. Good companions to refer to when traveling in the area. Stephens and illustrator Catherwood rediscovered many of the Maya ruins on their treks that took place in the mid-1800s. Easy reading.

Thompson, J. Eric. *Maya Archaeologist.* Norman: University of Oklahoma, 1963. Thompson, a noted Maya scholar, traveled and worked at most of the Maya ruins in the 1930s.

— —. *The Rise and Fall of the Maya Civilization.* Norman: University of Oklahoma Press, 1954. One man's story of the Maya Indian. Excellent reading.

Werner, David. *Where There is No Doctor.* California: The Hesperian Foundation. This is an invaluable resource for anyone traveling not only to isolated parts of Mexico, but to anyplace in the world without medical aid.

GLOSSARY

MAYA GODS AND CEREMONIES

Ahau Can — Serpent lord and highest priest

Ahau Chamehes — Deity of medicine

Acanum — Protective deity of hunters

Ah Cantzicnal — Aquatic deity

Ah Chhuy Kak — God of violent death and sacrifice

Ixchell — Goddess of birth, fertility, medicine and credited with inventing spinning.

Ahcit Dzamalcum — Protective god of fishermen

Ah Cup Cacap — God of the underworld who denies air

Ah Itzam — The water witch

Ah kines — Priests, lords who consult the oracles, who celebrate ceremonies and preside over sacrifices.

Ahpua — God of fishing

Ah Puch — God of death

Ak'Al — Sacred marsh where water abounds

Bacaboob — The *poureres,* supporters of the sky and guardians of the cardinal points, who form a single god, *Ah Cantzicnal Bacab.*

Bolontiku — The nine lords of the night

Cihuateteo — Women-goddesses who become divine through death in childbirth (Nahuatl word)

Chac — God of rain and agriculture

Chac Bolay Can — The butcher serpent living in the underworld

Chaces — Priest's assistants in agricultural and other ceremonies

Cit Chac Coh — God of war

Hetxmek — Ceremony when the child is first carried astride the hip

Hobnil Bacab — The bee god, protector of beekeepers

Holcanes — The brave warriors charged with obtaining slaves for sacrifice. (This word was unknown until the post-classic era.)

Itzamna — Lord of the skies, creator of the beginning, god of time

Hunab Ku — Giver of life, builder of the universe and father of Itzamna

Ik — God of the wind

Ixtab — Goddess of the cord and of suicide by hanging

Kinich — Face of the sun

Kukulcan — *Quetzal*-serpent, plumed serpent

Metnal — The underworld, place of the dead

Nacom — Warrior chief

Noh Ek — Venus

Pakat — God of violent death

Zec — Spirit lords of beehives

FOOD AND DRINK

alche — Inebriating drink, sweetened with honey and used for ceremonies and offerings.

Ic — chili

Itz — sweet potato

Kabaxbuul — The heaviest meal of the day, eaten at dusk and containing cooked black beans.

Kah — pinole flour

Kayem — ground maize

Macal — A type of root

Muxubbak — tamale

On — avocado

P'ac — tomatos

Op — plum

Uah — tortillas

Tzamna — black bean

Za — maize drink

Put — papaya

ANIMALS

Acehpek — dog used for deer hunting

Ah Maax Cal — the prattling monkey

Ah Maycuy — the chestnut deer

Ah xixteel Ul — the rugged land conch

Yac — mountain cat

Yaxum — mythical green bird

Bil — hairless dog reared for food

Ah Sac Dziu — the white thrush

Cutz — wild turkey

Cutzha — duck

Hoh — crow

Icim — owl

Keh — deer

Kitam — wild boar

Muan — evil bird related to death

Que — parrot

Thul — rabbit

Utiu — coyote

Tzo — domestic turkeys

Jaleb — hairless dog

MUSIC AND FESTIVALS

Zacatan — a drum made from a hollowed tree trunk, with one opening covered with hide.

Ah Paxboob — musicians

Bexelac — turtle shell used as percussion instrument

Chul — flute

Chohom — dance performed in ceremonies during the month of *Zip,* related to fishing.

Hom — trumpet

Tunkul — drum

Kayab — percussion instrument fashioned from turtle shell

Okot uil — dance performed during the *Pocan* ceremony

Oc na — festival of the month of *Yax.* Old idols of the temple are broken and replaced with new.

Pacum chac — festival in honor of the war gods

ELEMENTS OF TIME

Chumuc Kin — midday

Chunkin — midday

Chumuc akab — midnight

Haab — Solar calendar of 360 days which is made up with five extra days of misfortune which complete the final month.

Emelkin — sunset

Kin — the sun, the day, the unity of time

Kaz akab — dusk

Potakab — time before dawn

Yalhalcab — dawn

PLANTS AND TREES

Kan ak — plant that produces a yellow dye

Kikche — tree of which the trunk is used to make canoes

Kuche — red cedar tree

Ki — sisal

Kiixpaxhkum — chayote

K'uxub — annatto tree

Piim — fibre of the cotton tree

Taman — cotton plant

Tauch—black *zapote*

Tazon te—moss

Ha—cacao seed

Ploms—rich people

Suyen—square blanket

MISCELLANEOUS WORDS

Yuntun—slings

Xul—stake with a pointed fire-hardened tip

Xanab—sandals

Xicul—sleeveless jacket decorated with feathers

Ah Kay Kin Bak—meat seller

Cha te—black vegetable dye

Chi te—eugenia, plant for dyeing

Ch'oh—indigo

Ek—dye

Chaltun—water cistern

Halach uinic—leader

Hadzab—wooden swords

Mayacimil—smallpox epidemic, "easy death"

Pic—underskirt

NUMBERS

hun	one
ca	two
ox	three
can	four
ho	five
uac	six
uuc	seven
uacax	eight
bolon	nine
iahun	ten
buluc	eleven
iahca	twelve
oxlahum	thirteen
canlahum	fourteen
holahun	fifteen
uaclahun	sixteen
uuclahun	seventeen
uacaclahun	eighteen
bolontahun	nineteen
hunkal	twenty

INDEX

Italicized page numbers indicate information in captions, call-outs, charts, illustrations, or maps.
(Inclusive page numbers, i.e., "147-169," may also include these types of references.)
Bold-face page numbers offer the primary reference to a given topic.

ABOUT THE AUTHOR

Chicki and Oz Mallan

As a child Chicki Mallan caught the travel bug from her dad. The family would leave their Catalina Island home yearly, hit the road and explore the small towns, and big cities of the U.S.A. This urge didn't go away even with a good-sized family to tote around. At various times Chicki and kids have lived in the Orient and in Europe. Traveling with kids opened doors at the family level all over the world. Even when people don't speak the same language, they relate to other parents since kids are the same everywhere. When not traveling, lecturing, or giving slide presentations, Chicki, husband Oz and teen-age twins Patti and Bryant live in Paradise, a small community in the foothills of the Sierra Nevada mountains. She does what she enjoys most, writing magazine and newspaper articles in between travel books. She has been associated with Moon Publications since 1983, and is the author of *Guide to Catalina Island.*

ABOUT THE PHOTOGRAPHER

Oz Mallan has been a professional photographer for the past 36 years. Much of that time was spent as chief cameraman for the *Chico Enterprise-Record.* Oz graduated from Brooks Institute of Santa Barbara in 1950. His work has often appeared in newspapers across the country via UPI and AP. He travels the world with wife, Chicki, handling the photo end of their literary projects which include travel books, newspaper and magazine articles as well as lectures and slide presentations. The photos in *Guide to the Yucatan Peninsula* were taken during several visits and many months of travel on the Peninsula.

ABOUT THE ILLUSTRATORS

The watercolor painting on the cover and the banner art were done by Kathy Escovedo Sanders. She is an expert both in watercolor and this stipple style which lends itself to excellent black and white reproduction. Kathy is a 1982 Cal State Long Beach graduate with a BA in Art History. She exhibits drawings, etched intaglio prints, woodcut prints as well as her outstanding watercolor paintings. In the April 1982 issue of *Orange Coast Magazine,* a complete photo essay illustrates Kathy's unique craft of dyeing, designing, and etching eggs. Her stipple art can also be seen in Chicki Mallan's *Guide to Catalina Island.*

Diana Lasich is a Moon Publications regular with illustrations in many Moon books. She received her degree in Art from San Jose State University and continued studying as she traveled through Japan, where she learned wood block printing, *sumie,* and *kimono* painting.

Louise Foote is a talented artist, as well as official mapmaker for Moon books. She is also an archaeologist and has spent some interesting time on various digs around northern California concerned with American Indians. Louise executed all the maps, plus two sketches.

Discover 30 Centuries Of Civilization Surrounded By 6,000 Miles Of Beaches.

There are so many different Mexicana vacations. And all of them so affordable.

Over 30 destinations in all. With so many beaches along our Riviera and our Caribbean, they create a shoreline that could span North America twice.

Beaches lined with sunny outdoor restaurants, the rival of any in Europe.

Others inhabited only by coconut palms.

Board a modern Mexicana jet and travel back over 3,000 years. Witness art dominated by the oldest, largest pyramids on earth. Discover detailed works in precious metals that predate the Renaissance.

We were the first international airline in North America. Now, 65 years later, Mexicana flies more nonstops from the USA to Mexico than any other airline.

Experience the incredible variety of vacations in our beautiful country. On North America's most experienced airline.

mexicana
We've got more Mexico going for you.

HIKING, FISHING & FEASTING!

Backpacking: A Hedonist's Guide
by Rick Greenspan and Hal Kahn
This humorous, informative, handsomely illustrated how-to guide will convince even the most confirmed naturophobe that it's safe, easy, and enjoyable to leave the smoggy security of city life behind. *Backpacking: A Hedonist's Guide* covers all the backpacking basics—equipment, packing, maps, trails—but it places special emphasis on how to prepare such surprising culinary wonders as trout quiche, sourdough bread, chocolate cake, even pizza, over the fragrant coals of a wilderness campfire. This book won't catch trout or bake cake; it will, however, provide the initial inspiration, practical instruction, and cut the time, cost, and hard knocks of learning. 90 illustrations, annotated booklist, index. 199 pages. **Code MN23**   **$7.95**

FEATURED MOON TITLES

Guide to Catalina Island
by Chicki Mallan

Two hours by boat over transparent, fish-filled seas, sparkling Santa Catalina Island is an unspoiled temperate paradise right in Southern California's backyard. Leave Los Angeles far behind and find a bustling resort town, intimate cafes, the hot sun blazing on white-sand beaches and secluded coves, superlative sailing and diving, a wild interior of rolling hills and rugged peaks, scrub cactus and burly bison, enigmatic Shoshone Indian sites that still mystify the experts. *Guide to Catalina Island* provides all you need for an exciting, diverse experience. Hotels and camping facilities are listed with all budgets in mind, as well as information on where to eat to suit every palate and pocketbook. Historical background, maps, hiking trails, travel and recreation tips all make this compact guide indispensable for planning and enjoying your trip to Catalina—a real American island. 4 color pages, photos, illustrations, maps, index. 142 pages.

Code MN09 $5.95

Maui Handbook
by J.D. Bisignani

Ramble the rollicking streets of historic Lahaina where missionaries landed in search of souls, and whalers berthed in search of trade and pleasure. Scan the sun-dappled waters of the "Lahaina Roads" for the tell-tale spout of humpback whales as these gentle giants play and mate in their winter sanctuary. Luxuriate on glistening beaches. Swim and snorkel in reef-protected waters or dive into the mysterious world of a half-submerged volcanic crater. Grab a board and challenge the frantic surf at world-famous beaches such as Hookipa. Glory at the explosive brilliance of a Haleakala sunrise and hike its moon-crater floor to learn why the *kahunas* chanted to this ancient power center, revering it as "the house of the sun." No "fool-'round" advice is offered on Maui's full range of accommodations, eateries, rental cars, tours, charters, shopping, and inter-island transport. With practical money-saving tips, plus a comprehensive introduction to island ways, geography and history, *Maui Handbook* will pilot you through one of the most enchanting and popular islands in all of Oceania. 15 color photos, 70 b/w photos, 83 illustrations, 27 maps, booklist, glossary, index. 235 pages.

Code MN29 $7.95

Arizona Handbook
by Bill Weir

Giant cacti and mountain pines, ancient pueblos and sophisticated cities, deep canyons and soaring peaks—all these and more await you in Arizona, sunniest state in the Union. From the Grand Canyon, whose walls contain two billion years of Earth's history, to Lake Havasu, new home of the London Bridge, Arizona is famous for unparalleled year-round outdoor recreation. Millions of visitors a year can't be wrong, and *Arizona Handbook* covers it all. 8 color pages, 255 b/w photos, 81 illus., 53 maps, 4 charts. Booklist and index. 448 pages.

Code MN30   **$10.95**

Guide to Jamaica
by Harry S. Pariser

Jamaica is one of the most scenically beautiful islands in the Caribbean—and arguably the world. With an abundance of beach resorts and blue seas, the lush backdrop of 7,000-foot mountains completes the classic tropical paradise. Jamaica also has a highly distinctive contemporary culture: Rasta adherents and Maroon people, home of the lively native reggae dance music, a rich folklore, exceptional coffee, rum and *ganja*. No other guide treats Jamaica with more depth, historical detail, or practical travel information than *Guide to Jamaica*. 4 color pages, 51 b/w photos, 39 illus., 18 maps, 10 charts, booklist, glossary, index, 180 pages. **Code MN25**   **$6.95**

Guide to Puerto Rico and the Virgin Islands
by Harry S. Pariser

Puerto Rico and the U.S. Virgin Islands, often considered to be America's "51st States," are nevertheless *terra incognito* to most of us. Now discover them for yourself—from the wild beauty of St. John, an island almost wholly reserved as a national park, to cosmopolitan San Juan, where 500 years of history echo between ancient cobbled streets and ultramodern skyscrapers. Rich in culture and natural wonders, these are accessible and underrated destinations, never before explored with such thoroughness and sensitivity. Caribbean veteran Pariser turns up good-value accommodations, dining, and entertainment, with tips on getting to and around these islands inexpensively. Here is proof that "budget" travel really means getting *more* for your money, not less. 4 color pages, 55 b/w photos, 53 illus., 35 maps, 29 charts, booklist, glossary, index, 225 pages.

Code MN21   **$7.95**

OTHER MOON TITLES

Metzger, Steve. **CALIFORNIA DOWNHILL: A SKIER'S HANDBOOK.** 144 Smyth-sewn pages, 37 b/w photos, 21 illus., 15 color photos, 30 maps, 41 charts, index. Everything on ski resorts and facilities in glistening detail, plus transportation, accommodations, food, and additional attractions in each area.
Code MN31   **$7.95**

Stanley, David. **ALASKA-YUKON HANDBOOK.** 244 Smyth-sewn pages, 68 illus., 77 b/w photos, 4 color pages, 70 maps, glossary, index. The first true budget guide to Alaska and Western Canada.
Code MN07   **$7.95**

Bisignani, J.D. **JAPAN HANDBOOK.** 520 Smyth-sewn pages, 92 illus., 200 b/w photos, 35 color photos, 112 maps, 29 charts. A guide to the Japanese Archipelago from Okinawa to Rishiri Island.
Code MN05   **$12.95**

Dalton, Bill. **INDONESIA HANDBOOK. 4th edition,** 800 Smyth-sewn pages, illus., photos, maps, charts, appendices, booklist, glossary, index. An adventurer's guide through the world's largest archipelago.
Code MN01   **$14.95**

Stanley, David. **FINDING FIJI.** 127 Smyth-sewn pages, 78 illus., 36 b/w photos, 4 color pages, 26 maps, 3 charts, appendix, index. This guide covers land and seascapes, customs, climates, sightseeing attractions, transportation— everything in one practical volume. **Code MN17**   **$6.95**

Stanley, David. **MICRONESIA HANDBOOK.** 238 Smyth-sewn pages, 68 illus., 77 b/w photos, 8 color pages, 58 maps, 12 charts, index. This budget guide opens up the vast Pacific area between the Philippines and Hawaii, covering all seven north Pacific territories. **Code MN19**   **$7.95**

Stanley, David. **SOUTH PACIFIC HANDBOOK. 3rd edition.** 578 Smyth-sewn pages, 162 illus., 160 b/w photos, 8 color pages, 163 maps, 17 charts, booklist, glossary, index. The most comprehensive guide available on the Pacific, covering 30 Oceanic territories. **Code MN03**   **$13.95**

BOOKS OF RELATED INTEREST

LANGUAGE AIDS

Just Enough Spanish
This phrasebook concentrates on the simplest but most effective ways for travelers to express themselves. *Just Enough Spanish* covers such situations as asking directions, meeting and greeting people, and how to shop. Included is a pronunciation guide, and a key to likely answers you may receive to your questions. This comprehensive, easy-to-use book will prove to be an essential travel companion. Size: 4 x 6½.
Code PP15 $3.95

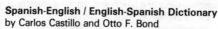

Spanish-English / English-Spanish Dictionary
by Carlos Castillo and Otto F. Bond
This handy pocket-sized dictionary from the University of Chicago includes Latin American Spanish words, phrases, and slang, making it invaluable to travelers in these regions. A special section deals with word usage, idioms and proverbs. Good value. Size: 4 x 6¾. 488 pages.
Code UC10 $3.95

Spanish—Language/30 Cassette
Language/30 is based on the famous U.S. military speed-up language learning method developed for government personnel preparing for overseas duty. Stressing conversational words and phrases, this course offers:

• Two cassettes and a phrase dictionary tucked into a long-lasting vinyl album.

• Approximately 1½ hours of guided practice in greetings, introductions, requests, and general conversation for use at hotels, restaurants, and places of business and entertainment.

• Native voices speaking with perfect pronunciation on companion cassette tapes.

• Two special sections by the famous linguist Charles Berlitz: one introducing the course, with helpful tips on its use, and the other about the social customs and etiquette of the country.
Code LG35 $14.95

MAPS

Hallwag Country Road Map—Mexico
Hallwag maps are known for their precise information and clear design. This is the surest, easiest map for people on the road. Exquisite detail of all Mexico's roadways; symbols denote airports, camping areas, other points of interest. Exclusive Hallwag index. Heavy-duty cover. **Code HL13** $6.95

Hildebrand Travel Map—Mexico
This sturdily packaged, folded map of Mexico is designed especially for the traveler. The map is entirely up-to-date and thoroughly researched. Map includes facts and information (in English) of special interest to the traveler—culture, climate, points of interest, currency, transportation, postal and telephone information, entrance formalities, as well as detailed street maps of important areas. **Code HD25** $5.95

Rand McNally 1986 Road Atlas
United States, Canada, and Mexico
Will you be driving to the Yucatan Peninsula? A good atlas is essential for the auto traveler. This atlas covers all 50 states plus Canada, Mexico, Puerto Rico, and Central America. Up-to-date, detailed, easy-to-read maps, valuable travel aids and bonus coupons to save you time, gas, and money. 128 pages. Size: 11 x 15. **Code RM02** $5.95

MOONBOOKS TRAVEL CATALOG

The Portable Store
for Independent Travelers

For the traveler, travel agent, scholar, librarian, businessperson, or aspiring globetrotter, here is the complete, *portable* travel bookstore stocked with the best and latest sources available: hard-to-find guides, maps, atlases, language tapes, histories, classic travel literature, and related travel accessories. Here is your guide to virtually every destination on Earth—from Paris to Patagonia, from Alberta to Zanzibar. By means of popular credit cards, personal check, or money order, all are easily available direct from our warehouse. Whether your idea of adventure is snorkeling in the Red Sea, bushwacking in New Guinea, or sipping espresso in a Venetian cafe...let your journey begin with the *Moonbooks Travel Catalog.*
Code MN27   **$2.95**

NEW AND IMPROVED!

MOON BELT

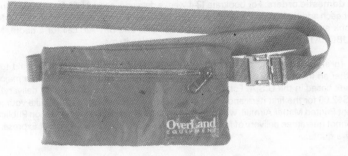

The Moonbelt Gets Better!

In our on-going effort to bring you the very best in travel books, maps, and accessories, we are pleased to announce a new and improved model of the best-selling *Moonbelt*. Produced by Overland Equipment, this new moneybelt offers improved features such as:

- Quick-release buckle. No more fumbling around for the strap or repeated adjustments. This handy buckle opens and closes with a touch, but won't come undone until you want it to.

- Heavy-duty Cordura Nylon construction. This fabric is strong and water-resistant, providing even more protection for your important papers.

This new moneybelt still slips under your shirt or waistband to be virtually undetectable and inaccessible to pickpockets, and is still the same useful size, 3½ x 8 inches. Available only in black. $6.95.

IMPORTANT ORDERING INFORMATION

1. codes: Please carefully enter book and/or map codes on your order form, as this will ensure accurate and speedy delivery of your order.

2. prices: Due to foreign-exchange fluctuations and the changing terms of our distributors, all prices are subject to change without notice.

3. domestic orders: For bookrate (3-4 weeks delivery), send $1.25 for first item and $.50 for each additional item. For UPS or USPS 1st class (3-7 days delivery), send $3.00 for first book and $.50 for each additional book. For UPS 2nd-Day Air, call for a quote. MOON PUBLICATIONS is not responsible for lost or stolen items.

4. foreign orders: All orders which originate outside the U.S.A must be paid for with either an International Money Order or a check in U.S. currency drawn on a major U.S. bank based in the U.S.A. For International Surface Bookrate (3-12 weeks delivery), send US$2.00 for the first item and US$1.00 for each additional item. If you'd like your item(s) sent Printed Matter Airmail, write us for a quote before sending money. Moon Publications cannot guarantee delivery of foreign orders unless sent via International Air Express. Write for a quote.

5. Visa or Mastercharge payments: Minimum order US$15.00. Telephone orders are accepted. Call (916) 895-3789 or 345-5473.

6. noncompliance: Any orders received which do not comply with any of the above conditions may result in the return of your order and/or payment intact.

ORDER FORM
(See important ordering information opposite page)

Name _____

Address_____

City _____

State or Country _____ Zip _____

Quantity	Full Book or Map Title	Code	Price

California Residents please add 6 percent sales tax

Domestic Shipping Charges for 1st item: $1.25

($.50 for each additional item)

Additional charges for International or UPS postage

TOTAL ENCLOSED

Make checks payable to:

MOON PUBLICATIONS P.O. BOX 1696 CHICO CALIFORNIA 95927-1696 USA

WE ACCEPT VISA AND MASTERCHARGE!
Please send written order with your Visa or Mastercharge number and expiry date clearly written

CHECK/MONEYORDER ENCLOSED FOR $ _____

CARD NO. ☐ VISA   ☐ MASTERCHARGE   BANK NO.

☐☐☐☐☐☐☐☐☐☐☐☐☐☐☐☐☐☐   ☐☐☐☐

SIGNATURE _____ EXPIRATION DATE _____

THANK YOU FOR YOUR ORDER

MN32